THE LIFE OF GEORGE MOORE

THE MACMILLAN COMPANY
NEW YORK · BOSTON · CHICAGO · DALLAS
ATLANTA · SAN FRANCISCO

GEORGE MOORE AGED 9
From a daguerreotype

THE
LIFE OF GEORGE MOORE

by

JOSEPH HONE

WITH AN ACCOUNT OF HIS LAST YEARS
BY HIS COOK AND HOUSEKEEPER
CLARA WARVILLE

NEW YORK
THE MACMILLAN COMPANY
1936

PRINTED IN THE UNITED STATES OF AMERICA
BY THE POLYGRAPHIC COMPANY OF AMERICA, N.Y.

CONTENTS

LIST OF ILLUSTRATIONS

AUTHORITIES AND ACKNOWLEDGMENTS

Before all other helpers I should mention Senator Colonel Maurice Moore, the brother to whom George Moore owed so much. He has not only given me free access to a correspondence, preserved by the family since George Moore was at school in England, writing to his parents at the age of nine, but has responded with unfailing kindness to my demands upon his memory. Other of Moore's relatives to whom I am under obligation for courtesies in the course of this work are Mrs. Kilkelly, Mr. Peter Moore, and the Dowager Lady Hemphill.

I am deeply grateful to Mr. C. D. Medley, Moore's executor, for his general help and advice. Mr. Medley has placed at my disposal the various unpublished documents relating to George Moore's work and life which are in his possession. He has given me permission to make use of all available correspondence, and to quote freely from Moore's books.

George Moore had in mind two biographers: the friend who in *Hail and Farewell* is called by his literary pseudonym of John Eglinton, and Mr. Charles Morgan. In turn, but for different reasons, these two distinguished men of letters were deterred from undertaking the task. Without their goodwill I should not have cared to begin the book. Nor would I have persevered without the friendship and assistance of Professor Henry Tonks, whose association with George Moore was longer and more continuous than that of any man now living excepting Colonel Moore. By him I was introduced to many of Moore's English friends, notably to Mr. D. S. MacColl, Mr. L. A. Harrison, Mr. Wilson Steer, O.M., and to Mr. and Mrs. St. John Hutchinson, to whom I must express my particular thanks for their encouraging influence. It has been impossible without

tedium to acknowledge in the text the source of every anec-
dote. But I have quoted from correspondence and remi-
niscence which have been generously supplied by the persons
I have named, and also, equally generously, by Lord Howard
de Walden, Sir William Geary, Sir William Rothenstein,
Sir John Thomson-Walker, Mr. Lionel Barton, Mrs. Belloc
Lowndes, Miss Nancy Cunard, Mrs. Virginia Crawford,
Professor Edmund Curtis, Mr. C. S. Evans, Mr. Dermot
Freyer, Mr. J. D. Hart (U.S.A.), Sir Alec Martin, Mrs.
Mona Jackson (Moore's secretary), Mr. Gerald Festus Kelly,
Mr. Desmond MacCarthy, Mr. Nelson Ward and Mrs.
Williamson. Two families with whom Moore was on terms
of intimacy for many years were the Charles Hunters and
the Edmund Gosses; and Mrs. Williamson and Mr. and
Mrs. Philip Gosse have been at kind pains in looking through
old papers on my behalf: Mr. Gosse also allows me to quote
from certain of his father's letters. Of those whom I have
been unable to meet I should mention especially some of
Moore's American correspondents and friends : the Marquise
Clara Lanza, Miss Viola Rodgers, Miss Honor Wolfe, Mrs.
Robinson Jeffers, Mr. Vincent O'Sullivan and Messrs. Liveright, for the active help which they have given in their
letters to me. Mr. O'Sullivan's abundant recollections of
literary London in the nineties have been of great service
in bringing the George Moore of *Esther Waters* and *Evelyn
Innes* to life for me. How much I am beholden to Miss Clara
Warville, Moore's cook, will be evident to readers of Chapter
XI; I also recall with relish the conversations of Mr. Reilly,
so long the bailiff at Moore Hall.

My debt to Mr. Desmond Shawe-Taylor is not limited to
the chapter which he has contributed on the literary achievement of George Moore. After I had completed a first draft
of the biography he was at my side in the work of revision
and emendation. As one of the younger generation, with a
deep appreciation and a close knowledge of George Moore's
writings, his criticisms and suggestions have been of peculiar
value. He has also aided me in reading the proof sheets.

Of those who can recall George Moore in the Paris of the
late seventies and early eighties not many survive. But a

few members of the circle of his earliest French friends were still living in 1922, when Mr. Barrett Clark made the unpublished notes on the " Paris of George Moore," which he handed to me with remarkable generosity, along with other interesting papers. Madame Duclaux and her sister, Miss Mabel Robinson, Moore's friends from 1877 onwards, have also both by their writings and their conversation helped me, with a friendly solicitude for Moore's memory, to surmount some of the difficulties presented by my earlier pages. In the matter of Moore's later associations with the intellectual life of France my chief debt is to M. J.-E. Blanche and M. Edouard Dujardin, those two distinguished Frenchmen, so long his compeers, who have elucidated for me many points of biographical and literary importance. I have made considerable use of Moore's letters to M. Édouard Dujardin, a complete file of which was furnished to me by Mr. Clark. In 1929 Mr. Crosby Gage of New York published in a private edition a translation by John Eglinton of a selection of this correspondence. My acknowledgments are due to Mr. Ellridge Adams for permission to draw upon the volume.

The friends whom George Moore made during his literary career in Ireland (1900–1910) are, for the most part, also my friends. All of them have been generous in giving me assistance; but I should mention in particular the kindness of Mr. R. I. Best, John Eglinton, the late George Russell (A.E.), and Mr. W. B. Yeats for the indulgence which they showed in many conversations to the importunities of a biographer, and record further obligations to John Eglinton for putting at my disposal his important correspondence with Moore. Other especially valuable Irish sources include: Mr. Ernest A. Boyd, Mr. Patrick Colum, Mr. C. P. Curran, Mr. John Garvey, D.L., Dr. Oliver Gogarty, Mrs. Noel Guinness, Lady Hanson, the late Colonel E. V. Longworth, Mrs. Murray Robertson, Colonel Ruttledge, D.S.O., Mr. James Stephens and Mr. Seamus O'Sullivan.

To the following books I am particularly indebted for the light they have thrown upon various aspects of my subject:

Epitaph on George Moore, by Charles Morgan (Macmillan & Co.), *A Portrait of George Moore in a Study of his Work*, by

John Freeman (T. Werner Laurie), *Irish Literary Portraits*, by John Eglinton (Macmillan & Co.), *An Irish Gentleman*, by Maurice Moore (T. Werner Laurie), *George Moore*, by Susan Mitchell (Talbot Press), *George Moore*, by Humbert Wolfe (Thornton Butterworth), *Conversations with George Moore*, by Geraint Goodwin (Benn), *Mes Modèles*, by J.-E. Blanche (P. V. Stock, Paris), " Souvenirs sur George Moore," by Mary Duclaux (*La Revue de Paris*, 1st March, 1933). Also : *Dramatis Personæ*, by W. B. Yeats (Macmillan & Co. and Cuala Press), *Our Irish Theatre*, by Lady Gregory (G. P. Putnam & Sons), *Edward Martyn*, by Denis Gwynn (Jonathan Cape), *Adventures of a Novelist*, by Gertrude Atherton (Jonathan Cape), *Contemporary Drama in Ireland*, by E. A. Boyd (Talbot Press), *Works and Days*, by Michael Field (John Murray), *Contemporary Portraits*, by Frank Harris (New York, 1919), *Pays Parisiens*, by Daniel Halévy (Bernard Grasset), *The Beardsley Period*, by Osbert Burdett (John Lean), *Le Mouvement Esthétique et " Décadent" en Angleterre*, by A. J. Farmer (Bibliothèque de Littérature comparée), *Zola and his Time*, by Matthew Josephson (Gollancz), and *La Fôret Symboliste*, by Aristide Marie (Firmin-Didot et Cie).

I wish to thank the following for their courtesy in granting permission to reproduce pictures in their possession : Bulloz et Cie for the drawing by Manet entitled *George Moore in Paris* ; Mr. Richard Sickert and the Tate Gallery for permission to reproduce Mr. Sickert's portrait of George Moore ; the Dublin Corporation for permission to reproduce Walter Osborne's portrait of Senator Colonel Maurice Moore, C.B., in the Municipal Gallery of Modern Art, Dublin ; the Manchester City Art Gallery for permission to reproduce Sir William Orpen's *Homage à Manet* ; the National Gallery of Ireland for permission to reproduce Thomas Wyatt's portrait, *George Moore, Historian* ; Professor Tonks and the Tate Gallery for permission to reproduce Professor Tonks's picture *Saturday Evening at the Vale* ; and Professor Tonks and the National Portrait Gallery for permission to reproduce *The Red Dressing Gown*.

CHAPTER I

MOORE HALL

I

THE OLD MAIL COACH ROAD leading from Dublin to Castlebar enters the county of Mayo a little beyond the hundredth milestone from Dublin. At the hundred and seventh milestone a road on the left crosses stone and bog for a few miles until the flat, reedy shore of Lough Carra comes in sight, the third and smallest of the three lakes—Corrib, Mask and Carra—which stretch in an almost unbroken sheet of water northwards from Galway Bay. Beyond the lake rises the blue ridge of the Partry Mountains. It is a soft wild country which the Welsh invaded in the twelfth century, and then de Burgo and his Normans; and Irish, Welsh and Normans have left the traces of their struggles and their defeats in the ruins of old castles and churches along the shores and on the islands, Castle Carra, Castle Burke, the Abbey of Ballintubber built in 1150 for Roderick O'Connor, last King of Ireland, the cell on Church Island under Partry where Marban, the hermit-poet, made his dwelling in the ninth century. A headland jutting southward into the lake divides it into two arms, and above the eastern arm, on a slope called Muckloon, there stands a square Georgian house of comfortable size with a prospect over numerous wooded islands to the far-off Connemara hills. A thick growth of ivy covers the walls, and from a distance Moore Hall still looks much as it must have looked when George Moore, the Alicante merchant, built it on his return from Spain in 1795; only a nearer view reveals the fact that it is nothing but a burnt-out shell.

2

The founder of Moore Hall belonged to a family which had been in Co. Mayo for three generations at least, and had some claim to be descended in the male line from the great Sir Thomas More, Lord Chancellor of England under Henry VIII. The claim is first made by this same George Moore who had made a small fortune in Spanish trade; while living in Alicante he drew up a pedigree which was registered in the office of the Ulster King at Arms. Although dates and proofs are absent, there is no question of the accuracy of this document as far back as the merchant's great-grandfather Captain George Moore of Ballina, " Vice-Admiral of Connaught " in the time of William III, whose grave may still be found with much difficulty in the over-grown ruins of a little Protestant cemetery near Straid Abbey. The pedigree goes on to say that this Captain George Moore was the son of Thomas More " of Barenbourg, Co. York " and Mary Apadam of Flintshire. We cannot tell where this information was derived from, presumably from family papers, but the pedigree makes a definite mistake in stating that " this Thomas More was son of John More who was son of the very celebrated Thomas More (in English Moore) Knight." The John More in question had in fact, by Anne Cressacre of Barnborough, Yorkshire, two sons named Thomas, but the names of their offspring are known, and neither of them had a son called George. The line of the elder Thomas became extinct in 1796; the younger Thomas, who became a Protestant clergyman, had three sons, Cipryan, Thomas and Constantine, of none of whom much is known. But although the Vice-Admiral of Connaught, Captain George Moore, cannot be the son of the Protestant clergyman, he may quite well have been the son of that clergyman's second son Thomas: the dates would fit, and in that case all that has happened is that one genera-tion was skipped in the pedigree, a possible slip in dealing with two Thomas Mores, father and son.

The evidence for the Sir Thomas More ancestry depends ultimately on the Alicante pedigree, and some would incline to reject the claims as insufficiently proved. Certainly they are not proved, but there is strong presumption against the supposition that the descent is fabricated, in two facts: (1) that the pedigree was made out in Spain whence such research as was necessary to discover the names and habitation of the Vice-Chancellor's grandsons would be at the least difficult; (2) that the family had possessed, for some time previous to the drawing up of the pedigree, in their earlier home at Ashbrook near Straid Abbey two portraits of Sir Thomas More, which were not destroyed until the destruction of Moore Hall itself.

The Moores of Ashbrook were undistinguished but they left some memory of fighting qualities among the people. " Scratch a Moore and your own blood will flow," it was said. They found wives among other Protestant families of small gentry or of clergy until the time of John Moore who in 1730 or thereabouts married Jane Lynch Athy of Renville, Co. Galway, and thus came into alliance with a Catholic and Celticised family, racy of the Connaught soil, members of the so-called " Twelve Tribes of Galway," the merchant princes who had ruled that city in medieval days.

John Moore and his wife had two sons, of whom the younger, George, being of adventurous disposition, migrated to Spain where many of his mother's relations already were, " wild geese " they were called, in flight from the disabilities which the Catholics of Ireland suffered in the eighteenth century. Whether George Moore (the matter was of interest to his great-grandson and namesake, and may therefore be mentioned here) was brought up in the religion of his father or in that of his mother, is unknown, but he passed as a Catholic in Spain and married while there a Catholic woman, Catherine de Killikelly, half Irish half Spaniard, who bore him three sons. At Alicante he manufactured iodine out of kelp shipped from the Galway coast, and exported wine; he prospered commercially, and returned to Ireland about the year 1790 with a very considerable fortune, his great-grandson used to say £250,000.[1] George

---

[1] Colonel Moore, the novelist's brother, writes: " George imagined the £250,000. It was no doubt more decorative than a smaller sum."

Moore invested the goodly sum in the purchase of land at Ballintubber and in other parts of Mayo and in the building of a big house; with him the Moores became an important county family in Mayo. He had also inherited the Ashbrook estates and would have built in that part if there had been a prospect. But there was none, and therefore he came south and selected the site of the pleasant green hill of Muckloon, saying that the scene was as fine as any that his travels had shown him. The lake is green on sunny days like a lake in the Pyrenees; and George Moore built a balcony over the porch so that he might enjoy the view, " in the cool of evening," he said, as though he forgot that he was not still in Spain.

3

The last years of this man's life were not happy: he went blind in his sleep, and one of his sons was a cause of grief. He had three sons: Peter the eldest had been always weak-minded, and now the second son John was induced to take part in the insurrection of 1798; he joined the French expedition under Humbert when it landed at Killala, and took the title of President of the Republic of Connaught after the British forces had been dispersed in the engagement at Castlebar. A swift revenge followed, he was made prisoner by the Governor and carried to Waterford to stand his trial, where he died. Friends could have contrived his escape, but he had refused to desert his companions in adversity.

The third son of the merchant, another George, succeeded to the property. He was of a reflective and studious disposition, a moralist, and with him literature made its appearance in the family. As a young man he had frequented the Holland House circle in London, and in later life he published a number of books, among them a *History of the British Revolution*, written from the Whig standpoint, and a series of edifying tales, illustrative of the passions. He married Louisa Browne, granddaughter of the first Earl of Altamont, of Westport in Mayo, and a relative of the Marquess of Sligo. In this way the Moores were connected with the high

Protestant aristocracy, although for some reason that is unknown Louisa Browne herself had been brought up by nuns. The marriage caused some scandal because the bride's cousin, Denis Browne, had been John Moore's most vindictive persecutor during the troubles of 1798.

Louisa suited her husband. A strong-minded woman, she took all the family affairs into her capable hands and permitted her husband to dream away his life in the library. Her word was law until she met her match in her eldest son, George Henry (George Moore's father), whom she sent to the new Roman Catholic college of Oscott for his education. George Henry distinguished himself at Oscott, writing excellent letters home and taking many prizes, especially in drawing. At the age of seventeen he composed a long poem on his native lake in Spenserian stanzas. Great hopes were entertained of him, and when he went to Cambridge his father published another book, " written solely for the use of my elder son now going to the University ": *A Treatise on the Art of Reasoning*. George Moore, anxious to minimise the Catholic ingredients of his heredity, used to say that his grandfather was an agnostic, but the philosophical work just mentioned hardly supports the assertion. It was in fact an attack on Kant and " the new German philosophy " for denying the existence of demonstrative proofs for a personal God. Kant had forgotten " what an exquisite and complicated contrivance, the mind, came from the hands of its Creator." A rationalising intellect is evident however in the work, and Lecky has shown that for a time the freethought of the Continent penetrated into educated Roman Catholic society in Ireland at the close of the eighteenth century. In their religious and political proclivities the Moores were Liberals.

George Henry proved a disappointment to his parents while at Cambridge. Instead of developing his literary and artistic talents he started racing and hunting, and spent more money than he should have done. Afterwards, while a student at Lincoln's Inn, his life was violently disturbed by a love affair with a married woman. This brought him into acrimonious dispute with his mother, whom he adored; and it was to avoid a break with her that he ran away to the east, followed, legend has it,. by his *innamorata* and her husband. While on his travels he kept notebooks, portions of which, along with some drawings of eastern life, have been published in his biography by his son, Colonel Maurice Moore. On his return from Damascus his mother once again began to write him reproachful letters until he said: " If you write any more I'll go back to the east."

George, the moralist, died in 1840, leaving behind him a manuscript history of the French Revolution, which he desired that his heirs should cherish and print. He had had no celebrity in his lifetime, he wrote in a preface to this work. " But a prospect of posthumous fame pleases me. . . . Having missed the applause and even notice of my age, I ought perhaps to be indifferent about the opinion of those who follow; their applause, should I ever gain it, will not reach me when the grave has closed over me. This is true, but we are so made that while we are living we think with pleasure that we shall not be forgotten after death." Lines which greatly touched George Moore when he was shown them some fifty years later, but the wish which they embodied was never fulfilled.

After his father's death George Henry Moore continued to race, and enjoyed many successes, both in Ireland and in England, including the Chester Cup. A much loved but somewhat eccentric brother, Augustus, who was also a sportsman, died as a result of an accident at Aintree; and when dying urged George Henry to " give up this reckless life." And Maria Edgeworth, who was a friend of the family, wrote " He will turn to quiet literary pursuits and he will feel in them . . . something congenial to his hereditary nature and pleasing and comforting to his mother." She discerned that the Moores had abilities and tastes superior to those of the Irish Western landlord as he is described in the rollicking and carefree pages of Lever's novels. No Moore in three generations had felt the temptation of strong drink.

The estate was already much encumbered, but the racing continued for some time yet. It was the Irish Famine of 1846–8 which brought Moore home and steadied him. The catastrophe shed a new light on his character which justified Miss Edgeworth's interpretation of it. George Henry Moore sold his horses and devoted himself to public effort. His generosities reduced his fortune still further; and he laid up trouble for his heirs by refusing to clear the estate of un-economic holdings, partly out of goodness of heart, partly because he wished to command the votes of masses of tenantry. The distresses of his country had caused him to turn his attention to politics, and in 1847 he came forward as Independent candidate for the representation of Mayo, and winning the support both of the landlords and the demo-crats was returned at the head of the poll. In 1851 when he was forty-one he married Mary Blake of Ballinafad, thus making another alliance between the Moores and a repre-sentative family of Roman Catholic gentry in the west of Ireland. His mother, now grown sad and meditative, con-tinued to live at Moore Hall. She survived long enough to enter into the consciousness of her eldest grandson, as an invalid whom two nurses used to carry out into the garden on a long chair when the day was fine. Her death was George Moore's first experience of grief. " I remember seeing my father sitting at a small table writing letters by the bed on which his dead mother lay. He was weeping bitterly."

4

GEORGE AUGUSTUS MOORE, the first child of the marriage, was born on the 24th of February, 1852. The child remained silent without crying for many days and it was feared that he might be dumb. He then became explosive, but re-mained inarticulate for a long time, and later was so back-ward in his reading and writing that he seriously impeded the progress of his second brother Maurice; he wore a blank expression at his lessons with Miss Westby the English governess, showing however a great deal of invention and spirit in his amusements. One day the two boys, embarking on the reedy and dangerous lake in an improvised raft, were almost drowned. On another occasion George bought a dozen gamecocks and made them fight, six against six and three against three, killing the beaten until only one was left. " It seemed," his brother writes, " like a dream remembered when I read his account in *The Brook Kerith* " (the story of the great main which Joseph of Arimathea witnessed in Tiberias).

George Henry Moore lost his seat in Parliament in 1857 on the petition of the Tory candidate. He could now live at home and watch his children grow; he gave George and Maurice two ponies, Spark and Twinkle, and stood behind them with a riding whip to make them jump fences. During the winter evenings he recounted tales of a romantic type that he had read in books, pretending that they had happened to himself, during his visit to the East. Mrs. Moore also liked to tell stories. She had hers mostly from Scott's novels, long passages from which she knew by heart: George may have inherited from her an uncommonly good memory. His father's stories excited George most, and after hearing one of them nothing would satisfy him until the servants found him a Circassian blade that he knew to be hidden away in some cupboard. With this he mounted his pony, and, waving it, he rode all day about the grounds of Moore Hall, imagining himself a Greek or Georgian warrior.

An amusing daguerreotype of the little boy survived for publication as a frontispiece for the limited 1921 edition of *Memoirs of My Dead Life*. It shows the child standing with one arm laid across the back of a chair and his hand in his belt. He wears a loose jacket and long trousers. Above the jacket is a soft, blue silk tie. The nose is long, the chin small and retreating, the hair is lank, the hands are peculiarly small, and the expression is definitely Irish. According to his parents George showed a remarkable resemblance to the portrait of his grandfather, not to the one in the dining-room, but to another which hung in the library and showed the moralist as a child, at Alicante, in Spanish dress. His knowledge that he was supposed to be like his grandfather was perhaps the cause of George's first interest in writers. He put questions about his grandfather to the servants and to his father. What did Grandfather write about ? How was it that no one read his books ? A third brother, Augustus, was said to take after the great-grandfather, the founder of Moore Hall, whose portrait, also done in Spain, with wig and vermilion coat, represented the characteristic Moore face, long and sheeplike and well-bred.

5

In 1859 George Henry Moore resumed racing; and his eldest son delighted in the lively movement of the stables, and used to say to everyone: " Do you think when I am grown up I shall ride at Aintree ? " An old mare, in use as a carriage horse, foaled unexpectedly, and the colt was named Croaghpatrick after Mayo's holy mountain, the peak of which shows from various points on Lough Carra, rising in the distance behind the house. Joseph Applely, the English butler, who had formerly been a jockey, prophesied that the fortunes of the family would be fully restored by this colt, which two years later was entered for the Steward's Cup at Goodwood, just about the time when it was thought that George should go to school. A few weeks before the race George Henry Moore and his wife went to England. They took George with them, and stayed at Cliff's, the trainer at Hednesford, whither Croaghpatrick had preceded them. George was left at Cliff's when the date of the race approached, and he has said that he enjoyed himself greatly among the stable boys. Mrs. Cliff saw that he put on his trousers and gave him a pony to ride out on the downs.

There was a great field, forty-five, for the race, and never had there been so many favourites; at the last Croaghpatrick, who had been at forty to one, advanced from the outside and became first favourite. The Cup fell to him, and Goodwood was followed by other spectacular successes, the results of which were the payment of Moore's election debts, the re-roofing of Moore Hall and the despatch of George to Oscott, which was more expensive than schools in Ireland but offered attractions to Irish parents who wanted their children to enjoy the advantages of the system without exposing them to the Protestant atmosphere of the ordinary English public school. All the masters were English priests. Formal manners and cleanliness of person received more attention than at Irish schools (at least this was the theory), and there was also the hope that the boys would return home without their brogues.

It was Moore's recollection as an elderly man that he was left a month at Cliff's; his father came for him after his victories on the turf, and pitched him headlong into the midst of a hundred and fifty boys. " Such," Colonel Maurice Moore observes, in the biography of George Henry Moore,[1] " are the strange freaks of fortune, or the devious ways of Providence. Literature in the twentieth century depending on the struggle of a horse or the efforts of a jockey half a century before; who can foresee the ultimate result of what seems the most trivial and transitory incident in life ? " The little George thought that he would enjoy the adventure. He left his father and his mother talking with the President in the pompous room reserved for visitors, and raced through the empty playgrounds (it was class time) delirious with excitement ; he could only think of the boys waiting to make his acquaintance. A few hours later they came trooping out of the classrooms, formed a procession, and marched into the refectory where, to his great surprise, a master told him that he must hold his tongue.

The description of Oscott fills several pages of *Salve* and takes the form of an exchange of reminiscences between Moore at the age of fifty-five and his brother Colonel Maurice Moore, who loyally defends Oscott against attacks. There is no doubt that Moore looked back on his school days with unfeigned bitterness; and to those who spoke to him of the matter he hinted that his experience of the " hated Roman Catholic college " was more lurid than would be imagined from the description in his book. He suffered spiritually as well as physically; but it is obvious that he was not cut out for a schoolboy : many boys were quite happy at Oscott and the discipline was not in fact as severe as at many other schools.

It was the winter half of 1861 when he arrived. The school stood high above Birmingham. Ice covered the water in the dormitory jugs when the boys rose at half-past six; and the

[1] *An Irish Gentleman*: Werner Laurie, 1913.

food was unappetising and insufficient. George was the youngest of all the boys and there was not even a matron to see to his childish needs. His first surviving letter, written eighteen months after his entrance, is headed " St. Mary's Colledge."

28th March 1863.

My dear Mama,

I made my first Communion this morning. You must send me some things please to send me a writing-case. I think that if you send all the things in a parcel and addressed to hear it would come all right for many of the boys have had parcels sent to them to-day. We breakfasted in the parlour this morning write and tell me where Papa has gone tell me what is the governess's name. I have had a bad cough but I am much better now I remain your affectionate son

George Moore.

His chest had already shown signs of delicacy, and the piercing draughts of the corridors and classrooms brought on a severe bronchitis. It was necessary to bring him back to Moore Hall where he nearly died. He was weak for a long time afterwards—so weak that Maurice could throw him in their wrestlings.

In this way he escaped many months of Oscott. He recovered his health under a course of cod-liver oil and was never again seriously troubled by his lungs. The zest for life returned, and the respite from school was the happiest period in his childhood. Long days were spent on the lake, where excellent pike and trout could be caught. He made a collection of wild birds' eggs, and wrote to his schoolfellows about his finds. There were wonderful picnics to Castle Island and to Castle Carra. Their father taught the boys to shoot, and the stables, jockeys and racing were a constant source of excitement; sometimes George was allowed to mount a race horse. Other of Moore's horses besides Croaghpatrick were doing pretty well, notably Master George, who was expected to win the Cambridgeshire, and a small private race course was laid down in the fields, below the woods on the west side of the house.

Again Moore was frequently away from home, but he provided his sons with tutors, one of whom, Father James Browne, a priest of the old school, redolent of the classics, was remembered with affection. He was short-sighted and good-natured, and it amused the boys to hide in the appletree on his approach and hear him say to the gardener: " Where is Master George and where is Master Maurice ? " " The story that my brother tells in one of his books about classical discussions with Father Browne and his precocious interest in Propertius is," Colonel Moore says, " quite fictitious."

On the return to Oscott at the beginning of 1865, George was accompanied by Maurice. George was put in the " Cæsar " class, his brother in the " grammar." Neither learned anything, perhaps the teaching was unintelligent. Maurice began at the head of the class and gradually sank to the bottom ; the other remained at the bottom of his until the end. Maurice Moore had been reading Cæsar before he went to Oscott ; he was now set to learn grammar and lost interest, leaving the impression that his abilities were beyond his performance. He knew French fairly well from his governess, but now gradually forgot it. George knew less French than his brother, but perhaps he knew more Latin, or rather his brother knew less. Though he played no more games than was obligatory, he must have picked up some knowledge of cricket, for when many years later he used to stay with Sir William Geary in Kent he used to watch the village matches and was, his host tells me, " a faithful critic of the bowling."

On their holidays George and Maurice were rated for dunces by their father. They put Father Browne to shame when a great dinner was given for the two families by the Blakes of Tower Hill, the Moores' nearest neighbours. All the young Blakes made fluent speeches, but George and Maurice were tongue tied. They also compared unfavourably with the Wilde boys, Oscar and Willie, who lived at Cong with their father in the summer time and used sometimes to row up the lake to spend an afternoon at Moore Hall. Nor could George find interest in the books that his father proposed for him; Scott, Macaulay, Burke. But he had a great literary experience at the age of eleven when he read *Lady Audley's Secret*. In 1863 all the world was talking about *Lady Audley's Secret*, and he has described in more than one of his books how he heard his parents discuss Miss Braddon's famous story as they sat opposite to him in the old family coach which was lumbering between Claremorris and Moore Hall. It was early morning (he had just made the long journey from Oscott) and he was sleepily watching the plovers as they rose out of the desolate waters of a bog which stretched away to blue mountains. The magic of the name " Lady Audley " aroused him, and the holidays were not far spent before he stole into his father's dressing room for the novel, which he read " eagerly, passionately, vehemently."

The incident gave him confidence in his instincts. Henceforth he would only know what he wanted to know, and as the terms passed at Oscott his teachers grew more and more exasperated. On the 22nd of December 1865 Northcote, the headmaster, reported of him as follows:

Of George, I scarcely know what to say—I mean as to his learning. As to his general conduct I really think school discipline seems to be having some effect as it has on every boy.

But of his progress in learning I can scarcely say too little. In Arithmetic he is positively the last in the House. And as to the Orthography, I send you a specimen of his examination papers, which will explain for why I *almost* despair of ever teaching him to spell. It is a translation (or mistranslation) of his Latin author—but I do not send it to you for the sake of the Latin part of the story; but that you may see how hopelessly *careless* he is in the spelling. It is not mere ignorance which teaching might hope to remove but the complete indifference with which the very same word is spelt in two or three different ways in the same sentence *proclaimed*, *proclamed*, *gentle*, *gentil*, *haughty, haighty,* etc.—In another paper, *Jesus* was spelt *Jeasus,* etc.

The habitual inattention and thoughtlessness necessary to produce such results as these seems almost to defy cure. I send you these specimens not to find fault with George, so much as to justify our own masters, whose labours have produced such infinitesimally small results. We have one other case in the house, almost equal to George's, and even in a much older boy; but I really think in that case a considerable improvement has been made this half year; indeed I am satisfied there has. I shall still hope therefore that renewed efforts, if only seconded by George himself, may effect something for him too. Wishing Mrs. Moore and yourself and boys all the joys and blessings of this holy season.

His father became admonitory. He threatened to deprive George of the next summer holidays, and ordered him to try to improve his spelling by writing home every day three good pages of a letter.

Jan. 25, 1866.

My dear Papa, I did not wilfully disobey your commands about writing you three pages of note paper. I could not do it it was quite impossible for me to do it every day if you will only try it for a week or two you will find it more difficult than you expect just you write me three pages every day and you will soon get puzzled about [what] you would say to fill up the three pages. Keep my pocket money if you will but dont keep me here during the vac I am sure that if I could only see you half an hour that I could convince you that I could not writ that letter of three pages besides my writing is much smaller than yours and I write much closer together than yours this letter would fill up twice as much space if I write wider apart I have made a great deel of improvement in spelling since midsummer do not be cross with me any more I will soon know how to spill perfectly the wood cocks must have been plentiful for you to shoot so many I am sure you will change your mind and take me home next summer just you try and write a letter every day and you wont find it so easy

I remain yours
George Moore.

Jan. 28th, 1866.

My dear Papa It appears to me that you think that I do not care two pins if I spell cat dog and dog cat but really the case is not so. I have made considerable progress both in spelling and writing since midsummer. It is of no good being cross with me any more if you will only correct the mistakes I make and send them to me I am sure that we by acting in concert will do a good deal more good than by scolding me and as for three pages a day it is not so easy as you might at first suppose if it was to different people it would not be so hard. I got a letter from my Aunt Browne who was kind enough to send me a post office order for a pound it was the hardest task I ever had to read her letter I will send you her letter by post I wrote to her the day following that I got her letter. Now my dear Papa we will be friends and you will not be cross with me any more. I am sure that we will do much good if you will only follow the advice of this letter. I hope that you are all well at home I suppose that the drawing room is finished by this time You must not expect a letter of three pages every day but I will write when I can If I could get a book of those everyday letters I could write one out every day and send it to you punish me if you like but dont be cross with me any more I have got such scolding letters from you lately that it has made me very sad but I dont like to be getting sentimental I am not generally so do not be too fast when you read this letter and send me another scolding one give my love to all at home

I remain yours affectionately
George A. Moore

Please send me a translation of my aunt's letter I could only make out a little of it.

The threats were repeated as the summer holidays approached, and George was distraught with fear. " My dear Papa," he wrote on the 5th of July, " if you do not take me home for the vacation while everybody else is going home I will be laughed at and I will scarcely be able to stop here. If you will take me home for the vacation I will try to improve myself. If you only knew what I will suffer by stopping here for goodness sake take me home. I hope you and all at home are well, I remain yours George Moore." And on the back of the sheet : " Everybody is going home but me."

6

It is not on record that George was punished by being left at Oscott during the summer holiday of 1866. But at the beginning of the second half year further complaints reached his father from Northcote. " There is nothing singular or outstanding in Maurice's backwardness," wrote the President. " . . . George however is deplorably deficient." The question of George's removal had already been raised, but Northcote thought they should wait until Christmas in the hope that in this interval the boy might make a decided step in advance. It was elementary teaching that George resisted; the rest of his class was now beginning Greek, and Northcote suggested that during the Greek hours he should be employed upon simple sums, spelling and the beginnings of grammar. In November " unquestionable improvement " was reported, and a composition was mentioned which disclosed a " certain measure of thought " and was better in spelling. Indeed, George won a prize, or found himself specially commended for, some literary exercise; to imagine the surprise of the other boys is easy: the classroom rocked with laughter, as though he had surpassed himself in eccentricity. It is the Colonel's recollection that George showed some little interest in history at this time and that the composition in question was on a historical subject.

Northcote was still worrying about him, and so was his father. " If I knew of any tutor," Northcote wrote, " whose *speciality* it was to deal with cases of this kind, I would recommend you to try him. . . . But I do not. . . . A change from Oscott to an ordinary private tutor would I conceive only be a change for the worse. He would lose the advantages of regular discipline and good company, without gaining any corresponding benefit." It may have been about this time that George showed reluctance in going to Confession and began an intrigue with a serving-maid. According to the story in *Salve* he wrote home saying that if the maid servant were sent away he would escape from school and marry her at once: news which made his father saddle the grey pony and ride as hard as he could to catch the boat train at Claremorris. In the President's study at Oscott, the boy was brought before the two men—Northcote, big and square, and so hairy that he was called the Gorilla, and a side-whiskered parent who inspired fear although his eyes were kind. There was a general reckoning and questions of religion as well as of behaviour were raised. " But, Dr. Northcote, I'm not sure that I believe in Confession, so why should I be obliged to go to Confession ? Dr. Northcote, you did not always believe in Confession yourself." The observation caused the boy's father to move quickly out of the light in order that the President might not catch the look of amused embarrassment which crossed his face. Northcote had been a Protestant up to the time of his wife's death, and he had a son at Oscott.

" Will you write to me on this subject ? " Moore questioned his brother in a letter from Ebury Street, dated the 8th of January 1912 when *Salve* was on the way to publication. " If you have forgotten the incident I will make you say you have forgotten." The Colonel had forgotten; but he could remember something about a pretty maidservant whom George was reported to have singled out for his attentions in the chapel by screwing his neck round in a way that astonished the other boys. In his early novel *A Mere Accident* Moore described a school-chapel which was evidently meant for the one at Oscott. " The maid servants kneel in that corner," says one of the characters. " They present a temptation where there are a number of young men. I have noticed that some of the young men look round when the maid servants come into church."

A bouquet and a tryst at the foot of the stairs was the most that it amounted to. Northcote's letters deal solely with the refractory scholar and say nothing of misconduct. Still there is no doubt that even before this George had let it be known both at home and at school that he had shaken off all belief in supernatural religion. The Colonel remembers him making the announcement one day on the staircase of Moore Hall. His mother only said that she was " sorry," and he was rather shocked by her apparent indifference. Many years later he described his family as detestable " from a religious point of view," because no member of it cared to go deeply into theology with him. He had no complaint to make of bigotry, but why, he asked, did his father not put a bible into his hands ? Very likely his parents believed that he was only trying to show off and horrify, and thought that the wisest method with him was to pretend to attach no importance to his opinions.

It was about this time, or possibly a little earlier, that he made the splendid discovery of Shelley which irradiated his world with a new light. Shelley was not a poet whom his father quoted, and George came upon him by·the accident of finding him mentioned in another of Miss Braddon's books —for after he had finished *Lady Audley's Secret* he read every new novel by Miss Braddon. In *The Doctor's Wife* the heroine loved Shelley and Byron, and George must needs love Shelley too. But why was he not attracted to Byron ? He explained afterwards that it was " echo augury "—" Shelley that crystal name and his poetry also crystalline "—which caused him to ransack the library at Moore Hall until at last he found a small pocket edition of the poet which opened at *The Sensitive Plant* " I think," he wrote twenty years later in his *Confessions of a Young Man*, " I had expected to understand better; but I had no difficulty in assuming that I was satisfied and delighted. And henceforth the little volume never left my pocket, and I read the dazzling stanzas by the shores of a pale green Irish lake. . . ."

After Shelley and Byron he asked for Kirke White, again being attracted by the sound of a name, but in this case he was disappointed and lost patience as soon as he had read two or three pages. He brought his copy of Shelley back with him to Oscott, and in the hope of being expelled for having an atheistical work in his possession, he showed the volume to a prefect, saying that he had begun to wonder if it was wrong to read it, as Shelley seemed to deny the existence of God. The book was confiscated, but this closed the incident. " My brother was eccentric at school," Colonel Moore writes to me, " and liked to do odd things even at the cost of being ridiculous. But his suggestion [in *Salve*] that he was expelled is misleading. He was never guilty of anything that deserved expulsion." The facts are that George Henry Moore asked the President to provide his son with special tutoring, but this being beyond the resources of the college, it was amicably decided between parent and schoolmaster that George had better be removed from Oscott.

Then there followed a year of hunting, shooting and attendance at race meetings. A proposal that he should adopt steeplechase riding as a profession was discouraged by his parents, and he never rode in a race, even on the private course of Moore Hall. For company he depended a good deal on the trainers and grooms of his father's establishment; Maurice Moore had gone back to Oscott, taking with him the third brother, Augustus, and the two other children, his sister Nina and Julian, the youngest of the family, were too small to be playmates of a boy of fifteen.

Another attempt was made to educate him. Father James Browne was again summoned; with Irish amiability he predicted that the day would come when the boy would give up hunting and everything for the classics. Mrs. Moore only laughed. " Am I then so stupid ? " George asked his mother. The boy was allowed the run of the library and his father encouraged him to talk of the poets, but George Moore already felt obscurely that literature should be loved for its own sake, and that his father, although a forcible critic of books, did not love literature in this way.

7

After a run of bad luck George Henry Moore was forced
to give up his stable for the second time. There was some talk
of a removal to Alicante where a house and some property
still remained in the possession of the family: but the temptation of politics deflected him from this project. He advocated
reforms in the system of land tenure, and by enlisting the
priests on his side was enabled in 1868 to win a memorable
election, which broke the political power of the Mayo landlords for ever. George accompanied his father to some of
the meetings and was present at the declaration of the
poll. The neighbours in the big places, numerous at that
time about Moore Hall, were very angry. " I don't think,
literally," wrote Moore's kinsman Lord Sligo, " that anyone
free from the power of the priest will vote for Moore—no
educated person at any rate." Before these events Moore
had been well liked by all classes and creeds, but now his
social position was seriously damaged, and few came to his
door except Nationalist politicians and priests, who indeed
showed a greater appreciation of his intellectual abilities
than his former associates. After his death one of the politicians said that he might have rivalled Berkeley in brilliance
if he had chosen to devote himself to metaphysical studies,
and a priest spoke of the wonderful entertainment he provided when he discussed the comparative merits of the great
Greek and classic authors, reserving his greatest eloquence
for descriptions of the perfection of Greek art. But as a
politician he suffered from an excess of pugnacity and a
reluctance to trust others, characteristics inherited in some
degree by his eldest son.

Early in 1869 the family moved to London for the convenience of Moore's parliamentary duties and after a short
stay in lodgings took a lease of 39, Alfred Place, just opposite
South Kensington Station. The three boys, George, Maurice
and Augustus, were a noisy crew, shouting and fighting in
the garden, and the quiet square regarded the Irish intrusion
as a nuisance. Moore himself was always back and forth
between London and Ireland. The suffering of the Fenian

GEORGE HENRY MOORE, M.P.: GEORGE MOORE'S FATHER

prisoners moved him deeply, and in a speech at Castlebar he showed himself a master of invective. " Her sceptre," he said, speaking of English Government in Ireland, " has been the sword, her diadem the black cap, and her throne the gallows." *The Times* threatened him with gaol, but he met the challenge by collecting an Irish crowd round him in Trafalgar Square and repeating the words. Politics however were seldom discussed in the family. George once asked: " Do you think, Father, that you could get Repeal of the Union if you had eighty members for it ? " But this was apparently the only occasion on which he showed any interest in his father's parliamentary career.

His chatter about racing matters was, on the other hand, unceasing; he spent much of his time in what he described as his two clubs, the Alliance and Exchange, both betting shops; and Applely, the ex-jockey who had been left in charge of Moore Hall, became a favoured correspondent.

July 29th 1869.

Dear Joe,

Great success at Goodwood I backed Stater and Restitution for the double event at 48 to 1 also Stater at 10 Was not that good : you said in your last letter that Restitution could not win with 9 st I dont know what made you think that because he was only giving 18 lbs to *Brigantine* for a year at that counting sex is not half enough over $2\frac{1}{2}$ miles I am indebted to you for St although you dont know it If you remember you told me that if a horse ran a severe race for *Ascott Cup* that he could never win at Goodwood You seem to have forgotten that yourself but I did not and it was of use to me you see and I also got good information too I backed the *Palmer* for the Chesterfield Cup I know he is a great horse and ought to win but 9st 8 is a steader I did not hedge this double event although everybody told me I knew *Restitution* was sure to win I saw *Baron Roschilde* Tell me something for the Caesarewitch and Cambridgeshire if you hear anything I and William used to have great disputes about the Stakes he

said that *War* and *Alpenstock* were the best in it but I
was lucky enough to stick to the *Stater* all through and
won a good bit It is a hard thing to win a double event.

I am yours truly

George A Moore

P.S. You will see in the account of the Goodwood Stakes
very well and made very strong *running* he is in the Lewis
Grand handicap 2 miles at 6 st 3 years old if I see him coming
in the betting I shall back him tell me what you think of
him and chance your *fair Wind* I have a very moderate
opinion of is in at 7st 6 don't know what to make of it.
Palmer is sure to win hope you are well if you want
anything on I will put it in for you

George A Moore

Shelley seemed forgotten in this environment. But there
was a small book case at No. 39, and George and Maurice
took a course of Dickens together. " My brother," says
Colonel Moore, " often read aloud to me, choosing mostly
the amusing parts."

On several occasions his father found time to take the two
elder boys to the National Gallery; he showed them round,
naming the painters and elucidating points in famous
pictures. It was the beginning of George's artistic education.
Colonel Moore remembers that his father once stopped
opposite a " Christ," and said " Call George's attention to
the foreshortening of the arm in that figure." This was to
draw George, who was putting on airs of superior knowledge.
" I was," Colonel Moore adds, " either too shy or too
ignorant to play-act. Long after Mother told me that Father
regarded us both as hopeless. He said, ' I fear those two red-
headed boys are stupid, perhaps Augustus and Julian will
do better.' "

But it was not until he met Jim Browne, who lived with
two sisters in a terrace off the Exhibition Road, that George
Moore conceived a real desire for art. " The great blond
man " was a member of the Mayo tribe of Brownes, and
therefore a connection of the Moores; one of his paintings,

" The Burial of an Indian Chief," had been bought for Moore Hall and occupied a prominent position in the top passage of the house. Jim had been painting his huge canvases for many years, and the Royal Academy (to encourage him, it was said) once accepted a work by him. He lacked the force of character and distinction of the true artist, but he talked very plausibly about art and women, was handsome, beautifully dressed and a society man: in brief, his conversation and style of living excited George Moore's imagination and caused him to think that the life of a painter must be the " jolliest " in the world, jollier even than that of a steeplechase rider. More than a glimpse of Jim Browne is given in the ridiculous figure of Mr. Barton in Moore's novel, *Muslin*.

The next step in Moore's artistic education was the School of Art in the South Kensington Museum, then building. Accompanied by Maurice he attended the evening classes. " We did not get much beyond drawing from the flat, ornaments, etc.," the Colonel says. " We then began to wander into the Museum where there was at that time a large collection of paintings. George soon made the acquaintance of the girls who copied them." He had a talent for ingratiating himself with young women, a talent which took him by surprise; for he was self-conscious about his appearance, having always been told that he was the ugly duckling of the family.

Girls of another sort were the immediate occasion of his despatch to an army tutor. Naturally, in these months of idleness, grave consideration was being given to his future, but he could not even say what profession he would dislike least. The discovery of Alma in tights and Kate in short skirts—photographs of the daughters of a small tradesman of Hammersmith that were left lying about the house— decided his father to send him at once to Jurles's off Marylebone Road, an army tutor famed at that time for his successes with the stupidest boys. Anonymous death on a battlefield, we are told did not attract George Moore, and he gave little attention to the instruction of Jurles. But he attended the classes with some regularity and at them he made two good friends (Colville and Belfort are the names given them in *Vale*), who shared his taste for betting and for horses and brought him into touch—or gave him the impression of being in touch—with the fast life and the fashionable beauties of St. John's Wood.

Jim Browne, however, continued to exercise an influence, and on an off day from Jurles, George Moore surprised his family by bringing back easel, brushes, paints, palette, and a coloured print of a flower girl from a shop in the Brompton Road, which sold artists' materials. He set up the easel in the back parlour and finished copying the print in about an hour. Then fetching his brother from the drawing-room, he asked him if the copy was not good; on hearing Maurice's reply that it was a daub, he pushed him unceremoniously from the room and told him that he knew nothing about painting, which was quite true. An hour later George had painted out the first effort and finished a new copy. Again Maurice was fetched and his criticism demanded as eagerly as though he were a high authority on art. No sooner had he repeated his previous opinion than his qualifications vanished and he was hustled once more from the room. Shortly afterwards, Colonel Lutyens, the inventor, and an artist of quality (father of the architect), consented to give the young aspirant a few lessons.

Jurles was about to complain of his pupil's idleness and to recommend his removal from the military academy when bad news came from Ireland. George Henry Moore had been called home from London on account of an agrarian disturbance which had broken out on his estates. Inspired by a dishonest bailiff, a combination of his tenants thought to blackmail their landlord by demanding heavy reductions of rent. Moore had won his seat in Mayo as a champion of the people and it was calculated that rather than risk his position as an Irish leader he would surrender to the agitation. The conspirators, however, had mistaken their man. Moore was a kind landlord, but he was not ready to be fooled or bullied, and in spite of his advocacy of tenant-right he clung to a feudal idea of his relationship with his tenants—that is to say, having done his duty as a landlord he expected a return of personal loyalty and affection. He was in great distress of mind when he crossed to Ireland a few days before Easter of 1870; but he was determined to evict every one of his Ballintubber tenants who refused to pay his rent in full. George remembered how he returned from the front door at Alfred Place to bid his son good-bye and in obedience to a sudden impulse put a sovereign into the boy's hand.

From Dublin he wrote to a friend, one of his neighbours in Mayo, to meet him and dine with him at Moore Hall on Easter Sunday and pass the day with him there. The friend replied that certain fixed arrangements prevented him, but that they would meet at Moore Hall on Sunday. Moore arrived home on Good Friday, having posted all the way from Athenry, some thirty-five miles, and next day he wrote to the friend to come early on Monday. In a letter of the same date to his wife, he said:

Moore Hall.
Saturday, 16th April 1870.

My dearest Mary,

I arrived yesterday and found the place looking well, considering that the trees are not yet in leaf. The climate and air are delicious, and it seems to me as if it were " good for us to be here," and that if we could build tabernacles for ourselves in this world we could find a paradise for ourselves here.

I shall send a telegraph message to you on Monday if I leave then. If you do not receive a message from me, come over by Monday evening's train; there will be a great deal to be done. God bless you; give my love to the children and believe me always

your affectionate and devoted husband
G. H. Moore.

On Sunday his neighbour received another letter from him which said that if he came at three on Monday it would be time enough. The friend accordingly arrived at that hour, but was handed a note by Appley which ran: " I am so unwell I cannot even see you to-day," and calling again on the next day, he found George Henry Moore speechless but still conscious, a priest, Father Lavelle, being present to administer the Last Sacrament. Moore had gone to his room tired out, early on Monday, leaving word that he should not be disturbed until the following morning; he was asleep when Applely knocked at the usual hour, and he still seemed to be sleeping an hour or two later; a doctor was called and diagnosed cerus apoplexy " such as statesmen often get," and Father Lavelle spoke of a heart broken by ingratitude and political frustration.[1]

A telegram summoned Mrs. Moore to Mayo, and she came with her eldest son. A contemporary record describes their arrival at Moore Hall. " I met," wrote the reporter of the *Freeman's Journal*, " the Rev. Conroy and the Rev. Lavelle who strove to administer all the consolations of religion to Mrs. Moore in her bitter sorrow and also to her eldest son, whose grief for his departed father was excessive in the extreme."

In *Vale*, written forty years or more later, Moore gave an account of the arrival at Moore Hall, of his mother's grief and of the impression which the death made upon him:

> I remember nothing till somebody came into the sum-mer room to tell my mother that if she wished to see him again she must come at once, for they were about to put him into his coffin, and snatching me by the hand, she said, " We must say a prayer for him." The dead man lay on the very bed in which I was born, his face covered with a handkerchief, and as my mother was about to lift it from his face the person who had brought us thither warned us from the other side of the white dimity curtain not to do so.
>
> " He is changed."
>
> " I don't care," she cried, and snatched away the hand-kerchief, revealing to me the face all changed. And it is this changed face that lives in my memory.

[1] The story has been told at some length because George Moore, very impressionable, was quick to imagine a case of suicide, and this led to a conflict with his brother Colonel Moore in their later years. See introduction by George Moore to Maurice Moore's life of G. H. Moore, *An Irish Gentleman*, and Prelude to *Memoirs of My Dead Life* (Moore Hall and Uniform edition) and also pages 307–8 of this book.

In the much earlier book, the *Confessions*, he had described his father as " the one pure image of his mind, the one true affection," adding that in the midst of his grief he had been conscious that he would not bring his father back if he could, for his father's death had redeemed him from the army and from Jurles.

George was chief mourner at the funeral; not many of the gentry attended, but the poor came from all over Mayo, and the coffin was borne on the shoulders of sixteen tenants to the chapel of Carnacun where the classical priest, old Father James Browne, officiated. When High Mass was over they took the body to the family vault, first built for George Henry Moore's father, at Kiltoome, the little hill of pine and beech, which is on the isthmus between the two arms of the lake, about a mile from Moore Hall.

It was known that the young Land League priest, Father Lavelle, proposed to deliver a political harangue at Kiltoome, and this perhaps was the reason why Lord John Browne, who represented the Sligo family at the funeral, bade George good-bye at Carnacun, and would not follow the cortège round the lake, pleading that he feared the cold March wind. At Kiltoome, Father Browne begged Father Lavelle to desist from speech making and there was some confusion, the multitude siding with the younger priest, who mounted the tomb and delivered a prodigious panegyric upon the dead man which occupied two columns of the next day's newspapers. " Woe, woe is Ireland. George Henry Moore is gone. The pale of death has fallen on her most gifted and devoted son. Oh, my country, now mayst thou weep—weep scalding tears from your million eyes until their very fountains are dried up. Long years of mourning after to-day art thou widowed indeed. . . . Those weeds of ages of thine he had resolved should be changed into nuptial robes of brightness and joy. . . ."

All eyes now turned on young Mr. Moore of Moore Hall, and it is no wonder that he felt self-conscious, and conjectured that all the dispersing mourners were asking themselves how far he would match his father in character and achievement.

8

" We cannot," he said to his mother a few weeks later,
" spend all our lives here, going to Kiltoome with flowers."
The property to which he had succeeded consisted of
12,371 acres in Co. Mayo and of 110 acres in Co. Roscommon, and its valuation was £3,596 per annum. The actual
rents received by Irish landlords were usually about 25
per cent in excess of this valuation; in the case of the Moores
the excess was smaller; but the rents when they were paid
provided an income of nearly £4,000 a year. Some of the
land was very poor, particularly on the Ballintubber estate,
and George Henry Moore had made matters worse by his
habit of sub-dividing land and giving holdings to the sons
of farmers, thus adding to the number of uneconomic
tenancies on his estates. The payment of rent was therefore
very uncertain, and moreover the property bore heavy
charges. In a chapter of the French edition of the *Confessions*
(1888) Moore wrote: " I found myself heir to a considerable
fortune, from three to four thousand pounds a year." He
deleted the sentence afterwards. After the deduction of the
interest on the mortgages not more than £500 a year was
left but this was enough to enable him to live what he thought
to be life. His three brothers would be obliged to fend for
themselves when they were grown up.

Even if he had wished for it there could have been no
question of his taking up the running where his father had
dropped out. The close of the first chapter of his life caused
him no pang. He retained vivid and happy memories of his
Irish childhood, but many years were to pass before he
began to dwell on these memories and to extract from them
a literary significance. Jim Browne had said: " If you want
to learn painting you must go to Paris," and the word Paris,
like the word Shelley, had intoxicated him. In the train that
bore them from Mayo, Moore told his mother decidedly that
he would forsake the army tutor and become a painter. Mrs.
Moore raised no objection but she did not facilitate her son's
plan to study in Paris, and being under age, he could not at
once obey the call. Lord Sligo, his guardian, and his uncle

Joseph Blake, constrained him, and he therefore continued in Alfred Place for another three years, as a young man about town with a good allowance.

In after years Moore wrote half-mockingly of his early aspirations for art, saying that his " studio " was little more than an amusement, a means of access to " tapestries, smoke, models and conversations," a more amusing way of seeing life than betting parlours. All the same his love of pictures was already very genuine. A Botticelli in the National Gallery held him, he says, in thrall, and he used to stand outside a Kensington house, where there was a modern collection, until he saw the owner come down the steps and enter his carriage; he would then knock at the door, with five shillings in his hand, to beg to be allowed to see a famous Rossetti.

The young man continued to model himself largely on Jim Browne, learning at that source his taste in dress, food and the figures of women; on one occasion Lord Sligo, who as a rule seems to have shown little interest in his duties as a guardian, protested against Jim's influence, but without avail. George's mother predicted imminent ruin. Toilet knick-nacks and scent cost him a good deal; he was minded to be a coxcomb, and to appear more " nice," less Irish, than his brothers and cousins. According to his own account he concealed nothing and boasted of dissipations, but being endowed with a very clear sense of self-preservation " there was no need for fear." In point of fact he did get into trouble more than once, not on account of women but on account of money. An impecunious musical and theatrical family of his acquaintance, four boys and their mother—one of them is said to have suggested Dick Lennox in *A Mummer's Wife*—inveigled him into backing one of their theatrical enterprises (they brought an entire company from Paris to play *Chilpéric* and other light operas), and he would have been in a serious financial scrape if he had not been able to escape his liabilities on the plea that he was under age. On another occasion he negotiated a secret loan with the largest of his tenants, the business being done through the cunning old butler Applely. The matter came to the ears of Mrs.

Moore, and Applely was dismissed from service. He retired to the village to which his Irish wife belonged, and eked out a miserable existence, but Moore was good enough to remember him when he came of age and to restore him to his pantry.

Moore liked to tell the story of his own life in his own way and with his own interpretations. " I remember," writes the American author and critic, Mr. Vincent O'Sullivan, " once spending an evening with him and with a painter named Dampier. George Moore was then well over forty. Dampier persisted in recalling to him a night passed with some girls in some dance garden (Cremorne perhaps), and told not without humour how Moore would pause now and then to urge his companions to unbridled revelry, pointing out that it was the duty of men and women to make merry and on occasion to occupy the same bed. Moore listened to this with some discomfort and at last said violently: ' Don't you ever forget anything ? ' " In the report which Moore has himself given of his early manhood he has not given the impression that he possessed high spirits or a capacity for violent enjoyment. He certainly owed nothing to artificial stimulus, and at no time in his life did he resort to wine or spirits in any quantity. The drinking habits, becoming at last dipsomania, of Kate Ede in *A Mummer's Wife*, though well portrayed, is no more the result of personal experience than Zola's drunkards in *L'Assommoir*. As to drugs it is certain that he never thought of them, and nowhere in his books are they mentioned as accessories or instruments.

His intellectual life was still very crude, but he hungered for great truths, and Shelley suggesting Godwin to him he proceeded in the line of the nineteenth century English liberal and positivist thinkers. He never mapped out a programme of study, but he turned over the pages of Darwin, Buckle, Mill, Lecky and George Eliot, and could quote these writers in support of his contention for disbelief. Like his father, who passed for an astronomer on the strength of having perused one work on astronomy, he was quick to glean such knowledge of the salient points of a book as would enable him to speak of it with an impressive confidence. His brother even remembers metaphysical conversations and an exchange of a copy of Berkeley's *Principles* for Plato's *Republic*; and he has himself related that he went on one occasion to the Derby with a party of " tarts and mashers," a copy of Kant's *Critique of Pure Reason* in his pocket. But he soon decided that science and speculative philosophy, science in particular, were things that he did not want to learn.

Mention of the *Critique* must remind his biographer, as it always reminded him, of a dear friend whom he made before his twentieth year—Mrs. Bridger, a wise and witty woman, the mother of " Colville," one of the young men with whom he had raced about London while he was supposed to be studying at Jurles'. The Bridgers were a family of squires settled at Old Shoreham, Sussex, for 200 years, and when Moore first went to stay with them the old squire was still alive and lived in the big house called Buckingham, a park of 70 acres, the scene of the opening of *Esther Waters*. Moore's friends occupied another property, Little Buckingham, and the family consisted of a mother and a father, young Harry Colvill Bridger of the long yellow moustaches and two sisters who still wore their long fair hair down to their waists. They were very kind, very unpretentious people, and George with his hunger for great truths passed with them for a remarkably learned young man. Mrs. Bridger, who mothered him, knew the truth, perhaps, for she laughed at him abundantly and though she seemed to be a religious woman she would not enter into religious discussion with him. One day he reproached her with being satisfied with mere belief, and quoted a passage from the *Critique*: she interrupted him and declared that she would henceforth call him Kant. The nickname was not adopted by the rest of the family, but she held to it, and as long as she lived she never addressed him in any other way. He said that if it had been possible he would certainly have asked her to marry him, and she must have been the first of the many women to whom he paid this compliment.

CHAPTER II

PARIS

I

ON THE VERGE OF THE STEP which was to determine
his future life, Moore showed no misgiving. The 24th February 1873 was the date of his majority and in a fever of haste
to carry out the project which he had nursed in his heart
since the day when Jim Browne had uttered the magic word,
he set out for Paris. We find him driving one miserable
morning from the Gare du Nord to the Hôtel Quai Voltaire,
an Irish valet with him, and he feels bound to apologise for
the appearance of the city before returning to his phrase
book. He carried with him several trunks and boxes full
of clothes, books, pictures, and he had in his pocket a
passport signed by Lord Granville requesting that Mr.
George Moore (British Subject) travelling on the Continent
with a man-servant named William Moloney (British Subject)
be allowed to pass freely and receive every protection. The
date of the passport, March 13th 1873, shows that Moore
did not go to Paris until he came of age, although in one of
his books he speaks of his life in Paris as a young man of
twenty. The name of his valet is given as Mullowney in the
Confessions and *Hail and Farewell*.

The Quai Voltaire was an old-fashioned family hotel
where Wagner had written the libretto of the *Meistersinger*;
Moore's apartments consisted of three rooms, one of which
he reserved for Jim Browne in the hope of enticing him to
Paris. As intended, he entered the Beaux Arts where his
first master was Alexandre Cabanel, a painter whose ideal
nudes excited his admiration. Although it was two or three
years since he had first planned to come to Paris, he had,
strangely enough, not acquired sufficient French to enable

him to explain that what he wanted was private tuition in Cabanel's own studio. He so disliked the rough and tumble of the Beaux Arts and the early hours (he was always a late riser) that after a few days he abandoned the schools and spent weeks walking up and down the boulevards looking at the photographs of the Salon pictures and wondering what he should do next. His valet advised him to return to his mother.

It seems that he made one other attempt to obtain private tuition, travelling out to Enghien to see a painter called Sevres, of whom he remembered hearing his father speak. This was his first sight of French country, and he was fascinated by tall poplars and green river banks and a lake reflecting the foliage and the stems of sapling oak and pine. In other respects the visit was not a success, first because Sevres could do nothing for him unless he came to live in Enghien and secondly because the mistress he imagined for Sevres—the Rubens-like Venus in the Salon picture of which his father had once shown him a photograph—failed to appear in the course of his interview with the artist.

Presently he moved from the Hôtel Quai Voltaire to a less expensive place, the Hôtel de Russie, which stood at the corner of the Rue Drouot and the Boulevard des Italiens. This hotel, which has been long since demolished, was recommended to him by his bankers. Moloney, the valet, was still with him—a Mayo peasant, formerly second man at Moore Hall, an excellent servant, Colonel Moore says, but with rather primitive manners. Byron abroad had a valet who sighed after beer, beef and a wife; and Moore's valet must do likewise, at least in the first edition of the *Confessions*. Moloney, in point of fact, had a wife in Mayo, but he did not sigh for her. He got on very well, too well, with the French. Paris went to his head and when Moore was obliged to dismiss him, he would not return to Ireland but obtained with Jim Browne's help a good situation in a London house.

Close to the Hôtel de Russie was Jullian's Academy of painting in the Passage des Panaromas, where Moore now became a pupil. Jullian had been in turn a shepherd, a

painter and an invincible masked man in a circus; the story
of his life has been told by Moore in a chapter of *Impressions
and Opinions* (1891), " Meissonier and the Salon Julian."
Here Moore attacked commercialism in art, Jullian having
become by the time the chapter was written an influential
man in the world of art, the managing director of a chain of
studios, the teaching in which provided the Salon each year
with dozens of mechanical drawings and paintings. It was
the well known painter Jules Lefebvre who recommended
Jullian, and at that time there were about twenty pupils in
the studio. Lefebvre and Boulanger used to pass round the
room among the easels, giving words of advice according to
the conventional Parisian technique. In these early days the
studio had still the character of a little family gathering, and
Jullian would sometimes conduct his pupils personally to
Meudon and Bas Meudon, and after a long day spent in
painting in the open air they would dine together at some
simple inn. The hot evenings would awake in Jullian some
memory of his beloved South and he would beguile the
company with memories of his adventurous past, and his
descriptions of the masked man taking fire in the hearts of his
pupils, they would demand instruction in attack and
counter-attack, and soon the moonlight was filled with
straining and prostrate forms. He had known Balzac, and
the stories he told of the great novelist may have sent Moore
to the *Comédie Humaine* which soon became for him his
mirror of the world. Most of those who came to the Passage
des Panoramas were English or American, but Moore picked
up a great deal of French in the months which followed his
entry into the studio. His approach to the language was
entirely by ear.

From the first there was no love lost between Jullian and
George Moore. " A typical Southerner," Moore wrote in
the *Confessions*, " the large stomach, the dark eyes, crafty
and watchful; the seductively mendacious manner, the
sensual mind. . . . To him my forty francs, a month's sub-
scription, were a godsend—nor were my invitations to
dinner and to the theatre disdained. . . . I felt this crafty
clever man of the world was necessary to me. I had never

met such a man before, and all my curiosity was awake. He spoke of art and literature, of the world and the flesh. . . ." Jullian when shown this passage in the *Confessions* is said to have retorted that there was " nothing that we could tell him that he had not already learned on his native bogs."

He had not been long at Jullian's before a young man of prepossessing appearance and gay light manners, introduced himself as a cousin of Jim Browne. This was the Lewis Ponsonby Marshall of the *Confessions* and of *Hail and Farewell*; his real name was Lewis Weldon Hawkins: a cosmopolitan, born in Stuttgart, brought up in Brussels, and a naturalized Frenchman. Hawkins painted with great facility and was loved for his own sake by a beautiful prostitute, whom he had brought with him from Belgium; for Moore the acquaintance opened new avenues for enjoyment and knowledge of life, and he spent a great part of the next six or nine months playing truant from Jullian's and amusing himself in cafés and dance-halls. He hero-worshipped, used and then dissected this enchanting youth —a not unusual progression in his relations with men. What induced Lewis to become Moore's cicerone is not related; but he had run through his money in two years of Paris and Moore with his five hundred a year must have passed for rich among Jullian's pupils.

2

There was a sudden return to Alfred Place in the Spring of 1874. It is explained in *Vale* that his departure from Paris was due to home-sickness; he had begun to pine for English food, for the English language and for his mother's house. In London he took a studio in Cromwell Mews where Millais who had been a friend of his father sometimes called. He used at this time to paint Rossetti-like women with long hair falling about their faces, and he got models to sit for him, one a pretty girl who used to be seen going to the Underground Station from one of the houses in Alfred Place: another his young sister, his portrait of whom was preserved at Moore Hall. It must also have been at this time that he attended Barthe's classes at Limerston Street and there formed a slight acquaintance with Whistler, who would sometimes look in, to draw a line or two to indicate the pose of the model and disappear as rapidly as he came. Among the students was Oliver Madox Brown, and he has told how his interest in the class declined after the sudden death of this young genius.[1] Whistler he did not like, nor could he yet bring himself to admire Whistler's work, so unbounded was his love of the pre-Raphaelites.

Jim Browne came to Alfred Place and described his compositions; but he had been displaced as an influence by Hawkins, who though absent in the flesh remained present in the spirit, determining not only the opinions but the dress and manners of his friend and to such an extent that, on his return to Paris, Jullian, catching sight of his Irish pupil on the boulevard, thought for a moment that he saw Hawkins. Another visitor at Alfred Place was a bulky youth from Galway destined to fill an important place in Moore's life. This was Edward Martyn of Tillyra Castle, Augustus's schoolfellow at Beaumont; and Martyn must have been drawing on his knowledge of the young George when he said years afterwards of his friend that he began out of nothing, developing from the mere sponge to the vertebræ and upwards. Colonel Moore's recollection is that during this stay in London his brother's conversation was chiefly of musical comedy, not of painting.

The studio cost more than £100 a year, and the Cremorne Gardens and Argyle Rooms were expensive amusements: His uncle, Joe Blake of Ballinafad, who collected the rents in Mayo, received frequent requests for advances of income. George was always being told that he ought to take an intelligent interest in his estate, but it was only when he needed ready money that his uncle heard from him. And apparently Joe Blake did not even trouble to send him yearly accounts. " I don't see any necessity for accounts," George wrote from Alfred Place, " I am sure we could go on for ever without

---

[1] Oliver Madox Browne died in 1874. In *Vale* Moore wrote as if he attended the Limerston Street classes two or three years earlier than this, but he often displaced events in his autobiographical narratives.

GEORGE MOORE *circa* 1873–5

but *enfin* it would be more satisfactory." He wanted advances on his income so as to pay off debts; if Joe Blake himself could not lend him the money, would he raise it for him in Ireland ? " I hope you will obtain it and immediately," he wrote, " I want the money even though you have to call an auction at Moore Hall (I am only speaking metaphorically) send me fifty pounds." Two pounds was all he asked for in another letter—" Send me two pounds for God's sake."

In later years, Moore, grown very cautious with money, did not like to acknowledge youthful extravagance, and attributed his early financial difficulties to the incompetence of his uncle, who had certainly no desire to be put to trouble on his account. " Let him get sense, and come home and collect his own rents," was Joe Blake's counsel to the family, but the young man recoiled from the prospect of a mediocre life by the lonely lake. He had not the means to cut a figure as an Irish landlord, and he determined upon a further sojourn in Paris. " I do not go there for instruction," he wrote to his uncle, " there is no such thing in painting, but because it is more convenient. As for spending the money that I did last time or running a rig of any kind, it is the most impossible of all imaginable things. I have greatly changed, I assure you. I shall not require more than £25 a month inclusive of every mortal thing."

However, as soon as he was back in Paris he resumed the companionship with Hawkins and continued to frequent the old haunts. He was still in outer aspect " the poor ignorant boy without preconceived ideas, without prejudice and without ambition," a memory of whom he summoned up fifty years later in *Avowals*. His spelling, grammar and punctuation were " as unconventional as a kitchen maid's."

Hôtel de Russie
Boulevard des Italiens.

March 28th 1875.

My dearest Mama

I am so sorry for not answering your letter So here goes for a scribble I cant correct so excuse faults, I know that you are lonely in London and I am sorry that I am not with you we are all away now. But I must be gay the Carnival is over the old King is dead. We had the greatest fun at the masked balls, I will tell you about it. The last one was the Micareme there was a large one at the Opera Comique Hawkins went as Faust I as Valantine a very beautiful girl as Margret and two others as Mephiste and Sibil we entered, all dressed, at different times first of all a fust was seen walking about then Mephiste was seen speaking to him then Margret then Velontin etc. everybody was noticing, thinking what a strange coincedence it was that all the characters should be there when we began speaking together and then wound up by all dancing a can can All the people formed a circle to see fust Margret etc. dancing a can can it was mentioned in the papers then we went to supper all together. Poor Nin I have not been to see her yet I am dying to but have not been able to afford it I went to see Miss Foy but have nothing to say pray forward my letters not the bills open them how is Maurice ask him to drop me a line I was on the eve of having a deal I thought I would have had one it is a long story I will tell you about it next time hoping you are well I remain yours affect

George Moore.

We find another account of the same ball in the pages of *Vale*, an instance of Moore's wonderful memory; he had forgotten nothing but the place. " I followed them one night to a masked ball dressed in the fantastic costume of Valentine in *Le Petit Faust*. Was it at Perren's I met *la belle Hollandaise* ? . . . She passed out of my life for ever and if I relate the incident of our meeting it is because I would pay tribute to her who revealed sensuality to me." Perren's was a famous old dance hall in the Rue du Bac. " It was there that I met most of the famous cocottes of the day," he said to Mr. Barrett Clark who, in 1922, was thinking of writing some illustrated sketches of the Paris of Moore. " I danced with them; I was a good dancer then. I see here a wonderful

article for you. Get photographs of these celebrated women—
you might describe Hortense."

During the summer of 1875 Moore's family visited Paris
and lodged with him at the Hôtel de Russie. " My brother
was painting at the time," Colonel Moore writes to me,
" and he used to be out most of the day, but in the evenings
I saw him in the hotel, and I remember that he talked
mostly about Corot and Balzac. Hawkins too I remember;
he was in low water, and was trying to make a living by
painting on porcelain; he called at the hotel on one occasion
and took us out to a respectable French house where he did
conjuring tricks and was the life and soul of the party. The
girls were kissed. It was all very innocent, and I did not get
the impression that Hawkins was the scamp whom my
brother afterwards described in his books."

This helps to date the passage in *Vale* which tells how
Lewis, when no longer supported by a successful courtesan, tried to earn an honest living by going to work in
a china factory run by a communist on the outskirts of
the town, and how Jullian, concerned at the loss to art,
proposed that Moore should leave the Hôtel de Russie and
take rooms in which his friend could live free of charge.
" I wrote to Lewis telling him of Jullian's proposal to me,
and next day he came up to thank me and to assure me that
he would try to justify the confidence I had placed in him.
He did not give me time to consider the sacrifice I was
making, and very wisely, but set out at once to find an
apartment that would suit us, coming next day to me with
the joyful tidings that he had found one in the Passage des
Panoramas in the Galerie Feydeau."

Here, following Hawkins's example, Moore rose early and
worked late, foregoing all his pleasures.

27 Galerie Montmartre.
Nov.—75.

My dear Mama, You ought to write to me sometimes
although I set a bad example you should not follow it. I
cannot I am sorry to say pay you a visit at Christmas. I
am working so hard that I have not time. I have only one

bit of news I am completely changed When I think of the
follies I have made I can scarcely believe it was myself.
I work ten hours a day. If I fail in painting it wont be my
fault. The pen is so bad I really cant go on I have rooms
of my own hoping all are well Yours affect, George
Moore. Please write by return.

25 April   Galerie Montmartre
1876.   Passage des Panoramas.

My dearest Mama—I hope that you have not thought—
not for one moment that it is want of affection that made
me neglect writing to you; indeed it is not: well I suppose
it is better to define it at once as idleness. I hope you are
well and that all is well, I hope no I need not hope I know
you think of me. I do of you. I am now really working hard
it was Hawkins who got me to do so. I have been now
some time I believe three months. Will you believe me
when I tell you before then I never met anybody who
knew except Mr. Cooper whom of course I did not listen
to. I did not know what a good drawing meant. I did
painting and drawing like everybody else, young ladies,
little boys and idle young men. Lutyens does not know. . . .

I am very sorry to hear that Anna was so foolish as to
buy the horrible aborochies [?] which Jim dignifies by the
name of pictures. When I first thought of painting I
thought him wonderful. After having learned a little I
thought him bad, but now since I have been shown and
told the meaning of painting I cannot find words to express,
to convey, to your mind a sense of the absurdity of that
man's work; it is absolutely below contempt, it is entirely
without any even the faintest shadow of merit. There is
no attempt at drawing, no I will not say that. I will say
there is not the slightest attempt to fix two lines together
there is no modeling no effect no colour. At first sight you
might be tempted to say there that there was composition
well there is a certain attempt that way as far as things
so badly drawn could be composed for good composition
requires a certain knowledge a certain fitting together of

figures of which he has not even the faintest conception.
You may perhaps think me unkind to speak so but it is
absolutely pure unexaggerated truth. . . .

Poor derest little Nine what a nice what a charming
little girl she is and how clever and amusing is still at tours
is she. Give my love to dusty and Maurice. Oh but bye
the way I met a Miss Blake in Paris a species of idiot she
knows you; she came and spoke to me and asked me to
dine; she is a cure and no mistake. I telegraphed to Joseph
in French Joseph sent me back the telegram and I assure
you I laughed, out of the twenty French words I wrote
only one in two arrived and one spelt wrong you can
imagine it the rest was double Dutch good bye derest
Mama believe me I think of you often and long you do
not know how much to see you. . . .

Though he disliked Jullian personally, Moore at this time
was satisfied with the technique and the ideals which the
studio at the Passage des Panoramas provided; and with
Hawkins and the general public he rushed to mock at the
Impressionists, when, in 1875, seventy drawings shown at the
Hôtel Drouot by Claude Monet, Sisley, Renoir and Berthe
Morisot realised 10,000 francs. The semi-classic objective
school, with its great subject canvasses, the fine draughts-
manship of Cabanel, Lefebvre and Bouguereau, had all his
admiration. " Cabanel," he wrote to his mother, " opened
my eyes and showed me how a person should make a
drawing . . . I thought that if I could run an outline round
a figure it was sufficient; but there is no use going to details,
you would not understand neither would I two or three
years ago . . . you do not know nor can you imagine the
work and the complexity attached to thorough artistic training. In England it is unknown; read about Father Flandrin.[1]
He was an example, not of an outburst of natural genius,
but of a thorough, sound artistic training in all its branches
. . . I will bet that Cabanel Lefevre Bulanger Gerome
Messonier or any trained artist will repeat what I have
written almost word for word."

[1] Jean Hippolyte Flandrin, died 1864.

Defeat fell upon Moore like the fatal pendulum in the pit, by inches. His own facility was unequal to his rival's although he possessed the rarer qualities of individuality and delicacy; but Hawkins showed himself singularly capable of education. So at least Moore wrote of himself in the *Confessions*; but in *Vale* he simply described how one day, horrified at the black thing in front of him, he laid down his pencil in despair and saying to himself that he would never take up pencil or brush again, he slunk back from Jullian's to his apartment, and bathed his pillow in tears.

Professor Henry Tonks sends me the following note on the subject of Moore's painting: " In our conversations he used to tell me much of his life as an art student in Paris and of the bitter blow it was to him when he finally decided that much as he loved the idea of being a painter, he was not fitted to become one. One day (he was then over forty) when Steer and I were dining with him, he told us that a model having called at his flat it came into his head that he would see if he had forgotten all about painting, so he asked her to pose for him. Of course we wanted to see the results; he at first blushingly denied our demands, but after much persuasion he gave in. The sketches in oil paint were certainly better than I had expected and made it quite clear that he had had considerable training."

3

The Galerie Feydeau now became as hateful as a prison, and Lewis was the gaoler. Lewis went away every morning at eight o'clock to work; and Moore met him at breakfast in the little restaurant near by. After breakfast Moore read Shelley and wandered about the streets. Jealously he imagined the time to come when Lewis, by his Salon successes, would be freed from financial dependence upon him and would leave him reduced to utter insignificance. On the other hand, if Lewis failed, this life in the Galerie might drag on for ever. He was as unhappy as he had been at Oscott; for on top of all he had come to realise that his friend's talent was only a superficial one, and that his sacrifice for art must be vain, whether Lewis succeeded or not.

To divert his thoughts Moore sought out a society where
Jullian and his pupils were unknown. He used introductions
from his family, or went among the Irish colony where he
met the brave old Fenian John O'Leary, who smiled on him
for his father's sake. It was not gay enough; and somehow or
other he contrived to slip from this milieu into what was
called " the circle of Alphonse Rothschild "; and names
like de la Tremoïlle (the first ducal family in France) and
d'Osmond began to appear in his correspondence with his
mother. How he managed it is not quite clear; but he was
good at making his way where he wanted.

The Duchesse de la Tremoïlle was a stout, plain and witty
old lady who entertained largely in her beautiful house in the
Champs-Élysées. Moore kept up his acquaintance with the
Duchess in after years and used to speak of her with considerable awe. J.-E. Blanche, the artist, says they may have
met first at Madame Howland's, the intelligent and beautiful
widow of an American, to whose house in old Montmartre
came distinguished people like Fromentin, Gustave Moreau,
Ricard and Degas. It was Degas who subsequently introduced Moore to Ludovic Halévy, well known in the Rothschild circle; and Degas may have also brought him to
Madame Howland's.

Unfortunately, Moore could not refrain from introducing
Hawkins to his grand friends; he had only intended an
outing, an exhibition, but Hawkins became so popular in
this society that invitations poured in upon him and he gave
up attending Jullian's classes, relapsing, at Moore's expense,
into his dissipations. He cut out his friend, and it was partly
to escape from the scene of his discomfiture that Moore
accompanied a Madame de Ratazzi to Boulogne, hoping
that Hawkins would be gone from the Galerie when he
returned to Paris. This Madame de Ratazzi, a granddaughter of Lucien Bonaparte, had been a public figure,
somewhat ridiculous and grotesque, at the end of the
Empire; she still kept a musical and literary salon and entertained many foreigners. Her seaside party included a
Madame de Coëtlogon, who had captured Moore's fancy,
and whose historic Breton name he used nearly fifty years

later for the mother of Héloise. Still another object of the trip is disclosed in Moore's letters to his mother. He was in pursuit of an heiress, a Miss Mary de Ross Rose, who was at Boulogne with her two aunts, Protestant Irishwomen from County Limerick. Miss Rose was not pretty but bright and intelligent.

My dearest Mama—You have not written to me for a long time. I should like to hear from you oftener. I have pushed my way into the Rose family, a matter of no small difficulty—they are the stiffest people I ever met. They are going to Boulogne in a week, I am going to follow, and will make it the seat of war; there is no doubt as to the money. Can you come over to Boulogne you would assist me very much or ask Anna to pass a week or two there. She could arrange it all. I found her photo in Mrs. Willingtons Album. It will be hard lines if I cannot succeed I know I am not particularly good looking but for the virtue of married woman I must hope that every man has not been as well received as I have been. What a great truth it is a virtuous woman is a woman who does not compromise herself. I have had often and often certain and that most certain of all proof that I have not been disliked by women it will certainly annoy me if I can not make this domned little girl like me. I suppose it will be like my luck. Being liked by a Princess or a Marquise bring little or nothing (if an honest man). I feel I wont succeed but we will see. Do you know the last Boulevard joke, a man is asked by the judge in court—Sir what are your means of livelihood—Answer—I compromise a lady Sir . . . Never . . . I was at the famous Princess Ratazzi masked ball the other day they are the most famous things in Paris. Her hotel is something wonderful and she spends between 60 and 80 thousand francs on a fete they are something extrodinary in their splendour. The gardens when lit up at night with a thousand lights all reflecit in the marble fountains, and the weird looking dominoes and masks winding in and out of the depths of red rose gardens between the marble colums and statues is like a page out of the Arabian nights. I am dining with her on Thursday. I went to church with Miss Rose last Sunday they dont give me a chance of making up to the girl. Strange to say with all my experience I am a little taken aback and am travelling over new ground. Let me know if you can come to Boulogne sur Mer or if Anna will go I will amuse her. Write dearest Mama by return of post With love to all I remain your affect son

George Moore.

10 Galerie Feydeau.

My dear Mama—I must really know all about Miss Rose. Anna can find out. When I wrote to you the first time it was a castle in the air. You have often spoken to me about marrying. Well now is the time. I found a girl who was said to have money. I have as we used to say in racing run up to the leaders. If I go to the front I will compromise myself. I really do not know how to proceed, what am I to do if my family do not do something I am at a loss. There is no use my scribbling ten pages asking if Anna or you should come over. What is to be done? It is for you to decide. I have been to the Bois this evening with them. They allowed me to walk in advance with Miss Rose and evidently perceived my game. I think I shall be accepted what is to be done

Write at once by return

With love to all I remain your affect son

George Moore.

10 Galerie Feydeau.

My dear Mama,

I am surprised at not hearing from you. I asked you to write at once and you are generally punctual at answering letters but you have inquiries to make.

Will you send me Josephs address; have you heard from him lately—A cheque was returned with not to be found on it. I suppose he is in Dublin—very disagreeable. I think

I have the race in hand with Miss Rose. I heard from a
lady who I met the other night at the Princess Ratazzi
that Miss R had 2000£ a year. Write there is a dear Mama.
Drop a line to Joseph; Address in Dublin it is the quickest
way and it is important. I would not like to be put about
for money for the moment a very little thing might mean
a big one—I remain your affect son

George Moore.

My dear Mama,

How one runs to ones Mother when in trouble; the
instinct exists the same at thirty as at three. I hope that
you will come to Boulogne You will amuse yourself and
will assist me. It is a pity I thought I was sick of everything,
but no, I dread marriage. What will I be when married—
nothing all my intrigues etc etc will cease, I am quite Parisian received in the society the most equivogue, the haute
monde of the last empire. I never cared for vulgarity like
William Murphy I never intrigued with maid servants The
society I frequent is the most viceous and the most splendid
in Paris un peu le rendez vous des femmes dont on parlait
trop et des jeunes gents oisifes imbeciles ou aventuriers
un lot complet de petites trahisons d'adulteres affrontes et
des mensonges criminels a fair danser Satan de joie—on
trouvez des embassadors etrangers toute les cocodette
celebres; le haut monde de la politique de la finance et des
lettres enfin la princess Mathilde et sa cour. All this
will have to be forgotten the last flame of a princess will
return to Ireland heigh ho it makes one sad. You will
write at once dear Mama and give me advice. I will
marry for seven hundred thousand francs not a half penny
less—You will write I remain your affect

George Moore.

Nothing came of the pursuit of Miss Rose. His Irish cousins
who knew the young lady and were fond of gossip, thought
that George proposed and was rejected. According to his
own account (which is to be found in a letter to his uncle Joe
Blake) he abandoned his endeavour when he discovered that

Miss Rose's income was only £800 a year. " I do not think
that is enough," he wrote. " There are plenty with more.
I might have a better chance. Write and tell me."

4

Upon his return to Paris in September 1876 he began to
think seriously about becoming a writer. He seems to have
been in a state of financial embarrassment at this time, and
he may have hoped to earn some money by literature. He
turned for help to an elderly literary Frenchman named
Lopez, whose acquaintance he had made at the Hôtel de
Russie—a former collaborator of Scribe, Gautier, Alexandre
Dumas *père* and a dozen others. Lopez had in fact already
presided at the birth of Moore's first published literary
effort, a comedy named *Worldliness* of which it is said that no
single copy now exists, and which appears to have been
written while he was still at Jullian's. Hawkins was the hero
. . . of a work that was inspired by Congreve and other
Restoration dramatists, whom Moore now discussed with
assurance and apparent familiarity.

A collaboration on the subject of Luther, a play in blank
verse, was next proposed (Lopez's mother was an Englishwoman, and he spoke the language fluently).

George Moore to Bernard Lopez.

Dear Sir,

Thanks for your kind letter. I am glad to see that you
are disposed to consider my offer to write a play for you
for the English stage. You want to know what my subject
is ? " That is the question." Forgive me the quotation for
I would hang anybody except you, dear Mr. Lopez who
dared to cite so hackneyed a phrase. To speak candidly,
I am afraid to tell you. You object at once, saying, " If I
am to write in conjunction with you, surely it will oblige
you to confide to me at least your subject." I admit what
you say is true; but before I unbosom myself entirely will
you let me know if you will shrink from writing the yet

unmentioned tragedy, when I tell you that the theme is essentially a religious one ? . . .

If I remember right, your reminiscences of the French censor are, indeed, bitter; but, I assure you, that in England a tragedy on the subject of . . . . could meet with no objection.

I await impatiently your answer.   Yours,

George Moore.

This letter is chosen from a series of letters between the collaborators which were affixed to *Martin Luther* as a preface when the play was published three years later in book form. Seeing that Moore and Lopez lived in neighbouring streets, there seems to have been no reason why they should have corresponded with each other about the work in progress. The letters were almost certainly an afterthought, a later concoction; but we may take it at all events that they reflect the nature of the conversations which took place between Lopez and Moore in Lopez's apartment in the Place Pigalle. Lopez may have corrected some of the spelling and the grammar; but the important thing to notice is the vigour and confidence and liveliness with which Moore expresses his opinions. " We find the country of Jonson, Shakespeare, Marlow, Beaumont, Ford and Massinger without a dramatic literature. . . . I will not stay to answer the voices who will shriek after me the names of Dryden, Lee, Cumberland and Otway. Yes, Otway was a poet who was a dramatic writer. There were during the reign of Charles the Second some great writers who wrote for the stage: Congreve, Witcherley —but at this name I must pause. Was it not he who invented the commerce of importation of plays from France, a trade not quite unknown in the present day, but the few names that may be called as witness against my statement only serve to strengthen rather than to refute my argument. All the Elizabethan poets wrote for the stage, with the exception of Spenser. If the age of Shakespeare be not our Augustan age, the title will certainly fall to the age of Shelley, if not to the age of Swinburne. He is a venturesome man who will endeavour to decide between the three. But great as was the age of Shelley, did it produce a dramatic literature ? No. Has it given us one great drama ? I say no, with the *Cenci* before my eyes, for it is not an actable play, it sins against construction over and over again; the opening scene between the Count and Cardinal moves so quickly that no audience could follow it. How very differently Shakespeare would write a preparatory scene. It is, nevertheless, a wonderful play, the greatest since the great dramatic age. . . . I will not speak of Coleridge's *Remorse*, of that the least said the better. Wordsworth never wrote a play except the *Borderers*, a tragedy of an unrivalled dullness, and Southey, I don't know whether he did or did not. . . . I take up *Bothwell*, and on the title page I read " a tragedy in two volumes ! . . ."

Here is the authoritative if unscholarly voice of the critic of *Avowals* and the *Conversations* ranging without dismay over the whole field of English literature to prove his latest contention. No less surprising is his approach to the subject in the first letter to his collaborator. " Let your thoughts travel back along the past six months; climb from reminiscence to reminiscence, until you come across a very wet day. . . . On the memorable wet day in question I heard you speak of Virgil, Horace and Homer, just as if you had passed your *baccalauréat* the day before. I have, consequently, hope that you have not forgotten the oysters, Sauterne, and the poularde financiere. A man of your excellent taste certainly could not; neither, perhaps, will the cigars and the Chartreuse be wholly unremembered." In the midst of so much that is to say the least immature, such maturity is something of a mystery, a flash in the pan. Two or three years before Moore was writing home the letters of an imaginative but uneducated child; and for many years to come both his letters and his published work remained crude and undisciplined. And it is not only the style of the prefatory letters to *Martin Luther* that is prophetic of the later Moore, but his insistence that the collaboration should reflect an attitude uncompromisingly Protestant. " You must make up your mind while you are writing our projected drama, to be absolutely and entirely a Lutheran, even at the risk

of ruining your nephew's chances of marrying an heiress.
There must be no shilly-shallying; there is no use in trying
to make an omelet without smashing eggs. Luther must not
only speak as Luther would speak, but he must likewise
be in the right . . ."

The discussions with Lopez were really the beginning of
the café-education which, as Moore used to say years after,
was his substitute for the University. He was soon con-
versing with people of much greater importance.

5

On his return from Boulogne Moore had found that Lewis
was still in the apartment. He was surprised at the " indelicacy " and made efforts to bring about a break. But
these Lewis ignored; and in the end it was Moore who suc-
cumbed and pleaded for forgiveness and a fresh start. The
fresh start was made in a new apartment, where the two
settled down, saying to each other that it would be " for
ever "; the one was to write, the other to paint. The essential
triviality of Lewis's character and of Lewis's art was now
obvious to Moore, but he could not resist the winning
ways and the lofty, dissolute air.

The move was into Montmartre, the rapidly changing
Montmartre of the late seventies, a memory of which has
lately been evoked by Daniel Halévy in his *Pays Parisiens*.
The pleasure seekers had already begun to invade the
quarter. In the Place Pigalle where once the spangle-coated
Italian models, tambourine in hand, idled and gossiped
around the fountain, while waiting to be called to pose, the
Moulin Rouge now whirled its sails. And what had been a
Faubourg to the " half world " was fast becoming its centre.
But there were still at the time we speak of little oases, lying
between the main thoroughfares which climbed the Montmartre hill, where an odour of the eighteenth century
lingered. The older inhabitants clung to their old houses
and to each other. It was in such a quarter in the Rue de la
Tour des Dames that Hawkins found and furnished an apartment for Moore. It looked out on to the backs of the good

houses in the Rue Rochfoucauld and Moore had for neighbours Madame Howland, the Halévys, Degas and Fromentin.

The furnishings of the Rue de la Tour des Dames signified an extreme hatred of the commonplace. The drawing-room was all in red with Turkish lamps and couches, and the two bedrooms were furnished with cushioned seats and rich Turkish canopies, censers, palms and great church candlesticks. In one of the bedrooms Lewis slept under a tree of gardenias in full bloom. A fourth room contained an altar, an organ, a Buddhist temple, a statue of Apollo and a bust of Shelley. The pets of the place were a Persian cat and a python which fed once a month on a live guinea pig. The description is in the *Confessions*; there is no means of confirming its accuracy. A man, long since dead, who visited Dublin many years ago, described to Moore's Irish friends a call which he had once made at the Rue de la Tour des Dames. He was silent about the furnishings, the cat and the python. All he remembered was that Moore had recently taken to his bed in protest against some violent criticism that had been directed against his book of poems, *Flowers of Passion*, and that he lay there, the sheets drawn over his head and his face turned to the wall.

It has to be considered whether Moore's portrait of himself as a young Parisian is not in part a literary satire. Huysmans' strange hero in *A Rebours*, Des Esseintes, not yet created,[1] owned a tortoise covered with jewels. Moore must needs anticipate Des Esseintes by keeping a python which feeds on live guinea pigs to the strain of the Vexilla Regis. "Our young man," writes Dr. Farmer in his book, *Le Mouvement Esthetique et "Décadent" en Angleterre*, "is not only a sensualist; he is also a pagan who trails with him remembrances of antique magnificence. He rejects Christianity with disgust, exacts the silence of marble courts, the shade of great columns, canopies embroidered with lilies. He wishes to revive the gladiators, to hear them cry Ave Cæsar, to see the blood flow. Why? Merely because d'Albert (the hero of Mademoiselle de Maupin) has proclaimed himself a worshipper of the pagan divinities, the admirer of Tiberius,

[1] *A Rebours* was published in 1884.

Caligula, Nero. This is the *côté bas empire*, at once sumptuous, delicate, ferocious. But Moore announces other complications and aims (here Des Esseintes appears) at discovering new malevolent traits. Above all he wishes to be thought perverse. ' I am feminine, morbid, perverse. Above all perverse.' The perversity is anodyne enough and seems to exhaust itself in effects of decorative art."

Moore could not have read Huysmans in 1876 but he had read Gautier, and there is significance in the passages of the *Confessions* which describe the effects upon him of the contrast offered by Gautier to his favourite English poet, Shelley. Shelley's idealism was not expressly rejected, but it ceased to serve a purpose in the " agitations of actual life " ; and now Moore began to suspect for the first time that a deification of flesh and fleshy desire was possible. There are only feeble echoes of Shelley among the poems which in the intervals of the composition of *Martin Luther* he had begun to write :

> *Like the fire*
> *Of a pyre,*
> *Like the tones of a vibrating lyre,*
> *Like the moon*
> *In swoon*
> *Of love on the bosom of night.*

A marriage of convenience is the subject of a long rhymed narrative in varying metres. Only Poe and Moore have dared to rhyme the name " Annie " and Moore does not repeat the American poet's success.

> *My soul was rife*
> *With grief when my lips spoke the name of wife.*
>
> .   .   .   .   .   .
>
> *Believe me Annie*
> *' Tis want of money*
> *That forces us apart.*
> *It is not any*
> *Capriciousness of heart.*
> *Pity me Annie.*

Lopez who encouraged Moore to talk of his writings advised
him to choose extreme subjects which would astonish the
British public by their originality. Moore bought a copy of
Les Fleurs du Mal and produced an *Ode to a Dead Body*. He
wrote other verses which bear the impress of Baudelaire—
the Baudelaire who worked in the horrible and declared that
the one supreme delight of love lies in the certainty of doing
wrong. Baudelaire's writing may have directed his attention
to Poe, a poet to whom Moore returned in his old age when
he was weary of *Les Fleurs du Mal*.

6

Moore returned to his work on *Martin Luther*, and one
evening the second act being then under weigh, Lopez and
he went to dine together at the Cabaret du Rat Mort. A
wild and dishevelled gentleman entered the café, and Moore
was introduced to Villiers de l'Isle Adam as an English poet.
Villiers, after a little conversation, scribbled something for
him on a piece of paper. It was an introduction to Mallarmé.
" You must know Mallarmé," he said, and Moore assented,
little thinking that the scribbled lines were charged with a
life's destiny.

Mallarmé, formerly a teacher of English in French
provincial towns, had at this time very few friends, and
Moore was lucky in thus coming across him by accident—
very few young Frenchmen had this opportunity. The poet
received him graciously in a fourth floor apartment at the
dingy end of the Rue de Rome, and suggested that he ought
to know Manet, who was to be found every evening at the
Nouvelle Athènes, for Manet would surely like to paint him.
In this way the chain was formed which stretched from the
Hôtel de Russie to Lopez, from Lopez to Villiers, from
Villiers to Mallarmé, and from Mallarmé to Manet. Mallarmé, he says in *Vale*, must have spoken to Manet about him,
for one night in the Nouvelles Athènes the painter came over
to him and asked him if the conversation distracted his
attention from his proofs.

The Nouvelles Athènes formed the white nose of a block of

buildings stretching up the hillside of Montmartre into the Place Pigalle, and was the centre of art in Paris in the latter years of Manet's life. Moore knew the café; perhaps he had already attached himself to some minor writers of the realistic school who were among its clients. The writers doubted their art and envied that of the painter; they used to rise in their places when Manet and Degas entered and passed to the superior table reserved for pictorial art. All the famous Impressionists except Cézanne, who roamed wild on the outskirts of Paris, came to the Nouvelle Athènes— Manet, Degas, Monet, Pissarro, Renoir, Sisley—and Moore soon acquired the habit of sitting with them and joining in their conversation. This was the "university" which launched him into the artistic and literary life of Paris. He has written so much of his French education that any further account of it must seem but a feeble repetition. Not only in the *Confessions* but in *Vale, Memoirs of My Dead Life, Modern Painting* and *Avowals,* he has told how he listened to Mallarmé, Manet, Zola, Monet, Degas and the others. "I did not take it all for gospel," he said to M. Jean-Aubry at the end of his life, "I already thought I knew a good deal: I was ignorant, of course, but I was already George Moore with something to say for myself though I did not know how to say it. How kind all the French were."

"He came, he talked with you; he, so wrapped up in his work, and apparently so full of himself, knew how to ask questions to advantage, how to listen; but even when he had not listened, when he seemed to have been full only of himself and his own idea, he ended by carrying away, absorbing all he wanted to know, and he astonished you later by describing it." This was written by Sainte Beuve of Balzac, but it might have been said no less truly of Moore.

7

In the summer of 1877, leaving his tragedy of Luther unfinished, he went to London with the object of finding a publisher for his verses. The visit was a short one; his mother was now at Moore Hall and he stayed at Morley's Hotel,

GEORGE MOORE IN PARIS
From the drawing by Manet

in Trafalgar Square. He found a publisher (Provost) for *Flowers of Passion*; and it was arranged that the book should appear with a skull, crossbones and a lyre stamped in gold upon the cover.

Mallarmé, who was at this time French correspondent of the *Art Monthly Review*, a periodical edited by S. T. Robinson, gave Moore an introduction to the poet O'Shaughnessy, and one day O'Shaughnessy brought him to Mr. Robinson's home. Here he met the two Robinson girls, Mary and Mabel, who remained his life-long friends. The former, now Madame Duclaux, has drawn upon her earliest memories of Moore in a charming contribution to *La Revue de Paris* for March 1st, 1933. His dress, she recalls, was that of a Frenchman (he had ceased to copy Hawkins who, one is sure, favoured an English cut); and he wore a beard, as in the somewhat later Manet portrait. " I was nineteen," says Madame Duclaux, " and working hard at Greek at University College; alone of my kind in a class of young men—my sister, a little younger than myself, was studying painting at the Slade. He was not handsome, there was something even vaguely comic in his appearance. Was it the long neck, the shoulders too sloping for a man of his height and strength ? Or was it his chin, too small for the forehead and nose (he himself says somewhere that the receding line of the chin always adds something comic to a face) ? But his chin was largely hidden by a fair beard. It was merely perhaps that he looked out of place in our learned little circle of artists and scholars.

" What was really ' amusing ' in the sense that painters use the word, was the colour of his hair. It called to mind the wild jonquil, being pale yellow without the least tint of red. . . . This fine hair fell on an absolutely white forehead, high and bulging. The grey blue eyes, a little too prominent, often wore the vague, spiritless expression common to the very observant, but sometimes they lit up and became strangely perspicacious, adventurous, or just derisory, the expression he must have worn when he jumped a hurdle.

" If Moore seemed strange to us, we must have seemed at east as strange to him. We lived in a little closed world.

Mabel and I that evening (as he often reminded us) wore with the same simplicity as a débutante wears white muslin, complicated gowns of the middle ages, laced under the arms with long cords of old gold and trailing all over the carpet. In short the costume of the statues on the façade of Chartres."

A letter to his mother, written on his return to Paris, suggests that he had begun to apply himself at last to the study of French grammar, but the pages may have been corrected by somebody before he sent them off.

61 Rue Condorcet, Paris.
(undated)

Ma chère mere,

J'ai reçu ta charmante lettre qui m'a fait un plaisir que je ne peux exprimer.

Je me demande a toute heure du jour si je merite un affection pareille, moi, qui suis si negligent. Je n'ai que le droit d'un fils, le meilleur du monde. Je suis très content de savoir que chère Nina s'amuse. Tu ne peux comprendre combien je regrette qu'il me fût impossible de vous voir cette été mais j'espère avoir ce plaisir cet hiver a Dublin. Tu m'as donné tant de nouvelles, que je suis honteux de ne pas en avoir pour te rendre. Ta lettre m'interessait beaucoup, elle etait si longue, tu ne m'a jamais écrit tant.

Mon livre va paraître en quinze jours d'ici, tu en auras un des premiers exemplaires, mais je te prie, ne le prêtes a personne, même s'il y a du monde là bas qui desirent lire mes bétises, qu'ils les achètent. J'espere que tu m'en passe vendre autant que possible ; je ne veux pas dire par cela qu'il faut dire a tout le monde, " payez cent sous pour le livre de mon fils," parle de mon livre et si on te le demande, dis " Je n'en ai pas un seul exemplaire mais vous pouvez l'avoir en écrivant à

Messrs Provost,
36 Henrietta Street,
Covent Garden

ou en faisant la commande chez votre librarie." Ce n'est pas pour le peu d'argent que j'y gagnerais, mais cela aurait un bon effet sur les relations avec mon éditeur.

J'ai quelque chose a te demander Julian (mon frère inconnu) qu'est ce qu'il est devenu, il me semble des années depuis que je l'ai vu, il doit etre tout à fait un grand garçon. Je n'ai pas son addresse, envoie le moi, et je lui écrirai, il sera étonné.

Je vous souhaite, toi et Nina, un hiver agréable à Moore Hall, écris moi bientôt et dis à Nina qu'elle me doit une lettre.

Tout à toi
George Moore.

The Rue Condorcet address is found at the head of several letters to his mother. His rooms in Rue de la Tour des Dames are never mentioned to Mrs. Moore; it may be that he did not wish it to be known at home that he was living in so grand a style. To his uncle Joe Blake, he wrote:

Have you seen my little volume of poems ? They made quite a little success. I am terribly abused for immorality but not for bad writing. I have made a little money by them which is extraordinary as all the London press received my book (*sic*). None could make out that I write badly although very indecently.

Edmund Yates, reviewing *Flowers of Passion* in *The World* under the heading of " A Bestial Bard," said that the author should be whipped at the cart's tail while the book was being burned by the common hangman. As Moore had in some degree courted such attacks his resentment was not wholly reasonable. Yates's assault was very savage, however, and it is not perhaps surprising that Moore should have got an idea into his head, which he afterwards cherished, that he was the destined victim of a gratuitous persecution. On his next visit to London he consulted some friends; one of them, Mrs. William Rossetti, a sister of Oliver Madox Brown, advised him out of her kindness to withdraw his book, and, touched by her concern for his spiritual and worldly welfare, he followed her advice.

8

It is made clear in the *Confessions* (although no dates are given) that Moore remained for a long time resistant to the influences—Impressionism in painting and Naturalism in the novel—by which he was now captivated. No doubt the change of heart began before he first heard the glass door of the Nouvelle Athènes grate upon the sanded floor. Manet became King of all for Moore, and for the rest of his life he never tired talking of him: his eyes were almost blinded by the brilliance of this light. Degas, taken as man and artist together, came next in his esteem; and of the great men whom he was to meet in the course of his life, these, Degas and Manet, were the two towards whose personalities he never showed a trace of disrespect or irony in his writings. He distinguished between them by calling the one a pure painter, an " instinct," the other an intellectuality, and he would ask what was any intellect compared with a gift like Manet's; but for their contrasting characters he had an equal admiration. He approved everything in Manet, the fashionable air, the boyish vanity, the blonde amusing face and sincere eyes; and behind Degas's mordancy and intractability he detected a sweet and genial nature, untouched by personal cynicism and misanthropy.

He knew Manet in the early days much better than Degas. Degas used to come to the Nouvelle Athènes late in the evening—about ten o'clock was his usual hour; but his home was impregnable except to his close friends. On the other hand Manet at once invited Moore to the studio in Rue St. Petersbourg, the flat close to his parents' house where his best impressionist work had been accomplished. This was a compliment, as at the time of his first meeting with Moore his door was strictly fastened against casual visitors. Perhaps Manet wanted to paint Moore as soon as he saw him. Shortly afterwards, however, when he moved to the huge studio in 57 Rue de Clichy, his habit became as public as formerly it had been private. The studio in the Rue de Clichy was a sort of club, the resort of journalists and of a pack of smart idlers, who arrived late in the day, attracted less by art than by the famous beauties who lounged on the sofa. Manet was ailing, and he worked fitfully with great pains in his legs; the society of lively young people pleased him.

What Theodore Duret, the historian of the Impressionists, best remembered about Moore were the gorgeous clothes, the silks and satins of Manet's model. " I was one of Moore's first friends in Paris," said Duret in response to an enquiry made in 1922, " I knew him when he had hardly yet begun to write. I remember him as a golden haired fop, an æsthete before the days of Wilde. He came to Paris to study painting, but he soon fell under the influence of the Naturalists and turned to writing. None of us thought anything of him as a writer, but he was very welcome wherever he went, for his manners were amusing and his French very funny. He tried to shock and astonish people; but he was always the gentleman, and would never associate with those whom he thought to be below his rank as an Irish landlord."

These remarks of Duret place justly and in its right light Moore's earlier life in literary and artistic Paris. If he had not afterwards written his French memoirs, would it be remembered that he had studied painting in Paris and known so many famous people ? Certainly his years in Paris counted for himself—they largely made him what he was. But what did they count for with the French, even with the French he knew ? Wilde, and also Whistler to a certain extent, were known to a public in France who had never read a line or seen a picture they had produced. Moore wrote about the French, putting all that he knew (and a little more) into his books, but the French wrote about Whistler and still more about Wilde. Moreover, Moore's first years in Paris were passed mainly among English or Irish residents or with French people who had cosmopolitan connections. His reminiscences of French artistic life in the late seventies and early eighties, even after he became a well-known and translated writer, have been very little supplemented by French accounts. But his fame was slow in crossing the Channel; Manet died in 1883, Villiers de l'Isle Adam in 1889, and it would not have occurred to anyone in the eighties to investigate the extent of his familiarity with these great men. It is certain at any rate that Manet and Degas, Mallarmé perhaps—later on Zola and Mendés—took some personal interest in him, and he went to their studios and houses : Duret's evidence is there to prove it. He was neither rich nor famous, but he had some gift for exteriorising himself, and was an unusual and interesting young man.

When in 1922, Mr. Barrett H. Clark embarked (with Moore's encouragement) upon his researches, Duret alone was able to give him first hand information as far as the " delightful seventies " are concerned. Through his bookseller, Mr. Clark communicated with the heirs of Madame Bouguereau (the Lizzie Gardner of *Memoirs* and *Avowals*) and received in reply a Tauchnitz edition of *Sister Teresa* and a copy of *Martin Luther*, both inscribed. There were no indications whatever of the whereabouts of Lopez's heirs. Daniel Halévy said that he could find nothing about Moore among the family papers; and he added that " my father [Ludovic Halévy] did not know Moore until well towards the end of his life "; there was no reply from the heirs of Paul Alexis, who was Moore's first and perhaps closest friend among the writers of Zola's school (see " La Butte " in *Memoirs of My Dead Life*); and neither J.-E. Blanche nor Edouard Dujardin, both of whom were considerably younger than himself, knew him in his Nouvelle Athènes days.

The fact is that Moore wrote into the memoirs of his early days in Paris much that he acquired on later visits. Through Zola, for instance, he became acquainted with the Goncourts, Daudet, Catulle Mendès, Coppée and Hérédia. But at the date of these acquaintanceships he was a visitor to Paris, not a resident there. From 1877, when he began to frequent the Nouvelle Athènes, to 1880, when he ceased to live in Paris, Moore had only one glimpse of Zola, who did not frequent the famous café; at a fancy dress ball—the same dance at which, dressed as a French workman, he had the conversation (described in *Impressions and Opinions*) with the " noble and melancholy " Turgenev, who liked to see the young amuse themselves. It was Manet who introduced

him to a thickly-built massive man in evening clothes; but
the chief of the Naturalists was not interested, and passed
on with a chilling bow. Neither time, place nor costume was
favourable to the exchange of ideas. In Moore's descriptive
account of Zola, written many years later, we are told that
" some months " after the encounter at this ball he proceeded to Médan to call upon the master. " You'll find him
at Médan any day you like to go there," Manet is alleged
to have said. But the approach was slower and more difficult
than one would imagine from reading the opening paragraphs of *A Visit to Médan*. When he was working in London
Moore reintroduced himself to Zola by letter, recalling
Manet and the *bal de l'Assommoir*; and it was not until he had
already done some journalistic propaganda in England for
the Naturalists that he received an invitation to come with
Alexis to Médan when next he should be in Paris.

Sometimes too Moore may have imagined that he had
left a greater impression upon casual French acquaintances
than was actually the case. For instance, he sent Barrett
Clark on a wild goose chase after Léon Hennique, one of
the last survivors of the Naturalistic school of writers. " See
him at once," Moore urged, " lose not a day. Flatter if need
be this old man who has now dropped so utterly from the
public view and from the memory of man. Tell him if need
be of my efforts to get his beautiful play *La Mort du Duc
d'Enghien* produced in England. Perhaps that will bring a
flash into his eyes. Tell him, too, that I will gladly come out
to see him if he wishes it. But no matter how little he
says to you, take it down, fix it in your memory, write it
down, amplify his phrases and sentences. I should come
into your paper only as a foil, an excuse, a shadow in the
background.

" On the other hand, Hennique may prove communicative; I can imagine him saying this to you, and in this
fashion: ' *Oui, je 'me souviens de ce jeune anglais—très gentil,
ce Georges Moore. Il parlait français assez bien à cette époque-là.
Il a collaboré avec Alexis, mais pas avec moi.*' Or else like this,
' *Oui, je me souviens: ce jeune homme était assez stupide.*' If you
know your business you will go out immediately and see

him—in his pretty little garden outside the Fortifications. Go straight to his house. There was Céard, too. He may be dead, I don't know. I was never very intimate with him, but he may help you. I hardly think you will get much from Céard even if he is still alive: he had a sour disposition and I don't imagine old age has improved that. But Hennique is your best chance. And then there's Forain— I am told he once made a sketch of me. Gervex is another possibility."

But a somewhat indifferent answer was received from the little house outside the Fortifications. Hennique was leaving for Brussels, and in any case had not much to say about Moore. " . . . Have I met him four times in all my life ? Not more. Once in the Rue de Douai, he was with Paul Alexis; another time at Zola's; a third time at the home of the painter Edouard Manet; a fourth at Edmond de Goncourt's; and that is all. He wrote me a long time since about one of my plays." "Dear me," said Moore when he was shown this letter. " Something was bound to spoil it all. I told you not to write, but to go. You missed him. Dear me, you ought to have gone to see Hennique."

9

We may conclude that Moore's personal acquaintance with the Naturalistic writers, although fairly extensive, was not, except in the case of Alexis, very intimate. It was during his last years in Paris that he became a whole-hearted believer in the cause of what he called in the *Confessions* " the idea of a new art based upon science, in opposition to the art of the old world that was based upon imagination, the art that should explain all things and embrace the modern world in its entirety." There had been Shelley, there had been Gautier, now for a third time he experienced " the pain and joy of an inward light," and Zola was accepted as the inspired teacher and guide. He had a book on hand, *The Roses of Midnight*, short stories in various metres; daylight was banished from its pages, and he began to feel that its " naturalisation " would be a difficult task.

The book is mentioned in another undated letter to his mother, the tone of which serves to remind us that Moore, in spite of the affection which he afterwards showed for his days in Paris, was not free from the fits of despondency common in youth. " Life gets pleasanter as one gets used to it," he said as an elderly man to a much younger friend. " There is no time so sad as the spring."

61 Rue Condorcet,
Paris.

My dearest Mama,

I hope you don't think me neglectful because I don't answer your letters—I am not, but I cant write letters nor get up in the morning. I wish I could see you it is terrible we dont see each other oftener, one of these days I shall go and see you and never leave you again. My life is a miserable one;—je vie dans mon ouvre—it is my only consolation, *Luther* is going to be a great success but I shall be terribly attacked for I have attacked all. I have corrected nearly all the proofs. My next book is three quarters finished *Roses of Midnight*. I have a novel on hand the title is *Aristocracy of Vice* it treats not of the demi monde but of the three quarter world the peaches that are at a shilling instead of half a crown; you wonder why for they are equally fresh large and ripe; look underneath, under the vine leaf and you will find an almost imperceptible black spot that is why they are sold at a shilling. Moore Hall you say is looking beautiful, I should like to live there, I would if I had money. If I were anybody else I might have made a marriage long ago. Good God how sick I am of myself on peux s'impoisonner avec les reveries comme avec des fleurs suerde inevrant exquise et sinistre. The cold in Paris has been dreadful. I nearly died of it. The streets are now a marsh of melted snow. Have you won anything in the lottery: I suppose you had tickets every one had except me.

I am going now out to have something to eat in a hurry so as to have a long evening to myself for reading and writing. I read now nothing but Balzac Hugo Shakespeare

the Bible and a couple of new novels every year and a volume or two of verse.[1] Goodbye my dearest mother—
George Moore.

P.S. Send me Lord Sligo's address for I intend to send him a copy of *Luther*.

During the winter of 1878–9 Moore went on another short visit to London; *Martin Luther*, it seems, was almost finished, and he hoped to find a producer for the tragedy. At Morley's Hotel he wrote the last iambic and also the dedicatory sonnet to Swinburne, which begins:

> " *Je t'apporte mon drame, o poète sublime,*
> *Ainsi qu'un ecolier au maître sa leçon—*"

and which he afterwards used to cite as proof of his early Protestantism:

> " *Accepte, tu verras la foi melée au crime,*
> *Se souiller dans le sang sacré de la raison,*
> *Quand surgit, redempteur du vieux peuple saxon,*
> *Luther à Wittemberg comme Christ à Solime.*"

He sent Lopez an account of his experiences, with a sarcastic comment on the state of the theatre in London and its dependence on adaptations and translations from the French.

> " I went to see my friends, the lyric poets. The dramatic poet is in my country a *rara avis*, so I did not look after him. I was very kindly received; all were glad to see me, and everyone was interested in *Luther*. I was accordingly invited to dine at . . . where I read some scenes from our play, which were very greatly admired, notably, the ' Diet of Worms ' and the fifth act, and all declared that we would find but little difficulty in getting the play produced, but advised me to publish it first as a book."

Who were the lyric poets, Moore's friends? Arthur O'Shaughnessy? Edmund Gosse? Rossetti? Was it at this

---

[1] Later he would assert that he was unacquainted with the Scriptures before middle age.

time that Moore called upon Swinburne ? He found a naked
man lying upon a bed, whom he thought for a moment was
his other self, and was so taken aback that he babbled out
" Does Mr. Jones live here ? " and fled.[1] The incident should
have occurred at this date, for a few months later, September, 1879, Swinburne passed into Watts Dunton's care at
the Pines, Putney.

As he had been advised, he printed *Luther* first, and then
sought for a producer. It tempted no producer, but as he
used to say in later years, the wonder was that he should
have " stumbled " through a play in blank verse, interspersed with songs, without coming to a full stop. The meeting in the wood between Catherine Bora and the monk was
well-imagined ; and a translation of Luther's celebrated
hymn was included which, he used to say " is as good a
translation as exists of it." The collaboration with Lopez
did not amount to much, a little advice and a few notes.[2]

Lewis no longer shared with him the apartment of the
Rue de la Tour des Dames. The story of his final dismissal
is told both in the *Confessions* and (with precise detail) in
Vale; it would be superfluous to repeat it here; all that need
be said is that Moore had found an æsthetic pretext for
sending his friend away; Lewis, when introduced to Manet
and Degas, had expressed his admiration of Lefebvre and
Bouguereau. They parted without anger. Moore used
occasionally to call upon Lewis in his new studio in the
Latin Quarter, and they used to meet in the flamboyant
cosmopolitan society of the Champs-Élysées between which
and the Nouvelle Athènes Moore now divided his attentions.

To Mrs. Moore (undated).

I go into the frenchest of french society now—houses
where an Englishman never is heard of. I dine twice a
week generally at the Princess de la Tremoille and at her
most select dinners, dinners of eight ten and twelve. The

---

[1] Moore's letter to Gosse describing this scene is in the Appendix to Gosse's
Life of Swinburne.
[2] Letter to Mr. E. A. Boyd, August 29th, 1917. The translation of the hymn
is in fact poor enough.

other day I was very pleased for a lady told me that the princess said that my manners were absolutely perfect. I was both pleased and astonished for it is astonishing it should be so; I can scarcely credit that the low society I have so much cultivated has not soiled me. Sometimes if I get away early I go to a low artists café, where with my two elbows on the beer stained (table) I scream the beastliest and slangiest french to groups of bohemians their is such an abime between the two that I often think " If the princess saw me now she never would believe me to be the same man who three hours (ago) was talking across her dinner table."

I have studied the art of conversation a great deal lately; it is extraordinary what there is to learn and how much all that has to be cultivated. My french gives me a good deal of trouble, in the street in the theatre and in nine tenths of french society it is perfect. I speak it of course just as I would my own language, but at the swell houses it sounds if not common very ordinary and bald; everyone there speaks with the sweet Racine elegance, that exquisite choice of expression it is really a pleasure to listen to it one may easily with a little stretch of the imagination believe oneself back in the never to be regretted time of Louis the 16th. Life then was really worth living, how charming it must have been never to meet anyone but ladies and gentlemen. It is a terribly fast society but people are fast as the Pompadours were fast, vice in silk and with good manners is better than virtue in a common dress and ill-bred. I left my card on Lord Sligo who of course returned my visit, but I have not since heard of him shall I send him *Luther*. But by the way, what do you think of it ? have you read it ? I am sorry that I am obliged to write the whole time about myself—but I dont know a soul that you know and can do nothing more therefore than ask a series of questions which is of course tiresome. I am playing my cards now to become the lover of the Marquise d'Osmond, she is very swell if not very young but I dont mind that (I mean the latter.) The first thing a young man who wants to get on in Paris

must do is to get under the wings of some lady with a good
name and in a high position that done with tact he can
wriggle himself anywhere. I should have been very glad
to take Arthur O'Conor about but he was impossible it
would take years of drilling to knock him into shape at
encre. I took him to a very shoddy place just to see how he
looked but I saw at once it would never do.

There is a father Burke who comes to see me, the kind
old man, but it is very embarrassing, he asked me to dine
at the Irish College—I of course backed out of the invitation it was too absurd.

He did not guess that his playtime was nearing its end,
and seemed to accept contentedly the modicum of literary
and social success that came his way. " I often wonder," he
wrote to his mother, " when we shall meet again ! Am I
ever to leave Paris? God knows ! It seems so like my home
now that I sometimes am startled when someone or something reminds me that I am a stranger."

CHAPTER III

LONDON: EARLY NOVELS

I

His butterfly life in Paris was rudely interrupted by a dismal letter from Ballinafad: he must come home, said his uncle, and look after his own affairs which were again in a confusion owing to the fall in agricultural prices and the refusal of tenants to pay their rents. The times were hard with the poor, and Moore had been allowed to anticipate income which it was now impossible to collect. Blake asked to be repaid, and added that he did not propose to risk his life by serving eviction orders on the Moore estate in order to collect the money. The war against landlords and their agents raged with particular severity in Mayo where at Westport, seventeen miles from Moore Hall, Michael Davitt had lately founded the Land League.

Moore has left us with two accounts of the effects upon him of Blake's " odious epistle." One of these is in the *Confessions of a Young Man* and was therefore drawn up at a distance of only a few years' recollection; the other is in *A Communication to My Friends*, the autobiographical essay upon which he was at work during the last few months of his life. In the *Confessions* he hurls reproaches at the ignominy of the modern world: a nobler antiquity was without humanitarian scruples. " That some wretched farmers and miners (*sic*) should refuse to starve, that I may not be deprived of my *demi-tasse* at Tortoni's, that I may not be forced to leave this beautiful retreat, my cat and my python—monstrous ! And these wretched creatures will find moral support in England —they will find pity. Pity, that most vile of all virtues has never been known to me. . . ."

The author of *A Communication to My Friends* was not

interested in the highly-flavoured philosophical condition of the æsthete of the Rue de la Tour des Dames, but sought to reveal his predecessor's character by the invention of incident. We are shown in this account a pretty apartment where a young man sits absorbed in happy thoughts which vanish quickly when a letter is brought in and read. The letter is from his uncle, and so he mutters " . . . always a fool, and a fool he will remain . . . interested only in his two-year-olds, and these he breaks down on the lumpy fields which he calls his racecourse, but I cannot waste any more time puzzling out a difficult handwriting. I am engaged to sit for Manet." The sitting goes badly; Manet scrapes out a morning's work, guesses that his model has had bad news, and says: " You are no longer *le plus Parisien de tous les Anglais*." Later on in the day the young man writes his uncle a letter about an imaginary half-finished novel, for which a publisher has offered him five hundred pounds, in this way hoping to keep him quiet until the next race is run at the Curragh. " If Joe Blake wins," the young man reflects, " he will forget about the state of my accounts." The actual letter which he wrote to his uncle has survived.

> I have never occupied (myself) with my affairs although urged to so by Maurice. I do not even know what my rent roll is. The question of the tenants refusing to pay any rent is terrible. What does it mean Communism? If I have never looked into my business at all events I have never committed any follies. I never spent more than five hundred a year and I was told when I came into the properties I had ever so much.

Soon afterwards, Joe Blake being in London, Moore crossed from France to meet him there and discuss the position of affairs. At Morley's Hotel they failed to come to an understanding, but Moore realised the existence of a crisis in his life. Before returning to Paris he saw the publisher Tinsley and called upon a young critic and poet, Edmund Gosse, a great friend of after years, a visit faintly remembered in *Avowals*. To Tinsley he spoke of the realistic novels he was minded to write and to Gosse he brought a copy of *Martin Luther*. In Paris he gave orders for the dispersal of the effects in his apartment and left before the auction in debt to his concierge for 100 francs.

There is an account in the *Confessions* of the sale at Rue de la Tour des Dames. It takes the form of a letter which he is supposed to have received from one of his women friends in Paris. The lady goes to the auction wearing a heavy veil; she buys the pastel (a work of Manet) and says that she will try to find some excuse to satisfy her husband. She mourns his loss, recalls soft moonlight nights and reproaches him for leaving his letters lying about; "men never appreciate the risks women run for them," she adds. All this was an excellent imitation of the epistolary style of an American lady in French society, who was a part of his fashionable life in Paris. He did leave her letters lying about, and those that she wrote to him while he was on visits during the next few years at Moore Hall were gathered together by the family and put among his own letters to his mother. He made love to her "not with conviction," so he said, "but successfully in the end." While her letters do not suggest that she was breaking her heart on his account, they show that she found him a very sympathetic confidant of her emotions and that she was exacting in her demands on his attention. "So you won't come to see me, *mon cher ami. Ça vaut mieux peut-être*. You are quite right to devote yourself to your art instead of trusting to the 'vacillating fancies' of a woman. Why do I want to see you, you say ! Does a woman ever know why she wants anything, least of all I who have almost given up trying to know myself. . . . But you know me very little, *mon cher ami*, my real self, that is. You know one side of me. Yes, the worldly frivolous side— but you do not know that very few women have as much earnestness of nature, as much intensity of feeling as I have. . . . I have very nearly singed my wings these last months, but have had the courage to fly from the flame. I don't know why I am saying all this to you, *mon cher ami*, except that I always had a way of ' saying things ' to you." At any rate it is clear that Moore's unhappiness at leaving Paris was not due to separation from any particular woman. Charming women of every description pervade all his literary and artistic reminiscences of Paris, but, as Daniel Halévy has said, "*Memoirs of My Dead Life* is not a book of love."

2

Moore's movements are uncertain until August 1880, when he is known to have been in Dublin with his mother. But he was living in London at some time in the beginning of the year for, as has only lately been revealed, he had a post on the *Examiner* of which Heinrich Felbermann—a cosmopolitan Hungarian, also lately from Paris and the friend of a good many of Moore's acquaintance there—was the new editor and proprietor. He was second secretary at two guineas a week; and Felbermann, who says he was "dear at the price," includes his name in a list of persons afterwards famous who passed through his hands.[1] The training cannot have lasted for long, because from August onwards Moore was in Ireland for several months. Mrs. Moore had taken a house for the Horse Show, and all her family were round her, as is recorded in Colonel Maurice Moore's diary. "August 1880, I had returned from South Africa with my regiment. Last Horse Show in the grounds of Leinster House. Family in Merrion Square—George, self, Augustus, Nina, Julian and Mother. Article for French paper that I wrote at G's instigation. G. said that I had curious style."

Uncle Joe was in Dublin for the Show and he handed George the estate accounts, saying that he was owed £3,000 which could be collected as soon as his nephew found an agent who understood peasants. "But who should understand peasants better than you do?" Moore replied, for he slighted his mother's family, putting the Blakes of Ballinafad with their harum scarum gentility into the category of squireens, a different race, he used to say, from the Moores. But his uncle steadfastly refused to continue the agency, and

[1] *The Memoirs of a Cosmopolitan*, by Heinrich Felbermann. Chapman & Hall, 1936.

Moore could neither tolerate, nor even comprehend opposition.

As he had never troubled to understand the estate he took his uncle's books to a lawyer, and the lawyer advised him not to sign the accounts, which had been kept without any system by one of the retainers about Ballinafad while Blake himself farmed and raced. Moore returned to Merrion Square, using language that caused consternation in the family. He forfeited sympathies by hinting that his uncle, whose reputation was an honourable one, had falsified the accounts; but as was often the case in his quarrels he had a real grievance to begin with: although the losses were really due to bad times, the family had done him a wrong during his minority by entrusting the property to this careless management. His mother was in agony lest he might engage in a lawsuit but at last he signed the accounts, saying as he did so that he would rather lose £3,000 than allow his thoughts to be distracted from literature. Colonel Moore went through the books at the time and satisfied himself that no money had gone astray. " My brother," he says, " had no idea of accounts, but had his suspicions when money failed to come in."

He went from Dublin to Mayo and spent the winter at Moore Hall with his sister, Nina Moore (afterwards Mrs. Kilkelly), his Mother remaining in Merrion Square. It was still on the cards that he might settle down at Moore Hall, but he shrank from the idea of looking after his properties. " I lie awake all night thinking of it," he wrote to his uncle, from the Palace, Elphin, where he was visiting some cousins, " I cannot trust myself, I dread a failure. You must understand we are all differently constituted. You would find yourself hopelessly at sea between the fourteen rhymes of a sonnet. You probably would not succeed in writing one. I would without difficulty. . . ." One day he was lunching with the Ruttledges of Cornfield, his neighbours, and he picked young Tom Ruttledge as Joe Blake's successor. There was a chorus of disapproval among his Blake cousins, first because George could not afford an agent and secondly because Ruttledge himself showed little promise of ability at the time. But Moore insisted upon obeying his instinct, and the choice proved to be a very lucky one for both. Ruttledge developed into a first-class man of business, acquiring many other agencies; he used to say that he owed his start in life to Moore. To pay the debt to Blake, Moore raised £3,000 by mortgage; and to support himself until he earned a living by his pen he sold some of the timber about Moore Hall (the woods needed thinning) for a few hundred pounds. With his new agent he made a tour of inspection of his property, a distressing experience which brought him up the desolate slopes of the Tourmakeady mountains and across water-logged plains where farms were rented at five shillings an acre. Tenants' deputations, headed by the local politician, called at Moore Hall, and instructed him in the grievance of the confiscations and in the history of Irish land tenure, explaining why no rents were being paid. He affected to be bored by such subjects; but he kept his eyes and ears open and formed his own opinions, as *Parnell and his Island* and *A Drama in Muslin* testify.

The organised peasant uprising threatened the Moore family with ruin, as it threatened all other encumbered landlords; but George Moore went in no danger of his life during the winter of 1880–81 and he was not obliged to follow the example of neighbours in carrying a revolver or applying for police protection. The Moores had never been hard upon their tenants. The anti-humanitarian principles of the Rue de la Tour des Dames were not put into practice on the estate. Moore was kind and indulgent to his tenants, so far as he came into contact with them, and continued his father's practice of refraining from evictions on his property.

Only once was he molested: while staying for a few days at Cornfield, he went with Robert Ruttledge, Tom's brother, to shoot at Castlemagarett, the seat of Lord Oranmore and Browne. Robert Ruttledge had rented the shooting, and for some reason or other the local branch of the League objected. As the party were returning home after a day's sport they had to cross a wooden bridge in the demesne; and when horse and trap were half across, the bridge collapsed and all fell into the river. The posts of the bridge had been sawn through. Luckily the water was not deep, and Moore and Ruttledge managed to extricate themselves, arriving home with nothing worse than a wetting.

Moore had come back to an Ireland very different from the Ireland he had known in his boyhood. He had grown up in a countryside which scarcely knew any inhabitants but the gentry and their dependents. He used to say in his later life that he had been born in feudalism, adding that the eighteenth century which ended in England in 1830 continued in Ireland until 1870. But he was quick to size up the new reality, ranking the cause of the landlords as a lost one, and citing Balzac's *Les Paysans* to the effect that the law must always be powerless to protect property against the combinations of tenants. In a lecture on Balzac and Shakespeare which he delivered in Paris many years later, he said " Avec une clairvoyance extraordinaire il [Balzac] a prévu tous les événements qui sont arrivés en Irelande depuis vingt-cinq ans." It appears that he passed as a dangerous radical among the Mayo gentry ; but he did not mind that for he liked to be thought different from his neighbours. His habit of automatically saying whatever occurred to him may perhaps be regarded as a tribute to Naturalistic principle.

But it was his dress in particular that created astonishment. He wore a little top-hat on the side of his head, highheeled boots, and wide trousers, looking like a caricature of a Frenchman in an English paper ; he kept to this costume even when he went out shooting, but he recovered respect by shooting as well as any one else. So anxious was he to be regarded as a stranger in his own country that he at first pretended that he had forgotten to speak English. He surrendered this pose after a while, but it was for a long time his habit to pass from English to French as abruptly as Dick Swiveller passed into scraps of verse. It seems that he thought indifferently in both languages. His brother Maurice suspected that he knew French only by ear (" I once brought him a French newspaper and he threw it aside impatiently ") ; this had formerly been true but was so no longer, although he could not yet read French with ease. In spite of his seven years' sojourn in France, an Irishman could still recognise him as a fellow-countryman. He had an odd way of detaching the last letter of a word and using it as the first letter of the next, " a narticle," he said for " an article," and in more ways than this, his spoken English had Irish traits. He was quite helpless with his hands which is rather surprising seeing that he was considered a good shot and a good rider, and that he played lawn tennis rather well. But his use of his hands in everyday life recalled a fish trying to use its fins. His complexion gave him the look almost of a baby and one with curious greeny blue eyes, and he had a poor figure, very sloping shoulders and long neck and body. His chin was receding, and he was given to explaining that such a condition was not a sign of weakness, for he was not a weak man; he did not mind what other people thought of his views and loved to be the single opponent in an argument. He had no great opinion of his appearance, in fact he often said that he was ashamed of it, but he was jealous of good looks in other men and, in later life, used to be very critical of portraits painted of him.

3

Poetry and a novel occupied his working hours. One day his sister came down to breakfast and found him in the best of humours. The post had just come in and it brought news of the acceptance by *The Spectator* of one of his poems—" The Sweetness of the Past." It was the first time he had been printed in an English periodical, and his sister remembers the lines: " I look to the past re-arisen, And joys come over in hosts, Like sea-birds from their roosts." The poem (*Spectator*, Dec. 11th, 1880) was reprinted in the *Confessions* as an example of the acceptable sort of English verse he was able to write as a young man; but with his habitual parsimony he treasured up the simile of the sea birds, using it again very many years later in the prose of *Ave*. " The present is no more than a little arid sand dribbling through the neck of an hour glass; but the past may be compared to a shrine in the coigne of some sea cliff, whither the white birds of recollection come to roost and rest awhile, and fly away again into the darkness."

That it is easier to write passable poetry than passable prose became one of Moore's favourite tenets, based, he thought, on his own experience. But he ran no danger of becoming a prolific poetaster, and to fill up his new (and last) volume of verse, *Pagan Poems*, he had to reprint some pieces from *Flowers of Passion*. The new volume was milder and less of a challenge to the conventions than the *Flowers*, but it contained some bizarre lines—

> *I am filled with carnivorous lust, like a tiger*
> *I crouch and feed on my beautiful prey.*

It failed to attract even hostile attention and the printer soon sold all the copies as waste paper; but for some time the author was known in London as " Pagan Moore."

The novel which he was writing during the winter at Moore Hall got completely out of hand and was abandoned in despair.[1] So that he had not much to show when he sallied forth among the London publishers and editors from the ugly and almost sordid rooms in the lodging house in Cecil St., Strand, where he settled in the spring of 1881. The rooms are very exactly described in the *Confessions*. His brother Colonel Moore, and his sister, when they came to London, used to stop with him, and both of them retain a clear memory of the Cockney drudge described in the *Confessions* whose dullness of mind and assiduity at her work were a perpetual astonishment, for poor " Emma " was very unlike an Irish servant.

Augustus, the third brother, also came to London with the intention of making a living by his pen. He was a young man of brilliant conversation, tall and with fascinating manners, the dashing member of the family. Like the other brothers and unlike his father, he was a poor scholar and at Beaumont he had tried to set the house on fire in order to

[1] The unpublished novel which is mentioned in the *Confessions*. A *Communication to My Friends* gives us to understand that Moore's first published novel, *A Modern Lover*, was almost finished before he left Paris; but the order of events in this autobiographical fragment is very inexact.

show his disapproval of English school discipline. In London Augustus quickly drew attention to himself by bringing out an annual called *Walnuts and Wine* which printed " Dolorida," an eight-line poem from the album of Adah Menken, the celebrated circus artist of the sixties who went by the name of the " Naked Lady," a friend of Swinburne's; Augustus attributed the authorship of " Dolorida " to the poet, much to the wrath of Swinburne's friends. Later on George and Augustus were a good deal together, but in the first years their ways led apart, for the playtime of " Masher Moore," as London called Augustus, was only beginning, whereas George considered that his had ended. If he sometimes consented to accompany his brother to a fashionable restaurant and dine there with prize-fighters and young lords in an atmosphere· of champagne, comic songs and chorus girls, he always vowed afterwards that he would not do it again, because he felt that the bluster and bluff of the restaurant turned his thoughts from the pages he had written or which he hoped to write on the following day. He wondered how this was, and at last discovered himself to be " irreparably æsthetic," which explained his aversions from his Galway cousins and the lords who drank champagne at Romano's. He did not even seek out his old friend Jim Browne, now in St. John's Wood, where he died of pneumonia, caught while he was modelling a huge snow lion in his garden. Of his showy friend Hawkins he now saw little or nothing. In the *Confessions* he comes over to avert a duel with Lord Rossmore, and this is the last we hear of him. A note in a German art-lexicon gives a few facts to satisfy the curious. He continued until the end of his life to exhibit in the *Salons* of Paris—genre pictures for the most part, also allegories, portraits and landscapes. Specimens of his work may be seen in the Luxembourg at Paris, and in the museums at Nantes and Troyes. He died in 1910—just before the composition of *Vale* : a significant date.

Very unlike the old life with Lewis was Moore's London existence—frugal, simple and laborious. Another motive, besides his æstheticism and determination to succeed, which induced him to avoid garish company, was a horror of debt; being by nature apt to expect the worst, he was certain that his tenants would never pay their rents again and that he must either earn a living or find his way to the workhouse. Often he was very unhappy under this self-imposed discipline, feeling that it would be all in vain and that he would fail as a novelist as previously he had failed as a painter and a poet. He suffered from a nostalgia for France. Old friends reminded him that he had once been the most Parisian of all Englishmen. " You must come to Paris and escape that dreadful British atmosphere," wrote the American lady of the auction of the Rue de la Tours des Dames: " Promise me that you will never become an uncompromising John Bull—as if you could. It was all a mistake about you. You were born out of your sphere. Your *côté parisien* was always the nicest, if not the best part of you. You were meant to have lived, loved and suffered in Paris, and now you are going to marry some square-backed, big-footed British matron, and have a dozen children *après la manière de votre pays*, and become a respectable *père de famille*, and think of us all in Paris as Pagans—it is all wrong, it is not your vocation, but what is to be done about it ? "

Moore remembered these compliments in the moods of his old age when he sometimes used to say that Providence (through the Land League) had done him a wrong by taking him from France to become an English writer instead of leaving him there to become a French one: the best work, he used to add, is done in conjunction with public opinion rather than against it.

4

But London greeted him in kindly fashion. " It is said that young men of genius come to London with great poems and dramas in their pockets, and find every door closed against them. . . . But when I, George Moore, came to London in search of literary adventure, I found a ready welcome." His only enemy was the " logical consequences of his past

education," the French wit in his brain, the French sentiment in his heart, the French idiom on his lips. " I was full
of France, and France had to be got rid of, or pushed out of
sight before I could understand England. I was handicapped
with dangerous ideas, and an impossible style, and before
long the leading journal [*Spectator*] that had printed two
poems and some seven or eight critical articles ceased to
send me books for review."[1]

No one ever mistook Moore for a Frenchman, and he
dropped the Parisian top-hat and high-heeled boots before
settling in London; he had not been cut off from English
influences during the years in Paris, and his family did not
find him greatly changed on his return. But anyone who
saw much of him in the eighties, and knew that he had lived
a good deal among Frenchmen, would probably have
attributed a number of his characteristics to a French
formation—the thriftiness, the dislike of travel and lack of
curiosity about foreign countries and people, the contempt
for all that did not interest himself. His attitude towards
religion then reflected the Parisian *boulevardier* of the eighteen
eighties who talked about Darwin and Renan in much the
same way that people nowadays talk about Einstein and
Freud. The way he talked about women was French rather
than English. For the *boulevardier* of the eighties it was highly
creditable to be known as *un homme à femmes* and few deprived
themselves of the pleasure of boasting of their conquests. The
type may be followed in the plays and novels of the period.
Variations from the truth, for which the listener made
allowance, were part of the game.

The plot of his first published novel came to him one day as
he was leaving Gatti's. He sat down at once to write it, but
it did not occupy all his time, and when the *Spectator* was
closed to him on account of his dangerous ideas, he looked
about him for odd literary jobs, contributing short stories
and essays to society papers; Augustus Moore was interested
in this class of journalism and a little later collaborated with
his brother in writing the English libretto for *Les Cloches de
Corneville*, by which he earned £30. (When G. R. Sims's

---

[1] *Confessions of a Young Man.*

library was being sold, a sixpenny copy of *Les Cloches de Corneville*, by George and Augustus Moore, fetched £90.) Moore read contemporary English fiction—Hardy, Meredith, Stevenson, James; also the more popular authors, Blackmore, Buchanan, David Christie Murray—and found little that was good to say of them. The scene of his effort to " become an Englishman " was the Gaiety Bar, to which he was introduced, it seems, by Tinsley, the publisher of Charles Reade and Miss Braddon; he would go there on most evenings to censure English fiction, inveigh against the artistic debauchery of the London theatre, and swear by Naturalism. The impressions of his days in Paris remained with him, his ambition to understand the English soul being at variance with his conviction of the superiority of the French civilisation. His circle of listeners was well enough, but rather common, and it had to be confessed that the Gaiety Bar was a poor substitute for the Nouvelle Athènes. Usually someone got drunk, and Moore would then leave the bar, for he hated drunkenness. However it may have been with him in Paris he never mixed with English Bohemian life, and Frank Harris, whom he presently met, marvelled at his extraordinary moderation. " He had the prudence of the Celt," another of his early friends, Sir William Geary, writes to me; " he was a tranquil spirit. Such lights-of-love as he speaks of in his autobiographical books had no influence to divert him from literature and art, and from self-education."

5

Some letters to Zola of this period in Cecil Street, two years or a little longer (1881–1883), remain: frequently, like so many of his letters, they are undated. They supplement Moore's own account of his early literary activities in London and show with what assiduity he sought to bring the Naturalistic novel before the notice of the British public. It has seemed best to translate these letters in order to avoid drawing undue attention to mistakes in Moore's French syntax, sometimes due to mere carelessness.

17 Cecil Street,
Strand.

Dear Sir,

I send you by today's post a short study which I have made on you and your works. It has but one merit and one originality. 1. it gives the truth, 2. it is the first eulogy which you have had in England. I am really proud of having been the first to sow this grain of truth, as you will understand, in view of all the silly things that have been said of you in the Paris journals how the ground here is encumbered with daily mounting stupidites in your regard (*l'encombrement de stupidites qui grandissent tous les jours en Angleterre sur votre compte*). People here have not had the advantage of reading your work, and so they go on repeating—you can guess what they repeat. My article is bad because I have tried to put the material of twenty papers into ten, but I believe and I hope that it will serve to open doors and enable me to place a more elaborated and a longer article, for it is always the old story of Panurge's sheep. I warn you that you will find terrible imbecilities in the article; I was forced to say them in order to get the article accepted and I thought that a little truth was better than none. But perhaps you don't remember me, so I shall give you some biographical details . . . M. Manet, one of my great friends, presented me to you at the ball given in honour of *L'Assommoir*, but I was always discreet enough not to annoy you with a visit. I know all your friends and it is probable that you have heard my great and intimate friend Alexis speak of me, perhaps also my friend Hennique. You see that we are in a country of acquaintances. One more word. A great London publisher has proposed that I should do a literal translation of *L'Assommoir*. Will you accept me as the translator if the business can be arranged ?

Zola delayed in answering this letter, and Moore wrote again when ten days had passed :

If you do not remember me you have only to apply to the *Voltaire* [the organ of the Naturalists] at the date of the

appearance of *Nana* and there you will find a letter on the
subject of the opinions entertained of you in England
addressed by me as an English man of letters to our friend
Paul Alexis.

Though Moore never translated *L'Assommoir* he must have
convinced Zola that he could be useful to him, for when he
paid a visit to Paris, in the course of 1882, he had the honour
of being bidden to the great man's country house, whither he
went accompanied by the loyal Alexis, as he has recorded in
" A Visit to Médan." They talked of the powers of the
circulating library in England and of Puritanism in literature, and Moore felt that he had made a good impression on
the great man. In a letter written on his return to Cecil
Street he said :

> You can't realise how we stand, you are unaware of the
> combinations which force us to be sentimental, to write
> flat and conventional novels and which prohibit *all*
> observation and analysis. It would take ten pages in which
> to explain the situation. If it were only the public [I] could
> destroy the inflexible prejudices which have caused the
> fall of the novel in England, but it is a question of libraries.
> (*Si se n'était que le public (je) pouvais abbatre les inflexibles
> préjuges qui ont fait tomber le roman en Angleterre, mais sont de
> libraries.*)

His mother was kept briefly informed of his literary
progress. " I am working incessantly at my novel," he
wrote in May 1882, " it takes a great deal of time to write
nine hundred pages particularly in my minute way of
writing. I am so glad about Nina [his sister had lately
married] . . . I must go back to the novel, so good-bye. You
are all right quite well *n'est pas.*"

6

His evident anticipation that *A Modern Lover* would be
subjected to attack from the libraries was fulfilled when the
book at last came out in the summer of 1883. It seems that

Smith's, cajoled by Tinsley, had taken *A Modern Lover* on
trust, and then discovered that it was unsuitable reading for
young girls. Fiction was then largely issued in the three-
volume form at thirty-one-and-sixpence, and this made
Smith's and Mudie's masters of the situation. Hearing that
Smith's were investigating the character of his novel Moore
precipitately took a cab and drove to the library. He demanded explanations. " You have only taken fifty copies of
my book, and Tinsley tells me you are not renewing your
order." " I did not suppress your book," the manager
replied, " I have still some copies in stock." " I daresay you
have, but you only took fifty, whereas Mudie's took three
times that number, and I believe it is your custom to take
three times as many as they. Why then did my case prove an
unfortunate exception ? " " Your book was considered
immoral," the manager replied; " two ladies from the
country wrote to me objecting to the scene in which the
girl sat to the artist. After that I naturally refused to circulate
the book, unless a customer said he wanted particularly to
read Mr. Moore's novel." " But, my dear Sir, the *Spectator*
quoted the very scene you object to as the most worthy in
the book."

The subject of *A Modern Lover* was the adventure of a
young artist in London; and no reader of Moore s memoirs
will doubt that his recent companion in Paris, Lewis
Weldon Hawkins, sat for the portrait of the ingenuous but
resourceful egoist who is helped all his life by women. Three
women undertake to work for Lewis Seymour's welfare, the
first a work-girl, the second a rich mistress, the third a wife
of high degree. Lewis betrays them all; but all contribute
something, and the young man ends on a high pedestal The
first worshipper retains her faith, the second loses hers
partially, and the third altogether. This is Moore's own
summary of the story in his preface to *Lewis Seymour and Some
Women*—the title given to *A Modern Lover* when it was
rewritten in 1917. It has been said that Moore plagiarised
Maupassant in *A Modern Lover*, but *A Modern Lover* preceded
the more famous story, *Bel Ami*.

Moore did not leap into fame with *A Modern Lover*, but he

was given no reason to complain of neglect or of unkindness on the part of the reviewers, and when the circulating libraries failed to subscribe for enough copies to defray the expenses of the issue, he was given space to air his complaint in the *Pall Mall Gazette* and other newspapers. Some of the comment upon the book seemed to conceal a note of relief. The *Spectator* wrote: " One is made aware by certain passages that Mr. Moore would fain imitate the methods of Zola and his odious school, but two obstacles are in his path— the faith of a Christian and the instincts of a gentleman; the author recognises and respects goodness, purity and disinterestedness, and if M. Zola or any of the hogs of his sty could write such an episode as that with which the story opens, the work-girl's sacrifice for the penniless artist, one would have as much hope for their future as for that of Mr. Moore."

Zola passed with the circulating libraries as a pornographer and nothing more, but the general public was growing restive under the Victorian convention of the novel, and intellectuals, making their idol of science, were in sympathy, if not with the whole practice of the Naturalists, at least with the theory of a fiction that should be based on observed realities and the commonplaces of life, and should follow " scientific methods."

What Moore thought of his book at the time is shown in a letter to Zola :

I have just published a novel which has had success. *A Modern Lover:* in the French papers they call it *Un Amant d'aujourdhui!* I don't know why my phrase has been altered. The fact that my novel has been successful may interest you; for, as I have already told you, I owe you everything. My book alas is not good. I know it well, but it has succeeded. I was obliged to attenuate dreadfully, but what else could I do ? I had to take a step and the step is taken. (*J'était forcé de faire des escomalages épouvantable mais que voulez vous ? Il faut faire un pas, il et fait.*)

In later life he considered his first success from quite a different point of view. " I wonder that I did not give up,"

GEORGE MOORE *circa* 1880

he told John Freeman in his old age, " I did not know—I simply did not know how to write. . . . But if you ask why, when I found I couldn't express myself in prose, I didn't give up prose, there's but one answer. . . . What is it ? Well, it was the story that held me in thrall, the story that was and is my *Belle Dame Sans Merci.* I've always been able to conceive and invent a story . . ."[1] It is possible that he was reading into his early experience a good many ideas about himself that he only acquired upon later reflection. The contemporary evidence indicates that the early Moore prided himself on his powers of observation and his readiness to use these powers in the service of an honest presentation of the raw facts of life, not on his gift as a story teller, and that he was not greatly troubled by considerations of good writing. He must have felt that he was encountering difficulties which authors with much more modest ambition escaped, but what these difficulties were he did not exactly understand. Oscar Wilde's remark that Moore took seven years to discover grammar, that he then discovered the paragraph, and so on, shouting his discoveries from the housetop as he went along, is well known. Words, however, always obeyed his call, and the interlarding of *A Modern Lover* with French sentences must be attributed to an affectation rather than to a difficulty of identifying his thoughts with the English language. The " excellent anecdote " revealed *A Modern Lover* as the work of a promising author, but the bad sentences and errors in English usage were accompanied, especially in the society passages, by an inflation of thought and feeling, the sort of perception of life which might have been expected to prevail among the young lords and chorus girls who supped with Augustus at Romano's.

Neither the commendation of the *Spectator* nor Sir Henry Norman's long, carefully considered, and on the whole appreciative notice in the *Fortnightly* could move Smith's from their position, and, dissatisfied with Tinsley's weak handling of his case, Moore directed his steps towards Vizetelly, the former correspondent of the *Illustrated London News* in Paris and a man of wide culture. To him he outlined

[1] *A Portrait of George Moore, in a Study of his Work* : Werner Laurie, 1922.

the subject of his next novel, *A Mummer's Wife*, the story of the leader of an opera company who lodges at a linen-draper's shop and rescues the pretty draperess from her drab existence of attendance upon an asthmatic husband. Vizetelly, who now earned a precarious livelihood by publishing translations of foreign books, Daudet and Flaubert (he had not yet dared to translate Zola), was very sympathetic, and welcomed Moore's suggestion—Zola was its real source—of evading dictation from the libraries by publishing in one volume at a cheaper price: ten shillings was the price arranged for, and a series of one-volume novels was planned in which *A Mummer's Wife* should take its place. Moore owed £40 to Tinsley, the sum he had agreed to pay if the libraries did not take enough copies to defray the expenses of *A Modern Lover*; but the stock was insured, and the lucky accident of a fire at Tinsley's warehouse put matters right for him, and he was able to share with Vizetelly the risk of bringing out in one volume the very long novel which he now proposed to write. The surprising publicity obtained by *A Modern Lover*, those long articles in the *Spectator* and the *Fortnightly*, was very encouraging, and he now felt sure that the moment had come for a genuinely Naturalistic novel of English life, and that only the man was needed.

We read in *A Communication to My Friends* that Vizetelly advised Moore to set out with notebook in hand in search of a suitable town, the uglier the better, a town without amusements of any sort, wherein to lay the opening scene of *A Mummer's Wife*, and that Moore then applied among his friends at the Gaiety Bar for introductions to some touring players who were bound for the town of Hanley. He toured for several weeks with the second company of *Les Cloches de Corneville*, visiting Hanley and certain factory towns; so he says in *A Communication to My Friends*. But Jimmy Glover, later of the Drury Lane Orchestra, who was the conductor of the *Les Cloches de Corneville* company, used always to claim that he was the real author of *A Mummer's Wife*, so many were the stories of operatic touring companies which he related to Moore; Glover, like James Davis, editor of the *Pink 'Un*, belonged to the circle of Augustus Moore, but George was fairly intimate with both for a time, and he dedicated *A Mummer's Wife* to Davis.

7

The greater part of the winter of 1883–84 was passed in Ireland. A month or two before Christmas Moore joined his mother at Moore Hall and stayed with her for several weeks. His brother Julian and his sister were away, and a cousin had to come to keep Mrs. Moore company. She has described to me how George would work from breakfast at *A Mummer's Wife*, and then appear at tea in a white dressing gown. As far as she remembers he had no amusements. He neither rode nor shot, his only exercise being an occasional walk in the dusk, perhaps to Tower Hill, their nearest neighbours, across the stones and mud, when to her surprise he would wear patent-leather shoes and blue silk stockings. After dinner he sat chatting with his mother and his cousin before the fire.

Little had been done in many years for the house and place, which seemed to George Moore to be typical of Ireland, the country of abandoned dreams. The famous stables whence had come the winners of the Chester Cup and the Steward's Cup were empty : the walled garden on the left of the house was over-grown with weeds, and the fine woods were uncared for. There is autobiographical interest in an article which he wrote a year later as a chapter for his book, *Parnell and his Island*; he is himself the poet who returns to Ireland with Verlaine and Mallarmé in his pocket and finds people who take his word for it that Wagner was a first-rate cattle dealer. The description of the pale, quiet reed-fringed lake rings true. In the evenings in an incompletely furnished dining-room of princely proportions, an old butler (Applely) hands round the trout that has just been caught on Lough Carra. After dinner the poet and his French guests spend their time putting the library in order — a library to which no new book has been added for fifty years.

Moore had told Vizetelly that when *A Mummer's Wife*

was finished he would begin a novel of the gentry, for he had been greatly struck by the contrast between the life of well-brought-up English girls and that of the French *jeune fille*. In this winter he decided that his gentry would be Irish, a clever lady whom he met at some party having excited his imagination by describing the Viceregal Court in Dublin and the girls who went to it with their dreams of conquest, so seldom fulfilled. He stayed with Edward Martyn and Mrs. Martyn at Tillyra, with the Ruttledges at Cornfield (where a room called the Pink Room was always in reserve for his writing), and at Browne's Grove near Tuam; then at the end of January 1884 he travelled to Dublin to take part himself in the Dublin Season. It was his subject that drew him to Lord Spencer's Court; his mother hoped, however, that he might find a wife among the " nice girls " about whom he proposed to write in his *Drama in Muslin*.

At Browne's Grove he had met a Miss Maud Browne, the daughter of a one-armed Crimean veteran, a famous clubman of the time, well known as an arbiter on all points regarding the deportment of young ladies. The sad destiny of the girl attracted his notice; she was in the care of an aunt who disapproved of him and whom he regarded as an ogress. Miss Browne was the little frightened thing who was to figure in *A Drama in Muslin*, the pale martyr of Lord Spencer's private dance, who has spoken to no one and who has not even a brother to offer her an ice. Various Browne and Blake cousins were convinced that George proposed to Maud, and that she did not dare accept him. To his sister he said: " I might have carried if off on the night of the Castle ball, but I had a scruple, the only scruple I ever had." Certainly he was not in the least in love; but Miss Browne was an heiress, and the aunt's attitude constituted a challenge. It was a more serious thing on the girl's side; a husband was found for her later, but she used to say ever afterwards that she " always loved George."

Upon first arriving in Dublin his thoughts ran on the clothes he would have to buy. A whole court suit ran to £45; but he succeeded in borrowing everything except the velvets.

In this way he saved £25 and he was able to recover £10 of the balance by selling the velvets when the season ended. He stayed at the Shelbourne Hotel, and every morning he wrote a portion of *A Mummer's Wife* in his bedroom. " I work very hard," he wrote to Zola, " and this time I hope to do a more solid piece of work. The success of my first novel (which has been noticed in the great reviews) has put me on my feet, and if I succeed, as I expect, in digging a dagger into the heart of the sentimental school, I shall have hopes of bringing about a change in the literature of my country—of being in fact Zola's offshoot in England (*d'être enfin un ricocher de Zola en Angleterre.*)"

February 17th, 1884.

My dear Mama,

Perhaps you were right. Anyhow I consider everything now over between me and Maud, but I shall never forget the horrible system of terrorism to which she has been subjected. The poor girl's life is one of those unknown tragedies which the historian must pass without noticing, but in which the history of nations is written as much as in the chronicles of battle or conquest.

But enough of the subject. Let the past be the past.

I have been to a state ball at the Castle, and have to confess that I thought it very grand and imposing. I was introduced to some nice people, among the number was Miss Grattan Bellew—I thought her charming, so bright and clever. I did not unfortunately dance with her, but her aunt asked me to call upon her. The Catholic lot I know by heart, and as I consider them low, commonplace and uneducated, I avoid them. I do not know if you ever heard of a Miss Cornwall. She is quite charming, and I see a good deal of her. Lady Bellew is staying with her. At the State ball I did not stir from the end of the room near the dais where I danced a few times with Lady Bellew, a young lady she was chaperoning, Miss Dease, the chamberlain's daughter, Miss Burke, Lady Fingall's sister and Miss Butler. Jane was sitting in sight without a creature to go near, Maud was without a partner, and as they were all

watching me I scored over them prodigiously. I had hoped
I was above such social triumphs, but the flesh is weak.

There was a Calico ball given at the Rotunda Never did
I see anything so low, so vile, so dirty. Dublin society has
lost all sense of what is *la vie comme il faut.* Men blacking
their faces to go and dance with ladies—it was awful.
Marriage is of course the ruling topic of conversation, and
poor Eddy causes them all the deepest inquietude.

I have been working at my book (*A Mummer's Wife*) and
am satisfied. I think that I shall this time knock *l'ecole
sentimentale* head over heels. Effie is laughing and shouting
as usual but very good naturedly. Anna Browne does not
interest me in the least. Jennie Ruttledge is not amusing
herself, I am afraid, but she is a very nice girl, much nicer
when she is away from Cornfield.

The Miss McDonnelly's are up here, they are as kittenish
as ever in manner.

Lady —— is amusing herself prodigeously with George
Brent, I don't spell the name right, Lady Bellew's son.

I have now told you all the news, and with many
affectionate wishes, I wish you till my next letter good-bye.

George Moore.

P.S. I am afraid you must find Moore Hall very lonely.
I am sorry I am not going back to live with you immediately. I must go to London, but next Autumn we shall
meet. I beg of you not to tell anybody of what I say about
the State ball—it would make me look absurd—it is one
thing to do a thing and another to talk about it.

Levee, State Ball and Calico Ball—all were to find a place
in the pages of *A Drama in Muslin.* In the book Mrs. Barton,
the ambitious mother, takes her two daughters, Alice, the
plain heroine of the story, and the lovely Olive, to the
distressing function at the Rotunda, deceived by some imposing names at the head of the prospectus.

Mrs. Barton fell into the trap, and to her dismay, found
herself and her girls in the company of the rag tag and

bobtail of Catholic Dublin; Bohemian girls, fabricated out of bed curtains, negro minstrels that an application of grease and burnt cork had brought into a filthy existence ... " I never felt so low," said the lady who always brought an A.D.C. from the Castle.

When it becomes known that the Bartons have been at this ball, that the beauties have been seen dancing with the young Catholic nobodies, their names are forthwith struck off the lists of the private dances at the Castle, and Olive's chances of catching Lord Kilcarney are diminished. Mrs. Barton was drawn in part from his aunt, Mrs. Anna Murphy, a rich woman who lived near Dublin and who also had two daughters. She showed no resentment at the portrait and indeed returned good for evil by giving him the pretty Louis Seize clock that is mentioned in one of the chapters in *Conversations in Ebury Street*. " Every time the bell of the clock rings I look up, to think, and not infrequently, of my dear aunt."

Certain old ladies, debutantes of that season, still remember dancing with him. " My recollection," one of them says, " is a red-headed affable young man, excellent company, but of sudden and uncertain temper. One never knew when or why he would become ruffled or bored, or annoyed with you."

8

On his return to London, Moore moved from Cecil Street into bachelor chambers on the north side of the Strand. Ireland had grown quieter, some rents were being collected, and he was making a little money with his contributions, chiefly on French literature, to the *Pall Mall Gazette* and other newspapers.

3, Dane's Inn,
Wych Street,
Strand.

My dear Mama,

Thanks a thousand times for the blankets. They are splendid. I found a conclave of housemaids assembled in my room for the purpose of admiring them. The oldest said she was sure they came from my mother. I asked her why, and she answered, " Am I not a mother myself, and do you think that I don't know a mother's present when I see it ? " And that is just the point I want to get at. You bought those blankets and put yourself to a lot of expense. Now I am so sorry for this; all I wanted was some from Moore Hall, where there are dozens I believe lying. Enfin a mother's a mother, and there is no use in quarrelling with her for that. So again many thanks. You did not allude to my last letter. I hope it did not offend you. What I meant was not unkind, but it is so difficult, and no one knows it better than a writer, how difficult it is, to give such verbal expression to vague doubt and shifting uncertainty as will establish an exact understanding between reader and writer. Somehow the impression conveyed is always more clear not to say brutal than is intended. My dear Mother, I did not mean to hurt your feelings. I only tried to speak what was uppermost in my mind. Pray write me a line on this subject and assure me that you are not offended. It would be so nice to live together again. You must be lonely, I know, and after all one really cares only for one's own.

Ever affect. yours,
George Moore.

There followed an excursion to Paris, an incident of which has yielded an amusing passage to a recent book of memoirs. Moore had business with Zola relating to the translations of his novels which Vizetelly began to issue in 1884, but he also found time to amuse himself. We see him, the morning after a costume ball, in dispute with the concierge outside the ballroom (*Milord n'a donc pas son maille cotch ?*), a Pierrot dressed in satin, a great bouquet of wilted roses in the muff formed by his wide cuffs. As there was no fiacre to be had in the empty Boulevard Malesherbes, the bedraggled Pierrot collapsed miserably on a bench hugging his bouquet. Someone who had been lucky enough to find a cab cried: " It is George Moore ! Let us bring him home with us "; but milord Pierrot, on the look-out, remained on the bench—no doubt hoping that some Cleopatra of his fancy would arrive in a bedecked barge to rescue him. The story is told by J.-E. Blanche,[1] the distinguished painter, whose early talent Moore was quick to perceive. They were continually together, both in England (where Blanche had many friends) and in Paris at the house in Auteuil with the fine garden, the home of Docteur Blanche, who is portrayed with such affection in the chapter " Spent Love " of *Memoirs of My Dead Life*. " My memories of Moore are rather vague up to 1882 or 1883," says Blanche. " I had been hearing of him for a long time, but when I was growing up he was talked about so much by the friends of my family that it is difficult to say when and where I first met him; perhaps it was in Gervex's studio, or with Ary Renan. No: on second thoughts I must at least have seen him at Manet's studio, rue de Clichy. I was only eighteen then, and Manet tried to make me paint a bun in his presence. I recall the excitement caused by Manet's macabre portrait of him nicknamed *Le Noyé Repêché*, and the elegant Roumanian woman whom everyone wanted to paint, Manet as well as Boldini and Helleu. G. M. used to watch over her, and choose the artists who seemed best suited to render her charms. He was very fond of my father. They always got along beautifully, and when my father died he wrote me a charming and sincere letter. I painted two portraits of him, one in 1888, the other in 1902—one of my best, which the model described as ' a drunken cabman,' and wished to have me destroy. Yet it was a most dignified picture and psychologically the most true of any that I shall leave behind me."

In the summer of 1884, at Dane's Inn, Moore completed *A Mummer's Wife*. There had been periods during his work upon this novel when Moore felt that he could not produce another line about strolling players and their habits; but towards the end he regained confidence and courage, and experienced the sensation of a man who was coming into his strength. " Everything goes well," he wrote to Zola at the end of September, " my novel is finished, and I think it is

[1] *Mes Modèles*: Paris. P. V. Stock, 1929.

twenty times better than my first effort; and what is more important it will be printed as a single volume, as you advised, and as I had at first thought would be impossible."

The writing in *A Mummer's Wife* was still poor, the sentences short and common. But the composition marked a great advance; and in Kate Ede, a sort of Madame Bovary of the potteries, and the huge good-natured commonness of Dick Lennox, her seducer from Morton and Cox's opera company, two vital characters were conceived. The life of the strolling players is vividly and accurately presented with a sympathy that never turns into sentimentality. In the middle of the book there is a slight tendency to monotony, which no doubt persuaded Moore to introduce a rather obvious diversion in the eccentric Mrs. Forest; but the psychological truth of the relationship between Dick and Kate, and of her moral and physical disintegration, is extraordinary. " She did not know what she wanted of him, but with a longing that was nearly madness she desired to possess him wholly; she yearned to bury her poor aching body, throbbing with the anguish of nerves, in that peaceful hulk of fat, so calm, so invulnerable to pain, marching amid, and contented in, its sensualities, as a gainly bull grazing amid the pastures of a succulent meadow." It is this tragic obsession that prepares the horror of that scene, after Kate's consent to enter a private asylum, when " Dick sat next her, kind, huge and indifferent, even as the world itself." A lesser artist would have made the world appear cruel to Kate's drink-sodden mind; but the good-natured helpfulness of friends, land-ladies, doorkeepers and street-walkers in the closing London scenes only increases Kate's sense of isolation by making it obvious even to her that her sole enemy is her own weakness of character.

Sir Henry Norman in his notice of *A Modern Lover* had said that Moore would have to carry his observations far deeper than black coats and the odour of shoulders if he would enter the order of the " new knights of fiction." This criticism could not apply to *A Mummer's Wife*, which was a genuine and successful attempt to apply French Naturalistic method to a description of English life. And in fact Moore was the first real adventurer on this ground; for the other English writers who sought assistance from the methods of the Naturalists shrank from carrying them out to their logical conclusion. Gissing would never have written of Kate Ede vomiting over her dress and the red velvet seat of the four-wheeler. Courage was needed for this in the high Victorian period.

9

In Ireland again during the winter of 1884–5, he spent the three months preceding Christmas with his mother at Moore Hall. Here there were no distractions, and often he would not rise from his desk until the sun set behind the great woods of the house. Blue mountains and a grey lake were before him as he worked; the first sketches of *A Drama in Muslin*, his " nice girls " book, and a series of articles on Irish life for a Paris newspaper were his tasks.

He had finally revised the proofs of *A Mummer's Wife* before leaving London, and alternating between hope and fear he waited for the press-cuttings from Vizetelly. The book came out in December, and Vizetelly sent good reports of the sales; it was therefore as an author who had made some noise in the world that Moore went again to Dublin in the New Year, on the quest of further documentation for his Irish novel. On the 18th of January he wrote to Colonel Dease, with whom he was acquainted, as follows:

I am actively engaged on a book, in the interests of which I came to Dublin last year to attend the Levee, the Drawing Rooms and the Castle balls. I was not fortunate enough to receive an invitation for a State dinner party. Now, as my book deals with the social and political power of the Castle in Modern Ireland, I should be glad to attend the Levee in February, if I could make sure of being asked to one of the big dinner parties. My books, as you are probably aware, are extensively read; this particular one will attract a good deal of attention. It would therefore be well to render my picture as complete, as true, as vivid as possible.

Perhaps in the previous year the State Steward had been warned that the young man with a hard loud voice, who expressed unconventional opinions to debutantes, would be an unsuitable guest at the Viceroy's table, although a large landowner in the west of Ireland.

There was an unworldly side to Moore's character, and it is quite possible that he at first supposed that the Castle would welcome the idea of being turned into Naturalistic fiction. When he perceived his blunder, instead of withdrawing in discomfiture (and this also was characteristic of him) he determined to extract all the possibilities both of impish fun and of publicity out of the situation in which he had unwittingly placed himself.

Everyone heard of the notes which " the hungry author " now began to send to the Castle by hand, bidding the messenger await an answer; and when finally the State Steward summoned up sufficient courage to say that " the lists are at present closed," Moore published the whole correspondence in the *Freeman's Journal*, a nationalist paper which was at that time engaged in bespattering Lord Spencer's administration:

The " at present " is amiable. Who are the people entitled to share in the entertainments given in Dublin Castle ? Every year large sums are voted in Parliament for the maintenance of this court Surely this is not done solely for the purpose of feasting and fêting —— and ——[1] I am of course unable as I am unwilling to argue that my social position entitles me to be asked to the Castle, but I cannot refrain from saying that Lord Fingall and Col. Dease would find it difficult to show I was not. Be that as it may, it was as a man of letters, it was for the purpose of studying, not of amusing myself, that I applied for an invitation. Was that the reason I was refused ? One would feel almost inclined to think so. . . . It would be presumptuous on my part to hope to unearth any fresh crime, the lists of shame are already filled. . . . The opinions I hold

[1] The names were those of some bureaucrats who, a year or two before, had been mixed up in an unsavoury scandal.

on the subject [of the Castle] will be found in my next novel, my writing table is covered with human documents —fragments of conversations overheard, notes on character, anecdotes of all kinds. I came to the Castle, not as a patriot nor as a place hunter, but as the passionless observer, who, unbiassed by political creed, comments impartially on the matter submitted to him for analysis. I confess I would have liked to have seen one of the State dinner parties, but we cannot have all things, and I am not sure that Lord Fingall was not right to refuse my application. Fame comes to us in unexpected ways, and I believe that when this somnolent earl is overtaken by that sleep which overtakes us all, and for which, it appears, he is qualifying himself daily as well as nightly, his claim to be remembered will be that he refused to invite me to dinner at the Castle.

Clearly he still regarded Zola as his master in method. It was not until some years later that he directed against the master that talent for satire which he now levelled upon the Viceregal Court. As a consequence of his row with the Castle he became quite a hero with the Irish Nationalists: " You are our best ally," an M.P. wrote to him, " against that stronghold of shame. I can only marvel at the unmatchable imbecility which allows its imbecile inmates to make an enemy of the leader of the realistic school in England. The final touch about Fingall's claim to immortality was worthy of Swift or Junius."

Extracts from the correspondence were copied into the English Press, and on his return to Moore Hall he received other letters of sympathy, one from Miss Mabel Robinson:

I hope your book is getting along quickly. I am longing to see your nice girls and to see whether they are as real and living as poor Kate. If so I am sure they will do very well without the dinner party for which I am sure your readers will trust your imagination.

Two important events occurred in this Spring—the appearance of *A Mummer's Wife* and his discovery of Pater's prose. The proofs were read at Moore Hall; just before he had finished their correction, he took the liberty of announcing in the newspapers that *A Mummer's Wife* would be introduced by Zola's preface. " You know that my struggle is difficult," he wrote to Zola, " and that every measure is necessary if I am to succeed. . . . So I am forgiven, dear Master, am I not ? "

Some important voices, Frank Harris's among them, were raised in whole-hearted approval, and William Archer, as Mr. Charles Morgan has related in his *Epitaph on George Moore*, came to tell Mr. Bernard Shaw that he had just been reading a wonderful Naturalistic novel by a new writer. " Nonsense ! But I know George Moore," was the reply; and according to Felbermann's recent *Memoirs*, Mendès and de l'Isle Adam were equally sceptical. The generality of reviewers deplored the unsparing realism with which Kate Ede's degeneration had been exposed and analysed, and it is really strange that Moore should have said at the time, and believed ever afterwards, that the book was helped to its success by an " enthusiastic Press." *The Athenæum*, for instance, allowed that Kate Ede was a powerful study in the commonplace, but held that the story as a whole was wearisome as well as painful. *The Academy* declared that a more repulsive tale had never been told.

By March *A Mummer's Wife* had gone into three editions. Moore attributed his triumph to the unconventionality of the book and to an article which he had published in the *Pall Mall Gazette* attacking Mudie and the library censorship :

Undated (Moore Hall) *To J.-E. Blanche.*

Mon Mummer's Wife a eu un veritable success. . . . I am sure for a fortnight the *Pall Mall* published letters from different people on the subject *il n'etait question que de George Moore:* but this was not all—every newspaper in England had an article on this subject from the *Saturday Review* downwards. The *Saturday Review* finished with " *Michel Levy saved France with cheap publications who will save England ?* " Besides the press spoke most favourably of the book. For example take the *Athenæum* and you can't go higher—if I had written the notice myself I could not have said more. The book is being translated into French by Madame Judith Bernard, the translator of Miss Braddon. . . . Needless to say I was not at Whistler's soiree; he sent me tickets or something that looked like tickets. *Il ferait mieux de faire de la peinture et de laisser ses blagues a Oscar Wilde et cie. Zalo* [Zola] *que j'espere va faire une preface a mon livre* [the French translation] *a eu la gracieusete de m'envoyer Germinal. Que penses vous—je suis a la moitie* . . .

The French leaves one in no doubt that Moore's knowledge of the language had come to him through sound. The faulty spelling, whatever the cause of the absence of accents, seems to have been largely due to carelessness, because the same mistakes are repeated again and again (*et* for *est*; for example). It pained Blanche, an excellent English scholar, that Moore should persist in writing most of his letters to him in French. Spelling and grammar were his difficulties, he never hesitated for words; he had the rhythm of the language which is rare for a foreigner, and always delighted in the discovery of a new phrase, though he did not always remember it accurately. " How wonderful ! " he would say. " *Quand on a une petite amie on est aux pommes;* " and chuckle over it for the rest of the evening. Next morning he was still rolling the phrase over his tongue. " *Quand on a une petite amie on est à la pomme !* "

He had promised to spend the whole spring at Moore Hall, but with the cuttings from Vizetelly coming in thick and fast, he resisted his mother's lamentations, saying that he must go to London to " see the Press in bloom " recording his name as an English writer. So at least he says in *A Communication to My Friends*, but a different explanation of his impatience to be gone is given in *Avowals*, where we are told that it was a reading of Walter Pater which caused him to break his promise to his mother; his thoughts were set on Kensington, on the Robinsons, in whose house in Earl's Terrace he would be sure to hear an interesting appreciation of a book which had just appeared, *Marius the Epicurean*. He had sent for this book from London, and had read it with

delight and surprise, for here surely was " the great atone-
ment for all the bad novels which had been written in the
English language "; it was the first prose that procured him
any pleasure in the English language; nor until reading
Pater had he ever felt the beauty of " mildness in life," or
realised that " by a certain avoidance of the wilfully passionate and the surely ugly we may secure an aspect of life that
is abiding and soul-sufficing."

10

Marius showed that æstheticism could be a spontaneous
English instinct; but Moore's standards were to remain
French for a long time to come, although his new hero was
altogether out of sympathy with the school of Zola. There
was a meeting with Pater during the summer in the Robinsons' drawing-room; and after this Moore pursued Pater, but
finding, he said, that the author of *Marius* was always sur-
rounded by old women he gave up, and came to the conclusion, expressed many years later in an article in the *Pall Mall
Magazine*, that behind the mask that Pater " did not lift,"
that he " could not lift," was " a shy sentimental man, all
powerful in the written word, impotent in life." His admiration for the artist never faltered, but he began to laugh at
the man behind his back.

Oddly enough, the year of the revelation of *Marius* was
also the year of Moore's greatest activity in support of the
essentially popular art and thought of the Naturalists. *Pot
Bouille* was introduced to the English public during the
course of the year under the title of " *Piping-Hot*, a Realistic
Novel," and with a preface by Moore eulogising the chief
of the Naturalists as " one of the mighty monumental
intelligences of all time " and the " Homer of modern life."

17.7.85. *To Mrs. Moore.*

All London has read *A Mummer's Wife*. When I enter a
drawing room everyone wants to be introduced to me;
I could dine out every night if I care to—I am pestered
with invitations.

Anna still continues her dinner parties, still continues to invite me, but I shall go no more unless she manages to rake up some new people. The dullness of her parties is dreadful to think of—the thought is like a nightmare. With all her cleverness on some points she has not a grain of sense. The Martyns are here and I seem to be getting on very well in the social way. May has the knack of making friends. I see a good deal of them—the other day we met at dinner at Mrs. Tylee's.[1]

Edward Martyn is hard at work at his poems—Julian never comes to see me now. Maurice I wrote to but he did not answer my letter. I suppose he went back to Galway a long time ago. He is so nice—I enjoyed his society immensely. Nina I hear has been very ill but she is now quite well I believe. Of Augustus I know nothing further than that he is travelling about the country with *The Woman and the Law*.

I am attacking the libraries again . . .

Literature at Nurse, or Circulating Morals was the excellent title of the attack on the libraries; he stood on unassailable ground in affirming the right of English novelists to escape from the restriction imposed on them by the commercial convenience of the libraries and enjoy the freedom accorded even in England to other artists. The substance of his argument appears in different parts of his later work, notably in *Conversations in Ebury Street*; but some telling material was not used again, for instance a collection of all the risky passages which could be found in the novels that the libraries kept on their lists; after each of which came the refrain—" Tell me, dear Mr. Mudie, for as is well known I am no judge, if this doll does not show a little too much of bosom, if too much leg does not appear below this petticoat. Do tell me, I beg you." The pamphlet called forth a leading article from *The World*, in which Moore was defended and Mudie severely criticised.

[1] The Miss Rose of the Boulogne courtship.

16.8.85. *To Zola.*

The literary situation is curious. I am still opposed, and yet my enemies cannot find a weapon with which to attack me. All doors are shut, and yet *A Mummer's Wife* continues nevertheless to sell. Certainly I have a great part to play— I am fighting that Englishman may exercise a right which they formerly enjoyed, that of writing freely and sanely. . . . Duret writes to me from time to time—and he has asked me if I was the author of the articles in the *Pall Mall Gazette.* I had nothing to do with that filth (*saloperie*) the truth of which appears to me to be doubtful. [These were W. T. Stead's articles on *The Maiden Tribute of Modern Babylon.*] All the same I am glad of their appearance from the point of view of literature since it destroys the sweet illusion of English virtue.

II

All through the summer of 1885 Moore was hard at work upon the completion of his *A Drama in Muslin.* Once he wrote to his youngest brother Julian, at Moore Hall, asking him to supply some Irish local colour. Julian, like his other brothers, had literary ambitions which George usually discouraged :

Take a large packet and a good pencil and write me in disconnected phrases the impressions as they struck you. Don't try to imitate me too much, that would not be alive, but write your impressions at once as they come, and above all things do not write anything after. A picture of Ballinasloe, the great meat market, would come in very well indeed. Write and let me know if you will do this.

Je prends mon bien où je le trouve, Moore used always to say. In one sense he had no pride, or, to put it better, his pride was that he refused no help that would improve his work. There are instances even in his later books of whole passages written by others at his request, and incorporated in some form or other in the narrative. When he was about to complete *Hail and Farewell*, a lady of his acquaintance told him of a visit she had recently made to Chinon. He did not appear to listen, but surprised her afterwards by asking her to write down what she had told him to help him with the end of *Vale:* he wanted sunlight to follow a long passage in which he had evoked the sombre landscape of the Mayo bog. The pages appeared, insinuated with great skill into the text as a relation of his own experience.

A Drama in Muslin was to have a frontispiece by Blanche who also designed the cover of the first edition of the *Confessions of a Young Man.*

Undated. *To J.-E. Blanche.*

I shall certainly be in London in the month of October and I shall certainly be enchanted to see you. I cannot promise you more, for, alas, I have never been so busy in my life . . . We shall find time to take walks together, but I am rather terrified about the portrait—it will take up a whole morning. Your success enchants me; it confirms the opinion which I have always entertained of the personality of your talent. If Degas admired your young girl, in red in the blue room, she must be good. We know our Degas. You must come to an arrangement with my publisher about illustrating my young girls' book. Have I told you its title ? *A Drama in Muslin.*

The subject will suit your talent admirably well. Have you heard that Alexis and I have had a little play accepted by the Odeon.[1] Best regards to Monsieur and Madame Blanche.

P.S. Hearty greetings to Sickert.

He was beginning to make friends among the younger English artists. Sickert, whom he met through Blanche, took him to meet Wilson Steer, as he has recorded in *Conversations in Ebury Street.* He has said that he found in Steer " the only painter in London who could fill the blank that Manet's death had left in my life." But the truth is that he began by being rather chilly about Steer's work, and when

[1] The translation of Gilbert's *Sweethearts.*

he first became art critic of the *Speaker*, he chided D. S. MacColl of the *Spectator* for his enthusiasm.

Dec. 1885. *To Mrs. Moore.*   Dane's Inn.
   I regret it is impossible for me to be with you on the 1st January. My book will begin to appear in the *Court and Society Review* on the 14th of next month and I do not like to leave London until it has started on its pilgrimage.
   I did not go to Edith's wedding—I did not care to go; nor do I go to see Anna very often now. I am going to eat my Christmas dinner with the Robinsons—you know who I mean. You will eat yours with Joe or Nina.
   What you say about my little story struck me very much I have got a good deal of satisfaction out of life but no happiness—those who see to the end cannot be happy.
   A Mummer's Wife, strange to say, is quite a pet book among the Aristocracy. All the Lords and Ladies want to know the author, and it is no infrequent thing for dinner parties to be given to meet the author of *A Mummer's Wife*.
   I sometimes see Julian. He is as nice a boy as ever lived, his only fault is idleness, and I think he is getting over that.
   I am so glad that Kilkelly[1] was gazetted. I sent Nina the *Court and Society* and I shall write to congratulate her.

The " little story " mentioned in this letter had been published in the *Court and Society Review*. An old man lives alone in lodgings in London. He has had but one love in his life, he had proposed and been refused; and now for years he has occupied himself only with his books and his writing. The woman's photograph remains on his shelf. One day, when he is out, she comes to enquire for lodgings; she is shown into the old man's room to wait, and sees her photograph. She has led a gay, dissipated life, but has settled down to look after her children. The old man comes in, and there is a dramatic recognition: the woman takes a room in the house, and the pair become friends, realising that they are too old for love.

   [1] Moore's brother-in-law.

The *Court and Society Review* was a struggling periodical, edited by Henry Barnett, a friend of Edward Martyn, and the serialisation in its columns of *A Drama in Muslin* was preceded by a long and rather amusing advertisement, written by Moore himself, in which the author " with Mr. Gladstone's manifesto concerning Home Rule lying before him " congratulated Barnett on having secured possession of the serial rights of a book which would charm a public, perhaps indifferent to wit, style and composition, by its " actuality "—a picture of Ireland all complete, Castle, landlords and land leaguers, and *painted by an Irishman.* Barnett's readers were further called upon to give ear to " the shrill wail of virgins " and " the thunder of a people marching to manhood," and to believe that one " out of a hundred delicately nurtured daughters " of Irish gentry was lucky if she should succeed in marrying a dispensary doctor or a police officer: a wild exaggeration of the truth. *A Drama in Muslin* does however contain as vivid an account as exists of social life in Ireland during the Land League, and is a document that the historian should not disregard. Nor can any reader of the original edition doubt that the reviser of 1915 (who cut out all the topical and many of the foolish things) spoke the truth when he said that his " predecessor " had been animated by a hatred as lively as Ibsen's for the conventions which drive women into the marriage market.

It is obvious that Moore was already deeply concerned with the various problems which confront the serious and circumspect novelist; he felt that he had achieved a little technical triumph in certain chapters of *A Drama in Muslin*, where, by the original method of combining scenes entirely dissimilar and yet dependent on each other, he had brought into relief the general design of his work—social tragedy in the lives of well-born girls enacted across a dark background of Irish political life. In *Madame Bovary* Flaubert had interwoven part of the Mayor's speech with Rudolph and Emma's love making, but Moore went further than this with scenes in which several interests played a part and where even the conversation of one set of the characters crossed with that of the others. In drawing a character Moore did not always copy one model only. Alice Barton came to him first in vague and fragmentary outline as the type of girl who would refuse to acquiesce in the view that to find a husband who would keep her was the first object of life. It is Bernard Shaw who has told Mr. Charles Morgan that in the early days of his acquaintance with Moore there was in all Moore's stories "a room full of mirrors and chandeliers and the story usually ended with some woman throwing a lamp at George and driving him out of the house." But even in the early days, Moore's interest in feminine society was more discriminating than Mr. Shaw's witty reminiscence would indicate. He often admired and made friends with women of the Alice Barton sort, who were striking out for themselves in the world, and he made Alice out of the five or six women who collectively were a realisation of the character. No doubt one of his models was Margaret Veley, author of *Damocles* and some other novels of distinction and promise. She dared to champion the Naturalistic novel in early days and Moore was touched by her courage and by her life of sacrifice and devotion to a consumptive sister; he has told in the *Confessions* how he met her in a Kensington drawing-room (not the Robinson's) " a tall shy woman, declining wittily, without regret, into middle age "; he at once preferred her to the " gentlemen's beauties " who only brightened up when young men came into the room. He used to go to Miss Veley with his manuscript and proofs and thought her the most beautiful character he had yet encountered.

12

The public showed less interest in *A Drama in Muslin* than in *A Mummer's Wife*, but for a time Moore preferred the new work to either of his earlier novels, and he was surprised when critics described Kate Ede as a more satisfactory study of character than Alice Barton. " Higher than Alice no woman could go; any higher advance must be attended by unwillingness to accept the double duties of life," he said in *Defensio pro Scriptis Meis*, a pamphlet which Swan Sonneschein

published in 1887; but in 1915 (Preface to *Muslin*) he wrote:
" A Puritan but not a sexless Puritan," expressing the same
idea a thousand times more simply. " Nobody was more
surprised than I," he wrote in his *Defensio*, " at the praise
bestowed on *A Mummer's Wife*, not indeed because it was a
bad novel, I was surprised to find that it was not, but because
no critic seemed cognisant of the merits and demerits which
I saw and which in turn delighted and tortured me. As the
public verdict continued to affirm itself, I will say, to realise
itself, the book I knew of was changed, metamorphosed,
disappeared, and another bearing no more than a distant
family resemblance to my *Mummer's Wife* was gradually
forced upon me. I have since forgotten the old, and accepted
and am content with the *Mummer's Wife* of critics and friends.
. . . In the case of *A Drama in Muslin*, the difference of
perception between the readers and the writer and of his
utter inability not apparently to convey ideas, but to convey
the idea which he wished to convey, was even still more
marked." Moore's estimate of the qualities of his own books
seldom agreed with that of the reviewers; at the same time
he was impressionable and open to suggestion.

The style—or rather styles—of *A Drama in Muslin* represented an attempt to escape from the plainness and literalism
of *A Mummer's Wife*, just as Alice Barton and Cecilia Cullen
were an attempt to render more spiritual and more complex
natures than those among which Zola had met with his
greatest successes. It is significant that when Huysmans'
A Rebours, which was to shatter Naturalism, appeared, Moore
reviewed it in the *Pall Mall Gazette* with as much enthusiasm
as the editor would allow. To Zola himself he said that,
although his new novel preserved the root idea of the school,
it contained novelties in composition and marked a great
advance in language compared with *A Mummer's Wife*.

In *Le Mouvement Esthetique et " Décadent" en Angleterre*, Dr.
Farmer has written an interesting page on the French
sources of *A Drama in Muslin*. He finds evidence that at the
time he wrote this book Moore had already realised the
insufficiencies of Zola's descriptive instrument, its lack of
shades and subtleties, for a rendering of the more poetical

aspects of life. The view is supported by Moore's correspondence; he wrote to Blanche: " Do you know the little cocotte in *L'Education Sentimentale* ? She is as true to life as Nana, more true to life." Not only such masters as Flaubert, but comparatively obscure contemporaries were now playing a part in Moore's literary evolution. Réné Ghil, the symbolist, believed in the correspondence between sounds, both vocal and instrumental, and colours; and this theory has inspired the description of the Dublin dressmaker's shop which prepares Mrs. Barton's daughters for the Castle ball :

> Lengths of white silk clear as the notes of violins playing in a minor key; white poplin falling into folds statuesque as the bass of a fugue by Bach; yards of ruby velvet, rich as an air from Verdi played on the piano; tender green velvet, pastoral as hautboys heard beneath trees in a fair Arcadian vale; blue turquoise faille française fanciful as the twinkling of a guitar twanged by a Watteau shepherd; gold brocade, sumptuous as organ tones swelling through the jewelled twilight of a nave; scarves and trains of midnight blue profound as the harmonic snoring of a bassoon . . .

An orchestra of feminine dress which amused the Miss Robinsons and to which they added, in the margin of their copy, some final touches of their own: " Everything was represented there, from the light clarinette of the embroidered lace handkerchief to the profound trombone of the red flannel pantaloons." " Oh how could you write such a thing, Mr. Moore ! " the sisters exclaimed, as they read the passage out to Moore on his next visit to Earl's Terrace. " He fell into the trap," Madame Duclaux records, " and defended the phrase which he had never used. We enlightened him . . . but he bore no malice, and was enchanted that we should interest ourselves in his literature, his great and sole preoccupation." [1]

Zola's influence, however, was still predominant; the

[1] The anecdote is from Madame Duclaux's charming article on Moore in the *Revue de Paris* (March 1933).

notion of the display of stuffs is evidently taken from *Au Bonheur des Dames*; and the chapter on the Castle Ball, with its accumulation of detail, showed that Moore could successfully emulate the power and skill in the representation of crowds for which the author of *L'Assommoir* was justly famous. A mere imitator of French writers, however, Moore never was, even in *A Mummer's Wife*. Moreover, he always made an individual use of his sources, and for style he was now casting his net widely. In the preface to the 1915 edition of *Muslin* he found in the original version "an evident desire to write well, a headlong eager, uncertain style, a hound yelping at every trace of scent." And what strange scents had been laid across his path we may see from that passage, reminiscent of the euphuists, in which the crippled Cecilia Cullen assails Alice Barton with reflections on the depravity of the world and the joys of Heaven :

Yes, I have left for ever the life of desire and have entered into that of prayer ! There, there are no frozen morns nor fiery noons, but long pensive evenings, and all who live there are thrilled with happiness, and all who dream there dream of mansuetude and calm. And there we walk as in a garden of straight walks, seeing the happy end from afar; heedless we pass by the dark coverts of doubt and the red flowerage of too keen rejoicings. There sadness may not endure.[1]

13

At this time Edward Martyn—the " dear Edward " of *Hail and Farewell*—had come over from his castle in Galway to Pump Court in the Temple, where he shared rooms with Sir William Geary, a young barrister whom Moore had already met at Tillyra, an Oxford friend of Martyn's. At Dane's Inn Moore was close by; and in the evenings all three would eat together in the restaurants near the Temple, and afterwards went to each other's rooms to talk and listen. Sir William Geary has sent me a note on the early days of a

[1] Omitted from the revised edition of 1915.

friendship which lasted for fifty years. Moore told " briefless, marvellous stories of his Paris life "; once he related how he had fought a duel. With memories of Lever in his mind Sir William Geary asked him how far he was from his opponent, ten or fifteen paces ? "No," replied Moore, "that would be dangerous. We were thirty-five paces apart; each went scatheless."

" I and the world were glad that he had taken care of himself," Sir William Geary writes. " Critics of Moore have suggested that his writing about Martyn in *Ave, Salve, Vale* was a grievous breach of hospitality. But Moore has raised a permanent monument to Edward Martyn, 'dear Edward,' and dear to me. He has preserved the likeness of a most loveable friend, with weaknesses maybe, as we all have, but no meanness, no vice, one who might be called a man after God's own heart. Every word Moore wrote of Martyn makes one love Martyn more, and that is a noble tribute to a friend." Dear Edward was a very young man, only lately down from Oxford. Visits to Tillyra had aroused in Moore a profound interest in this eccentric Irish landlord and his mother, a stone-mason's daughter, who, having brought a fortune to an ancient house, could not endure the thought of its extinction, and was in consequence, always trying to persuade her son to marry. In all else Martyn obeyed her implicitly, but not in this. He was a strange mixture: a born celibate without vocation for the priesthood, a Roman Catholic consumed with literary ambition, whose religious scruples had lately caused him to destroy a poem on some classical subject. But literature was again in the ascendant, and he was now engaged upon a vast allegorical satire, modelled on Rabelais. A better educated man than Moore, his devotion to polyphonic music, Wagner and Ibsen and his courteous manners seemed to contradict a blunt-witted and thick-set appearance, a voracious appetite and the religious conformism of an Irish peasant. The friendship was a strange one, but the friends had this in common: each was simply and solely himself, not a mere member of the Irish gentry. Moore used to complain: " He thinks I'm damned and doesn't care," and indeed there was a good deal of the careless derisive tolerance of the Irish in "dear Edward's" nature. But he was sharp enough if his own spiritual interests were in danger of being compromised: and when Moore's Irish novel was coming out in the *Court and Society Review*, he threatened to withdraw his assistance if any passage should contain an offence against faith or morals.

They went to Paris together in January 1886. Moore was educating Martyn in art. He introduced him to the Impressionists, and Martyn brought back a Degas and a Manet to his newly built Gothic Castle in Galway. At the Salon they chanced to encounter Zola. Martyn used to relate with some amusement that he was not introduced, being left to his own devices, while Moore, preening himself on being the cynosure of all eyes, walked round the gallery with the great man.

3.2.86 *To Mrs. Moore.*

I have just returned from Paris where I spent a very pleasant fortnight with Edward. We saw a great many painters and pictures, writers and books. I persuaded Edward to buy two pictures. Zola was very kind to me, and I saw a great deal of him. We went to the Salon together on varnishing day and attracted a great deal of attention. I saw some of the French translation of my book—it satisfied me pretty well. The book continues to sell very well, and I got £65 out of Vizetelly for the first three months. Another [cheque] is nearly due but it wont come to so much. He says I shall make a hundred and fifty out of it.

I saw Maurice for the first time yesterday. [Maurice Moore had been with his regiment in India for some years] He was up to his usual standard of niceness which is as you know a high one. He seems to be a very clever fellow. I wonder that he does not try to do something.

14

His habit of paying a long visit each year to Ireland now ceased. There were two reasons, one the offence which his

Irish novel was reported to have given. The other was the new life which he was making for himself in England. As a *roman à clef* dealing with Irish society, the book caused scandal in Dublin. At the castle dinner party to which he had not been invited, Moore made " a goodly company of time-servers, panders and others" forget their fears of the Land League " in the fragrance of the soup and the lascivious pleasing of the waltz tunes." Some of Moore's cousins in Galway were downright in their condemnation, and in England he was threatened with an action for libel on account of the opening description : a prize giving day in an English convent, which was named. The girls were shown acting in a vulgarly staged *King Cophetua and the Beggar Maid:* and as they watched the spectacle, the nuns " forgot themselves . . . and gloried in having been at least bride providers for men." The nuns consulted Charles Russell, the famous lawyer, and the passage was omitted from later editions. There was a sketch of a priest, obviously meant for the parish priest of Ardrahan, which obliged Mrs. Martyn to tell her son that Moore must never again enter Tillyra Castle while she lived. " This is very unpleasant," Moore wrote to his mother, " but it can't be helped. Of course I regret nothing. I pursue my way uninfluenced by any considerations. In this lies my strength, and you will be glad to hear of my success. My triumph grows daily greater. London for the moment lies at my feet."

He now wore the air of a man who has arrived. It was not that he entertained an extravagant opinion of his achievement ; he felt (especially when he remembered Pater) that he had much to learn, but he was George Moore, a successful novelist, and what is more, a serious one—perhaps by his own standards the only serious English novelist, and he thought that bravado helped him on. The Robinsons noted a change even in his appearance when he called at their house. He was no longer the young artist with the flowing tie, nor the harassed journalist of the Strand lodging house, but a considered and considerable person. But the better complexion of his affairs did not induce him to alter the frugal habits of life to which he had accustomed himself;

MARY MOORE: GEORGE MOORE'S MOTHER

he wore ill-made clothes, " and yet," says Sir William Geary,
" when I have seen him in the theatre lounge at a first night,
as he stood in evening dress, though his opera hat was bat-
tered, somehow or other he gave the impression of being
the most distinguished person present."

He was ripening slowly; but that famous devastating
simplicity of his, that character of being utterly himself,
would sometimes give way to an affectation of æstheticism,
an unwonted touch of Bunthorne. Madame Duclaux recalls
an arrival at Earl's Terrace. Moore entered, shook hands
with his hostess, Madame Duclaux's mother: looking round
him, he said, " I like this room," and then spoilt everything
by adding: " the wall paper sets off my yellow hair." The
beautiful Mrs. Stillman, the muse of the pre-Raphaelites,
was talking to Mrs. Robinson. She slowly turned her head,
Madame Duclaux continues, *pour foudroyer Moore d'un regard
de Minerve courroucée*. But Moore, who had come to talk
about Pater, was conscious neither of Mrs. Stillman's beauty
nor of her disdain. He was enveloped, like a silk worm in its
cocoon, in an isolating dream, his dream of literary perfection.

15

The summer of 1886 found Moore at " The Inn, Southwick, near Brighton." This address resulted from a chance
encounter in Regent's Street with Colvill Bridger, the
Colville of the autobiographical books. " Colly " asked him
to come down to Sussex and resume an old intimacy. Since
his pursuit of art to Paris in 1873, Moore had neglected these
friends who had come into his life when he was a boy at
Jurles's; but all his old love of them sprang up again on the
instant, and he went down to Shoreham that very afternoon
with Colly. The squire and his wife (the clever laughing
woman who called Moore Kant), the two daughters, Dulcibella and Florence, and the son—he liked them all; but they
were the last people anyone would expect to be his companions, kind and simple people who never spoke of books,
Saxons whom in his mind's eye he could see coming over

with Hengist and Horsa, a silent family with the exception
of the mother, and a welcome change, he said to himself,
from his chattering Galway cousins. The English village
grouped around a green, with its horse pond and cottages
of roses and ivy, its gardens of sunflowers, was a new experience and enchanted the Balzacian Irishman. Towards
evening he would follow the line of the undulating downs
to the pretty house of his friends—the so-called Italian house
sheltered among elms that is described in *Esther Waters*—
where he was always welcome. Here he planned a new novel
entitled *A Mere Accident*, the scene of which he set in Sussex,
and finished a book upon Ireland for Charpentier, the French
publisher, some chapters of which had already appeared in
the *Figaro*. He stayed the whole summer in this place,
making many acquaintances among the local people.
The smaller house, Little Buckingham, where Moore had
first known the Bridgers, was let to a dentist who had two
sisters; one of whom the squire afterwards married. Like
Dulcibella and Florence these girls coquetted with Moore:
his letters home reflect his content with his new surroundings.

Undated. *To Julian Moore.*

I am glad to find you minded to take life seriously.
There is a pretty stiff exam, for a consulship, International
law etc. You will be expected to write at least one language
correctly. Can you do this? Drop me a line by return
of post and I will do the best I can. Of course what you
say about Lady Ardilaun being ashamed that [her]
relations are brewers is all *nonsense*, silly Dublin scandal.
I know Lady Ardilaun very well indeed and I know she
is above such folly. I am sorry such folly is attributed to her,
but what can be expected but dirt from Dublin. My last
article on Ireland is a description of a visit to Ashford.
I crack the Ardilauns up to the skies. My translaters say
it is the best thing in the book.

Undated. *To Mrs. Moore.*

Of course I knew from the first that the consulship was
visionary but he [Julian] insisted I should write to Lord

Ardilaun. Does Julian continue to talk about literature, or has he abandoned that dream ? I wish he would try and write something for by so doing he would learn how to think and how to form sentences.

I am more sorry than I can say that the Ruttledges are under the impression that I described Cornfield in the *Figaro*; I never thought of doing such a thing; I described Moore Hall in the *Figaro*, but that was all, I did not see the Irish papers. Did they approve of my articles ? What did the *Freeman* say ? I find it very hard to make an income out of literature. This year I only made a trifle over four hundred pounds, and this is very little when you consider my reputation for I am well-known not only in England but in Europe. This makes me feel often very anxious . . .

My summer has been very pleasant—a summer of tennis and girls and literature. For I have worked hard and have finished a new book, a book on Ireland for the French market. It will be published in Paris by Charpentier and I do not think I shall allow it to be translated into English. You do not say anything about either Nina or Maurice. I hope the latter (*sic*) will not continue to have babies for I do not know how she is to support them.

Colvill Bridger, who was an officer in the Sussex militia, now proposed to apply himself to rabbit farming, and Moore offered his collaboration. The grounds of Buckingham were not suitable for the enterprise, and so a farm was bought on the downs and Colvill began to build the small house, Freshcombe Lodge, which Moore afterwards shared with him. His life there and his part, not very onerous, in the care of the rabbits are described in some amusing pages of *Ave*.

The Christmas of 1886 he spent with the Bridgers.

16.12.86. *To Miss Dulcibella Bridger.*

I am looking forward to seeing you—Snow should be on the ground but I heartily hate Christmas weather. I am most anxious to see Colly's house but to walk on the hills in snow time would be pitiful work. I am very pleased with my descriptions of the hills in my new book. It will

amuse you for it is all about Buckingham. I shall call it
A Mere Accident.

Do you see as much as ever of the MacDonalds ? When
you meet them remember me to them. I preserve an
excellent souvenir of them—by the way that last phrase
is French done into English. Is little Buckingham let yet.
I wish I could afford to take that place, perhaps I will if
this book is a big success.

Now what else have I got to say—well nothing—ah,
yes that I am looking forward to *seeing you at Christmas.*

He was still in Sussex at the New Year.

3.1.87. *To Julian Moore.*

I received this evening your card. It amused me.
Perhaps you would like to hear something about the
rabbits.

Well a friend of mine is going in for rabbit farming on
the top of the south downs; the houses are being built,
the land prepared. It is a very lonely place and it would
be difficult to live there alone, so he asked me to live with
him; and he is to give me a small share in the business
in return for my collaboration. I do not know if I shall
remain in the business but I am going to give it a try.
I do not think it will interfere with my literary pursuits,
and perhaps concerning them you would like to hear
something too— Well my book on Ireland will be published
in France early in February; I fancy that it will create
a sensation. If it does I shall be able to dispose of the
English rights on very favourable terms. I have finished
a short book entitled *A Mere Accident* which I shall send
to the printers very soon immediately I am convinced
that there is no hope of selling the serial rights. And now
about yourself. I am glad you are with mother at Moore
Hall. You could not be in a more suitable place, for there
you will have leasure to think, observe and read. I wish
you would write and tell me what you are doing. I was
very sorry about the consulship, but I knew from the first
that it was all moonshine. Lady Ardilaun by the way

wrote me a long letter the other day, the kindest letter possible to imagine. From Maurice I have not heard for a long time; I wish he would write now and again. I hear rumours of flirtations, but that is all. Nina I hope has not brought any more children into this miserable world; for what she will do with them later on I cannot think. Home Rule is of course certain.

Write me a long letter and tell me about yourself.

A few weeks later Charpentier brought out the Irish sketches. *Irelande en Eau Forte* was to have been the title, but this was changed at the last moment to *Terre d'Irlande*. The French preface by Moore is dated Brighton, August 1886. In it he spoke of the nine years spent in Paris in the society of the greatest artists and writers of the time, and paid a particular tribute to Manet. He complimented his translator, Rabbe, who apparently had already done Shelley into French, and France, the land of excellent translations, as against England, the country of wretched translations. No one and nothing in Ireland meets with Moore's commendation except Lord Ardilaun, and Lord Ardilaun's castle at Cong, the beauty and luxury of which had evidently left him spellbound: in his last autobiography, *A Communication to My Friends*, he again sang the praises of the great brewer-philanthropist. We read much of Celtic savagery, and once more assist at the satirical observation of provincial society. The Anglo-Irish gentry are shown sinking into a squalid bog. Local gossip and scandal were used unashamedly to build up his Irish types: the landlord, the M.P., the priest, etc. These essays—the ordinary reporter would give his eyes to produce anything as good—appear to offer fairly positive proof that Moore had no thought that he would ever again live in Ireland, especially as he reprinted them in English in the following year.

Parnell and his Island still showed all the familiar signs of Zola's influence—notably in the chapter on the Irish peasant: the preoccupation with smells, the story of the pig and the child's entrails, and all the other working details which render a picture of sordid decay. Though *La Terre* had not yet appeared Moore claimed that the mud cabins and mud of Ireland offered as good a subject to the artist as a picturesque village around a green close. Throughout 1886 he had still been in correspondence with his old master, from whom he hoped for a preface to Madame Bernard's translation of *A Mummer's Wife*. His own preface to Vizetelly's translation of *La Curée* gave no hint of a weakening of his allegiance to Naturalism. But after *Parnell and his Island* he wrote no book in which the direct inspiration of Zola can be detected.

16

The next novel, *A Mere Accident*, came out in 1887, about the same time as the English edition of *Terre d'Irlande*. It depicted a young Sussex squire, a religious ascetic without vocation for the priesthood. John Norton is the heir to many acres, and his mother is always trying to make him marry. He collects Renoirs and Monets, admires Wagner and Palestrina, and reads Pater; he is also, like Huysmans' hero in *A Rebours*, a student of Schopenhauer and of the Latin Christian authors: he hates life. It was a portrait of Edward Martyn, Martyn anglicised, rendered wholly æsthetic and much reduced in physical bulk. A short novel and quickly finished, it turned out a dead failure, the mere accident by which Norton escapes marriage (the outrage of a tramp upon the innocent young girl who has become his fiancée) provoking almost unanimous reproaches from the reviewers and drawing from Pater, to whom Moore sent a copy of the novel, the comment that the object of violent acts was not very clear to him. " Or something like that," Moore says in *Avowals*, " and he may have added that the object of art was to enable us to escape from the crude and violent."

This novel was an event of some importance in Moore's career, not only because he returned to the same subject on two later occasions, but also because the choice of such a hero showed that he now wished to carry out something other than that typical representation of society which was the object of the Naturalistic school. The book would

certainly have never been written if Moore had not read
Huysmans, and been impressed by the superior breadth of
mind and culture of this former disciple of Zola, who was
now in revolt against the " absolute materialism " of Médan.
" I have spent the summer," Moore had written to his
brother Julian while he was working on *A Mere Accident*,
" reading all the Latin authors of the Middle Ages from the
second to the eighth century for a chapter of my book."
All in a summer—what seven-league boots had this
student! The chapter however created the right impression
and a scholar of Roman Christian poetry has described it as
wonderful. It is certain that Moore put in some hard work
with books in English and French on the period, and that he
must have acquired some knowledge of Latin while doing so.

Music as well as Latin played a part in the novel; and
here we are faced with one of the vexed questions of Moore's
career. " I don't think," his musical friend Edouard Dujardin
writes, " that he had any ear, and it always seemed to me
that his interest in Wagner, on whom we had endless
conversations, was mainly literary." We have the testimony
of Colonel Moore: " The members of our family were all
unmusical—Father, Mother, and all the children; George
no better than the rest. He could not hum a tune correctly,
and what he wrote about music was what he heard others
say. Perhaps he had some taste, but he had no ear." And as
late as 1897 Moore left Mr. Vincent O'Sullivan under the
impression that his ignorance of musical theory, history and
everything else was profound. " I once asked him if he liked
Wagner's earlier style—meaning of course *Rienzi*, the
Holländer and parts of *Tannhäuser*. Perhaps I mumbled the
last two words ' earlier style.' But his reply was that he had
never heard of ' that opera.' I never heard him mention any
composer but Wagner, and once when I sounded him on
Debussy and Fauré their names did not seem familiar to
him."

All this may be true; nevertheless *Evelyn Innes*, his later
musical novel, is convincing as few musical novels written
by non-musicians have ever been. It is not only the almost
complete absence of slips which is remarkable, for Moore

always took enormous pains over the background of his stories and was adept at picking the brains of others; but there are many passages which persuade the reader that he really understood something of the subject. Mr. Innes's Dolmetsch-like enthusiasm for the old music and Ulick Dean's exposition of the ancient modes ring as true as tnat musical world which was the natural ambit of a social man of letters in the 'nineties: the fashionable operas of Bizet, Verdi, Gounod, (how good is Ulick's criticism of Evelyn's Marguerite !) and above all the all-pervading excitement of Wagner. And there is a direct conflict of evidence over the question of Moore's ear: for he himself stated (in a letter to his friend John Eglinton) that he heard an excursion party in a French train singing the fatuous, pathetic little snatch of tune which so happily rounds off " Wilfred Holmes " in *Celibate Lives*. Perhaps the truth is that his interest in Wagner, though as genuine as that of many amateurs of Wagner to-day, was literary in origin; but his writing on this composer, as well as his unsympathetic comments (in *Memoirs of My Dead Life*, " La Butte ") on an unnamed novelty, clearly *Pelléas et Mélisande,* make it plain that his senses remained on the alert when listening to music: he did not lapse into the vague reverie so common to literary musicians. On the other hand his interests were strictly limited: Mozart and Beethoven are scarcely mentioned in his work, and his selection of Bach and Scarlatti for the music which a wife might have played to him in the evenings is no more than a tribute to his general love of the eighteenth century. Music for him meant Wagner, first and last; but so far as it went his interest in the art was genuine as well as discerning.

17

The golden summer of 1887 was passed in the company of his friends at Southwick, with the *Confessions of A Young Man* before him on the table at the village inn. While there he received the news of the publication in the *Figaro* of the famous " Manifesto of the Five " against Zola. The manifesto was signed by J. H. Rosny *aine*, Descares, Paul Bonnetain,

Gustave Guiches and Paul Margueritte, and it denounced *La Terre* as a work of impotent filth: a piece of indecency which was not even based on personal documentation but on documents collected by proxy. Moore, who had not yet read *La Terre*, wrote immediately to the master.

25.8.87. *To Zola.*

Yesterday I heard that Bonnetain and other young people have addressed a letter to the *Figaro* on the subject of *La Terre*. That is a pity. If you have the paper handy send it to me with your reply. I shall read the volume and as usual write an article, this time a rather more important article

And as regards Charpentier do you think he intends to publish *A Mummer's Wife* (*La Femme d'un Cabotin.*) After all the work that Alexis has done it would really be a pity if the book were lost. . .

Zola spoke of the signatories to the manifesto as his " tail." " Had it been Huysmans or Céard," he said, " it would have been different. . . . These men formed my tail. The tail has now detached itself."

Huysmans denounced the document as the work of ill-bred persons, and the incident, although it had large repercussions, should not be held in any way accountable for Moore's own defection from Zola, which does not appear to have been premeditated. " The Five " were not his personal friends, nor did they inspire the disrespectful comments on Zola's work which are found in the *Confessions*. " What I reproach Zola with is that he has no style; there is nothing that you won't find in Zola from Chateaubriand to the reporting of the *Figaro*. He seeks immortality in the exact description of a linen draper's shop; if the shop conferred immortality it should be upon the linen draper. . . . And that terrible phrase repeated over and over again—the Conquest of Paris. What does it mean ? I never knew anyone who thought of conquering Paris except one or two provincials."

Among the new influences which were drawing Moore

away from Zola's Naturalism was that of Edouard Dujardin, the young editor of *La Revue Wagnérienne* and *La Revue Indépendante*, and the author of *Les Lauriers sont Coupés*, the first example of the interior monologue in modern literature. Mallarmé and Moore were early admirers of Dujardin's talent, Moore saying of *Les Lauriers sont Coupés* that it was Henri Monnier rendered readable, "the inner life of the soul revealed for the first time." *La Revue Wagnérienne* aimed at acquainting the French public with Wagner's music—and not with his music only but with his poems and theoretical works as well. It was the organ of the Symbolist movement and showed on one side the influence of Stephen Mallarmé: the Symbolists *ipso facto* were Wagnerians, whereas the Naturalists were generally indifferent to all music, Wagnerian or other. When *La Revue Indépendante* was founded Moore at once contributed an article, and in the editor he found a prince of good fellows, a forthcoming man, who restored his faith, rudely shaken by Pater, in his genius for intimacy. Dujardin is described in *Conversations in Ebury Street* and has also appeared in other of Moore's books: metaphysical as well as musical, an Englishman in appearance rather than a Frenchman, long-limbed, small-headed, broad-shouldered. "Art with him has always been a rite accomplished in secret, without thought of money or even glory. A man of large appetites and fine sensibilities. . . . In the days that I am remembering Dujardin was a pervervid youth, whose joy was to preach and instruct, and at any hour of the day or night he was available."

18

Moore still kept his rooms at Dane's Inn, but he was oftener in Sussex than in London; in the autumn of 1887 he ceased to lodge at the inn and became the guest of the Bridgers at Buckingham, the prettiest house imaginable, with a wide Italian staircase going up to an open landing, the bedrooms on either side of two curtained pillars. Looking backwards he regarded this period as one of the happiest of his life. ". . . One day, walking in the garden with one of the girls," he was to write in his *Memoirs*, "a sensation of home came upon me. I seemed always to have known these people; they seemed part and parcel of my life. It was like a sudden and enchanting awakening of love; life seemed to lengthen out like the fields at dawn and to become distinct and real in many new and unimagined ways." He would accompany the two daughters of the house to dances, and bathe with them at Devil's Dyke; and in talking over this life in his old age he did not forget to mention a succession of love affairs. But it was Mrs. Bridger for whom he felt a real emotional attachment. She was now a woman over fifty; fifteen years earlier he had thought her a little dowdy, now he was surprised to find himself noticing what dresses she wore and told her which he liked her best in.[1]

Towards Christmas, Moore moved with Colvill Bridger to the farm on the Downs. "The last delay was happily not a long one; a few weeks afterwards the house was declared ready to receive us, and the rabbits went away in several vans, Colville and I following on foot, talking, as we went by Thunders Barrows Barn, of the great fortune that always lay about waiting to be picked up by the adventurous."[2] It amused Moore to have a share in a rabbit farm; his part, it seems, was to shoot the rabbits when they were ready for the market. Expenses were shared. Colvill drew up minute accounts of the ingoings and outgoings; he had a passion for book-keeping, but it was soon found that the profit to be made on shot rabbits would not pay the interest on the large sum of money that had been expended on the house and hutches. Moore had a pony sent him from Ireland; there were rides across the downs in the course of which he learned the scenery of many of his novels. In the evenings, Colvill's conversation not being particularly stimulating, he used to walk across to the big house under the downs and play a game of billiards with the squire. He could make breaks of thirty and forty, never more than fifty.

He was preparing the *Confessions* for publication in Dujardin's review. It has been stated that the book was originally

[1] "A Remembrance" (*Memoirs of My Dead Life*).
[2] *Ave*, p. 308.

written in French, but this was not so. The only French of
Moore's which it contained was the dedication to Blanche,
which Blanche considered atrocious. Portions of the book ·
were printed in the first instance by an English monthly
magazine, *Time*. " Will you kindly forward me a number of
La Revue Indépendante," Moore wrote to Th. de Wyzewa,
" I am most anxious to read your criticism of *A Mere
Accident*. The book will not be a great success, but what I am
now publishing *en feuilleton*, the *Confessions of A Young Man*,
is attracting a good deal of attention."

2.12.87. *To Dujardin.*

(From Freshcombe Lodge)

I will gladly write to Martyn, but I think the attempt
wil be useless. Martyn is a very intelligent boy, very
intelligent, but impossible where the religious question is
concerned . . .

I thank you and Wyzewa with all my heart for the
excellent and amusing article on *A Mere Accident*. The book
has not been understood either in England or in France
as I would have liked, I must have blundered somewhere
—a phrase in Wyzewa's notice indicates the place I think;
I shall change the end, or perhaps extend the book a little
in the new edition. I found the close of your novel excellent, and well written, admirably written, the description
of the sleeping woman is wholly admirable. On the other
hand I find Rosny's novel vulgar and abominably written.
Rosny is without education. . . .

19

The long peaceful Sussex days ripened in Moore that deep
love of " dear sweet Protestant England " which he celebrated so happily in the *Confessions*. " The red tiles of the
farmhouse, the elms, the great hedgerows, and all the rich
fields adorned with spreading trees, and the weald and the
wold. . . . The villages clustered round the greens, the spires
of the churches pointing between the elm trees. This is

congenial to me, and this is Protestantism. England is Protestantism, Protestantism is England." On Sundays he accompanied the Bridgers to the parish church, and he confessed his instinctive feeling for Protestantism in words that presaged a dramatic episode in his later life.

22.12.87. *To Mrs. Moore.*

I have now taken up my abode I hope for good in Sussex. I wrote to Julian a long letter descriptive of my life here so there is no use in re-describing it. I am very fond of my friends and have entirely adopted their life— have said in fact thy people shall be my people thy God shall be my God. I put on a high hat, take an umbrella and march to church every Sunday. I do not believe but I love protestantism. If it is not the faith of my brain it is the faith of my heart. You will not I know feel much sympathy in these sentiments but you will agree with me that it is better to acquiesce in outward forms than to protest and so give scandal and offence. . . .

The interest in theology which he subsequently showed was not yet evident, and Protestantism was found compatible, to judge from certain pages in the *Confessions*, with a worship of the Pagan spirit taught him by Gautier, and with a continuing awareness that intellectually he was nearer the French than the English. Like Frank Escott in *Spring Days*, his new novel, he spoke of atavism, remembering that the Moores were of English descent, and attributed his hatred of Catholicism to ancestral memories as well as to the experience of Oscott. It was limitless, the strongest fibre in his nature, he told Julian Moore, and he congratulated the family when his brother Maurice's engagement to an Irish Protestant girl, Miss Handcock of Galway, was announced. There was an element of social prejudice in all this (one recalls his dislike of the " Catholic set " during his Dublin season), Irish Catholicism being without style; but his Protestant love did not debar him from admiring the

devotional poetry of Verlaine, or from following with
sympathetic interest certain literary manifestations of
Catholicism which the French Symbolist movement encouraged in its reaction against the crude positivism of the
earlier Naturalists.

The Protestantism was a gesture of defiance; the affection
for England was the affection which the unorthodox Irishman is always liable to feel. It did not indicate that he wished
to alienate himself from his family, but like the elder brother
in " Wilfrid Holmes," a story which he wrote many years
later, he was conscious that he owed everything to merit and
his own exertions, and for that reason was not always a
sympathetic counsellor. His youngest brother was now at
Moore Hall with their mother, a strange existence Moore
often thought. Nothing was too good to say of Maurice, who
was bound for India with his regiment. " He is much nicer
than anyone I ever knew or heard of, read of or imagined.
It is awful to think we shall not see him again for years."
Of himself at this time he said that he lived in the " giddi-
ness " of artistic creation. He had " got rid of his mistress "
and all his thoughts were set upon his work. He had let many
chances of marriage go by and he did not now believe that
he would ever marry. His books were selling pretty well,
and he had arranged that *Spring Days*, as soon as it was half
finished, should appear in instalments in the *Evening News*.
It was, he said, a light and gay book, different in tone from
any of his other works. In February he was still on the
rabbit farm, and from there he sent an advance copy of
the English *Confessions* to Dujardin.

10.2.88. *To Dujardin.*

I sent you a copy but the book has not yet appeared.
I am enchanted that you have decided to publish it in
the review. I am pleased with the novel which I am writing
at the moment, but may be mistaken, and so I prefer to
give you some thing that I know to be good. I have
published some fragments of the *Confessions* in a magazine
with the best results. I hope to see the first instalment in

your next number because I am going to announce the publication in all the newspapers here.

Dujardin writes " The translation of the *Confessions* was done by a man whose name I have forgotten and who did not belong to our circle. Everyone agreed that it was very bad, and we decided to revise it before it was printed as a book by Savine. I did the revision, keeping throughout in touch with Moore, who was well satisfied with the result."

The English edition—" a book which to-day finds readers " Moore wrote in 1932, " and it is rare, I prided myself as I wrote this line, that a book finds readers after six months,"—drew from *The Academy* the enquiry why a disagreeable young man of bad education should have thought his memoirs worth writing. In the first edition it was a mythical " Edmund Dayne " who related in the third person his life and opinions, and the reviewers took pleasure in quoting a passage in which Dayne referred to the persecutions of his works : "Shelley and Byron came first, and now it is the turn of Edmund Dayne." But the book was widely read, and what was more it drew an appreciation from Pater. Pater wrote twice; once on seeing a copy of *Time*, when he wrote to say how much he admired the appreciations of modern French poetry, and again after receiving a copy of the Swan Sonnenschein edition.

20.3.88. *To Maurice Moore.*

India is a long way off; I never knew it was so far before, latterly I have felt the distance very keenly . . . but there were practical reasons in the delay *viz* there was no use writing until I had the *Confessions* to send you—forgive the egotism—and the book was delayed from week to week . . . I now send you the book also a French review— very æsthetic, the organ of the Symbolists and Decadents which publishes a translation. The translation is not up to the mark but it is the best I have had. All the liveliness of the original seems to me to have evaporated, all the irony and subtlety of expression has been replaced by heavy and ungrateful sentences. You know the language very well and I daresay it will amuse you to compare the two when you have absolutely nothing to [do]. The book is much admired—more admired than anything I have [done]. Pater wrote to me—well, just as he did not write about *A Mere Accident*; all the reviews have so far been enthusiastic —I sent you *The Academy*. The writer does not like the Strand episode, others say it is the best thing in the book. *Spring Days* is almost completed. . . . I have been working very hard, harder than I ever worked before, for I promised [*Spring Days*] to the *Evening News* and for the first time a daily paper publishes a feuilleton. The first number I believe appeared to-day . . . I like the pony very much indeed; she is a sweet little thing and very much admired. She is quite sound for the hills, for gentle work, though I daresay she would no longer be any use for polo playing. Riding her has given me a taste for riding and I sometimes go out with the South Downs, not on her but the Squire's hunter which he himself lends me whenever I like. It is a miserable thing that you should live so far away . . .

Of Julian or mother I hear but little; they live at Moore Hall in their mysterious way. Julian is very good in that respect but it would be more satisfactory if he were to try to do something; still we must be grateful that he is not a blackguard lounging round bar rooms in London. Occasionally he sends me stories to read, they generally contain an idea, which I could make use of. . . . Augustus is getting a divorce. . . . Another libel action broke up *The Bat*, Davis will never be able to return to London, and Augustus is trying to continue the paper under the name of *The Hawk*, but I am afraid nothing much will come of it. He is clever enough and I have been trying to start him on a story and I hope he will carry it through. In London to do any good you must make at least one success on the bookstalls, then you are all right. . . .

Edward Martyn is completing his great work[1]—I have seen some of it and from what he tells me I judge it to be

---

[1] *Morgante the Lesser*, a satire in the manner of Rabelais, published anonymously in 1890.

magnificent but Geary who has seen some of it says it is nonsense . . .

The first letter from Pater was lost, the second was reprinted in the preface to the 1904 edition of the *Confessions* and again in *Avowals*. Pater spoke of the originality of the *Confessions*, its unfailing liveliness, its delightful criticism of French literature, and its " questionable moral shape," adding that in the case of so satiric a book he " supposed " that one was hardly expected to agree or disagree. The letter at first put Moore in the seventh heaven of delight, but after a while a sentence in it—" I wonder what you may be losing both for yourself and your writings . . . by what I must call a cynical, and therefore exclusive way, of looking at the world "—began to assail his mind with doubt, causing him to wonder whether Henry James was not right in saying that the author of *Marius the Epicurean* evinced a tendency to hunt with the Pagan hound and run with the Christian hare. Moore's attitude towards Christianity in the *Confessions* is certainly " exclusive "; he thinks that it has brought nothing into the world but chastity, a fraudulent humanitarianism, fear of life, and a code of morality which has made the modern world so ugly and hypocritical a place.

Pater seems to have understood Moore's intentions when he called the *Confessions* satiric, for Moore had already applied this epithet to his book in a letter to Dujardin. It would not do, therefore, to consider too deeply Moore's own consistency; to enquire, for instance into the agreement of the praise of the Pagan world for its " cruelty " and unrestrained individualism with the tributes to goodness and disinterestedness which are found in other parts of the book. The goodness which always pleased Moore was instinctive and and innate, not an abstract and rationalised habit of morality, and the *Confessions* disclose throughout what Pater called (in a review of *Modern Painting*) Moore's deep preference for " the personal and uncontrollable," " the opinion and sensation one cannot help," an acute observation which offers a clue to the attraction which the philosophy of Schopenhauer had for him at this time. For Schopenhauer too set the instinct

above the intellect, finding the true key to the riddle of
existence in the unconscious will. At this time Schopenhauer
had great vogue in France, having come in on the Wagnerian
wave; and Rémy de Gourmont has described the intoxication
with which the Symbolists received his revelation that the
world was bad and yet existed only relatively to themselves.
" It is I who am the world," says Frank Escott in *Spring Days*.
Too much importance should not be attached to this influence upon Moore, who, however, certainly shared and
continued to share the Frankfurt philosopher's aversion from
Judaism and belief in the superior wisdom of India. Years
later the Jesus of the end of *The Book Kerith* was to be conceived as a sort of Buddhist sage to whom all desire, even the
desire of God, is evil; and when adding sixty pages to the
third edition of the *Confessions* he emphasised the importance
of these new pages, since they enabled him to accentuate
the philosophy of the book, that of Schopenhauer, who
" alone helps us to live," and " alone shows us the real
good and leads us from the real evil." Perhaps too one may
discern resemblances between Moore's character and that of
the Frankfurt philosopher, who was irascible, very prudent
and (although he founded his morality upon compassion) a
great egoist. His spirits, however, do not appear to have been
seriously affected by his reading of the great pessimist.
Disillusionment and indifference were, he told a woman
friend, a state of mind from which he seldom suffered.
" Needless to say I know that nothing lasts, but what does
it matter ? The need of the moment is the greatest of all."

20

Balzac, Moore would now say, was the novelist who
summed up in himself the whole art of story-telling. The
rest, even the Symbolists and Huysmans, were " like walnuts
and wine, an agreeable aftertaste." It is clear, however,
that Moore still wished to escape the consequences of a break
with Zola, whom he continued to address as his " dear
master," and while he was in Paris in April 1888 he was
delighted to accept an invitation for Alexis and himself to

pass the day at Médan. The *Confessions* was just then coming
out in *La Revue Indépendante*, and he did not feel quite at his
ease in the train to Médan, but calculated that his considerable powers of blandishment would bring him unscathed
through the interview. Zola was prepared for him and had
marked the offending passages. " But," said Moore, " what
you have just read out is from a chapter called ' La Syn-
thèse de la Nouvelle Athènes ' and represents not my
opinion but the opinion of the various ratés who assemble
there." Zola answered by pointing to an earlier passage in
the *Confessions* which contained a frivolous description of the
Naturalistic principles, showing Moore himself as a young
man in Paris, hardly able to believe his eyes as they read
that one should write with as little imagination as possible
and that the Republic would fall if it did not instantly
become Naturalistic. Zola was kind but firm. " You call your
book *Confessions*," he said, " and whoever does that, means
that he is going to tell the truth." He was not angry, and never
had he appeared so great in Moore's eyes as at this moment.
But with the saucy sentences before him he would not write
a preface for *La Femme d'un Cabotin*. " Children," he added,
" devour their parents, it is the law of nature "; and this
morality brought tears to Moore's eyes. The story is very well
told in " A Visit to Médan," but it may be that Moore
magnified Zola's personal interest in himself. " There was
never any real intimacy between my husband and Mr.
Moore," Madame Zola told Mr. Barrett H. Clark in 1922.
" They had merely agreed to make each other's work known,
the one in England, the other in France."

It is difficult to say whether Moore at the epoch of the
Confessions still retained any respect for Zola as an artist;
his article, " A Visit to Médan," with its final satiric judgment on the master's work, was not written until many years
later. He certainly no longer believed in the absurd fallacy
of approximating art to science, but then Zola too had by
then abandoned this theory. *La Terre*, Moore had said in a
letter to Dujardin, " makes me smile," but perhaps he still
admired some of Zola's earlier books, and when revising the
French of the *Confessions* he changed some of the phrasing

with the object of being " more just " to Zola. More remarkable is the fact that after his dismissal, in the very same
year, he gave loud praise in a review to Zola's *Le Rêve*. This
very insipid novel was designed by Zola to show the seceders
that he could depict the more spiritual aspects of life quite
as well as they could and Moore accepted the will for the
deed.

In after years it was different: Moore could then say little
or nothing of Zola that was not a taunt. " Huysmans and I,"
he once observed to Vincent O'Sullivan, " lie on the floor
and kick up our heels when we think of him." " The man
had no art," he told Barrett Clark in 1922. " A clever man,
but too damned thorough. I remember one evening he came
to dinner at the home of La Valtesse, a famous cocotte . . .
Zola was collecting notes (my God, what masses of notes !)
preparing to write *Nana*. He was in search of local colour.
I don't think he felt at ease there, and evidently he had come
for strictly scientific purposes; at any rate he scarcely looked
at the woman, but asked at once to see her bedroom; and
what do you think he wanted there ? To measure it, get its
exact dimensions ! Good God ! Art is a coquette, and Zola
never knew it."

It is reported, however, that on the day that Moore heard
of Zola's death he said, very honestly, " That man was the
beginning of me."

CHAPTER IV

LONDON: THE TEMPLE

I

SOME COPIES of the *Confessions* found their way to New York and lay for a while on the counters of Brentano's in Union Square. Mr. Brentano was considering the publication of an American edition, and he spoke of the matter to a young novelist, the Marquise Clara Lanza, when one day, in the late spring of 1888, this lady happened to enter his shop. Madame Lanza had never heard of George Moore, but she took a copy of the book home with her, and was entranced by its contents. Her influence prevailed upon Brentano to proceed with his project, and as soon as the publisher and author were in communication she wrote to tell Moore of the part she had played in the affair, and of her admiration for his book. He was very grateful, and a correspondence ensued which provides many details of his literary and personal life during the next three years. His longest and most carefully considered letters were usually written to women. He was flattered by their attentions, and especially was he flattered in this case, for he discovered (on enquiry among Americans in London) that his correspondent was a reigning beauty in New York.

He was at Freshcombe Lodge, the rabbit farm, in July, and from there he wrote an account of *Spring Days*: " the tale of a city merchant who is worried about his daughters—a sort of comic King Lear." The story, he said, was in itself quite harmless, but it contained " a few passages to which the chaste city of New York might take exception "; nothing, however, would be easier than to eliminate them for Mr. Brentano.

In August he spent four days at Dieppe, where Blanche's

parents had a house. Blanche himself was there and Dujardin, and Gervex, the painter. He carried back with him to England the most delightful memories of arguments with Blanche (their ideas of art never wholly corresponded), of the seashore, the pines and walks about the town with Gervex, and Dujardin's kindness in translating for him some new " copy "—a chapter specially written for the French *Confessions* to show how he thought of women as a boy. *Spring Days* was published very soon after his return, a slight work originally undertaken as the prelude to a trilogy.

The scenes of the book are set in Sussex, near Brighton; he had written an English suburban variant of *A Drama in Muslin*. The city merchant, Mr. Brooke, talks of sacrifice but always refrains from dividing his fortune among his three daughters who miss their chances of marriage. Frank Escott, the heir to an Irish peerage and the Oxford friend of Willie, the brother of the three girls, hangs about the house, and in one passage Maggie, Sally and Grace fight for the sheets in which he has slept. Willie contracts a secret marriage with a humble young woman whom he calls " the missus," and with her keeps a shop for fruit and vegetables in Brighton; as a solid Saxon he is contrasted with the more showy Frank Escott, and, like Moore's friend, Colvill Bridger, his happiest hours are spent among account books. Escott, perhaps, is a portrait of Amico Moorini, the disciple to whom Moore in his old age used sarcastically to attribute the inferior portions of his work. When Frank is in low spirits he thinks of the wife who should be sitting opposite to him and saying: " Poor old man, come sit on my knee." " One of the most notable defects of Frank's character was an impotence to divine or judge the consequences of a decisive action. . . . He was conscious of things, not of the consequences of things. . . . This blindness was obvious to the least observant, and tempted the least thoughtful to think; and all who knew him strove vainly to understand why at one moment he appeared to be so entirely selfish, and at another so impulsive and generous. . . . Those whom he was with were his all, the rest of the world was to him as nothing. He would snub a duchess and continue talking to an insignificant girl."

The subject of the first part of the proposed trilogy was to be young men in London pursuing the world's amusements; that of the second, servants from the servants' point of view; that of the third, the hopes and disappointments of old people who see their children growing up: and the servants would move with the Brooke family from Sussex to a house in London. But to judge from what Moore says in the autobiographical fragment of his old age, *A Communication to My Friends*, the idea of writing a story of servants had seized him soon after the publication of *A Drama in Muslin*. One day he was walking along Fleet Street, reading a newspaper as he walked, for an article had attracted his eye. The author of the article bespoke his readers' interest in the manifold services which are demanded of servants; and his thoughts " galloped away on something like an inspiration from the muses." He asked himself if servants, who in English literature are never introduced except as comic characters, might not be introduced as the principal characters of a novel.

This was the germ of *Esther Waters*, but it is not revealed in *A Communication* that *Esther Waters* was intended at one time to take its place in a sort of *Comédie Humaine*. For how long Moore entertained the idea of writing a trilogy it is impossible to say. There was no hint of anything of the kind in the preface to the first edition of *Spring Days*, where all that was promised was a sequel in which the various characters of *Spring Days* would reappear, and where the Don Juan " idea of man " would be treated weightily, not as the poets treated it, but with due regard to its subtle psychological interest. The subject was so large that he had to create the characters in *Spring Days* before he began his story. " The three principal characters," he wrote to Madame Lanza, "are Mike Fletcher, Frank Escott and John Norton. I might call the book *The Seekers of Oblivion*. . . . If I ever write a great novel, it will be Don Juan." Mike Fletcher, an Irish journalist, was to seek oblivion in love, John Norton (the hero of *A Mere Accident* revived) in religion, Frank Escott in the fireside.

2

Spring Days was not a success. To quote from Moore's
preface to the revised edition of 1915, all the welcome it
got " were a few contemptuous paragraphs scattered through
the Press and an insolent article in *The Academy*." The writer
in *The Academy* said that he opened the novel with distinctly
friendly feelings, being under the impression that Moore had
been the victim of persecution, but found himself confronted with the worst novel ever written. No one was more
surprised than Moore when many years later, succumbing
to the entreaties of certain friends, he re-read *Spring Days*
and found many points for praise in a story " as free from
sentiment and morals as Daphne and Chloë " : at the time
he made no attempt to resist the general verdict.

23.9.88. *To the Marquise Clara Lanza.*

Everybody is abusing *Spring Days*. The papers say it
is the worst book I have ever written . . . A writer may
elect to put his life into one book. (Baudelaire did this
in his *Fleurs du Mal*.) Or he may elect to spread himself
over fifty volumes. (Balzac did this in the *Comédie Humaine*.)
But once a writer elects to spread himself over a number
of volumes it seems to me that he must not only create
new methods but he must from time to time recreate old
ones. I am a great admirer of Jane Austen and I said
to myself, " I will recreate Jane Austen's method in
Spring Days." It was an attempt not to continue, but to
recreate *Pride and Prejudice*, *Emma*, etc. Apparently I have
failed horribly.

A great grief of the reviewers was the absence of a sense
of humour from Moore's narratives. There was nothing in
them to raise a smile, much less a hearty laugh. His work
ran counter to the good-natured tradition of the English
novel and to the prevalent belief enforced even in *The
Athenæum*, that " any joke is better than no joke." Moore
joked with difficulty, the reviewers declared, and on the
same ground complaints were lodged against his ventures

into sublimity, such as Mike Fletcher's meditations on life
" on one of the meanest of the planets " and the description
of Frank Escott in love, an interesting passage (omitted
from the revised *Spring Days*) which shows Moore's familiarity with the phraseology of the Wagnerian opera. Many
years later, in the *Avowals* conversation with Edmund Gosse,
all this was remembered philosophically. "A living and
moving story related by a humourist very soon becomes a
thing of jeers and laughter, signifying nothing. We must
have humour, of course, but the use we must make of our
sense of humour is to avoid introducing anything into the
narrative that shall distract the reader from the beauty,
the mystery, and the pathos of the life we live in this world.
Whoever keeps humour under lock and key is read in the
next generation, if he writes well, for to write well without
the help of humour is the supreme test." This needed to be
said, and was very well said. Some readers may have found
it strange, as coming from the author of *Hail and Farewell*;
but although *Hail and Farewell* is a work of humorous
genius, it is far from being a book of bright and abundant
laughter. The humour in it is not a spontaneous sense of
the comic, but results from presenting ideals and individuals
in a ludicrous light. To this sort of humour Moore was always
prone, as is proved by many of his early essays, for instance
by " A Visit to Médan " and " Mummer Worship," where,
as with Huysmans, things are deformed by vehemence and
indignation, real or assumed.

His critical articles were now attracting considerable
attention. Of one he spoke with particular pride : " Mummer
Worship," a satire on the pretensions of the stage to domes-
ticity, which was published in the *Universal Review*. The
spectacle of the successful English actor—with villa at St.
John's Wood, cards from the parson, silk hat, and son at
Eton—had put him in a real rage. He continued to like this
essay until the end of his life, and " Mummer Worship "
is now to be found, among a few other occasional papers,
in the Appendix to the final edition of the *Confessions*. But,
to tell the truth, " Mummer Worship " takes a good deal
of colour from the period and is rather a snobbish piece of

work. More interesting is the appreciation of Turgenev (which appeared in the *Fortnightly Review* towards the end of 1888) where the definitions of the Naturalistic school are shown to be not only brutally material but contradictory in themselves. It is now evident to Moore that the indifferent objective reproduction of things is a dream and not even a beautiful dream: Flaubert's so-called impersonality is the vainest of delusions, and Turgenev, even in his narration of physical phenomena, gives utterance to a thought, and manifests his own spirit.

3

Moore went on with his Don Juan novel, but his letters on this subject sometimes betrayed uneasiness, the consequence of the dismal failure of *Spring Days*. To his mother he wrote:

> It is the best thing I have ever done. I do not think it can be mistaken for anything except the work of a person who has endeavoured to think for himself. That it is peculiar goes without saying. I was born, I live, I shall die a peculiar man. I could not be commonplace were I to try. The bitterest thing is what I think of myself:— it is not the work of genius, not that of great talent. It is the work of a man affected by that most terrible of all maladies, a dash of genius. We are the unfortunates who finish alone in the fight and upon whose bodies others ascend the peak of genius. . . .
>
> My novel is a new method. It is not a warming up out of Dickens and Thackeray. It is a method that will certainly be adopted by other writers, but will the first effort meet with recognition. I scarcely think so. . . .

It was a tale of London in the 'eighties, young lawyers in the Temple and a great many prostitutes. Mike Fletcher, the illegitimate son of a French father and an Irish mother, edits *The Pilgrim*, a journal for men about town, not unlike *The Hawk*, Augustus Moore's journal, which was founded at this time. Frank Escott joins Mike on the staff of *The*

Pilgrim. One of their friends is John Norton, a priggish young Catholic, interested in Schopenhauer, who rebukes them for their loose lives and conversation. Mike stays with Norton in Sussex, hunts and joins in country house life, creating havoc everywhere he goes by his invariable successes with women. Wearying of all this he returns to London, where he visits the Escotts and wins money from them by cheating at cards. He suddenly hears that he has been left a property in Berkshire and a fortune by an old mistress. He is something of a mystery in Berkshire " county society." Following the vaguest hint he goes to Nice to look up Lily Green, his ideal of womanly purity whom some time ago he persuaded to leave her convent. She is consumptive when he finds her : she dies as they are planning to run away to Italy, a passage which recalls the final scene in *La Dame aux Camelias.* Mike goes to Africa and lives two years among the Arabs, an echo of the poet Rimbaud's flight to the shores of the Dead Sea, a story which enchanted Moore. He comes home, stands as M.P. for Cashel, where he was born, and is elected. He spends all his time drabbing and playing cards, but is very jealous both of the Escotts' domestic bliss (which, after the manner of Huysmans' hero in *A Rebours* he wantonly tries to destroy) and of John Norton's medievalist oblivion (he goes one day to Norton's country house with a party of " tarts and mashers " and finds Norton playing the *Dies Irae* on his organ). Mike, after long cogitation on the subject of suicide, shoots himself.

In the autumn of 1888 Vizetelly, who was to publish the masterpiece, was brought to Bow Street, at the instigation of the Vigilance Society, on the charge of publishing English translations of Zola : *Nana*, *Piping Hot* and *The Soil*. Lord Oxford (then Mr. Asquith) prosecuted, and the case was referred to the Recorder. *Pendente lite*, Vizetelly, on Moore's advice and with his help, issued an anthology designed to show that, on the grounds alleged against Zola's work, the Bible, Shakespeare and most of the English classics should be suppressed : a *reductio ad absurdum* which became Moore's stock argument against the censorship. " Is there no book you would condemn," John Balderston asked thirty

years later in the discussion in *Avowals*, " even such as certain
are given to collecting ? " " We are discussing literature, not
indecency," Moore replied, " and there can be no possible
excuse for mistaking one for the other. It is not true that
pornography and literature overlap, that the frontiers are
indistinct. Real literature is concerned with the description
of life and thoughts about life rather than acts. The very
opposite is true in the case of pornographic books. It is true,
however, that in real literature a good deal of license is asked
for by the author. . . ."

4

Having given up his quarters in Dane's Inn, Moore now
became Sir William Geary's tenant at 8, King's Bench Walk
in the Temple. He continued to visit his friends in Sussex
fairly regularly, but the rabbit farm on the Downs no longer
occupied any of his attention. There is not a great deal to
record of his external life at this period. Frank Harris provided him with his chief intellectual entertainment and won
his perfervid admiration: " the most brilliant conversa-
tionalist who ever lived," was his description of Harris.
" To listen to him is an enchantment, a cerebral debauch,"
he wrote to Madame Lanza. He was on the eve of making
many valued friends in the English art world, but for the
time being he found London a dreary place except when
Harris scintillated. And Harris did not arouse affection.
" I am happy only with my French friends," he said in one
of his letters to Madame Lanza. " I often think of going to
Paris and settling there for good."

Women, as always, occupied a prominent place in his
thoughts. Hope was " born anew in every new face," but
his heart was not engaged, and one has the impression that
he suffered from the lack of romantic colour in his life. He
made the most of his epistolary friendship with Madame
Lanza. " I went on a shooting party with the editor of the
Fortnightly [Frank Harris] into Kent," he wrote to her.
". . . There were many people staying in the house. I talked
about you. . . . This friendship which is so real to us, I felt
was a little out of their reach. And I was not sorry for their

want of comprehension, for it seemed to make the tie only
the more strongly personal and intense." The account which
Harris gives in his memoirs of shooting with Moore may
refer to the same occasion. Moore, he says, on being struck
in the eye by a pellet, received jeers instead of sympathy
from the other sportsmen, one of whom said: " What can
he expect when he goes out shooting with gentlemen ? "
It may be that Moore had created a prejudice against himself by his over-communicativeness of the night before. But
Harris, whose presence at the party does not suggest that
the company was punctilious, relates the incident as an
illustration of the contempt of English aristocrats for the
artist, even when the artist was, as in this case, a sportsman
himself and a gentleman born.

A lady at this time asked Moore how long love had ever
lasted with him. " Two months," was his reply. But he
demurred to being classed among those who regard sex only
in the simplest form. They were " common livers." " Sex,"
he wrote to Madame Lanza, " is full of mysteries and subtleties. Who has not seen a young man paying compliments to,
and sincerely admiring an old woman—a beautiful old
woman ? " Another opinion he had formed was that the
friendship between man and woman which survived the
shipwreck of passion was deeper and stronger than platonic
friendship. But he could be brusque enough to his old flames
when they bothered him; and he now dismissed from his life
the woman whose letters he imitated in the *Confessions*—the
American with whom he used to read Browning in his flat
in Paris and who attended the auction there. " When I bade
you good-bye," he wrote, " I tried to make you understand
that it *was* good-bye, but as you have seen fit to write, no
alternative is left me except to say good-bye again."

Holding these views, Moore agreed with the philosopher
who called marriage the grave of love, but he looked on
marriage as Nature's way out of many difficulties, and he
would quote Turgenev's advice to young people with
approval. Fortunately, except at rare intervals, he was fully
alive to the fact that his temperament precluded him from
inviting anyone to share his life. He once gave an amusing

account of his conduct during such an interval (the earlier eighties, perhaps, date the story) to a lady in Dublin who asked him if he had ever thought of marrying. To this he replied that he had done so once and that the person was a well-brought-up young woman, a poetess, with whom he often took walks. One day he made up his mind to propose to her, and to do so during the walk. The walk started, and he felt that he must redeem the promise to himself, but the walk continued and the proposal was not put. He looked along the road and said to himself: " At that bend, I speak," but the bend came, and was passed. Again he looked ahead; there was a bridge in sight, the ideal spot, but even at the bridge the proposal would not come. In despair he resolved to write. . . . After many attempts he wrote a letter and gave it to his landlady. A moment after, full of misgivings, he flung his window wide and called back the woman, so that he might add something. He then thought that it would be more fitting to post the letter himself, so he walked out to put it in the nearest box. " No," he said to himself, " I'll go to a box further on," but no box seemed worthy except the one at the General Post Office, and that being too far off he returned to his room with the letter still in his hands. His listener reproached him: " That girl has perhaps lived all her life loving you and she never had the joy of knowing that you responded." " No," he replied, " she married another man."

5

His rooms in King's Bench Walk, a sitting-room and a bedroom, were at the top of three flights of creaking disjointed stairs. Vincent O'Sullivan, when he called upon him here, was astonished by their dreariness. The study had not even the melancholy counterfeit of luxury that is found in a dentist's waiting-room. Apart from the view from the front windows across the court of the Temple, it was about as attractive as a room in a cheap hotel. And Ruttledge, Moore's agent, when he was over from Ireland, used to chaff him and say: " There are very few who would be content to live in a cockloft such as this." He was a heavy man, and the three flights distressed him. Moore reminded Ruttledge of the financial folly of other Irish landlords; and he reminded himself that it was natural for authors to live in garrets, wear old clothes, and spend two and sixpence on their dinners. Poor folk were always running in and out of Temple Lane, picking up a living in the garrets; and he tells in *Ave* how through his laundress he became acquainted with many of them. They awakened spontaneous sympathies in him, and by doing them kindness he was making honey for himself (the reference is to his studies for *Esther Waters*) without knowing it.

"I live a very quiet life in the Temple, looking out on the scenes described in *Mike Fletcher*," he wrote to Madame Lanza shortly after his installation. "Alas, I am thirty-seven or very nearly. The heart wears out and life is not so new or as joyous as it used to be. . . . I am writing an article called 'Our Dramatists,' in which I shall get rid of a great deal of gall. Nothing exasperates me so much as the modern play."

Having admired one of Madame Lanza's novels he wanted to dramatise it, but confessed with his usual candour in such matters that he could not write a play unaided. He was to write a synopsis of each act—there were to be four or five—forward them to his collaborator in succession, and when they were returned to him he would put on the finishing touches, the polish. The work started excellently, but he soon wanted to try his own hand at dialogue:

19.3.89. *To the Marquise Clara Lanza*

. . . Your dialogue is good in substance, but it is more than faulty in form. It is not dramatic dialogue. It could not be spoken; it would not be listened to. In its present form, the play would be hissed at the end of the first act, if the actors got so far. There is no use mincing matters, that is the truth. Now I think I can convert what you sent me into a beautiful play; indeed, I feel sure I can. I like the subject and the treatment of the subject as much as ever. . . .

I do not believe I have written to you since you sent

me your last photograph. I admired it exceedingly. You are much better thin than fat. I confess I have a weakness for thin people and I would sooner put up with any discomfort in the way of eating than grow fat. The way to keep down flesh is not to drink at meals. Zola reduced himself three stone by this simple expedient. Drink two hours after meals and avoid a crumb of bread.

Moore refers in this letter to a real sorrow which he suffered at this time: in March 1889, Mrs. Bridger, the mother of his Sussex friends and his own very dear friend, died. To Madame Lanza he said: " I should have written long ago if my time and thoughts had been free, but I have been sadly harassed these last weeks. My friends—the friends with whom I live so much—lost their mother, and I have been with them, talking of death. Their mother died by inches. We used to sit down to lunch and wonder if she would live through the afternoon. How disgraceful life is ! The life of the body at every moment degrades and dishonours that of the soul."

His tribute to Mrs. Bridger, " A Remembrance," was written a year or two later, but was not published until it found its place in *Memoirs of My Dead Life* in 1906. Here he told how he was called one gusty March afternoon to Shoreham by a telegram. His friend had long been ill, but she would neither take care of herself, nor complain, and her " quick dance of movement " was still " a grace and a joy." Now she was dying, but she did not die on the night he arrived, nor the next night, nor the next. While they waited he " thought often of the degradation that these lingering deaths impose upon the watchers. . . . For, however great our grief may be, we must eat and drink, and must even talk of other things than the beloved one we are about to lose. We may not escape our shameful natures."

After the death of Mrs. Bridger, Moore's sojourns in Sussex became shorter and when the squire married a second time they ceased to have any regularity. He was getting a little tired of the unintellectual Colly, one fancies. But he continued to feel an affection for the two sisters, with one of whom, Dulcibella, he remained in correspondence almost until the end of his life.

6

The year was full of tumult. Moore fell out with Quilter, the editor of the *Universal Review*, and with Robert Buchanan; and his methods of negotiation with Brentano, the American publisher of the *Confessions*, resembled a series of explosions. The quarrels with Brentano and with Quilter were a misfortune, but it gave him unmitigated satisfaction to be at blows with Buchanan, the detractor of Swinburne and the Pre-Raphaelites. The *Confessions* had incurred the swashbuckling Scotsman's moral disapproval, and Moore replied to a personal censure in an article which in Harris's opinion " ran Swift pretty close." He would have been happy but for certain dubieties regarding *Mike Fletcher*. He was worried about the quality of this work and still more worried about the publication, for Vizetelly was again being prosecuted. In the previous year the Recorder, although of opinion that the translations of Zola were obscene and had been " published for gain and deliberately for gain," allowed Vizetelly to go free, in view of his age, under recognisance of £200 and a promise to withdraw the books from publication. But the old man found that his business was going from him, and he began to reprint the offending novels in unexpurgated editions: the Vigilance Society once more intervened, and Vizetelly found himself at the Old Bailey. Although he was the author of one of the translations, Moore's name was not brought into the case; he would have liked to give evidence, but no witnesses were called, for as before Vizetelly was advised by Counsel to plead guilty: he was sentenced to three months' imprisonment.

The case made an ineffaceable impression on Moore's mind. He visited the prisoner, and the sight of the poor old man, whose health was already broken, filled him with a disgust of English hypocrisy which he communicated to the not unwilling ears of his brother Maurice and of Edward Martyn. Vizetelly said to him that the jury was a good one and would have acquitted him, but why had the lawyer

advised him to plead guilty ? Moore was convinced that both
the publisher and his legal advisers were the victims of a
far-reaching conspiracy, and the case presented itself to him
as an example of cunning and hypocrisy, humanity at its
very worst.

In May he was in Paris, and writing to his mother, he
repeated his wish that he could live there. " Paris is as
beautiful as a siren, and friends new and old are an enchantment to which I grow more and more susceptible." In the
course of his stay at a musical reception at Baron Salvadore's
house he met the American novelist, Mrs. Gertrude Atherton, as she has reported in her amusing book of memoirs :
her note on the encounter shows that he was still considered
to be a shocking author. He was the only young man present,
and she the only young woman ; the pair retired to the
dining-room, where they talked for three hours of Zola and
the censorship, and of Flaubert, who was now one of the
canonical scriptures. In Mrs. Atherton's estimation, Moore
was anything but handsome : " very tall and very blond,
with a long colourless face that looked like a codfish crossed
by a satyr." It is curious that she should have thought him
so tall, but perhaps the sloping shoulders and long neck
contributed to give this impression of him to those who were
below medium height. In any event, Mrs. Atherton's conservative friends were aghast, one of them saying to her next
day : " You went off into a room alone with a man who was
arrested for writing obscene literature." Moore was not to
be gainsaid in the pursuit of his new acquaintance, particularly when he was told that Mrs. Atherton was going to a
convent in Boulogne to write a book. As he could never
resist a convent, he declared that he would follow Mrs.
Atherton to Boulogne. " I shuddered," says Mrs. Atherton,
" at the thought of George Moore's face on one side of the
wicket and a nun on the other." She managed to elude the
collaboration in a play or novel, which was inevitably
proposed.[1]

Degas reappears in Moore's life for a moment, and then
vanishes from it for ever. It seems that Moore, hearing that

[1] *Adventures of a Novelist* : Jonathan Cape.

Degas liked the *Confessions*, called at the painter's studio with the object of writing about him, but Degas, who held that an artist should have no private life, would not consent to see him again. And there were other estrangements from his French friends. Zola as a result of the *Confessions* had gone partially out of Moore's life; for the same reason Goncourt and Catulle Mendès vanished altogether. Goncourt recalled the visits of a young man who used to take notes of the conversations upon his cuffs. These visits now ceased, and so did the walks under the moonlight in the Place Pigalle with Mendès, disparaged in the same book as the type of false artist, a sort of French Robert Buchanan. Towards Degas Moore bore no resentment. " A more delicate nature never breathed," he wrote a year before his own death to Daniel Halévy, " though for some reason unknown to himself he took the devil's pains to persuade the world that he was an old bear without a civil word for anyone."[1]

When he returned to London Moore appeared to be much refreshed; his next letter to Madame Lanza is written in a happy-go-lucky strain. The meeting with Mrs. Atherton was duly reported.

> Mrs. Atherton said: " I think I know a friend of yours. . . ." I felt quite proud and pleased. She says you are the most beautiful woman in New York, and I know you are one of the cleverest. *Ah, quelle nostalgie d'Amerique !* . . .
>
> Mrs. Atherton is going to spend the summer in a convent in Boulogne, I think I may run over there. She is amusing and talks readily of you. I have written you out of my thoughts as they pass, as they dart through my mind. I have not considered for a second what I should say or how I should say it.

7

Two tasks before him were articles on the Vizetelly prosecutions and on Balzac, both for Frank Harris. It was not

[1] Appendix: *Pays Parisiens* by D. Halévy.

found possible to print what he wrote on the Vizetelly case, but the article on Balzac appeared at the end of the year in the *Fortnightly Review*. " You cannot write well," he said, " about what you irreparably love " : but the article, to which he gave the title of " Some of Balzac's Minor Pieces," was a very good one, and helped to re-establish his reputation as a literary artist. After its publication in the *Fortnightly*, he revised the essay, and used it in its new form as the opening chapter of *Impressions and Opinions*. Passages from the original are still preserved in *Conversations in Ebury Street*. They were fine enough to compel the approval of Moore's most exacting critic—himself.

Ward and Downey now agreed to publish *Mike Fletcher*, and an arrangement was come to with a New York firm for an American edition. " Ward and Downey say it is my best book," Moore informed Madame Lanza, " and the friends who have seen fragments say so too. I have done my best, inspired by the desire to leave one good book, one really great novel, quite first rate." Along with Cardinal Manning and Lord Randolph Churchill he was asked to contribute to one of the opening numbers of the *Daily Mail*, a testimony to his growing position as a popular controversialist. A wave of confidence swept over him, and he spoke of going to America to give readings from *Mike Fletcher*. " Do you think the Americans would come to listen to it ? " he asked his New York friend, " or would a lecture be more attractive ? Or could the two be merged in one entertainment ? "

But the next months brought unrelieved disaster. The American publisher smashed. Moore's comments were unrestrained. Madame Lanza recovered the proof sheets of Moore's novel, but she met with a disheartening reception at the offices of other publishers, and it was a small mercy when a Greek, bearing the name of the Minerva Publishing Company, agreed to issue *Mike Fletcher* in a cheap way and to guarantee the sale of a certain number of copies. While waiting for the English publication Moore began a play— the story of a strike—the work which became *The Strike at Arlingford*.

The English edition of *Mike Fletcher* was published in the

autumn, and the friends to whom Moore had read fragments did not disguise their disappointment when they saw the work as a whole. Frank Harris had encouraged Moore to believe that he was creating a hero of tragedy in a solemn cad and second-rate poet, but he now declared that *Mike Fletcher* was not as good as *A Mummer's Wife*; and on further reflection he became " loud in his abuse." " I fancy," Moore wrote to Madame Lanza, " he may be overstating the case against the book . . . It is impossible that a man who writes as well as I have done, and am still writing, should be the author of three hundred pages of twaddle." " I realise now that *Mike Fletcher* is not good," he said in his next letter, " I wish I had known how bad it was and I wouldn't have published it." The Greek publisher in New York complained that he could not sell one single copy, and was sure that he had been duped—that the author of *Mike Fletcher* and the author of the *Confessions* could not be one and the same person. However, Moore insisted on his rights, and Madame Lanza has related how her household was awakened one morning at three by a cable: " Where are my royalties ? Send draft immediately." She managed at last to extract fifty dollars from the Greek, and her draft for this sum was the last that was heard of the American edition, for the Minerva Publishing Company dissolved a few weeks later. " Please don't bother about the wretched book." Moore wrote to his American friend. On the whole he kept his spirits in a remarkable way; it was a catastrophe which would have shocked and discouraged most authors.

In England the book had a small commercial success. But once having turned against the story Moore's bad opinion of it never faltered, and *Mike Fletcher* proved to be the only one of his novels which he never wished to revise, and the only one of his books, not excluding the poems, of which in his old age he preferred never to speak. The fault he found with *Mike Fletcher* was its want of order and development, and he put the blame on his subject. " My next novel," he wrote to Madame Lanza, " will be more human. I shall bathe myself in the simplest and most naïve emotions, the daily bread of humanity." His story about servants was now shaping in his mind as a kitchen-maid's fight for her child's life in a racing framework. But before venturing on the new enterprise he wished to prepare a book of essays for publication, and also to finish his play.

24.11.89. *To the Marquise Clara Lanza:*

The leader of the Socialists falls in love with the owner of the mine. He is a sort of Hamlet of the West End. The comic character is an impropriety hunter. Harris thinks it is the biggest thing I have done—he only saw a very incomplete scenario. I have not quite finished the work yet. I must if I wish to succeed with it, for I want to go to America and to do that I must make some money. Dear, oh, dear, how ill I feel. I have spent the whole day reading Stendhal—*Le Rouge et Le Noir.* I shall write an article in the *Fortnightly* about him. . . .

Two months later he thought that the part of the Hamlet must tempt the vanity of any actor. And if *The Strike at Arlingford* were done in America he would go there, and then he would see his fair correspondent.

18.2.90 *To the Marquise Clara Lanza*

What a pleasure that would be ! Sometimes I think it would be better not to see you, for naturally there is the risk that we might not like each other. But these are only Hamlet mutterings. We should like each other well enough. There is too much in common between us, and besides we know all about each other. You know I am not a vulgarian, a Cockney, whose slightest word would make you shudder. Even my enemies would not accuse me of being a cad, and then I know all about you. Heron-Allen told me the other night that you were the cleverest and most witty woman he had ever spoken to. By the way, he is much improved. He is not nearly so affected as he was and is really a good sort. Of course, he was intolerable when he was practicing chiromancy and you only knew him then.

What you said about the " scandals " was exactly what I have said a hundred times. Three thousand miles of ocean do not prevent us from thinking alike. Of course ! I see no reason why those who prefer to drink salad oil to champagne should not be allowed to do so. Yet the charm of a nice woman is so sufficing, so infinite, that the perversion necessary not to see it is to me as unfathomable as the belief in the mystery of the Trinity. Art and women affect me much in the same way, and I should say that you might say the same about art and man. . . .

But really the things I write to you startle me at times. Never did one person reveal himself more nakedly than I do to you. But why shouldn't I ? I shall never have another friend like you. By the way, when I go to New York, I shall not only have to get on with you but also with your Chinese dog. I suppose that friendship with him is outside of all possibility. Well . . . I shall go to Paris in May and I shall see such nice friends. What a pity it is that you will not be there at the same time ! I am sorry you have so many family ties—husband and children. Life is better without a family surely. If I were married, I could not write you this letter, and this letter is symbolic of a great deal.

It is just to say that Moore was grateful to Madame Lanza for her efforts on his behalf and that he tried to be of service to her in return. He had admired her novel *A Righteous Apostate*, and now he spoke of her work to London publishers and to Augustus Moore, the editor of *The Hawk*.

19.4.90 *To the Marquise Clara Lanza*

My brother is very pleased with your story, so pleased that he speaks of sending you a cheque for it. I am glad of this because it will please you. He spoke about it the other night. We were sitting at dinner in the " Rainbow," an old fashioned tavern, and as we were talking two men came up to speak to him, both of whom he introduced to me. I hate casual introductions and am apt to bow and turn aside. But one of the men said : "I know a friend of

yours, Mr. Moore—Madame Lanza." I need hardly say
I brightened up at once and asked him to sit down and
have a glass of wine. He could not stay, and I only had
three minutes' talk on the subject nearest my heart. He is
the editor of *New York Truth*. I hate needless introductions,
don't you ? First, the people do not amuse me. I am tired
of being told that they liked *A Mummer's Wife* and I can't
remember their faces afterwards. I cut them dead and
involuntarily make enemies. I am cursed with the worst
memory for faces of any man on earth. Nevertheless, I
think I should know you if I were to meet you, but then I
have *thought* about you.

The Strike at Arlingford was finished, and he had submitted
it to Hare, the actor-manager. He had talked so much of it to
all his acquaintance and such wide publicity had been given
to his vehement and indignant views of the English theatre
that he could not account for Hare's silence of three weeks.
" I do so hope he'll take it," he confided to his American
correspondent. " It will be so pleasant to have a great deal
of money. I have always had plenty of pocket money. . . .
But I have never had large sums in the bank, or been able to
say—' Well, I'll go to Italy and spend five hundred pounds.' "
In May, the two women writers, aunt and niece, Kathleen
Bradley and Edith Cooper (known as " Michael Field " in
their books), after a chance encounter with Moore in the
Louvre, put their impressions of him on paper—" hue un-
healthy, hair honey coloured, nose the strong man among
his features . . . I like the sincerity of his light eyes and the
candour of his speech." Moore formed an acquaintance with
these ladies in London and admired their work, particularly
a play *William Rufus*, and since they were religious-minded
and morally fastidious women and Moore had the character
of being loose in principles and practice, their comment
upon him seems worth recording. Already they had made
an earnest round of famous authors, but they now found that
at its best Moore's conversation had a value and range
beyond Meredith's. " He is likeable, spite of oaths and confessions. He is in the world, and yet no liar. . . . There is

' blood ' in his dealings with literature. His tongue, not his manner, could give offence—he has the obstinate tactlessness of speech that comes of his race . . . a man of good original instincts, however much his way of life may have deflected them."[1]

While in Paris he had his portrait painted by Blanche (the first of the two portraits done of him by this artist), and he accompanied Ludovic Halévy to Antoine's Théâtre Libre for performances of *Ghosts* and the *Doll's House*: the sight of Antoine's great work caused him on his return to London to attack the trivialities of the English drama with a renewed vigour. It was also on the occasion of this visit that Dujardin should have brought him to see Verlaine whose poetry he adored; but the project for some reason miscarried, much to his chagrin. Hearing of the mischance, Arthur Symons mentioned the matter to his friends, who were therefore considerably surprised when Moore wrote an account of Verlaine in his garret, unbinding and displaying an ulcerated leg to himself and to Dujardin. A meeting did take place at a later date, and when the poet was asked by Mr. Vincent O'Sullivan to give his impressions of his English visitor, he replied that he remembered a man with clean cuffs. This was repeated to Moore, who seemed rather pleased, but asked: " Is this his only recollection of me ? "

8

" You ask me to tell you about my book," he wrote to Madame Lanza in July. " Well, it is all about servants— servants devoured by betting. It begins in a house in the country where there are race horses. Towards the end of the book—past the middle—the servants set up a public house. They cannot get custom unless they have betting. Then come the various tragedies of the bar—the hairdresser who cuts his throat—the servant who loses thirty years' character for six shillings—the woman who pledges the plate to give her lover money to bet with. The human drama is the story of the servant girl with an illegitimate child, how she saves the

[1] *Works and Days* by Michael Field. Murray. 1933.

child from the baby farmers, her endless temptations to get rid of it and to steal for it. She succeeds in bringing up her boy, and the last scene is when she is living with her first mistress in the old place, ruined and deserted. The race horses have ruined masters as well as the servants."

Esther Waters (the book was not yet so named) was laid aside in August when Moore was called to Ireland for a few weeks. What his errand was is uncertain; it was probably business connected with his property and the family. He found his mother and his youngest brother Julian at Moore Hall; and saw for the last time the secretive Joseph Applely, the correspondent of his betting days in London, who had alway given his mother an impression of the uncanny. When the old servant died a few months later Moore wrote to his mother: " The last real remembrance of my child-hood is gone." In the early pages of *Esther Waters* he was drawing a portrait of his old friend.

> Of Mr. Leopold she [Esther] saw almost as little as she did of the people upstairs. He passed along the passages or remained shut up in his pantry. Ginger used to go there to smoke; when the door stood ajar Esther saw his narrow person seated on the edge of the table, his leg swinging. Among the pantry people Mr. Leopold's erudition was a constant subject of admiration. His reminiscences of the races of thirty years ago were full of interest; he had seen the great horses whose names live in the stud-book, the horses the Gaffer owned, had trained, had ridden. . . . Mrs. Barfield shared her cook's horror of the pantry, and often spoke of Mr. Leopold as " that little man."

Augustus, the editor of *The Hawk*, was the one member of his family of whom he had seen much in recent years. *Mike Fletcher* had been dedicated to Augustus, " in memory of many years of mutual aspiration and labour." And from time to time Moore wrote for *The Hawk*, " a smart journal for young men about town," which in spite of this description and its tendency to provoke discord and lend an ear to scandal, had managed to gather round it a considerable number of distinguished contributors. "Augustus is doing well," Moore now reported to his brother in India, " and Julian is arranging the orchestral portions of his opera." He was himself " writing better than ever "—a long novel about servants, servants devoured by racing; *le petit côté des courses* was obviously a good idea, because racing novels had hitherto been " confined to lords and earls." But he was deceived in nothing, and he knew well the invariable end of artistic cravings: the natural affections were all that the world had for giving.

1.8.90. *To Maurice Moore.*

You have every reason to think me a madman for surely the peculiarity of leaving those you love best three whole years without a letter can only be defined as madness. I do not attempt either to explain or to excuse—I know what the facts are—I know that there is no one who means so much to me as you do, and yet I have been unable to bring myself to write to you for so long a while. . . .

So you are married. When shall I see you both ? India is a curse, a kind of amateur death, so completely does it divide men's lives. You said you would be coming home in a year, but for how long ? I hope for life, or else when we take our departure for good and all we shall bow our-selves through the final exit as comparative strangers. . . .

I do not think I shall do anything of real value. The others delude themselves, they confuse temporary reputa-tion with the real reputation that time grants slowly but always with inflexible justice. The fools quarrel as [to] whom they should sit next at the author's dinner. I see over the heads of such possible vanity, I have the senti-ment of great work but I cannot produce it. *Voilà ma confession*, what I strictly believe to be true.

Whilst he thus dwelt lovingly on the thought of Maurice, irritability began to disclose itself in his relations with Augustus. Two pugnacious people had been too much in each other's company, and Augustus used to say: " If you

wish to be friends with George see him once a year." But
Moore vowed that he was in total ignorance of the origins
of their dispute. " [Augustus] must cease to think the whole
world is in the wrong," he wrote to his mother on the 2nd
of November. " That is the trouble in a single phrase." He
now wished however to dissociate himself from *The Hawk*,
which was earning too great a notoriety by its quarrelsome-
ness. On one occasion, Whistler, who always ridiculed
both brothers, was provoked by some reference to himself in
its columns, and seeing the editor in a theatre, he ran at him
from behind, crying with hand uplifted : " This is the way a
hawk strikes " ; but he missed his footing and fell.

Augustus was about to marry for the second time and he
proposed to take his bride to Moore Hall for the honeymoon.
This seemed to Moore an odd arrangement, seeing that they
were not friends. " But I desire nothing better than to be
friends with him and I ask nothing better than to go to
Moore Hall to entertain him and his wife, and the only
condition I make is that he shall behave himself. To edit
The Hawk from Moore Hall is a thing that I most distinctly
object to."

All this was to his mother. She heard other complaints,
for the family finances were distinctly on her son's mind at
this time. He admitted that Augustus's fiancée was a lady,
but she had not a penny-piece. And how was Julian doing ?
He thought of Julian with kindness, and wished to be
apprised of his progress : " how far had he got towards being
able to write a song ? " But was it not surprising that Julian
showed no desire to go out to Africa to seek fortune ? And
his sister, Mrs. Kilkelly ? " Nina I should like to hear something about. I hear she is about to have another baby.
Surely this is not true." Maurice alone gave satisfaction.
" There is no one like Maurice," he continued to say.

Even his mother was sometimes the victim of his impatience, and when she asked him why he did not write
oftener, he reminded her rather sharply that he lived largely
by what his writings brought in, which gave him little time
for correspondence, and that if he had to earn his living, it
was on account of the disastrous advice she had given him

for the management of his property during his minority.
These reflections led him to a question of business:

15.11.90. *To Mrs. Moore.*

You are aware that you get five hundred a year out of
the property and that I get less than two hundred. It is
not with any intention of causing you pain that I allude to
these facts but it is necessary to take them into consideration in determining your course in the matter I have to
lay before you. I have accidentally discovered that two
sums of money—I have reason to believe insignificant
sums of money—are lying in my father's name in two
public departments. I do not know if these monies are
yours or mine by my father's will. Will you find out to
whom this money belongs by right and if it belongs to you
will you, having regard to the enormous losses which I
have sustained, and in which you have not participated.
forfeit your right to this money and assign it to me.

To this proposal Mrs. Moore at once assented. But the
moneys proved to be a mare's nest. They were not lying in
the Funds or anywhere else, and instead of £400 all he
received was a bill of costs from the solicitor through whom
he had instituted the enquiry.

Everything still went awry with him. A scheme to collaborate in a novel of 60,000 words with Ella Hepworth Dixon
proved to be impracticable. She was the daughter of a
former editor of *The Spectator*, and Moore had placed his
Pagan Poems at her feet long ago. Hare would not produce
The Strike at Arlingford (Beerbohm Tree, for whom it was
originally intended, had also rejected the work); and now
Wilson Barrett announced a play called *The Dock Strike*:
The Idol of the People, which he expected would be his own
play mutilated and transformed. He vowed that he would
never write another play. But his interest in the drama waxed
rather than waned, and it found an outlet in the part which
he took in the management of the Independent Theatre,
which was now founded, on Antoine's model, for the
elevation of English taste by the production of foreign

masterpieces. The chief credit for the scheme should go to
J. T. Grein, but Moore, a very diligent and useful member
of the Committee, was inclined to regard the theatre as his
own child, and when Augustus criticised in *The Hawk* the
finances of the enterprise, he was very angry. Rather
wildly, he chose to accuse his brother of having reflected upon his honesty; he spoke of obliquious journalism,
and was deaf for some years to all pleas for a reconciliation :
a disposition in his will and a sentence or two in his last
autobiographical essay show however that he always
preserved a latent tenderness for Augustus.

9

Esther Waters was now laid aside, and owing to the anxiety
which he found in the state of his purse, Moore spent the
winter of 1890–1 in writing *Vain Fortune*, a serial for the
Lady's Pictorial, and in collecting some of the best of his
recent essays on literature, art and the drama for publication
in book form. " I had an invitation to go south," he wrote to
Madame Lanza at the end of March, " and the company
was pleasant, but I had to forego a whole winter's amusement . . . I was so busy. I have worked with such stupid
persistence."

The success of *Impressions and Opinions*, his collected essays,
rewarded him.

24.4.91. *To the Marquise Clara Lanza.*

My book, *Impressions and Opinions*, continues to be well
received here. Everybody likes it, and it is being said that
I am much better as an essayist (I am afraid the word is
wrongly spelled, but you are used to my bad spelling by
this time) than as a novelist. I shall disabuse them of that
idea presently. There is more in me than they think.

You are mistaken in thinking that I have written a pot
boiler. I have not. I have written a short book with nothing offensive in it. " Offensive " is the word the proprietor
of the paper used. In every other respect I have written
to please myself. The story did not lend itself to a single

coarse word, so in truth I made no concession to anyone. . . .

The *Lady's Pictorial* published the story under the *nom de
plume* of " Lady Rhone "; the illustrations were by Maurice
Griffenhagen. *Vain Fortune* was written twice over before it
appeared serially, and during its run in the *Pictorial* Moore
rewrote it once more for an edition which he had arranged
to have published in the autumn under his own name by
Henry & Co., a firm of which his colleague of the Independent Theatre, J. T. Grein, was a member. Mr. Grein,
who watched him at work, recalled for me shortly before
his death his impression of the most pertinacious of authors.
" Time after time Moore, who had no secretary in those
days, would tear up his pages and begin all over again."
The readers of the *Lady's Pictorial* were deprived of the
conventionally happy ending. Moore described his story as
an illustration of the senseless cruelty of nature, and indeed
Vain Fortune is almost Hardyesque, so heavily are the dice
loaded in favour of malign fate. It was a tale of an unsuccessful author in contemporary London and of a young girl's
passion which comes to naught. Hubert Price has written a
play, a play which rouses interest, and yet fails lamentably;
and when all hopes are dead, his uncle, who has adopted a
distant member of the family, Emily Watson, suddenly takes
it into his head to disinherit the young girl and to leave his
great fortune to the nearest of kin. The now penniless Emily
should obviously marry Hubert, and she falls in love with
him pathetically; he provides for her and is kind to her, but
prefers her companion, a mature and intellectual woman,
who encourages him in his literary illusions, and the story
moves to its close in Emily's suicide, the news of which
reaches Hubert while he is on his honeymoon with Julia.
" He remembered how he had taken everything from her—
fortune, happiness, and now life itself . . . Then a thought
revealed an unexpected analogy between himself and his
victim. In both lives there had been a supreme desire, and
both had failed . . . He did not think that he would live
long. There were men like him in every profession—the arts

are crowded with them. One hears of their death—failure
of the heart's action, paralysis of the brain, a hundred other
medical causes—but the real cause is lack of appreciation."

While this story of frustration was still appearing in the
Lady's Pictorial, Moore himself enjoyed a little triumph, for
Impressions and Opinions met with considerable appreciation
from all quarters. " My book," he wrote to Madame Lanza,
" has been praised more than any book I have seen reviewed." In spite of the aggressive face which he presented
to the world he was almost humbly grateful for a small share
of justice.

> 29.7.91. *To Mrs. Moore.*
>
> I send you by this post this week's *Athenæum*. It gives
> me the front page and five columns. The honour is
> unexpected and I am afraid undeserved. You probably
> do not know that the front page in the *Athenæum* is only
> given to writers in the very front rank. Praise does not
> elate me but it is a pleasure after having been made for
> years the target of every fool's abuse to find that the
> reaction has come. I did well not to take the advice of
> every silly person. I had something to say and I said it
> regardless of the shrieking of the crowd. I have more to
> say and I shall say it regardless of the praise that may be
> given. The *Athenæum* is as you know the first literary
> journal in the English language and the article on *Impres-
> sions and Opinions* will do me more good than if it had
> appeared in *The Times*. I was particularly touched by the
> last sentence, and it is only natural that I should be, for
> I have had to bear a great deal more than you think.

The sentence ran: " Any critic who recognising Mr.
Moore's talent, and believing that his intellectual short-
comings are due to carelessness, not inability, and will
disappear, anticipates a noteworthy future for him, must
needs wish that he shall put away all that is less worthy of
an eminent career."

The book deserved all the good things that were said of it.
Moore was now at once more cautious in the expression of

his dislikes and more inflamed in the expression of his loves than he afterwards became; and some may miss from *Impressions and Opinions* the wit, the epigrammatic quality and the amusing intolerance of the later critical prose. But the philosophical foundation is more solid than that of *Avowals, Conversations in Ebury Street* and *Pure Poetry*; for Moore was now in the full tide of his reaction against the materialistic theory of art as impersonal documentation, to some of the fallacies of which he again lent an ear in his old age—in *Pure Poetry* for example, where he perverted the principle of art for art's sake in order to establish an impossible case for " objectivity." In *Impressions and Opinions* criticism is regarded as the story of the critic's soul rather than as an exact science, but many admirable general truths are enunciated; this perception for instance of the nature of the poet's creation : " The vulgar do not know that the artist makes but little use of his empirical knowledge of life, and that he relies almost entirely on his inner consciousness of the truth. . . . In the somnambulism of his genius he lived peopling a perfectly imagined world . . . the world is but one's thought."

It would, on the other hand, be a mistake to suppose that at any time Moore rejected Naturalism understood in the larger sense as a typical manifestation of the French spirit, which dates even from the fables of the Middle Ages, and in the nineteenth century embraced such diverse imaginations as Balzac, Flaubert, de Goncourt, Huysmans and even some of the Symbolists, and found its parallel in painting with Manet. " The Naturalism of Flaubert, of the Goncourts, and of Maupassant," M. Edmond Jaloux has recently written, " was, in the thought of those authors, to form a work of art before being an exact document: it is this which gives them their general tendency, and isolates them from a certain contemporary tendency, in which the proletarian novel plays a part, where all idea of *literature* is absent . . . In England we perceive that both the Naturalist and the Symbolist revolutions were effected between 1885 and 1900. . . . The triumph was due in part to George Moore. . . . Arrived in Paris . . . George Moore discovered at once the preface to *Mademoiselle de Maupin* (who was to become a sort of gospel for his young friends of the *Yellow Book* and the *Savoy*), and Zola, *Les Palais Nomades* of Gustave Kahn, and the painting of Manet. Fifty years later when I knew him he could still talk with rapture of the wonder with which Manet's painting filled him; his eyes were still dazzled."

10

With *Vain Fortune* Moore suffered a set-back. He made the mistake of causing Henry & Co. to publish a limited and large-paper edition as well as the ordinary edition—a pretentious gesture which encouraged his enemies to come again into the open: he was rather badly mauled. But although *Vain Fortune* does not show him in the plenitude of his powers, it is not (as has been more than once stated) " the worst of Moore's novels." The scenes of literary life in London are vivid, and the drawing of Emily Watson—the girl who must die before she becomes used to life—has beauty and pathos. The book had a curious history from the first, and Henry & Co. had scarcely published it before Moore went to them and bought back his rights in the book for £100; he wanted to re-write it once more, and the revised version appeared with Scribner in 1892 and with Walter Scott in 1895 as " a totally new story." There were French and Dutch translations, the French by the Rosny brothers in the *Revue Hebdomadaire*, the Dutch by Madame Couperus, who claimed to have accomplished the feat of uniting two of the texts without the alteration of a single comma. Very many years later John Freeman in his *Portrait of George Moore* drew attention to some merits in the book, marvelling that *A Modern Lover* should be preferred by its author. And another of the approvers of *Vain Fortune* has been James Joyce, who in some passages of sententious appraisal of Moore's career (*The Day of the Rabblement*, 1901 : Joyce was then nineteen) singled out the forgotten novel for especial mention. But Moore himself acquired a chronic distaste for *Vain Fortune*, and in his later life would never listen to any protestations on its behalf. Once Mr. Vincent O'Sullivan, having invited him out for the evening, brought him for dinner to the hotel in which (in one of the versions) Emily Watson commits suicide. O'Sullivan thought to pay Moore a compliment in this way, but his guest took the gesture in bad part, and the reminder of *Vain Fortune* was the prelude to a most disastrous evening, during which Moore made O'Sullivan as uncomfortable as possible by speculating in a loud voice on the intimate lives of their neighbours at the *table d'hôte*, a middle-aged gentleman and a very old lady.

With *Vain Fortune* off his hands (more or less) and in an easier financial situation after the success of his essays, Moore was able to devote the greater part of the winter of 1891–2 to his big novel. " All day I have been trying to write a scene," he reported to his mother in December, " and I have not written ten lines. Until I *see* my subject I cannot write." Nevertheless, the early chapters of *Esther Waters* were brought to paper by the end of the year, and he felt pretty sure that at last he was exercising a true vocation—that he was in distant sight of a masterpiece. " There is nothing to do now," he confided to his mother, " but to push the bolts of my door and to bury myself in my work . . . I have worked hard, and am feeling lazy, and Society is insidious, and the temptation is sometimes intolerable. I have half a mind to fly from London and write the book about betting at Moore Hall."

He had now published four successive novels without gaining much credit from any of them; not one of the four was to find a place in his collected works. Five years had passed since the writing of the *Confessions*, and in the whole period he had enjoyed but one advance in his fortunes, *Impressions and Opinions*. If we turn to the account of his literary career on which he was at work during the last months of his life, we find that, except for the mention of *Spring Days* in a footnote, *A Communication to My Friends* contains no reference to any book which he published between the *Confessions* (1888) and *Esther Waters* (1894). Indeed, the story in *A Communication* is so told as almost to give the impression that *Esther Waters* was the immediate successor of the *Confessions* and of *A Drama in Muslin*. At the time he attributed his

adversities to experimentation with his talent, and represented *Esther Waters* as the recovery of a simple human theme
after those various ventures into the exceptional and exotic
which began with *A Mere Accident.* " All experimentation is
over now," he wrote to Madame Lanza, " and henceforth I
shall only sow seeds in the garden that is suitable to my
talent." " Even in the hands of a man of talent," he had
recently said in his essay on Balzac, " the abnormal easily
slips into sterile eccentricity, which is the dreariest form of
commonplace; but let the man of talent choose an ordinary
everyday story, and in developing it any originality of mind
and vision he may possess will appear to its very best
advantage."

In a review of *Impressions and Opinions* Arthur Symons, then
a rising critic, took the occasion to survey Moore's career as a
whole, and his article, which appeared in the *Academy*, is of
some historical interest, for it enables one to form an idea of
the position occupied by Moore at this date in the eyes of
those who shared his standards and ideals, and were combat-
ing with him the English tendency to introduce moral, or
(it would be better to say) practical considerations into
judgments upon art and literature. Symons found that Moore
had produced one masterpiece, *A Mummer's Wife*, and
another book which was " amazingly clever," the *Confessions*. In everything that he wrote, said Symons, there were
signs of a great talent as well as of a tireless industry and a
single-minded devotion to art : even in the worst of his books,
ear and feeling for a phrase were to be detected ; and yet he
had an inexplicable capacity, not only for offences against
literary good taste, but also for astounding incorrectness, the
incorrectness of a man who knows better, who is not careless,
and yet who cannot help himself. " Cannot help himself ! "
Like old Northcote at Oscott when he read the schoolboy's
exercises, Symons scarcely knew what to say.

It is doubtful if Moore " knew better " ; he was learning as
he went along by the method of trial and error ; and one of
the reasons why he had to be at such labour was that he had
never acquired the habit of being careful. Nor was he ever
ready to acknowledge that he would have been spared a

great deal of labour and waste of time if he had been more receptive to formal education and more attentive to his schoolmasters as a boy. In later life, especially, carried away by his own experience, he held that a man is self-taught, and that what he wants to know he can find out for himself. He was very quick at recognising the man whom he thought likeliest to tell him what he wanted to know, and has even given (in the introduction to *Daphnis and Chloë*) an account of such a meeting between master and pupil, he obviously being the pupil. But we are almost made to believe that he is the master ; and it was vain to tell him that however ardent a boy may be to learn the trade of a carpenter, unless a master takes the trouble to see that he holds his chisel or uses his saw rightly, he will waste much time, and perhaps never become a good carpenter.

CHAPTER V

LONDON: A SOCIAL PHASE

I

FOR SOME TIME PAST Moore's art criticism had been attracting attention. He had occasionally written on art matters for *The Hawk* in its early days, and after that he had become a regular critic on the staff of the *Speaker*. His first contribution to that periodical was on the 21st March, 1891 —the subject being an exhibition of the work of Diaz in Bond Street. He had then rather drastically revised an earlier enthusiasm—the title of the article being " A Lesser Light."

Concurrently Mr. D. S. MacColl was art critic for the *Spectator*, and Moore and he together may be said to have conducted the propaganda of the 'nineties for the work of the French Impressionists in England. The critic of the *Spectator* had the advantage of a larger circulation, and Moore himself, though he had the prestige of having been person- ally acquainted with Manet, regarded MacColl as the leader, as did also the " hearties " of the art world, and when a counter-attack was made on the occasion of the exhibition of Degas's " L'Absinthe " at the Grafton Gallery (a series of articles by Spender, in the *Pall Mall Gazette*, and letters from Richmond, Quilter, and others), it was shown that MacColl was held to be the more dangerous man of the two. But Moore in later times was given almost all the credit for the persuasion of English taste in the new direction, perhaps because he reprinted his *Speaker* articles almost at once, whereas his colleague brought out no book until 1902.

As in his youth in Paris, Moore was now once again profoundly interested in painters, whose society he eagerly sought. The Hogarth Club, which Wilson Steer, D. S. MacColl, William Rothenstein and others of the " New English " artists frequented, became one of his favourite resorts; he was always happier among painters than among writers, and the new friendships which he made while he was art critic of the *Speaker* greatly enriched his life. One finds his account of these friendships in the chapters in *Conversations in Ebury Street* : his literary portraits of Steer, Tonks, Sickert, MacColl and L. A. Harrison are as charming as anything in his varied memoirs. With Tonks he was not yet acquainted when he began to write for the *Speaker*, and L. A. Harrison entered the group much later. The friendship with Tonks dated from the winter of 1894–5. " Steer introduced me to him," Tonks writes, " bringing him one evening to my rooms in the King's Road, Chelsea. I had left my old profession of medicine and having been appointed a teacher of drawing by Professor Browne at the Slade School of Art, I regarded myself as a painter. Though at all times the strangest character I had ever met, and utterly unlike anybody else, Moore when I first knew him was most agreeable company, much readier than he afterwards became to listen to the views of others, and always pleased to find a painter who seemed to him to have something to say. The friendship then made lasted until his death, though I am often surprised that it did, as he became in many ways a changed man before he died, largely owing, however, to his bodily sufferings."

It is worthy of mention that while he was writing for the *Speaker*, Moore looked about him for employment in some museum, and at one time actually presented himself for the directorship of the Fine Arts Gallery in Manchester. " It would be fun," he said to his brother, " to have the post." " As well as I remember," Colonel Moore writes to me, " he was rejected on the ground that he was likely to buy too many Manets." That Moore valued his knowledge of painting is beyond doubt, and in later life he frequently complained that he had not been made a Trustee of the National Gallery. One day, this question arising among his friends, Tonks said : " Moore, what would you do there when your acquaintance with the names of painters is so limited,

what for instance do you know of Foppa ? " Tonks chose this
name as the first one that came into his head, and because
it sounds a little comic. Moore thought a minute, and then
said : " You are right. I don't know anything about him, but
I could look him up." " He felt," Tonks writes, " that with
his great love of painting and also with his early training as a
painter he would be much more useful at the Gallery than
most of the Trustees. On the other hand I do not think he
would have been of any use on any Committee, certainly not
in his later life when he seemed incapable of quietly listening
to the opinions of others and waiting till his turn came to
give his opinion. If he disagreed with something said, he
would answer at once and perhaps afterwards sulk, if his
views were not accepted. With all his interest in painting he
never went to Italy, and, as there are Italian painters whom
it is impossible to see at their best anywhere else, he missed a
great opportunity. I think he felt this because he often
talked of going there, the difficulty was with whom was he
to go. I think perhaps, a fairly docile lady who knew the
language and the country would have been best, someone
who would have talked with him in the evenings of love and
of the pictures they had seen during the day. But it would
have been difficult for anyone as the little I have seen of him
going anywhere even by omnibus makes me think of him as
always in a muddle on those occasions. Such a small matter
as settling which was his portmanteau at the end of a train
journey would lead to confusion."

2

The contributions to the *Speaker* were very interesting,
written in a free and easy manner, and almost always from
the heart. They showed how sincere was Moore's love of
painting. A friend told Tonks that he traced all the interest which he had in pictures to coming by chance on what
Moore had to say of them in *Modern Painting*, the selection
from the *Speaker* articles which was published in 1893.

Successful criticism could not however satisfy Moore, and

Esther Waters remained his principal, his great pre-occupation. " I wish you were oftener in London," he said to his brother Maurice, who had now returned from India, a Major in the Connaught Rangers, " I never see you and you are what is best worth seeing. There was never anyone like you, except Margaret Veley, and she is dead. . . ." But he would not join a family reunion at Moore Hall, nor would he allow Augustus Moore to be invited there after the " shocking manner " in which the *Hawk* had written on the subject of the Independent Theatre. " Do you go to Moore Hall," he wrote to his soldier brother, on the 28th of June, 1892 ; " so long as the place is mine it is yours in every respect. It is quite impossible for me to come. . . . I am trying as hard as I can to get on with my work which is coming on very well. If the book comes out right my position will be secure. . . . The moment I finish it I will see you in Ireland or anywhere else you like."

Later in the year he read *Anna Karenina,* which he described as " the greatest novel ever written." In September he spoke of a projected Mediterranean cruise in a yacht belonging to some rich friends, whose name he did not divulge. " Say nothing about the yacht," he begged his brother. It does not appear that he went on the cruise, but in the last months of 1892 his attention was diverted from his novel by his being offered an opportunity of realising a long cherished ambition to appear before the world as a dramatic author. G. R. Sims, a doughty champion of the popular drama, who considered that the production of Ibsen and other foreign masters was of no advantage to the English stage, offered a hundred pounds to the Independent Theatre if the directors dared to produce a play by Moore " written all by himself." The Independent Theatre was impoverished and the proposal came as a godsend. " I like an adventure," said Moore, " and I'll never again find a man who is willing to pay a hundred pounds for a play by me." He took *The Strike at Arlingford* from the drawer where it had lain since it had been rejected by Beerbohm Tree and other managers, and with surprising speed he reduced the five acts to three and had the play ready for rehearsal by the beginning of 1893. It was presented on the 21st of February at the long since vanished Opera Comique in the Strand.

G. R. Sims sat in the box for which he had paid a hundred pounds. In the front row of the stalls, no doubt hoping for the worst, were the leading dramatic authors who had been pilloried in *Impressions and Opinions* for their " illiterate puerilities." Behind them were the critics, headed by Clement Scott. They too were disposed to hostility, for Moore had just delivered a damaging attack on English dramatic criticism in the *Pall Mall Gazette*. Moore was so nervous that he stayed away from the theatre. " Everything was against me," he wrote to his brother after the performance, " and it was not a failure. Sims bet a hundred—it was not to be conventional, it was not to be this, not to be that; I was writing it, I was not writing it, etc. etc. A real success under such circumstances was impossible. *Macbeth* and *Hamlet* would not suffice to satisfy such anticipations. Worst of all I could not get proper actors. It is being translated into French, and if it is a success in France my enemies will have a bad time of it. By God, I will rub it in."

William Archer praised the play in the *World*. He found more flesh and blood in it than in Bernard Shaw's *Widowers' Houses* and made fun of the Fabians who were shocked by Moore's failure to distinguish between Trades Unionism and Socialism. An old friend, Arthur Kennedy, had helped in *The Strike at Arlingford*, for Moore felt that though he could write a scene in a novel he could not write a scene in a play and, as we shall see, nearly all his later dramatic experiments were collaborations. On one occasion, at about this time, he called upon Henry Arthur Jones—an author of whom, exceptionally, he had spoken favourably in *Impressions and Opinions*—for advice upon a scenario which he had in mind. Jones refused outright to render him any assistance. " I would not think for a moment of collaborating with Moore," he said. It was not that Moore was ignorant of stagecraft, but he was very stubborn in holding to the opinion that a play which read well must also act well. He would not admit that an actor's point of view had any importance.

3

Walter Scott, a new publisher, who had purchased Vizetelly's copyrights, brought out *The Strike at Arlingford* together
with new editions of *A Mummer's Wife* and *A Drama in
Muslin*. There was a request from George Alexander for a
play, and an offer reached Moore for the serial rights of
Esther Waters. His days were very busy, especially as he was
now adapting himself for a more social life than the one
which hitherto he had led in London. Edmund Gosse was an
old acquaintance of whom he was making a friend; he began
going to the critic's Sunday supper parties, where he met
many notabilities.

3.7.93.   *To Edmund Gosse.*

I talked too much and am full of repentance. I must
have bored you, tired you if I did not bore you more or
less. I hope it was less. I send you two books. *A.M.W.*
[*A Mummer's Wife*] is I suppose the best thing I have done.
It was liked very much in France and by the best people—
Zola, Coppee, Banville. It is therefore probable that you
will like it more or less. My Racenian drama [*sic*] is what I
like. I do not know that anyone else likes it, I am afraid
they do not, but I do, I can't help myself. . . . I should
like to know what you think.

Modern Painting proved to be a success. The press as a
whole received the book with applause, and a thousand
copies were sold in the summer of 1893. " I have a review of
your book in type by the greatest writer in the world," said
the editor of the *Daily Chronicle*, stopping Moore one day in
the street. Moore asked: " Whom do you think the greatest
writer in the world ? " " Not whom I think but whom you
think," Sir Henry Norman replied, " but one of these days
you will see the name in the paper, and you will agree with
me that the writer of the article is the greatest writer in the
world." The notice—it was Pater's of course—gave Moore
much to think on. The article was good, it delighted him,

like everything that Pater wrote, but he could not help feeling that it did not compare favourably with the short articles that Pater contributed to the *Guardian*. He felt a little ashamed of himself for not admiring the article more than he did, and began to think that the source of it lay in Pater's desire to acknowledge that he had written, as he put it, very pleasantly about himself. But Pater's mind did not move in such mediocre honesty, and another reason, and a more pleasant one, rose up in his mind. Pater knew that he was disappointed at not receiving as much of his personal affection as he had wished for, and wrote this article as a way of recompense for what was his due.[1]

For a while longer Moore continued to contribute more or less regular art criticism to the Press. His last article in the *Speaker* appeared on the 29th June, 1895, and was an appreciation of Mark Fisher. *Modern Painting* was never revised, nor did Moore allow the book to appear in the collected edition of his works although he came near doing so. It was too topical in parts, too much of a tract for the times. These extracts from two of his letters to MacColl written in 1893, suggest that he valued the book largely as a contribution to a cause.

I did not send you my book because I knew you could get it from the *Spectator*. I shall be much obliged if you will write something about it either in that paper or elsewhere. I believe that Harris would take a short article from you on the subject. Nothing, however, would be better than an article in the *Spectator*.

Your review of my book is of great importance; the *Spectator* is the very best paper for it to appear in. So I will venture to beg you to do it at your very earliest convenience. Every copy of the book sold means the propagation of our ideal. You do not write nearly often enough in the *Spectator*. A good deal has been done and a great deal more could be done by writing. I have begged of Sickert to write, but he will not. . . .

[1] *Avowals.*

GEORGE MOORE
From the painting by Richard Sickert

MacColl's notice in the *Spectator*[1] was a full page. It praised Moore's inveigling descriptions of pictures and the warmth of his convictions, but threw some doubt on his logic, and also reproached him for appearing to carry the argument for nationality in art to extremes. In *Impressions and Opinions* Moore had attacked the French system of artistic education, the Beaux Arts and the studios of Jullian, and he now spoke of the fall of art in France, comparing the New English Art Club to a seed blown over from a French garden catching root in English soil, with English colour and fragrance already in the flower. But it was one thing to warn English aspirants against the academies of Paris, and another thing, as MacColl observed, to convey the impression that the young painter should cut himself off from all methods of seeing and rendering developed in other countries than his own.

One could extract sentences from *Modern Painting* and find that Moore repeated them almost word for word when six years later he determined to aid in the revival of a Celtic language and to seek inspiration in a return to his native country after long exile.

4

In 1893 he was already meditating upon the application to his own case of the doctrine of nationality in art. How explain his repulsion to Ireland, and the fact that in *Esther Waters* he was writing the most English of all novels ? " I hate Ireland," he wrote to his brother who had inherited much of their father's patriotism, " and I have no wish to hear anything about Ireland." But he began to take an interest in the history of his family because it seemed to him that this history might account for *Esther Waters*. The Moores, he remembered, were comparative newcomers in Ireland, and it seemed to him that he might trace his love of England to " atavism." He confided his bewilderment to his brother: " I doubt if the upper classes in Ireland are Celt." All the same he seems to have been conscious that

[1] 18th November, 1893.

he was not an Englishman, for he spoke of the love of England that he was " pouring into *Esther Waters* " as " monstrous and preposterous." " How I love that dull-witted race ! " In a letter to his brother, after describing the " servant girl "—" one more effort, the most serious I have yet made to do a book, you know what I mean, a real piece of literature "—he foreshadowed a project of depicting the Saxon in his " habit of instinctive hypocrisy."

31.7.93.

. . . Pecksniff done seriously, and if the feat does not seem impossible, with love. This extraordinary civilisation—the Bible in one hand, the gin bottle in the other, the cotton factory behind him, starting from the cricket field. A great project but one of enormous difficulty—I am afraid unrealisable, but dear me, is it not shocking that I can't write to tell you that I long to see you without the spectre of literature growling and barking all the while ?

Nothing in *Esther Waters*, he said, pleased him more than the account of the Derby, " 30 or 40 pages : no racing, only the sweat and boom of the crowd—the great Cockney holiday."

He continued to dwell upon his ancestry, a curiosity which he afterwards turned to excellent literary account. His brother was patient with him and informative, and it is unlikely that, without his brother's sympathy, he would ever have undertaken those voyages to the past which give so much enchantment to his later books. A cousin, Martin J. Blake, now sent him from New Zealand the pedigree of the Moores which purports to show the descent of the family from Sir Thomas More. This pleased him and he put more questions to Maurice. His brother reminded him that family piety should prompt them to seek a publisher for their grandfather's *History of the French Revolution*. It was not possible to find the £500 which the old scholar had left for the expenses of an edition, but Moore offered the book for Heinemann's consideration, without much enthusiasm, for a more tempting subject, he remarked to his brother, would be a history of their family. The rise and fall of a family was as interesting as the rise and fall of a nation; why should they not trace it in collaboration ? The narrative should be brought up to date, so as to include the living, in whom he found an exasperating echo of his own strangeness.

By August 1893 the end of *Esther Waters* was in sight. The last chapters were being written and Moore looked forward to publishing his book in the spring. In a letter to his brother he described the nightmares which afflicted him: he was over-worked, but hopeful. " As you say fame has preceded fortune . . . but I think I have written a novel which will take the wind out of every sail in the offing and out of it. The impression of my work that my last letter seems to have conveyed is somewhat grandiose. It reminds me more of a book I am minded to write than of the book I have written. One of my dreams is to write the book you describe—the serious side of Pecksniff. The book I have written is the story of the fight of a servant girl for her child's life. *Esther Waters* is Alice Barton in another form. . . . I have written 29 chapters; there are 32."

A few days later, at the beginning of September, he took a short holiday in France, reporting a love-adventure upon his return. Which one ? the reader of *Memoirs of My Dead Life* will ask. It could not be the corn-coloured 18-year-old girl of Baltimore from the chapter entitled " Bring in the Lamp," because the hero of this story of a tryst at Vincennes is not a man of forty but a youth. But Moore often ran things together in his autobiographical recitals, setting his scene backwards or forwards in time without respect for the facts, moving events of his love life from their real into a fictitious place, as the need of the literary design and perhaps prudence might dictate. His brother can throw no light upon the adventure ; indeed he was so accustomed to recitals of this kind that he listened to them no more than to the ticking of a clock.

21.9.93. *To Maurice Moore.*

I had a most delicious love-adventure—generally my loves are mature but this is a young girl of 18. I think the

most beautiful girl I ever saw in my life. Beauty generally
doesn't fetch me but this one did. What she could see in
me to rave about I cannot think—a *blasé roué* like me,
rotten with literature and art to which Wagnerism has
lately been added. Wagner's operas are now my great
delight and relaxation. I daresay I do not understand but
what does that matter? I regard music as other men
regard a game of billiards. My golden-haired siren is an
heiress, she wanted me to marry her but I said that would
be dishonourable, that I never went after women for their
money. Only five days, but when the lady is amorous,
and the aunt complacent or witless a great deal can be
done. *J'ai revé dans le grotte où nage la sirène.* That women
may lose their virtue certainly makes life worth living.
Forgive this light chatter. . . .

Zola visited London in September, and Moore offered
him the hospitality of his rooms in the Temple. Zola's
arrangements were already made, and he could not come to
Moore, who however met his old master at a big dinner at
the Authors' Club on the twenty-eighth of the month. The
chairman, Sir Walter Besant, spoke of the Naturalist chief
as a conqueror: " He has passed *par la terre* as a conqueror
and London will soon lie at his feet." Zola's visit was a great
success. He was honoured in the most unexpected places,
and Moore pursued his reflections upon the charming illogi-
cality of the English nation and his own " sneaking regard "
for Pecksniff. They had prosecuted Vizetelly for publishing a
pornographer and now trumpets were being blown in the
pornographer's honour at the Mansion House, and rockets
were let off at the Crystal Palace. " The idea of conquest
seems inherent in Zola," he now wrote. " Five-and-twenty
years ago he wrote a book called *La Conquête de Plassaus*. The
idea of conquest cropped up again in *L'Œuvre* and this time
it was Paris that was conquered. And now it seems that Zola
meditates the conquest of the world. . . . The newspapers
reported that Madame Zola, astonished at the length of the
London suburbs, said: ' This is a town that should suit you,
Emile.' "

" Impressions of Zola," afterwards revised and rewritten as " A Visit to Médan," a brilliant and mocking piece of work, appeared in January 1894 in the *English Illustrated Magazine*. It was decorated with photographs of the hideous chambers of the great villa at Médan, characteristic of Zola's pretensions to æstheticism. " I have been asked to write an intimate and personal article about my friend Emile Zola," Moore began; and he went on to describe the first encounter at the *bal de l'Assommoir*, the first visit to Médan " a few weeks later," and then the last visit there when the preface for *La Femme d'un Cabotin* was refused. He himself had once entertained the so un-English idea of conquest (Balzacian, by the way, in its origin rather than Zolaesque), and of the author as the modern Alexander, and the sardonic turn in the middle of his paper was characteristic—Zola must be made ridiculous because he reminds Moore of things in his own past which he now hates.

5

In any notice of Moore during these years it is impossible to escape from speaking of Mrs. Pearl Craigie, the novelist. He used to give a characteristic account of how he came to make her acquaintance. She wrote to ask him if he thought that one of her stories could be dramatised, and signed her letter John Oliver Hobbes, supposing that everyone knew that this was her *nom de plume*. Moore left the letter unanswered until Arthur Symons told him that John Oliver Hobbes was not the name of a man but of the daughter of a rich American patent medicine manufacturer, a very beautiful woman, clever, fashionable and musical. Moore then called upon her at once, and the acquaintance rapidly ripened into love on his side at least. They were continually together throughout this winter. They made excursions to the country and began to collaborate in plays, one of which, *The Fool's Hour*, was published, in April 1894, in the first number of the *Yellow Book*. She was perhaps the first woman of the world who had paid Moore serious attention and he seems to have lost his head and his foothold in the affair altogether. He talked much too much about Mrs. Craigie, often to the most undesirable kind of people, and the fact that she was seeking a release from an unhappy marriage in the divorce court made matters considerably worse. The baronet in *Sister Teresa* used to explain that if he talked of a woman publicly the reason was that he loved her. Moore too thought it excuse enough, and so did many Frenchmen of his time, Barbey d'Aurevilly for example. But Mrs. Craigie, though answering to the Victorian description of a " gentleman's beauty," was a woman of strict principles who also valued her social position; and the ensuing gossip hurt her gravely. Her letters, though carefully edited by her father, who wished to present her as a woman of fashion moving unblemished in the most aristocratic circles, nevertheless reveal about this time a sense of despair and of frustration, and of what she calls in one of her books the cruelty of people to one another.

Mrs. Craigie certainly influenced Moore in various ways, good and bad. She furbished him up, and perhaps she started him on his career as the fashionable author who followed *Esther Waters* with a novel of music and flamboyant high life. A man of forty, he started to learn the piano. "You can't know anything about music," he declared, " unless you've done a little counterpoint yourself." After he had passed through Mrs. Craigie's hands he was hardly likely to write another *Mummer's Wife*. But he soon became critical of her world, and ruthlessly analysed one of her works to Vincent O'Sullivan. To his friend's objections he replied: " My dear fellow, you don't seem to realise that I have collaborated with her. Now when a man has collaborated with a woman it is the same as if he had slept with her. She has no secrets left to reveal."

"Duchesses," he used to say, while he was writing *Esther Waters*, " duchesses ! Everyone writes about duchesses. My book is about a servant girl. There is nothing pretty or namby pamby about her." " Then you don't like Bourget ? " said Mr. Vincent O'Sullivan, who was the recipient of this confidence. "Bourget is a shit," Moore replied, dropping into the Swiftian scatology which so horrified Oscar Wilde during the short periods when he was on speaking terms with him. He was never encaged by a lion hunter or taken about as a show, but he developed a liking for the world of fashion and for country houses. Sir William Eden, then famous as an arbiter of elegance, sportsman, and amateur of art, fascinated him by his magnificent eccentricities, and a meeting with Miss Maud Burke, afterwards Lady Cunard, for whom he conceived a romantic affection which lasted all his life, caused his movement into Mayfair to gather momentum. Eden refused to read Moore's novels, but he had a great respect for Moore's opinions on art; and Moore praised Eden's water-colours. The story (1893-4) of Whistler's portrait of Lady Eden has been told so often that it would be useless to repeat it here. In Whistler's phrase Moore figured as " hind, henchman, expert and go between," in the famous " Baronet and Butterfly " case. It is sufficient to say that Moore's support of Eden's reasonable contentions caused the natural antipathy which had always existed between him and the painter to develop into deadly enmity. Whistler challenged Moore to a duel, and Moore replied that he could not fight a duel as they were not allowed in England and he was always seasick when he crossed the Channel.

At this time also Moore astonished his older friends by becoming a member of Boodles, the High Tory and aristocratic club in St. James's Street, no doubt at Sir William Eden's instance. Considering the raillery to which he had subjected the English club habit in *Confessions of a Young Man*, it seemed like a surrender on his part; but although he used the club a good deal, and was even proud of being a member, he looked like a rather distinguished fish out of water, and gave the impression that he would have been very much happier sitting in a café with a nice unpretentious girl by his side and the manuscript of the work on hand on the table. He used to scandalise the other members by taking his manuscripts to the club tied up in a parcel and by disputing small items of his bill as though he had been in a swindling restaurant. One evening he was seen to refuse the

offer of a servant to stamp his letters. The occupant of the
next chair raised his eyebrows slightly, and Moore said con-
fidingly: " I always like to stamp my letters myself, don't
you ? " " No." was the reply, " I give them to the porter."
" Then you don't know what you've paid." When after a
few years he resigned his membership he explained that he
had been driven from the club by a member who insisted on
accosting him with the question: " What are you going to
do with your two year olds ? "

Moore had a fancy for toffs, and sometimes thought that
he would like to be a toff himself. But he was not really very
keen, and never took the trouble to get it right; sometimes
he would stop playing altogether, as when he cheerfully
admitted to Sir William Eden that he preferred rabbit
shooting to deer stalking, an admission, he said, which
made his presence unendurable to the baronet for a while.
Those who met him in his rooms in the Temple still received
the impression of a poor man. Ordinarily he dressed negli-
gently, and it is said that up to the time of his success with
Esther Waters, he still wore paper collars. " In the first year
I knew him," Vincent O'Sullivan writes, " I tried to interest
a New York manager in his play, *The Strike at Arlingford*. The
negotiations were not successful; but Moore was pleased with
the quite disinterested efforts I made to sell the play and his
attitude towards the financial aspects of the negotiations
convinced me that if not hard up he was in need of money.
When London hostesses took him in hand, he made an
effort to improve his clothes, but in a way that still suggested
the struggling author. I remember that once in Paris, after
he had been narrating a conquest, I said to him : ' All that
must cost you a great deal.' ' Not at all,' he replied, ' I
never waste money on women beyond a bunch of flowers,
a dinner, trifles like that.' "

He was at bottom a man of great simplicity, to whom the
pleasant commonplaces of life were a source of never-failing
interest. The event of the day for him was the discovery of
a phrase or the germ of a story—some little invention.
Someone once told him that Zola was so bored on his con-
stitutionals that he was obliged to count up figures in his

head or estimate the distances between the lamp-posts. It surprised him. " I am never like that," he said; and on solitary walks he was always thinking about something in particular, or watching for an incident that would excite his inward comment and set him speculating or telling himself a story.

6

Esther Waters was ready by the late autumn of 1893, but Moore rewrote the second half of it upon the proofs. In the meantime the *Yellow Book* was founded, and it showed, as Mr. Osbert Burdett has said in his essay on the Beardsley Period, that the author of the *Confessions of a Young Man* had been a true precursor, having formulated much of the æsthetic ideal of this significant periodical. D. S. MacColl had suggested the foundation of a magazine which should give young writers and young artists a chance. In February 1894 a dinner was given to the American humorist, Bill Nye, at which Beardsley, Harland and John Lane were present. After dinner they adjourned to the Hogarth Club, where they were joined by Frank Harris and Moore. Lane was urged to bring out the periodical and finally consented on the condition that Harland and Beardsley would act as editors.[1]

Esther Waters appeared in March and was dedicated to Maurice Moore who received a charming letter from the author a few days before the publication by Walter Scott. Many other titles for the masterpiece had been considered, among them " Travellers' Rest " and " Mother and Child." " Esther Waters " was an afterthought due to a chance conversation with a working woman in the Temple who bore the perfect name. Moore hoped for a popular success; he told his brother that the most he had yet made out of literature was six hundred a year—" and I daresay Augustus makes as much."

[1] Mr. Alfred Thornton in contributions to *The Artist* (April and May 1935) has told the story of the foundation of the *Yellow Book*.

My dear Maurice,   9th March, 1894.

I am glad to be his godfather. I see you are full of your
little son. I have always heard married men say there is no
happiness like children. All the love I have for giving I
give to you my dear Maurice, and my regret is that we
seem condemned to live our lives apart. There is no one
like you—no one so loyal, so good. I do not know what
you mean when you speak of your heaviness of mind. I
know no one so clever, your mind is not heavy. It is your
modesty that makes you see yourself in a false light. It is
you not I who have the family brains—I always say so as I
daresay mother has told you. You have not taken the
trouble to acquire the scribbling habit and that is little or
nothing. Fifty years will wipe out all that I have
written. The best thing I have done is certainly *Esther
Waters*. I always intended to dedicate the book to you
if it came out well. I think it has. You will receive it
next week. I should like to write a longer letter but if I
add another line I shall miss the post.

Affectionately
George Moore.

The admirable novel, so full of humanity and affection,
met, on the whole, with an excellent reception; and few
doubted thereafter that Moore was endowed with an original
power and individual genius above those of any other contemporary English realist. It was commended by Lionel
Johnson and by Hubert Crackenthorpe, one of the cleverest
of the young *Yellow Book* writers. Lionel Johnson, who
ordinarily did not like modern French influences, wrote in
the *Daily Chronicle*: "The synthesis—to use a dreadful word—
the synthesis of the book is perfect." Moore was particularly
gratified by " Q's " appreciation in the *Spectator*, for " Q "
set *Esther Waters* above Hardy's *Tess*, declaring that it was
" the best book of its kind in the English language," and
then wrote privately to say that this was an insufficient
appreciation. Moore read *Tess* while he was writing *Esther*

Waters, and the scene where Angel carries Tess over the plain merely increased the distaste for Hardy which he had already shown in the *Confessions*. That the two books should have been compared is strange, one being primarily the statement of a metaphysical grievance, the other a human document. There were dissentients, a curious alliance represented by Captain Ames, the tallest guardsman in the Army, David Christie Murray, the Victorian novelist, and John Corlett, the editor of the *Sporting Times*. Ames said that he was not interested in reading about servants. Murray, who bracketed Moore and Hardy together as coming under the same baleful influence of France, denied that *Esther Waters* showed any gift of observation.[1] Corlett denounced George Moore as a Puritan killjoy, the degenerate son of a noble father who had owned many racehorses— Croaghpatrick, Corunna, Wolfdog, and the rest. " The best way to answer my enemies," Moore wrote to his brother, " is by publishing a masterpiece, and as I have many enemies the effect of *Esther Waters* is rather amusing to watch."

On the 21st of March Moore was " too unhappy to write," he said in a brief note to his brother. The cause was not literature, and it may have been dissatisfaction with the progress of his courtship of Mrs. Craigie. In May when this lady was about to set forth for the Viceregal Lodge, Dublin, Moore wrote to his brother, then stationed at Boyle, Co. Roscommon, saying that he would like to pay him a visit there if Mrs. Craigie were also invited; he wanted to show her Moore Hall, and " you know how I hate travelling alone." He " supposed " Boyle was a town and that there would be a hotel where Mrs. Craigie's maid could lodge. Nothing came out of the project, and it is likely—exact dates are lacking—that it was now that the break with Mrs. Craigie occurred. She suddenly said to Moore while walking in the woods with him that she did not wish to see him again.

He complained very bitterly : " Why have I suddenly and without a cause had the door slammed and bolted against

[1] *My Contemporaries in Fiction.*

me ? What have I done ? How have I offended ? " Sir
William Geary suggested that the authoress was a frequent
guest of the judge of the Divorce Court, wherein she was a
petitioner, and that it may have been hinted to her that she
had better be off with the old love before she was on with
the new. " True," Moore said, " I could have understood
such a temporary separation, but I should have been told
the reason. And I was turned off without a word." " He was
pitiably moved; it was the only time," Sir William Geary
records, " that I ever saw him so affected. I went away from
England then for over a year and when I returned I asked
him if he had ever found out why he was dismissed so harshly,
so rudely, so unmercifully. He replied that when a woman
falls in love every previous thought or promise or obligation
dissolves like a burnt thread, and that he had been driven
out by a handsome worldling."

The tale is an old one; all are dead now, though doubtless
some may remember what was interesting forty years ago.
" Moore was not handsome," Sir William Geary writes.
" He had not graceful manners. He was born a gentleman
but had not that polish and charm which germinates in the
fertile soil of Eton and Oxford. There came upon the lady
a young politician who possessed and displayed all that
Moore had not. He had the fine flavour of an ancient race
and honours at Oxford, he was cultivated in Greek and
Latin and educated by travels in the East. He was born in
the purple, in Parliament and an eloquent speaker, associating with the best in the land, handsome and distinguished.
So Moore was outclassed and jilted, the lady drove out Moore
in favour of his more brilliant supplanter."

In truth, Moore gave many accounts of the affair, not
only in his conversations at the time and later, but also in
the story " Mildred Lawson " in *Celibates* which was published in 1895, in " Lui et Elles " (*Memoirs of My Dead Life*,
1921 edition only) and in " Henrietta Marr," his mature
rendering of " Mildred Lawson," which was published in
1922 in the volume called *In Single Strictness*. In all these
accounts a successful politician, suggested by his rival Lord
Curzon, figured. And it was certainly said at the time that

the gossip which mixed up her name with Moore's interfered with Lord Curzon's intention to marry Mrs. Craigie, and if that was so her momentary infatuation for Moore did her the harm which she must have felt most, for she was socially very ambitious. In April 1895 Lord Curzon married Miss Leiter, and Mrs. Craigie was their guest in India when he was Viceroy. But the disappointment of her higher hopes did nothing to mitigate Moore's anger, and she now became " the only disagreeable woman I ever knew " : a cold-hearted woman, he said, who led him on just to satisfy her vanity, as Mildred Lawson did with Morton in the story. Perhaps she might have married him if he had behaved more wisely. He certainly gave many of his friends the impression that in this case he might have been ready to waive his objections to marriage. " I was desperately in love," he said to Mr. Barrett Clark in 1922 ; " I'd like to deny it, but I cannot."

As the sequel will show, Moore's anger and sense of humiliation did not prevent him from seeing Mrs. Craigie again when the occasion presented itself. Looking backwards in old age, however, he expressed a wish that his biographer should present this affair as an experience merely preparatory to a real and lasting devotion. During his social phase Moore talked very freely of many well-known women, no doubt sometimes building up a whole love episode on trifles—a smile, a pressure of the hand, such as women give not to the man but to the celebrity who can be of use to them in one way or another. But whatever the basis may have been on which he constructed his indiscretions, the ladies concerned sometimes retaliated and left their gallant high and dry. Vincent O'Sullivan tells a typical story of Moore and a lady in the nineties who, not being content with riches, must be a novelist as well. Upon the publication of one of her novels Moore, who seldom reviewed books and professed a total indifference to contemporary English literature apart from Walter Pater, did, upon some impulse, write in one of the weekly reviews either an article or a letter dealing with this lady's novel. In its course he said : " When Mrs. . . . used to show me her productions I invariably implored her to open her dictionary. ' The dictionary, dear Madam, the dictionary.' " A few days after the notice was published O'Sullivan saw Moore who confided to him his anxieties. " A woman," said Moore, " who has been one's mistress is capable of saying anything at all when she is angry." " Perhaps she is not angry," said O'Sullivan. " If you have the slightest notion," replied Moore, " of what a woman is who has been one's mistress and is abandoned, you would not speak like that." Saturday came, and O'Sullivan opened his paper with some curiosity. There was a short letter from the novelist. She kept to the technical questions in dispute, but just at the end added a line: " My acquaintance with Mr. Moore is very slight and, such as it was, it came to an end some time ago."

" She is coming now," he would say to his male visitors, " she will be here soon. If she found I was not alone you know what it would be." Once or twice he was caught out. One evening he went to the theatre with Blanche and they planned to have supper together afterwards, but during the performance Moore announced that he was going home with the leading lady, a fat, middle-aged demi-mondaine— " My God, Blanche, isn't she beautiful? "—and at the end of the play he walked off to the rear of the theatre, deaf to his companion's protests. Blanche followed him at a little distance, saw him stand a minute or two at the stage entrance and then make off alone towards his hotel. " My God, she was wonderful, *wonderful*," he said to Blanche next day. In other matters he gave the impression that he was an exceedingly truthful man—indeed that he had the dangerous form of truth-telling which some casuists have held to be worse than an economy of the truth—but it is certain that he did deliberately mystify people, partly for the fun of the thing and partly because there went with his overwhelming desire to reveal his inmost self a considerable suspiciousness of others. We may legitimately conjecture that there is autobiographical colour in " the deep discomfort " which Ulick in Moore's fourteenth-century story *Ulick and Soracha* feels at the thought that Tadgh may have found out a great deal about him. Returning from France to seek out Soracha he asks himself if he will be able to keep his secret from his servant. " An obscure clandestine little fellow, who never questions a messenger or is tempted to look into a letter left lying about, but who comes all the same into knowledge of every kiss given, and the name of every new acquaintance no later than twelve hours after I have learned it myself. Even into my mind he seems to peer and so readily that I am afraid to think in his presence. But this time I shall outwit him . . ."

7

After the publication of *Esther Waters* Moore had for a while no ambitious work on hand. He tried to make something new out of *Vain Fortune* and he rewrote *A Mere Accident* for inclusion in a volume of short stories to be called *Celibates*, which he was now building up. He continued to work very hard, like an American business man, driven on by stern will power, and was often sitting at his desk until past midnight. He would then feel that he must have conversation and would go out to seek it with Edward Martyn who still had rooms in Pump Court. One night Martyn, who had just come back from Ireland, spoke of the Gaelic League[1] and of his dear wish to write plays in Irish. Moore was in a receptive mood—" A new language to enwomb new thought "; and he could not sleep that night for thinking of the great novel that he might have written if he had followed a child's impulse (the memory of it floated up like a wraith from Lough Carra) to learn Irish from the boatmen at Moore Hall. But London was to hold him for a long time yet.

Notwithstanding his popular success he was still dissatisfied with his literary position. Mudie had accepted the book, but on account of the scene in the lying-in hospital Smith's reader had raised objections, and the thought of the opposition was gall and wormwood to Moore. He described his renewed wrangle with the library in what may have

[1] The Gaelic League was founded in 1893.

been his last letter to his mother, now an old lady and ailing:
" Thank you, dear mother, for your letter. It is full of the
sweetest kindness and affection. How good you are . . . I
cannot say as much for myself. I feel my own selfishness very
acutely. But there are excuses. You know that the public is
opposed to me, and how Smith has encouraged the ignorant.
. . . When this new book *Celibates* is finished, it is now being
finished, I hope to visit Ireland. I want to see you and
Maurice and Nina."

Mrs. Moore died at Moore Hall on 25th May, 1895.

My mother died certainly on the most beautiful day I
had ever seen, the most winsome, the most white, the most
wanton, as full of love as a girl in a lane who stops to
gather a spray of hawthorn. How many times, like many
another, did I wonder why death should have come to
anyone on such a bridal-like day. . . . The day moved
slowly from afternoon to evening like a bride hidden
within a white veil, her hands and her veil filled with white
blossom; but a blackbird, tiny, like a humming-bird, had
perched upon a bunch of blossom, and I seemed to lose
sight of the day in the sinister black speck that had in-
truded itself upon it. No doubt I could think of something
better were I to get my mind upon doing so, but that is
how I thought the day I walked on the lawn with my
brothers, ashamed and yet compelled to talk of what our
lives had been during the years which separated us.

So several years later he wrote in " Resurgam,"[1] where
also he dwelt upon an unhappy love affair which made it
difficult for him to mourn for his mother as he might have
done in normal circumstances, because " a man cannot
lament two women at the same time, and only a month ago
the most beautiful thing that had ever appeared in my life,
an idea which I knew from the first I was destined to follow,
appeared to me—a love in which all the partial loves of my
youth seemed to find expression." But his relation with his

[1] *Memoirs of My Dead Life* (1906).

mother had been on the whole a happy, even a charming
one, and he felt the loss. She, his contrary in every opinion
and sentiment, never quarrelled with him, her Catholic
piety was as sweet natured and unintellectual as the evan-
gelicism of Mrs. Barfield in *Esther Waters*; it did not seem to
occur to her son to engage her in the arguments with which
he generally tackled the conventional. It had been under
considerable pressure from Maurice Moore that he had left
London, and in " Resurgam " he confessed to his terror
lest he should arrive in time to see his mother die. The
funeral pomp, the shroud and the Irish wailing repelled
him, and all that he wrote to his brother after returning to
London shows that his sensitive mind continued to harp
upon obsequies and the particulars of death. " Remember,"
he wrote to his brother, " I have but one wish—to be
cremated and my ashes scattered, Hampstead for choice."
By the time that he wrote " Resurgam " the simple instruction to his executors for his escape from " the horrible
vault " at Kiltoome had been elaborated into an imagination of a great funeral pyre on Castle Island, Lough
Carra.

He took the occasion, while he was in Ireland, to break,
with Tom Ruttledge's knowledge, the settlement of the property and to leave himself full owner. This was not concealed
from Maurice Moore who later on asked Ruttledge why he
had advised it. Ruttledge replied that it was usual enough. " I
attached little importance to the action at the time," Colonel
Moore writes to me, " but our uncle Llewelyn Blake did the
same thing many years later, and in discussion with George I
then said that anyone had a right to do what he liked with
money made by himself but that money made by his
forefathers should remain in the family. G. did not say
much."

The whole property had originally been settled upon
Maurice Moore as second son, failing children by George. If
George Henry Moore had not died before his eldest son came
of age, George would have been pressed to renew the settlement at twenty-one, but as the settlement had not then been
renewed it could now be broken. Whatever the motive of the

step it indicated no cooling of brotherly affection. Moore remained on the best of terms with Maurice and was in constant communication with him during the months which followed their mother's death. It was also his desire to assure the material future of his sister and of Julian his youngest brother, and he gave help to Mrs. Kilkelly in the education of her children.

29.7.95. *To Maurice Moore.*

I got a letter from Gerald Balfour. He says he will give every consideration to your candidature . . . Mrs. Asquith and I hit it off fairly well. I think she would like to oblige me. If the Liberal Government had remained in I was sure I could have managed it. I intended to cultivate this society and perhaps will be able to help you to a still better appointment when the Liberals come in. . . . You are the one person I really care for . . . I am greatly distressed that the sorrows of life weigh upon you . . .

There was one point at least upon which he agreed with Dr. Johnson and with received opinion; all his letters home stressed the importance of living within one's income, and the folly, indeed " the outrageous wickedness," of touching capital, and he held up his hands in horror when he was told that his sister proposed to make an investment in gold mines instead of in the Funds. Moore Hall was left empty. Maurice Moore was stationed not far off at Boyle, and he could keep an eye on the place, but Julian Moore came to London and George introduced him to some editors. He published an article in the *Fortnightly* on " Book Collecting as a Fine Art," which, said his eldest brother, " reveals a gracious mind," and he pursued his studies of the English illustrators, Cruikshank and Rowlandson, and his investigation of the itineraries of Iseult.

Journeys End in Lovers' Meetings, a play by Mrs. Craigie and George Moore, was performed at Daly's Theatre in the course of June of this year. According to Moore's account he not only provided the idea of the play (it was founded on a

French version of some story in *The Rose Garden*) but he
wrote it out, dialogue and all, the lady adding only some
pretty little epigrams and speeches, " her little liver pills,"
he called them. Mr. J. T. Grein, in his obituary notice of
Moore, said that *Journeys End in Lovers' Meetings* was Moore's
one successful play, and he was given full credit for it as co-
author on the programme and in the reviews, but it was
printed afterwards by Mrs. Craigie without any reference to
a collaboration, much to his indignation. Mrs. Craigie, who
had now obtained a divorce, was much under the religious
influence of a Monsignor Browne, the original of the Monsignor in Moore's new novel *Evelyn Innes*, and had become a
Roman Catholic; it is curious that she should have wished to
see Moore again, but he used always to say that it was she
who " insisted " and he who was foolish enough to accede,
and that the " whole damned business " then began once
again—and just after he had succeeded in falling in love
with some one else ! This time however it was not so serious
on his side, for his letters show that he was thinking more
about his new book than about anything else.

Celibates, which followed *Esther Waters*, foreshadowed
Moore's later successes as a short story writer, but failed to
enhance his reputation at the time. There were three stories
in the book, " Mildred Lawson," " John Norton " (*A Mere
Accident* reconstructed) and " Agnes Lahens." The best of
them was " Mildred Lawson," of which Henry Harland said
that it would have been worthy of Flaubert if Moore had
known how to write. The third story has found admirers.
John Freeman likens it to Turgenev—but Moore never
rewrote or republished it as he did the two others. The
subject is a young supersensitive girl who is driven into a
convent by the life which she leads with an ineffectual father
and a cynical and worldly mother. *Celibates* fell flat, but
Moore's disappointment did not endure for long, as his mind
and imagination were fully occupied with *Evelyn Innes*.
Never before had he worked with such ease. *Evelyn Innes*
began with sixteenth-century music and passed to a convent
of cloistered nuns, promising to be at least as long as *Esther
Waters*.

15.8.95 *To Maurice Moore.*

It is a pleasure to write this book. Hitherto I have had to drag myself to the writing table, now I can't drag myself away. I am making myself ill. The composition of this book is a pure joy. I cannot think what has come over me to write like this. It must be very bad or very good. I shall do a great book this time or cut the whole thing.

My young lady is trying to get away from her husband —for a time. A week's adultery we agree would be charming. Some good friends of ours are doing their best but it is difficult to arrange.

I am writing this letter because I am afraid to go to bed. I should not sleep. I have worked myself into a state of nerves.

I think you are pretty safe to get the appointment. You will then have £800 a year. When you have that I shall not relax my efforts to get something better for you. If Asquith is Prime Minister there will be little difficulty. But why are you not happy ? It distresses me so much to hear you are not Happiness is the first thing, prosperity is an over-word. You had better do what you can for Nina. Anything you like I'll agree to . . .

The next month some newspaper published a report that he was about to marry Mrs. Craigie. " The report that I am going to marry Mrs. Craigie is only gossip," he wrote to Maurice Moore on the 9th of September. " I long ago resolved never to marry and from that resolve I shall not swerve. I am too much interested in other men's wives to think of getting one of my own."

His brother did not think that he seemed to be the right person to write a religious novel. Huysmans too smiled on hearing of Moore's new enterprise. He said to William Rothenstein : " George Moore has been here. He doesn't know the difference between one order of nuns and another, and yet he talks about writing this book." It was not the discipline of any particular order which interested Moore but the mystery of the cloistered life. Books were no use to him. " I should like to meet someone who has been in a convent," he wrote to W. T. Stead. " A professed nun would be best of all, that of course would be difficult to obtain. . . . I do not propose to write a word that would give offence to any nun of any order; to do so would be to ruin my book."

Through Stead at this time he met Mrs. Virginia Crawford who had many friends among nuns and was able to supply him with much of what he needed. She helped him not only with *Evelyn Innes* and *Sister Teresa* but with other books, and remained his friend to the end of his life. He could, he said, describe a scene that had been related to him better than if he had witnessed it, a remark which is significant of his method of work and also bears out Steer's view that " Moore's landscapes are based on pictures rather than nature."

8

The year witnessed his great triumph in the long-drawn-out struggle with the libraries. Twenty-four thousand copies of *Esther Waters* were sold, and when this success was followed by a postcard from Mr. Gladstone approving of the book's morality Smith's capitulated. The story is related with great gusto in *A Communication to My Friends*.

It seems Moore called in an accountant who checked the sales, and reckoned that Smith had lost about £1,500 by refusing to take *Esther Waters*. The partners of the firm then sent word to their librarian that it would be well in future to avoid the heavy losses of banning books, especially books that Mr. Gladstone would be likely to read and publicly approve in the *Westminster Gazette*. There is evidence here of the sincerity of Moore's desire to free English fiction from the shackles of the libraries, for after the firm establishment of his reputation in *Esther Waters* it would no doubt have been to his advantage that the thousands who wished to read his books should have to buy them instead of borrowing. The days when the boycott of the libraries could hurt him were

over, but he would not renounce his fight for the principle.
And he was shrewd enough to see that a commercial argument would turn the scales more surely than all the idealism
in the world.

He told an interviewer from the *Daily Chronicle* that
Esther Waters was written out of " a love of humanity, a
desire to serve humanity "; and Mr. Havelock Ellis has
related in *My Confessional* how, crossing the court of the
Temple one day, he met Moore, who stopped him to talk
with deep emotion of the cases, then being ventilated in the
newspapers, of young women compelled by the hostile
attitude of society to destroy their illegitimate babies. Such
tender human sympathy, Havelock Ellis says, was among his
most pronounced traits. He must have felt that he had made
a slip in the interview with the *Daily Chronicle*, for although he
used to say that *Esther Waters* " radiated goodness," he was
henceforth careful to add that he had been innocent of any
intention to do good. *Esther Waters* stood on its own ground as
a work of art, but Moore would remark with some pride that
this book had actually alleviated more material suffering
than any novel of its generation. The context of this remark
was the establishment of the Fallowfield Corner Home for
Homeless Children by a hospital nurse who had been moved
by the description of the struggles of the unmarried mother
in *Esther Waters*. He failed to reflect that the existence of this
Home discounted his dogma that " literature has no effect
upon conduct," as did also his own definition of *Evelyn Innes*
(in *Memoirs of My Dead Life*) as " one of the most powerful
literary aphrodisiacs ever written " : rather an over-state-
ment, one would think.

He continued to keep up his correspondence with Madame
Lanza, hoping, though a little doubtfully, that one day they
might meet. " I often think of you and I sometimes talk about
you. . . . Is there any chance of seeing you ? Sometimes I
think I should like to see you. We have known each other so
long by means of correspondence that it might be something
of a shock to meet you in the flesh, perhaps. . . . " When at
the end of 1895 her husband died and she announced her
intention of settling at Naples, Moore was quite upset at her

choice, and his reply was singularly unlike the conventional letter of condolence.

You are a real good sort. It was most kind of you to write to me advising me of your husband's death. I have neglected you, I know; but the neglect has not been intentional, that you know. I have thought of you and determined to write many times. . . . It was very good of you to write. But tell me why are you going to live in Naples ? What a strange idea ! Why do you not come to Europe—to London, or Paris ? But Naples ! How strangely you arrange your life. But everything is unaccountable, nothing can be explained—why do you like me ? Why do I like you ? And there is a liking and a sincere liking on both sides. What a mystery life is, and to get some of that mystery into my books is now my aim. But why Naples ?— I believe that you are a rich woman—all the money you have is your own, isn't that so ? Then why Naples ? Far better bring up your children as Americans or as English than as Italians. But they have not been brought up as Italians: they are to be converted into Italians. How inscrutable are the designs of life ! What could be stranger than the fact that I am writing you this letter.

Your plans are certainly unfixed. You say that you may go to Paris and then on to London. I hope so. I wish I had met you long ago, when you first wrote to me. But perhaps no ! However this may be I shall think of you affectionately, and if the chance should come, shall be pleased to meet you. " Be pleased——" the words seem cold. Should I have said " delighted " ? Of course after all these years there would be some misgiving, and yet no—I have always liked you and should like you face to face as much as far away. There's an instinct about those things which doesn't deceive.

How you astonished me ! Your husband dead, and you coming to Europe to settle in Naples ! But you will write to me when you get this letter giving me farther particulars. You will, I hope, never forget George Moore.

You will write to him from Naples and, and—well goodbye, Clara.

9

No longer could he derive pleasure from his early work. Vincent O'Sullivan, the American critic, to whom he talked about his books, writes: " I found him modest about his personal qualities (except his prowess as a conqueror of women) and uncertain to an almost irritating point about the worth of his books. I spoke of *Mike Fletcher*. ' Why do you keep on talking of that book ? ' he cried out vehemently; ' you know that it pains and annoys me ! ' I replied that I spoke of it because I found it interesting. But he would not agree. He had done his best to put the book out of print in England and was indignant that the Americans should presume to keep it alive. Another time it was *A Mummer's Wife*. ' Do you really think that book is good ? ' he asked doubtfully, and added, ' There is one of my books, *A Modern Lover*, in which I think there are some really good things.' And he complained bitterly of the people who persisted in associating his name with Zola. ' Nobody who knows anything would say such a thing. They would know that if I have a master it is Flaubert. Open *Esther Waters* and read that scene where she meets her son after a long separation. What an embrace ! That, my dear friend, is pure Flaubert.' "

The heroine of *Evelyn Innes* was an opera singer, and Moore made of Arthur Symons, who knew a great deal about music, one of his principal confidants at the time that he was writing this book. One day he appeared in Symons's chambers at the Temple and said that he was on his way to a luncheon party given by some woman well known in Society; he then asked, with the characteristic drawing out of the vowels of the words he wished to emphasise: " Does anyone here know an opera singer ? I am writing a story about an opera singer. I must have a model. What can you *do* without a model. To write a book about an opera singer without knowing one, and even sleeping with her, is to expose oneself to defeat." His wish was at least partly gratified: " I am not dining with my aunt," he wrote one day in 1896 to Mrs. Edmund Gosse, " but with Melba. She is to tell me about her voice." The novel also needed archaic documentation, for Mr. Innes, the father of the opera singer, was a connoisseur of old music and old musical instruments; and J.-E. Blanche has related how when Moore was in a tantrum nowadays it was useless to try to soothe him by playing the Liebestod from *Tristan*; he must be provided with Bach, Palestrina or conversations upon the subject of harpsichords and violes d'amour.

Symons, who at first adopted a deferential attitude towards the older man, in the end incurred Moore's grave displeasure on account of his obstinacy in holding to certain opinions which were not Moore's. Moore said: " When a man, after proof upon proof has been given him, persists in brazening out his errors, there is no more to be said. I told Symons: ' When you see the right side you can come to see me again.' He went away in a rage. I have no wish to see him again." But for a time Moore was very intimate with the young poet and critic, even dependent on him. He found Symons's rooms in Fountain Court—so much pleasanter than his own in situation and arrangement—a very agreeable stopping-place on the way to and from King's Bench Walk. Symons was without Lionel Johnson's formal academic education, but he was interested in what interested Moore, modern French literature and painting, theatres and music halls.

A new impression of Moore shaped itself in the minds of his literary acquaintances when it became known that he was going hunting in the North Country. They had not suspected that he practised any sport, or even took any exercise. He was going to stay with Sir William Eden, and proposed to ride to hounds. This showed pluck, for he had never been a first-class man to hounds, or very keen, and Eden was an outspoken critic in the hunting field, and of anything connected with horsemanship. " I remember my surprise," Vincent O'Sullivan writes, " when he asked me to recommend a tailor for hunting clothes." O'Sullivan's surprise is interesting, because it shows how little Moore was disposed to supply his acquaintances with useless information. As far as mere riding was concerned he did very well indeed, earning the compliments of the house party and thoroughly enjoying himself. So at least he told his brother, a horseman too; he added, however, that he " could not jump across a road, avoid three ploughed fields and come in just in front of the hounds " (*sic*). Eden to him was " the most interesting man in the world," but conflicts were frequent, for Eden's temper was even more uncertain than his own. " Eden is perfectly charming," Moore wrote to Mrs. Charles Hunter, another North Country friend. " I feel that it was perfectly hateful of me to lose my temper and write him letters that would annoy him when he had the gout. I should dearly love to tell him so. But it will be better to keep my counsel."

Some of *Evelyn Innes* was written during visits to the north of England, where Moore was the guest not only of the Edens but of Lord Grimthorpe, a favourite companion—one of the few who called him George—and of Mr. and Mrs. Charles Hunter. The Hunters lived at Selaby, a country house between Darlington and Barnard Castle; they were neighbours and great friends of Sir William Eden, and they became Moore's friends also. He appreciated their kindness and hospitalities, and the letters he wrote to Mrs. Hunter, and, afterwards, when their home was at Hill Hall, Essex, to Mrs. Williamson, her daughter, show him in his happiest and most affectionate nature. The Hunters were then almost entirely absorbed in sport and country life, and he adapted himself to their interests and joined in their pursuits; in return they formed a sympathetic and eager audience when he talked or wrote to them of his art and of his hopes of *Evelyn Innes*: " The subject unfolds itself like the dawn. Light is breaking in every direction and I am dreaming a lovely dream. But will any of my dream transpire ? Shall I communicate my dream ? I often ask myself the question."

From Selaby, too, he rode to hounds, and once he got very severely kicked on the leg at the meet, but he made no fuss and went well during a short spurt. He then rather pathetic-ally remarked : " I think my leg is broken, and my boot is full of blood. . . ." He was laid up for some time, and did not return to the hunting-field again. His brother offered to

send him some horses from Ireland. These he refused, saying:
" My business is with *Evelyn Innes*."

He now decided to leave the Temple, and, his thoughts
turning to Dulwich as a possible residence, he arranged a
walk with Steer from Pimlico to that suburb, which he knew
already, owing to his having laid there certain scenes from
Esther Waters. He wanted to verify something that he had said
about haystacks in those parts. After making enquiries of
various policemen he found his haystack, and on the walk
home he was so pleased with the success of the expedition
that he suggested to Steer that they should share a house
there together and keep a pony cart, in which they would be
able to drive to London. For the good of both, perhaps, this
did not come about, and Moore chose a flat in Victoria
Street. A note to Mrs. Hunter from Boodles', written in the
spring of 1896 when he was about to make the change, shows
the agony of doubt and confusion into which he was thrown
by the details of practical life:

> I am sorry to receive your telegram this morning. I
> should have liked to have seen your husband. I have not
> forgotten his kindness to me when my leg was bad. I have
> had a horrid day, no place to wash my hands, horrible
> disorder. Yet there are people who change their houses and
> flats every three years.
>
> When you return to England I hope I shall see you.
> Kind regards to your sister [Dame Ethel Smyth]. Tell
> her I have a plot for a one act opera which I shall not use.
> It is entirely at her service.

This was perhaps the opera libretto on which he corresponded with Dujardin. " A magnificent subject," he told his
French friend. " If the subject pleases you we can write it
together. It is very heroic. I've heard a symphonic piece by
Vincent d'Indy which pleased me greatly; something of that
nature. Do you think he could write an opera ? "

In the " large handsome low-ceilinged flat " at 92 Victoria
Street he seemed happy, and the housekeeper whom he
found understood all his little ways very well. Although he

had lost the American copyright in *Esther Waters*, he could afford some luxury, and part of the savings he had made over a number of years were spent on " a grey portrait by Manet " (which he at first supposed Lord Grimthorpe would wish to acquire), " a mauve morning by Monet, willows emerging from a submerged meadow," and a Berthe Morisot. He used to say that *Esther Waters* had done him evil by withdrawing him from poverty and from contact with the poor, yet he had a great love for his chairs, his Aubusson carpet, his pictures and his china, and would interrupt a conversation at once if his guest showed a disposition to treat them casually. "What do you think, Moore, of . . . ? " " My dear friend, I cannot think so long as you sit on my eight guinea chair."

10

The story of his first two years in Victoria Street may be told briefly. No great change took place in his habits, except that he was more often out of London than formerly. The new house, Le Val Changis, of his delightful and surprising friend, Dujardin, now become a historian of primitive Christianity, often tempted him across the Channel; holidays in the north of England were still a feature of his life; and Edward Martyn's mother having died (she had, it will be remembered, forbidden him to enter Tillyra) there was a comfortable house ready to receive him if he wished to go to Ireland. In July 1897 he reported on *Evelyn Innes* to Dujardin; he had written some " fine scenes " since the Spring and an " admirable confession " for his opera singer. In November all his working hours were still being employed upon the book. Paul Bourget's social successes in London provoked him to anger, and he sent Dujardin a scatological comment (in French verse) on " le high life en dog cart " which made a lion of that novelist.

W. B. Yeats had taken him in hand, and was telling him that England owed everything to her adventurers, nothing to her gentlemen. They had met some years previously, at the

Cheshire Cheese, Yeats has said; and in 1893 Moore had
written to his brother asking him to call on the Irish poet,
" whose work I hold in high esteem," when he should next
be in Dublin. Arthur Symons must often have spoken of
Yeats to Moore before 1897, the year in which Edward
Martyn's plans for the formation of an Irish Literary
Theatre first began to mature. Martyn now brought Yeats to
the flat in Victoria Street, and Moore's sympathies were
quickly enlisted, because both Martyn and Yeats had
written plays which he admired, Martyn (under his eye) *The
Heather Field* and Yeats *The Countess Cathleen.* He ran all over
the West End of London, showing Martyn's play to the actor
managers, and had Yeats listen to him as he read out
Evelyn Innes in Symons's rooms. " Yeats and Symons," he
reported modestly to his brother on the 18th April, 1898,
" find it far better than they thought I could do. It is
inferior to Tourgournoff [*sic*] and Balzac, but I think it is
better than trashy Thackeray and rubbishy Dickens and
pompous Eliot.[1] But it cannot be properly judged till the
second half of *Sister Teresa* is written. But what matter?
Shakespeare absorbed dramatic poetry, Balzac the novel,
Wagner absorbed dramatic music—we are the moths that
flutter in the light of suns that shall have no setting."

Evelyn could not marry her first lover, Sir Owen, without
telling him about Ulick, the Celtic musician, who believes in
Angus and Lir and the great Mother Dana. But Ulick?
Should she marry Ulick and accept the gods? She could not
marry Ulick without telling him that she had been unfaithful to him with Owen. Should she send Owen away and
marry Ulick, or would it be better to send away Ulick and
marry Owen, if Owen would marry her after he had heard
her confession. . . . She ought to send them both away. . . .
But could she remain on the stage without a lover? So drawn
out were her perplexities that the story threatened to run to
a thousand pages, and Fisher Unwin, who had now become
Moore's publisher, shying at the prospect, it was decided to
publish the novel in two parts with two titles. *Evelyn Innes*, the
first part, was before the public in the summer of 1898, the

[1] But he had written respectfully of Thackeray in *Impressions and Opinions.*

story being brought down (in this edition) to Evelyn Innes's return to her father's house. She has been a boarder in a convent, but does not propose to become a nun. She has sacrificed Owen and her career as a singer in order that she may live a chaste life, but her conversion does not explain her choice to herself, and she feels that her natural preferences are still for lovers and worldly pleasures. " I should have sent you my book sooner," Moore wrote to Dujardin on the 20th of June, " but its merits were at first contested by some hasty and malicious critics. . . . I was next door to believing that I had spent three years on the invention of an imbecility. . . . Things are now going better." *Evelyn Innes*, dedicated to W. B. Yeats and Arthur Symons (" Two Contemporary Writers with whom I am in sympathy ") ended by being one of the most successful of Moore's novels, 15,000 copies being sold in the six-shilling form; he was very soon preparing a third edition for the press, with masses of corrections and a reconstruction of the love scene between Ulick and Evelyn.

Musically, *Evelyn Innes* has always met with approval. But as a scene from society life, it is rather " rue de Rivoli," to use an expression which Moore applied later to d'Annunzio, (whose *Triumph of Death* he at this time admired). Even in the late Victorian time, Sir Owen Asher with his forty suits, his golden moustache and slight hips cut a rather ridiculous figure. The baronet presents the prima donna with a pair of " almost thoroughbred " horses, and, incidentally, affronts the town at midday in patent leather boots with tan tops. " I am not surprised," said Oscar Wilde, when his attention was drawn to the dreadful sartorial solecism. " The next time Moore will get it right. He conducts his education in public." Robert Ross, who was present, replied: " Well, the public pays for it. They have a right to know how he is getting on."

Having published *Evelyn Innes*, Moore wrote a preface to Martyn's *The Heather Field*, " the first appearance of humanity in English prose drama of the day." He chastised the critics, William Archer included, who had failed to perceive the merits of this play, Ibsen transplanted to Irish soil, a dreaming country gentleman driven to madness by his wife's practical sense. Inseparable as they were it was Moore's sense of obligation to a work of art rather than his friendship which caused him to labour with an almost fanatical zeal on behalf of the *Heather Field*. A performance in Dublin was in sight by the end of 1898, and Moore was invited to find and rehearse a cast. He worked almost as hard for Yeats, whose *Countess Cathleen* was also to be played in Dublin; in retrospect he mocked at his own efforts (there is a comic account in *Ave* of the finding of the actors and of the rehearsals) but his services were acknowledged by Yeats, who wrote two years later (*Samhain*, 1901) that the work of founding the Irish theatre could not have been done without him and his knowledge of the stage. Indeed Moore's intelligent interest in every aspect of the theatre comes out clearly in the dialogue with William Archer which Archer published in 1904 as part of a volume entitled *Real Conversations*. Archer thought Moore affected and absurd in objecting to Tree's elaborate Shakespearean pageants and had just, he tells us, published an article eulogising the " appropriate and beautiful background " of his *Twelfth Night*. But time and Mr. Granville-Barker have vindicated Moore's judgment, and his remarks now suggest a pioneer of simplicity in the theatre. Of *A Midsummer Night's Dream* he said: " The interest of the audience was held by a tap that had been left running, and that drowned the voices of the actors. When I want to hear a tap running, I go to the scullery, not to the theatre." Tree's *Twelfth Night* was " a small play enlarged, like a photograph, till it was out of all drawing, and every trace of composition had disappeared . . . played in a very verdant landscape with rhododendrons " which reminded him of " the emptying of a pot of red currant jam into a pail of green peas. No shadow anywhere."

So forcible an opponent of the conventional theatre was naturally regarded by Yeats and Martyn as a considerable recruit to their movement; and conversely the attitude of Moore towards Yeats at this time is roughly indicated by the relationship of Evelyn Innes and Ulick Dean, her rescuer from the materialism which she feared must result from her association with Sir Owen Asher. Sir Owen had given her Spencer and Huxley to read, but Ulick, by his eloquent descriptions of the Celtic gods and the mysticism of Blake, showed her that Spencer and Huxley were not the only alternatives to the Roman Catholic theology in which she had been brought up. The two strands of Moore's life are symbolised by the two men, Owen and Ulick: his social phase in the one, and his returning home to poor Ireland in the other.

CHAPTER VI

IRELAND: GREAT EXPECTATIONS

I

At the beginning of May, 1899, Moore crossed to Ireland for the performance in the Antient Concert Rooms of *The Countess Cathleen*. He was the third director of the Irish Literary Theatre, Yeats and Martyn being the two others. A pamphlet, the work of one of Yeats's political enemies, had been published which appealed to Catholic and patriotic feeling to put a stop to "blasphemy"; the writer objected particularly to a scene in which the Countess sells her soul to merchants disguised as demons in order that a starving people may be fed. A more serious criticism of the theology of the play had also appeared, after the rehearsals, anonymously in an Irish newspaper; it was written by a Monsignor, not as Yeats has stated by a monk or as Moore has stated by a friar.[1] Disturbances were expected, and a close watch was kept on Martyn by Yeats and Lady Gregory, lest this devout Catholic should resign from his directorship of the theatre, if the play were authoritatively convicted of heresy. Yeats procured the approval of Father Finlay and Father Barry for *The Countess Cathleen*, two ecclesiastics against one, hushing Martyn's scruples, and this it seems disappointed Moore, for he had written an article, "Edward Martyn and His Soul," which he meant to publish when Martyn resigned. Yeats reports him as saying: "It was the best opportunity I ever had. What a sensation it would have made. Nobody has ever written in that way about his most intimate friend. What a chance. It would have been heard of everywhere."

---

[1] Yeats in *Dramatis Personæ* 1896–1902, and Moore in *Ave*. Moore and Yeats were very anxious to discover the name of the author, but never succeeded in doing so.

Cardinal Logue, however, had condemned the play (though without reading it), and there were interrupters in the gallery of the dim hall which first reminded Moore of a picture by Sickert—" the melancholy of this dim hall I had never seen before, except in some of Sickert's pictures " —and then " of a cats' and dogs' home merged into one." *The Heather Field* which followed was an immense success, and it appeared that a great new dramatist had arisen in Martyn and that Moore had been right in his battle with the English dramatic critics. Max Beerbohm confessed to a mistake in an article on the plays which he contributed to *The Saturday Review*, and others who had come from England did likewise. Everyone was in high feather at the dinner which T. P. Gill, Editor of the *Daily Express*, the organ of the Irish Renaissance, gave in honour of the new movement a few evenings later. It is described in *Ave*; Moore read " an historic entertainment in the appearance of the waiters," but there was " not an opera hat " among the guests. The extreme ends of Dublin had " yielded to Gill's persuasiveness." John O'Leary, the old Fenian, was there, Douglas Hyde, the Gaelic leader, T. W. Rolleston, John Eglinton and many others who were afterwards to be Moore's foils in the Moore-hero novel, *Hail and Farewell*, and Trinity College dined with them. Yeats has also written about the banquet, saying that his memory differs from Moore's in various details, including the question of opera hats, and since Max Beerbohm was among Gill's guests Yeats is probably right. Moore did not exaggerate the platitudes of Gill's speech, and he reported his own discourse very accurately, but his account of his impressions of the scene and company undoubtedly owed a good deal to the reflections and experience of later days. It is more than hinted in *Ave* that he had already a lively sense of the comedy of his situation, but the evidence of his Irish associates and of his own correspondence between 1895 and 1900 reveals him as a man who was in deadly earnest, determined to interpret the facts of Irish life according to his desires, and fully persuaded that something was in the air which offered him a chance of influence if not of leadership.

His speech dwelt upon the coincidence of great art with periods of national re-awakening; and he proclaimed his faith in all aspects of the New Ireland—in Sir Horace Plunkett's co-operative movement in agriculture, as well as in the Irish language movement and the poetry of W. B. Yeats. Nothing amused him so much when he was writing his Irish autobiography, as the thought of Plunkett, characterised as the man who brought dreamland into politics, but at the banquet he made a particular point of his admiration of Plunkett, finding in what he afterwards called " the co-operative egg " the keystone of the arch of the Irish Revival. Plunkett was unable to be at the banquet, but he sent a message reminding the men of letters present, that " we practical folk keep a poet in our office, and from him our most fruitful inspirations are derived." Moore already knew this poet, A. E. (George Russell), the mystic with the long grey pantheistic eyes, who was one of the magnets drawing him to Ireland.

His speech was nervous, even apologetic; he felt, he said, like a man who having deserted his mother in her poverty returned to her when she had become wealthy, a remark which brought a snarl into the voice of the next speaker, a truculent lawyer, J. F. Taylor, who expressed an ironical satisfaction that " we Irish have reached a level which makes it worth while for Mr. Moore to return to Ireland. . . . When Mr. William O'Brien (a politician outside the Renaissance when Moore's speech had attacked) was making the sacrifice of Mr. Yeats' *Countess Cathleen*, damning his soul for his country, where was Mr. Moore? In London, in Paris . . ." It was the first time that Moore had ever made a speech in public, and Yeats who has described the scene, says that his opponent though not on this occasion quite at his best was " the greatest orator I have ever heard."

2

Edward Martyn was at work upon another play, *The Tale of a Town*, a satire on Irish public life; he and Moore were making this year one of their expeditions to Beyreuth, and the long hours of the railway journey were whiled away in argument upon style and construction. Was it on this occasion that Moore met Cosima Wagner and discovered that she was the most wonderful woman in the world ? He wanted to give expression to what he felt for her, and so he bought the little Tauchnitz edition of *Esther Waters*, and gave it " nicely bound " to the heroine of the Wagner epic, a touching act, although Beardsley when he heard of it burst into derisive laughter. " How like George Moore ! And does he think she will read it ? "

Life in London became more and more discouraging. With Kipling's star in the ascendant, his short-lived belief in the susceptibility of England to art faded out altogether. He hated all manifestations of the new Imperialism, and watched with disgust the preparation of public opinion for the Boer war and the growth of a national mood in which his own works would be sure to be overlooked. " Someone must tread upon our beetles," he wrote to Mrs. Gosse. But he did not yet guess that his quarrel with England, a lover's quarrel, would force him to remove to his native country. Visits to Martyn's Gothic castle in Galway, with occasional descents upon Dublin for rehearsals, were all that would be required of him as one of the directors of the Irish Literary Theatre.

In September, at the time of the outbreak of the Boer War, Moore was again at Tillyra, and in a quandary because Martyn showed resistance to his advice on *The Tale of a Town*. The rather comic story has been told by Moore in *Ave* and by Yeats in *Dramatis Personæ*. On the strength of the success of *The Heather Field* an expensive theatre had already been engaged for the performance of the new play. But the new play was unworthy, and Yeats asked for explanations. How could the author of *The Heather Field* stumble in this way ? Moore went over to Lady Gregory's house near by, and confessed that he was part author of *The Heather Field*, but had kept silent in the general interest. Not a line of the play was actually written by Moore, but he had shown Martyn the way throughout. " This was a Moore of whom I had known nothing," Yeats writes in *Dramatic Personæ* . . .

" Moore in his moments of self-abnegation was convinced and convincing." The extent of Moore's collaboration in *The Heather Field* will never be known; later on Martyn implied that it was not after all very great, and it needs to be remembered that Moore had singular views as to what constitutes part-authorship. Thus in a controversy several years later with another play-writing friend on whose work he had offered criticism and advice, he claimed that anyone even amending a situation should have a right to sign a play. On this ground, as the friend in question pointed out, there were very few of Moore's own books which were not collaborations.

In the end Martyn gave in and said that Moore might do what he wished with the play, but must sign it himself. As Moore did not fully understand the political subject, it became necessary for him to invoke aid from Yeats. Yeats was invited to Tillyra, and Moore's heart began to bleed for Martyn. " The poor man sitting alone in his tower, brooding upon failure. I expected Yeats to say something sympathetic, but all he said was: ' We couldn't produce such a play as that.' " The work, under Moore's sole signature and with a new title, *The Bending of the Bough*, was produced at the Gaiety Theatre on the 19th of February, 1900, and greatly pleased all the young idealists. Lady Gregory in *Our Irish Theatre* quotes from her diary: " No one is really offended, certainly not the Nationalists, and we have not heard that the Unionists are either." In a speech at the time, Yeats described the play as " that whirl-wind of passion." But the English actors were mystified. They learned the words, but never discovered that the play had any subject whatever, and were taken aback by the cheering of speeches which meant nothing to them. In a letter to his brother, who was campaigning in South Africa, Moore said:

I am afraid Martyn suffered a good deal. He says I spoil[ed] his play but that is an illusion. I recast the play, but not enough. I should have written a new play on the subject. . . . Then Edward said he could not sign it, and he refused to let it be played anonymously so I had to sign it.

Unquestionably, Martyn suffered. But it would seem from his correspondence and unpublished manuscripts that he bore more resentment against Yeats and Lady Gregory than against Moore.

3

A luncheon party was given by the Irish Literary Society, at which Moore read the paper which was afterwards reprinted in *Ideals in Ireland*, a collection of papers on the new Ireland by Yeats, Lady Gregory, Douglas Hyde and others. In this paper he compared the Irish language to a spring rising among the mountains, increasing into a rivulet, and then becoming a great river flowing through the fields. The English language was like a river which had arrived at a great town. Such water must be filtered, and Milton was the first filter of English, Pater the last. Pater knew that English had reached the same stage of decay as Latin in the second century, and since Pater's death English had passed " through the patty pans of Mr. Stevenson into the pint pot of Mr. Kipling." The passage shows that Moore was able to bring certain opinions, to which for several years past he had been attracted, into relation with his crusade for Irish. Huysmans is quoted in the *Confessions of A Young Man* to the effect that a language long current wears itself out and ceases to be able to support a literature.

These considerations were more or less private to Moore, for, as he was presently to discover, the Gaelic League was without the slightest interest in æsthetic questions, and Yeats had no sure belief in the importance of the Irish language. At first, however, his own interest in Irish was not of a purely literary order; and he concurred with those who attributed all Irish distresses to the disappearance of the native speech. And to show that his opinion did not go one way and his actions another, he had said in his address to the luncheon party that although he was himself too old to learn Irish and had no children of his own he would at once arrange that his brother's children should learn Irish. " I have written," he said, " to my sister-in-law telling her that I will undertake this essential part of her children's education. I will arrange that they have a nurse straight from Arran, for I am convinced that it profits a man nothing if he knows all the languages of the world and knows not his own." His audience giggled at these sentences, but as he said when writing to his brother he expected that it would, and he added: " I meant them seriously. Evelyn [Mrs. Maurice Moore] will be astonished when she reads them this morning."

His horror of the Boer War was even greater than his love of Irish. It was painful to witness, and he would pass whole days without looking at the newspapers. " I live in a sort of nightmare," he wrote in one of his letters, " when I think of the war. If I were to allow my mind to ponder on it as others do, I should go off my head. . . . We are not all constructed in the same way." At other moments he was exalted by the thought of the spiritual change which his pro-Boer opinions signified. He was another man, he told his brother; " what once seemed wrong now seems right and what once seemed right now seems wrong." The sentence was a paraphrase of the words used by Jaspar Dean in *The Bending of the Bough*: " It is such a joy to allow the truth into one's mind. It was like a sudden change of light, all that had seemed right was suddenly changed to wrong, and what I had thought despicable became right and praiseworthy." He thought of making propaganda against England in America, and when the aged Queen came to Ireland, in the summer of 1900, to acknowledge the heroism of Irish troops in South Africa, he wrote a letter to the Dublin papers to explain why he felt obliged to receive her in silence.

It is no wonder that in *Ave* he could give " no reasonable account " of his condition at this time, and that he fell back on a story of mysterious voices in the Chelsea Road bidding him to go to Ireland. Yeats, one fancies, egged him on a little, while finding him an embarrassing ally. Lady Gregory mentions in *Our Irish Theatre* that the old historian Lecky

said to her: " What silly speeches your celtic people have
been making." " Moore?" queried Lady Gregory. " Yes,"
Lecky replied, " and Yeats. Oh, very silly."

4

Another descent upon Dublin in this year was in response
to an invitation to be present on the platform at some big
Gaelic League demonstration. Though he had not been
asked to speak, Moore was at pains to prepare a paper on
the literary value of the languages of small peoples; and
readers of his Irish memoirs will remember the comic way
in which he describes Dr. Douglas Hyde's evident reluctance
to see him get on his legs. Dr. Hyde recalls the occasion very
well, and admits that with his " Thanks, thanks, thanks
for coming " he hoped to discourage Moore from making
a speech. Five or six thousand people were in the audience,
and the crowd wanted honest oratory, not the theories of a
man of letters. " I thought Moore a great big child," says
Dr. Hyde, " but when he came to Dublin he certainly set
us all an example of hard work."

Amusing as the episode appeared in retrospect, Moore
was conscious of a rebuff at the time. It was always easy for
him to think that he was disliked, and there were in fact
some complaints against Yeats—they came chiefly from the
London Irish—for having introduced the author of *Parnell
and his Island* and of *A Drama in Muslin* into a patriotic movement. Moore felt that his brother alone understood him—his
brother who was fighting against the Boers in a war which
they both detested.

21.5.00. *To Colonel Moore.*

That the war will be over soon is the best news I have
heard for a long time. Nothing will give me greater
pleasure than to see you again. . . .

It is the Irish language which interests me more than
anything else and if you will let your children be taught
Irish I will pay. I call the tune so it is only fair that I

should pay. I do not know if I should write to Evelyn about it. I am afraid she would not sympathise for she would not understand. Nor should I have understood years ago. Opinions change, we do not know how. The new opinions spring up like grass in the soul. . . . The speech which you liked was yours, it was you who gave me the ideas twenty years ago, some of them twenty-five years ago. I published the speech in the *New Ireland Review*. But it did not read well. Yeats told me I must repeat myself in a speech and I failed to get rid of the repititions when I rewrote it. The comedy was a great success. . . . There are fifty things I should like to say, but can't. Anything you send me will needless to say receive my best attention. Learning the Irish language with shells bursting about you is—well I don't know what it is, lurid is I suppose the right word.

Later in the year, he received a letter from Colonel Moore telling him of the ruthless orders given to British troops to combat the Boers in their guerilla warfare. He spoke to W. T. Stead of a letter which he had had from the front. But Stead could do nothing, because Moore would not give him the writer's name. Lest he might get his brother into trouble he refused to surrender the manuscript, but finally took it to Dublin and dictated the contents to a stenographer of the *Freeman's Journal*. *The Times* copied the account; two newspapers at the Cape reproduced *The Times* article, and their editors were sentenced to imprisonment. " I nearly fainted," says Colonel Moore, "when I read my letter to George in *The Times*. Twenty years later, happening to be again in South Africa, I went to the office of one of the editors, who was now a Cabinet Minister, to apologise to him."

Moore continued to impress upon his sister-in-law the importance of bringing up her sons to speak Irish. As Mrs. Moore was living in the west of Ireland, she should have no difficulty, he thought, in getting a good teacher for the children.

14.7.00. *To Mrs. Maurice Moore.*

You have read all about it in the papers of course and have been expecting to hear from me on the subject. Maurice has written to me and he is anxious that his children should be taught Irish. . . . To make Irish their instructive language, it will be necessary for them to begin Irish at once. I ought to have written to you on this matter long ago but because I have delayed there should be no further delay. I will pay for a woman from the Arran school, £12 or £15 a year, whatever the costs, to teach the children Irish. There is no necessity to send to Arran. Dr. Hyde tells me that very good Irish is spoken about Moore Hall. Will you enquire about the woman who speaks the best Irish and engage her to speak Irish all day to the children. They will soon pick it up and next year I hope they will learn to read the language. Maurice has sent me some very good articles home—he writes very well and I had no difficulty in disposing of them.

It was in vain that he tried to fix his thoughts on the composition of *Sister Teresa*. England seemed to rise up before him, the embodiment of a vulgar and shameful materialism from which he turned in horror, and this passionate revolt was only aggravated by memories of his former love. He went down to Sussex and stayed with friends whom he had of late neglected, the Bridgers, for he hoped that among them he might forget the war. But at dinner on the first night of his visit he fell into a political argument; and the next day, riding across the downs, he found that he could not recover his pleasure in the English countryside, the pretty lanes and red tiled cottages, his thoughts turning to the dim wastes about Lough Carra, to Martyn's castle and the Burren hills, and to the lake at Coole out of which thirty-six swans had risen when Yeats spoke of his play, *The Shadowy Waters*.

We have other accounts of his last months in London, and all of them show him in a state of tension. He felt some sadness in leaving London where he had many friends. " I also hated the war in many ways," Tonks writes, " and we

often spoke on the subject. I regret very much that I made
no notes of his chance meeting in my house, while the war
was still on, with a distinguished young soldier, who afterwards held high rank in the Great War. I can only remember
that, although their views were entirely opposed, he and
the young soldier never discovered their disagreement;
perhaps it was that they both preferred to talk on a subject
of such profound interest rather than to listen. If Moore
wanted to learn something he would listen very carefully,
but he more often wanted to talk than to listen, and he was
very ingenious in discovering ways of intervening."

The decision to settle in Ireland was rendered more agreeable by the knowledge that one of his friends—an Englishwoman, who shared his Irish ideals—was also ready to make
her home there. Miss Clara Christian, an artist of gifts, had
in recent months come much under his influence. In his
Irish memoirs she is the lady called " Stella," who lives in
the house at Rathfarnham, beyond the outskirts of Dublin,
and gives her days to gardening and to painting. A woman
of independent means, not pretty but distinguished looking,
tall and with a pleasant grave expression, when Moore first
knew her she was the inseparable companion of another
woman artist, whose work is now widely known and appreciated. The companionship, which had been long and
devoted, did not survive Moore's intervention, and when
Miss Christian came to Ireland she came without her friend.

5

Ely Place is a short street ending in a cul-de-sac. The
houses are in the Georgian style, built of dark brick, tall
and reserved. In the centre of the row, looking down Hume
Street to St. Stephen's Green is Ely House, once a nobleman's mansion with a lovely light staircase and fine interior
decorations. At the cul-de-sac end there is a terrace of five
houses, sometimes called Smith's Buildings, dated 1820, of
more modest size and uniform in their design. They have
the long narrow windows of the later eighteenth century.
Until quite recently high iron gates and railings divided

the terrace from the abutting street, and gave it an air of seclusion and quiet. It was No. 4 of this terrace, the second house from the end, which was George Moore's home during his ten years' residence in Dublin. The front windows faced west and overlooked, directly opposite, a garden railed in by iron palings, covering in extent the whole length of the terrace. Here in spring the apple trees, pink thorn, laburnum and lilac make a profusion of blossom. There was a little slum at the back of the house, and from the drawing-room level on the second floor, the author of *Sister Teresa* had an oblique view into the high-walled enclosure of a convent.

A. E. found him the house, and helped to instal him. Moore could not have been better suited, and it astonished him to discover that the author of *Homeward—Songs by the Way* should know all about kitchen ranges and cisterns. He had feared that his hatred of the Boer war was forcing him almost to the brink of ruin : but the rent was only £100 a year, with a few pounds extra for the fine garden with the largest apple tree in Ireland. He had a friend near by, the cultivated and hospitable old doctor, Sir Thornley Stoker, who lived in Ely House amid a collection of rare furniture. He described his content in a pleasant letter to J.-E. Blanche : " I have said farewell to my artificial life . . . The wind off the sea and from the fields makes me feel another man . . . I have no lack of friends who will come in and talk to me after dinner. I am being given a reception which shows that I am not despised. I shall be able to write in the newspapers, and mix actively in politics—but I think that I am going to teach the Irish what art and painting are."

The account in *Salve* of his settling-in shows that he did not feel so confident that he was wanted in Ireland as he gave Blanche to understand. Many of the Gaelic enthusiasts put him down as an alien—Irish no doubt, but Imperial Irish— and indeed he had grown to look very like the absentee landlord who is either a retired British Colonel or a retired civil servant. Little notice was taken of him at the offices of the League, where he found that his name was unknown to the secretary of the staff : " Seamstresses, seamstresses," he murmured. A. E. said to him that there was other work to do besides that of the League; but he replied that no other work would interest him, and went on harrying his sister-in-law about the children's Irish. James Joyce, from a point of view very different from that of the League, also saw no reason for Moore's arrival in Ireland. " Mr. Moore's impulse," he wrote, " has no relation to the plane of art."

The Irish-speaking nurse for whom he promised to pay proved a failure. She contented herself with rattling off long sentences to the boys; no one could pick out the meaning of a word, and when the local Mayo schoolmaster was engaged in her stead, he began with the letters of the alphabet. The only persons left were too dirty to let into the house. " I am in despair," Colonel Moore wrote from South Africa, on the 25th of March, 1901, " but do not write too hastily. I daresay Evelyn does her best . . . I wish you would take the matter up and send a nurse who can speak Irish, I do not know how you will set about it but I can only say that you are nearer the scene of action than I am and I know that when you want to do a thing you usually find a way pretty quickly." This letter disturbed Moore greatly, and being resolved to show that he meant always what he said and exactly what he said, he went to his solicitors and altered his will.

25.4.01. *To Colonel Moore.*

It happens, my dear Maurice, that the first letter that I wrote from the above address [Ely Place] is to you. I received your letter about the children's Irish yesterday, and I posted the enclosed letter to Evelyn yesterday. . . . I shall write to her Mother and Brother on the subject. I don't want to marry, and nothing will induce me to marry except the desire that a Moore shall be born, whose natural language shall be Irish . . . I am jealous of your knowledge of Irish—you will always know the language better than I. I suppose you speak it with the soldiers. There must be many in the regiment who know Irish. . . .

24.4.01. *To Mrs. Maurice Moore.*

I have to-day revoked the will which I made in their (the children's) favour. If I die now your children will have

lost £1,000 a year and you will be responsible for it.
However, the matter can be remedied and the remedy lies
in your own hands. If you write me a letter within the
next few days, assuring me that you have taken steps to
have your children taught Irish as their language—mind
you, no smattering of Irish will do—I wish their first
impressions to be conveyed to them in Irish—I will revoke
the will which I have just made; and I will agree to give
you a year to make up for the time which you have wasted.
If between now and this time next year, your children
speak Irish fluently, I shall henceforth consider them as
my heirs and not unless. If they do not, I shall leave all the
money I have to leave and all the property away from
them, and you will be responsible for this disinherit-
ance . . .

It must be clear to you now that the first thing that
concerns your children is to learn Irish, that whether the
nurses are dirty or ill-mannered are matters of no moment
whatever, that henceforth their business is to learn Irish.
I beg of you to let me have your mother's address, for I
shall send her a copy of this letter and I shall write to your
brother on the same subject. . . .

6

It surprised him that his sister-in-law did not answer his
letters, and took no notice of his invitations to stay with him
in Dublin for a week. " She is doubtless very angry with me,
why I cannot think," Moore wrote to the Colonel. " I can
leave my property to whom I please and if I choose to leave
it to her children on condition that they speak Irish fluently,
I am only imposing a condition that any mother in Ireland
would gladly accept . . ."

Colonel Moore, to whom Moore largely owed his present
ideas, must have felt by now that he had conjured up a
spirit which he could not control. Yet, for all he knew, when
next they met, his brother might dismiss the Irish language
with a wave of the hand. This was more or less what actually
happened, and indeed Moore often became particularly

disputatious and overbearing when he was trying to convince himself on a matter of which he was not himself very sure. The sky, however, cleared : his stipulations were carried out ; a suitable Irish nurse was found, and a little later, a native-speaking teacher took over the task of teaching the two boys, and he then turned his attention to the question of Irish in the national schools, and devised means for bringing Trinity College, that stronghold of the classical culture of Anglo-Ireland, to its knees. " The Rotunda," he wrote to his brother, " was crammed even to stenching point on the night of the Oireachtas. We are fighting the battle of the schools day by day, and Trinity College is a worry, and I am thinking of publishing a long descriptive article on Professor Mahaffy, but these personal attacks are disagreeable to me and I shall not write if I can possibly avoid doing so."

Dr. Mahaffy, whom Moore must have met at Gosse's Sunday supper parties in London, was an irrepressible critic of Gaelicism ; and an outrageous article from Moore's pen " descriptive " of him did presently appear in a saucy journal of Nationalist and Catholic opinion. It was a lamentable performance for which Moore soon repented, for he hated the idea of doing material wrong to anyone, and he was filled with horror when someone said to him, with a scant regard for truth, that his article had so impressed the Chief Secretary as to injure very gravely Mahaffy's chances of being appointed to the Provostship of Trinity College. Later, he found another reason for regretting his action ; he would so have enjoyed the learning and worldly wit, which in Dublin could best be found at Mahaffy's dinner table, and what excellent conversations he could have had with this very liberal clergyman on the subject of St. Paul !

This was not the end of his misadventures as a patriot. At the time of his moving in, all the five houses in Upper Ely Place had white hall-doors. Moore, to the just annoyance of the other residents, ordered that his should be painted green. Two young women, sisters, threatened a lawsuit against Moore, or the landlord, on the ground that the five white hall doors was one of the reasons for their taking a house in Ely Place. Moore's retort was to go out at midnight and seek

to disturb the ladies in their sleep by rousing all the dogs
within earshot with a rattle of his stick on their area-railings.
One night, while he was so engaged, the sisters' dog bit him
and he had to get Thornley Stoker out of bed to give him an
injection. Another resident, the eccentric Cunningham, who
is described in *A Story Teller's Holiday*, sided with the two
sisters and paid an Italian to grind an organ outside No. 4
during Moore's working hours. Moore then declared war on
their favourite cat who was in the habit of using his garden,
saying that the cat threatened the life of a blackbird which
sang there. To protect the blackbird he set a trap for the cat,
and both parties appealed to the Society for the Prevention
of Cruelty to Animals. The grotesque warfare ended in
Moore's discomfiture, for his trap caught the blackbird.

With Sir Thornley Stoker he was on terms of facetious
familiarity. The old doctor had a kind heart; when Moore
annoyed him he would pretend that he only knew of him by
hearsay. " There is a ruffian in our street," he said one day
to young Dr. Oliver Gogarty. " He will presently try to make
your acquaintance and expect free medical treatment.
Remember your apothecary's oath." Lady Stoker fell ill, and
her malady was diagnosed as likely to be long and painful,
Moore thought he should say how sorry he was. He was
dining at Ely House that night, and on entering the drawing-
room he found the other guests busy with their polite
enquiries. This irritated him, for he wanted the conversation
to become interesting. He greeted Sir Thornley and said:
" Please convey my sympathy *once for all* to Lady Stoker."
The story bears a resemblance to another of much later date
which has been told me by Tonks. A friend called on Moore
to break some sad news, the death of an old friend. Moore was
much moved and started walking up and down the room,
describing in eloquent words the virtues of one he had
admired so much. The friend listened most carefully, but at
last interrupted him by saying: " But Moore, I did not say
Gosse, I said Ross." Moore stopped, thought a moment, and
replied: " Well, I can't go over all that again."

But so many anecdotes were told of Moore in Dublin that
it would take a volume to relate them all. They passed from

mouth to mouth, " improving " as they went, and taking the proportions of a saga. Much must have been invented, for instance the story of his experience with the local printing firm to which he gave his new version of *Evelyn Innes* so as to help Irish industry. The foreman took a love scene home and rewrote it according to his notions of propriety. Moore read the scene aloud to A. E. from the proofs and showed some petulance when A. E. said: " It seems very icy." Another cause which he had at heart was the reform of Irish cooking, but his attempt to come to an understanding with his first cook on the subject of an omelette led to a scene so atrocious as to cause the woman to dash from the house and call in a policeman. His next cook gave satisfaction with omelettes and he was very kind when her sister fell ill, and paid the expenses, but it was not a place she liked, and there were so many " rumours " about Mr. Moore, she said, that she was glad to leave and go back to her mother.

His fury against the war continued unabated:

On the subject of the war (he wrote to his brother) I think I am going a little crazy, for I refuse to speak to anyone except those who are against the war. I met a man the other day whom I had known all my life, he told me that war was a beautiful thing; and that this was an exceptionally fine example of war. I said " I shall never speak to you again." This seems unreasonable, but to feel as I do on this subject and to be friends with those who think otherwise would be false to myself. Our ideas are our friends. What are our friends but the embodiment of our ideas ? Our ideas are the most precious things we have, and they are the only things we carry away with us when we leave the world.

7

Sister Teresa was ready in 1901 as well as a new version of *Evelyn Innes*. Huysmans said when he heard that Moore was working on this novel that he feared little could be done to make English convent life interesting in fiction and *Sister*

Teresa bore out the truth of this remark. But although Moore still took great pains with his external details he now aimed at revealing his characters by the explanation of their mental processes rather than by exact pictures of their actions and environment. *Evelyn Innes* and *Sister Teresa* are psychological novels. On this new ground Moore met with a considerable success. The reader of *Sister Teresa* is told repeatedly that having escaped from her lovers to the convent Evelyn is pursuing a moral idea. " Her problem is to live or to put life aside " ; and the Christ to whom her thoughts go is " neither the victim nor the bridegroom, but the young man who appeared in Galilee preaching a doctrine which alone could save men from themselves." While the scene shifts, it is very skilfully shown that Evelyn is always fundamentally the same, never " converted," and conversely never without her scruples of a Catholic; the two books have been aptly described as a study in what Moore once called the most terrible of all forms of sensuality—the religious. He seems to have found it difficult to decide how he should bring the story to a close. He was minded at times to make his heroine marry Owen Asher and bring up children, her experience in the convent becoming as the years passed the great reality in her life. But he doubtfully rejected this solution, and in the first edition Evelyn makes her vows and, after coming near in an anguishing scene to breaking them, she is left, somewhat unaccountably, at peace. On the last pages she has decided that " the important thing to do is to live, and we do not begin to know life, taste life, until we put it aside. . . ."

The alterations in *Evelyn Innes* were interesting, particularly the substitution of A. E. for W. B. Yeats as the Irish musician who talks about " the Gods." Evelyn's break with Ulick is now described more briefly and the young musician's views on Shakespeare, Blake and Shelley, suggestive of Yeats rather than of A. E. are omitted. In the 1901 edition Evelyn admires the tall thin figure of Ulick; she wonders if she would like him better without a beard. He wears an old suit of grey clothes, a loose necktie and a soft felt hat; Evelyn likes him thus, but " one did not think of Ulick's clothes," for " Ulick's naturalness made everyone natural."

At a hotel one night " at midnight his simplicity prevented her from throwing herself into his arms." Ulick and Evelyn go to Ireland together, bicycling into Louth and Meath on a visit to the sacred places of the old Pagan civilisation, Dowth and New Grange, to which A. E. had recently conducted Moore.[1] Ulick is a pantheist who speculates upon the divinity of Earth:

> *I look with sudden awe beneath my feet*
> *As you with erring reverence overhead—*

and upon one of his expeditions with Evelyn in an encounter with two Presbyterian ministers, he gives some evidence of anti-clericalism:

> I am afraid you have led us wrong, said one of the clergymen, and Ulick answered him—Gentlemen of your profession should know the meaning of " the blind leading the blind."

A. E. would have been incapable of Ulick's insolence, but his conversation undoubtedly encouraged Moore to regard priestly power as the bane of Irish life.

A. E. charmed Moore both by his personality and ideas. " It was," he wrote in his Irish autobiography, " just as if somebody had suddenly put his hand into mine and led me away into a young world which I recognized at once as the fabled Arcady that had flourished before man discovered gold, and forged the gold into a ring which gave him power to enslave. ' While we strive after happiness, he holds it in his hands,' I said. . . . It seemed clear to me that he was the one who could restore to me my confidence in life; and when he left me a certain mental sweetness seemed to have gone out of the air, and thinking of him, I began to wonder if he were aware of his own sweetness. It is as spontaneous and in-stinctive in him as . . . A breath of scent from the lilac bushes seemed to finish my sentence for me."

[1] The tour is described in *Salve*.

Had he searched he could scarcely have found a man whose material and spiritual experience was more dissimilar from his own. At their first meeting A. E. was a young man of thirty-four, lately come to that belief in the divine symbolism of the Gaelic myths and in their resemblances to Hindu wisdom which was to inspire a career of Irish prophecy. His heredity was Northern Irish and nothing impressed Moore more than the story of how as a lad he had stopped one day upon the road to ask why men should be condemned by a law which they had never promised to obey, thereafter nourishing himself upon the Sacred Books of the East and treating Christianity (with some condescension, perhaps) as one of the minor religions. Yeats had known A. E. at the Art School, and then as a leader among Dublin theosophists, and through Yeats A. E. was introduced to Sir Horace Plunkett and given employment in the Irish Agricultural Organisation Society, and that Society henceforth seemed to move around invisible suns. Moore was stirred to wonder, even to enchantment, before this man who combined practical gifts and a nimble brain with a deep religious and poetical impulse. " I love him," he would say, " I love everything he writes." He could even read A. E.'s prose—books with such titles as *Priest and King*, or *The Hero in Man*, which expressed the august if somewhat uncritical moral intuitions of his new friend. And when he thought that A. E. looked ill he immediately suggested paying for a holiday in Italy.

Signs of the enchantment were beginning to appear in Moore's work. We read in the 1901 edition of *Evelyn Innes* that " the plants lifted their leaves to the light. *Everything* knew it, even the stone in the centre of the earth ; she watched the distant woods submerged in the light of the sun . . . her immortal spirit seemed to ascend into the immortal light." And a few years later in the *Lake* : " Trees always interested him and in one of his walks he began to think of their great roots seeking the darkness, and of their branches lifting themselves in love to the sky. He and these trees were one, for there is but one life, one Mother, one elemental substance out of which we have all come." A. E. did not readily acknowledge a disciple in Moore, and was inclined to question the wisdom of bringing him into the movement. Outside æsthetics he took him for a materialist in life and thought, but he grew fond of him and admired him as a rare being who always acted from his own will and centre. " We talked on all subjects," A. E. once said to me, " but our favourite subjects were painting and immortality. I think that he wished to be convinced of survival after death, but he asked for evidence that would pass in a police court, and it was no use applying the Socratic argument and appealing to an inner sense."

A. E. became the chief of Moore's literary friends in Dublin, and next to him came, also from the North and of Puritan heredity and formation, John Eglinton, a librarian in the National Library, whose real name was W. K. Magee (" A good spanking little name," said Moore. " Why does he wish to change it ? ") While he was still in London Moore's attention had been drawn to the excellence of John Eglinton's prose in *Two Essays on the Remnant,* and to certain contributions in the *Express* which showed a greater flavour of the classics and also a more prudent way of conducting thought than was customary in Ireland. Here, they told him, was the Irish Thoreau. Distinguished prose, Moore agreed, but at that time he was still disposed to regard as impious any Irishman who could not see the Celtic gods; and as John Eglinton for his part refused to believe that a man of Moore's antecedents could confer any moral or literary benefits on the Irish Renaissance, the first encounters of the two were not altogether a success. Moore, however, was not long in Dublin before he realised the interest of John Eglinton's personality: " a gnarled solitary life," he would say, " a sort of lonely thorn tree, thorny and tenacious—the thorn breaking into flower." He doubtless foresaw the advantages of having as a friend one who would have the courage and would take the pains to admonish him should the occasion arise. And John Eglinton without sacrificing the independence which Moore admired—resolutely remaining to the end in a dubious attitude towards Moore as an artist—experienced a certain satisfaction in being on confidential terms with the elder

man of letters who had " arrived." They showed a remarkable compatibility of temper, and the variety of their
opinions and tenets was of no ill consequence to a friendship
which proved to be one of the smoothest in Moore's
experience.

8

In W. B. Yeats Moore thought that he had found another
Dujardin. Yeats too was a metaphysical man, a poet who
transfigured metaphysics, and like Moore's French friend,
he found a joy in instruction. They were engaged upon a
new dramatic adventure: *Diarmuid and Grania* (begun before
Moore's settlement in his native country), a prose play
in three acts, founded on the Ossianic story of the lovers'
bed on the hill of the Fenians. They differed continuously,
and the compromise that was eventually arrived at—that
Moore should supervise the construction while Yeats wrote
the dialogue—must have been little more than a nominal
arrangement, since changes in the writing exacted changes
in the construction. Yeats wanted to eradicate descriptions
and ideas, as inappropriate to a heroic play, but the second
act was descriptive, and no sooner was the work put on the
stage than he proposed a structural alteration of this act.
The one hankered after a Grania of folk and the other
imagined a play in the style of *Die Walküre* or *Tristan und
Isolde*.

At one point Lady Gregory or Yeats, or both, suggested
that certain parts of the play might be suitably put into
dialect; and Yeats may have suggested a translation into
Irish (like the prose of Douglas Hyde's *Love Songs of Connaught*) as a basis for this dialect. Moore cried: " I could
write all this much more easily in French "; and he was
begged to do so in Heaven's name. " Translating you will
improve my French, and we won't have any more quarrels
about style," said Yeats. Later, Moore expanded these con-
versational incidents into the story of a wonderful project:
Lady Gregory would translate the French text into English,
and after the English had been put into Irish by a native

writer, the Irish text would be translated back into English by Lady Gregory.

At Moore's request Elgar composed some beautiful music for the scene in which Diarmuid is borne away to the funeral pyre, and when the play was shown to famous London actors and actresses it provoked many compliments. For the honour of Ireland *Diarmuid and. Grania* had first to be performed in Dublin: Benson's company undertook the performance on the 21st October, 1901, and after that there was no more nibbling from London theatres. In retrospect Moore treated the whole episode very lightly, but at the time he was much pleased with the finished work. In letters to a German correspondent, Dr. Heilborn, he spoke as if the play were entirely his own and said that he liked it better than anything he had written except *Esther Waters*. " There is no reason why it should not be a success in Germany. . . . Everyone who has seen it loved it. Mrs. Pat Campbell, one of our best actresses, offered me a good deal of money for the play if I allowed it to be produced in London. I refused."

Local critics found the play too modern in atmosphere, not " Irish " enough; and perhaps they made up their minds beforehand that any treatment of heroic legend by Moore would be deficient in delicacy.

To Colonel Moore.

They first of all enjoyed the play, and having enjoyed it they repented in sackcloth and ashes, and I really believe that the repentance was much greater than their enjoyment of the play. At the end of the week they all discovered that the irrelevancies of the legend (the folklore) which had collected round the essential story had been omitted. They also discovered that Grania was not as perfectly virtuous as an Irishwoman should be.

From this time on disparaging comments on his life in Ireland and on Ireland itself began to make appearance in his conversation and in his correspondence. But he was still much in earnest about the language; he kept in touch with

Douglas Hyde and other Gaelic leaders, and urged on them the importance of providing the people with good books in Irish. The *Bible* and *The Arabian Nights* were two of his suggestions. At the beginning of 1902 he offered Hyde his garden for the performance of a Gaelic play, *The Tinker and the Fairy*.

To Colonel Moore.

I am very much interested in a party. I want to give a party. The garden in front of my house belongs to me and it will hold five or six hundred people easily; and there are apple trees; and nothing will be easier than to build a stage. . . . On this stage I want to have performed a play in Irish. I want to have a Gaelic-speaking audience. I think this would be a very good thing, and I think it would annoy Dublin society very much; which will add considerably to my pleasure.

He attended rehearsals and left a charming impression upon the young people from the League who were to act in his play. But he had never before given a party and when the day came—" But what am I to do ? " he said, opening his arms, like a bird that lifts its wings, a characteristic gesture. He decided to do nothing, and stood about in the crowd of his guests with a helpless smile on his face. The stage consisted of a few boards laid one on the other, six inches high. His hostile neighbours looked down on the scene from their upper windows. They mocked loudly when the sounds of a strange language reached them from the garden.

Soon after this the Irish Literary Theatre was wound up after three years of work. No one could tell what form the dramatic movement in Ireland would henceforth take, but there was a general feeling that it would be well to cease from dependence upon English professional actors. Yeats and Martyn were at loggerheads, for Martyn held that Irish actors when found should be trained for the modern drama of society and Yeats wanted to vary peasant plays with the poetic drama of legend. The brothers Fay—amateurs who earned their living in offices and performed farces in coffee-houses after the day's work—determined the issue. It was discovered that the one brother had a beautiful gift for the speaking of verse, and that the other had a natural genius for interpreting the life of Irish countrymen. By the end of 1902 the Fay's Irish National Dramatic Company was recognised as the successor of the Irish Literary Theatre.

Martyn thought it was an illegitimate successor, and to some extent this seems to have been Moore's view also. Henceforward the movement was dominated by Lady Gregory and Yeats, both as masterful as Moore himself, and far more prepared for responsibilities than Martyn or Moore or A. E. In *Samhain: 1902*, Yeats said that they "had dropped out of the movement," but whether either of them was asked to stay in it is uncertain, and Moore's anticlericalism was growing so vocal as to make him unfitted to be a director in any public enterprise. He had admired the talents of the Fays when he saw them in a play by A. E., but he thought they would be more usefully employed by the Gaelic League to go up and down the country doing plays in Irish than in Dublin. And he felt very sore when Yeats did not come back to him with a modern psychological play for which his collaboration had been asked some months previously. During the summer they had met in Galway at the Gaelic festival which is described in *Salve*; on his return to Dublin Moore telegraphed to Yeats to say that he would get an injunction if Yeats used the scenario as he was writing a novel on the subject himself. He could scarcely have been serious, but Yeats took him seriously and hastily published *Where There is Nothing* in order, as he explained afterwards, " to save from a plagiarist a subject that seemed worth the keeping till a greater knowledge of the stage made an adequate treatment possible." He left out an incident which Moore had suggested. A few months later, John Quinn, an American supporter of Irish movements, induced the two writers to be on speaking terms again, but henceforward there were reserves on both sides.

9

The writing of a number of short stories rather than the breach with Yeats makes the year 1902 a landmark in Moore's literary history.

One day, not long after the performance of *Diarmuid and Grania*, John Eglinton put it to him that he should write of Irish life in the manner of Turgenev's *Tales of a Sportsman*. This would be his true contribution to the Irish Revival. He was one of the older men in the Revival; unlike Yeats and A. E. he had lost sight of his country for a while, but had now returned with memories of his childhood and developed powers of criticism and observation.

Moore's heart sank when Turgenev's name was mentioned. " As well ask me to paint like Corot," he said, but he set to work on the stories, saying to himself that in this way he would provide the League with something that could be translated into Irish. The first, and one of the best, of the tales was "The Wedding Gown." A text book for the schools was intended, and he found a prince of native speakers to translate "The Wedding Gown," and some of the other stories for the *New Ireland Review*, a magazine edited by a Jesuit, Father Finlay, of whom he was very fond, a member of Sir Horace Plunket's circle: he sent copies of the *New Ireland Review* to his English friends hoping that they would believe the Irish was his (and indeed at this time he took a few lessons in the language). Religion and sex were forbidden subjects, but he remembered that Turgenev wrote stories about things, without moral and literary tendency, like the story of the horse that was stolen, and his English friend, " Stella," encouraged him to go on. " These stories," he was to say in *Salve*, " might never have been written if it had not been for Stella's interest in them."

It will be remembered that early in life Moore discovered a sympathy with Protestantism, a sympathy of the heart he had called it. However, when writing *Evelyn Innes* and *Sister Teresa* he tried to cultivate as an artist an imaginative understanding of the emotions and beliefs of Catholics, and in his contribution to a book called *Ideals in Ireland* he praised the

fidelity of the Irish people as a whole to their religion as a
sign of their resolve to resist Anglicisation; he appeared on his
first arrival in Ireland to be pro-Catholic. But he was not
long settled in Dublin before he began to raise objections to
the Roman Catholic Church in Ireland on political grounds,
and to side with the anti-clericals and Protestants who put
the blame for the failure of Irish nationality, the melancholy
waste in Irish life, emigration and so forth, on the Puritan
excesses of the Irish priest. Then he looked around him and
began to count the number of religious institutions he
passed on his daily walks. Soon he was writing stories on the
relations of priests and people, and it became impossible to
publish any more of his work in the *New Ireland Review*.

He wrote his stories primarily because he had stories to
tell, not to influence a cause, and in some of them the priests
were quite favourably depicted. Gradually however *The
Untilled Field* developed into a portrait of Ireland, Ireland
clerically supervised and without a language of her own. He
was still interested in the country, he said. " Ignorance is
everywhere," he wrote to his brother, " and intellectually
the country is unwashed—that is why it is interesting." While
he was in this mood he was a godsend to all the people who
wished to explain Ireland and improve their neighbours—
and they were the majority of the people whom he met. " I
don't believe," writes one who saw him a great deal at this
time, " that Moore has the slightest idea what Plunkett or
any of us were doing—he could not understand because it
would never have occurred to him that any of us were such
fools. The only person he really understood in Ireland was
Thornley Stoker and perhaps Hicks, the cabinet-maker—
they had common interests in old glass and furniture, and
through them Moore picked up some bargains, but missed
more owing to his indecisions. On the side of art he understood Walter Osborne, and Hughes the sculptor reminded
him pleasantly of Paris."

10

The Untilled Field in its Irish dress was brought out by a
Dublin publisher in 1902 as "An T-ūr-Gort, Sgéalta." It was

a nice-looking little book and Moore was gratified to see his name in Irish on the title page: Séorsa Ó Mórda. He got T. W. Rolleston, a distinguished man of letters who knew the language, to translate the beautiful "Wedding Gown" and one or two of the stories back into English and found them "much improved after their bath in Irish. ' She had a face such as one sees in a fox ' . . . how much better than ' She had a fox-like face.' " Rolleston's work was by him when he prepared the English text which Fisher Unwin published in the following year.

There were thirteen stories in the original English edition of *The Untilled Field*. They continued, especially those of them which had been best suited for Father Finlay's review, to please Moore until the end of his life. This inscription is in a copy which he gave to Mr. Philip Gosse in December 1931: " To Philip Gosse. Philip, Edmund Gosse said that the story entitled ' The Window,' was the best short story ever written. I did not agree with him. I prefer ' So On He Fares.' George Moore, an old family friend." (The long chain of stories called " Some Parishioners " in the first edition was later divided into four parts, the last of which is " The Window.")

The completion of the book (in September 1902) left him a little weary. " Fourteen priests in ten months are too much," he wrote to Dujardin. " I'd like to paint, to model, to write in French. . . . For the moment I've had enough of the Gaelic League . . . I shall come to Paris for sure. . . ." The Irish edition of *The Untilled Field* had scarcely raised a ripple on the complacent surface of the Gaelic waters. To his brother who was still in South Africa he wrote: " The only thing I look forward to with any degree of interest is seeing you again. My other interests are puny."

His other interests now included biblical exegesis, and when he visited Dujardin at Fontainebleau the conversation chiefly turned on this subject, no longer on music. Dujardin, having become Professor of the History of Primitive Christianity at the Sorbonne, was now engaged on a study of Judaic origins, *La Source du Fleuve Chrétien*, and the very title ravished Moore. " You know how greatly your book interests me," he wrote upon his return to Dublin. " What endless talk it led to on your terrace. . . . And do you remember my awful *gaffe*? By Jove, it was a *gaffe*. I have the highest hopes for your book. I am always thinking about it."

The handsome Colonel returned from South Africa and stopped for a while at Ely Place, to be shown about with pride to Moore's friends, as an elderly man might show his bride. He had been through the fiercest fighting on Colenso Hill and at Spion Kop, and ought to write, Moore thought, a book of camp life. Their grandfather's manuscript history of the French Revolution was to be published at last; they were to do this and that together. The Colonel's letters to the press on questions of public interest, earned his brother's compliments, and Moore went about saying: " He has the talent—I the vocation."

Differences soon declared themselves. Colonel Moore wanted to work for the Gaelic League and could not agree with his brother that Catholicism stood in the way of all Irish progress. In this opinion Moore was now unalterably fixed.

—.6.03 *To Dujardin.*

I am very sorry that you cannot come here for my house is charming and excursions from village to village on our bicycles would be good for us. My arm is no better but one day or another I shall be forced to ride again. I have utterly renounced my Celtic aspirations. Of the race there remains but a tattered remnant, a shred in which one finds a great deal of rabble, I mean the priests. Life has no other goal but life, and art has no other end but to make life possible, to help us to live. As soon as one puts one's hopes in another world, life becomes dreary and ugly and art makes itself scarce.

A few weeks later he wrote again: " It is just because I am living in Ireland that I await your book with such eagerness." He was always hoping that J.-E. Blanche or

Dujardin or Lord Howard de Walden would visit Ireland for his sake. Dujardin was to be shown the Mayo and the Galway castles of his Norman ancestors. But it was rarely that anyone came to stay with him, even from England; in 1903 however he had a visit from Mark Fisher, who came to paint landscapes in Ireland. While at Ely Place Fisher painted a portrait of his host, which Moore liked better than any other that had been done of him; perhaps because it made less free of his characteristic features than most.

In England and abroad his fame was extending; he had written a fashionable book in *Evelyn Innes*, a book for those who enjoyed the fashionable novels of the day. The Tauchnitz edition inspired the admiration of a foreign lady of noble birth who opened a correspondence with him. She showed interest in the man behind the work, approaching Moore in a mixed spirit of flattery and raillery which he rightly found delicious. The lady had begun to pick out heroes from Tauchnitz at a very early age, but this was the first time she was in communication with an author, for when she wrote to Tolstoy she forgot to post the letter. " My dear Baronne," Moore replied to her enquiry, " I am not horrid. I used to fear I was when I was very young, but now I know that I am not." " I wondered at first if you were a priest," she wrote. " Not a monk of course, but something in the nature of a Monsignor, or just a man who was interested in all sorts of people—in nuns as well as in prima donnas, in race horses and in poor working folk." Later on she sent him her photograph; he began to call her Gabrielle, and wished to know if he might mention her wonderful letters to Sir William Eden. " Don't call me Gabrielle," she answered. " I am not a courtesan. Do I call you Henri ? " In one of his letters he spoke of *The Untilled Field*. " You have lived only in castles and convents. I hate convents. *The Untilled Field* will have told you that. There are some good things in that book. You will like it better when you take it up six months hence. It is a dry book and does not claim the affections at once. The old woman who puts up a window in her church and hears the saints singing is intended to represent Ireland. ' The Wild Goose ' is being

translated into German. I have refused permission to translate so often that at length I yielded."

He was busy with another Irish story, *The Lake*, a further
scene from clerical life; begun while he was writing *The
Untilled Field* this story had proved to be too long and perhaps too complex to be included in that volume. It showed,
he said, the essential not the daily life of a priest, but the
closing episode—the priest's swim across the lake, his old
clothes left on the one shore, his new awaiting him on the
other—had been suggested by an incident of real life. There
was a Protestant clergyman in Dublin, formerly a Roman
Catholic priest and at this time a conductor of Protestant
missions among the poor, of whom the same story of escape
was told. And Moore had committed two engaging larcenies
of nomenclature. His priest bore the familiar name of Oliver
Gogarty, and another of the personages—the scholar
Ralph Ellis (in later editions Walter Poole) who does
not appear, but of whom much is heard, was the author
of a work of exegesis named *The Source of the Christian River*.

The Lake absorbed him. While writing the earlier stories
he seems hardly to have realised what good work he was
again doing, but with *The Lake* he felt that his artistic life
was being renewed. Therefore, although Ireland refused his
help and indeed as a Catholic country was beyond his help,
it was not necessary to admit that he had made a mistake
in coming there. " He went to Ireland intuitively, as he did
all things, for the sake of his art," writes Mr. Charles
Morgan, in his *Epitaph on George Moore*; and passages in
" The Way Back " (the last story in the original *Untilled
Field*) show that he was already in 1902 beginning to take
a biographer's view of the reasons which led to his migration.
Harding, the ironical, worldly novelist who appears in
several of the early books, has created a sensation in London
by announcing that he must return to Ireland.

" Your biographer " [says his friend Rodney] " will be
puzzled to explain this last episode, and, however he may
explain it, it will seem a discrepancy."

" I suppose one should think of one's biographer," and

they laughed and talked of a time when everybody would choose his biographer and live accordingly.

Harding proceeds to answer his friend's pessimistic comments on the Catholic Celt by quoting the Irish proverb: " No man ever wanders far from his grave sod," and when they tempt him with the prospect of an Italian tour he replies: " You won't be angry with me when I tell you that all your interesting utterances about the Italian renaissance would not interest me half so much as what Paddy Durkin and Father Pat will say to me on the roadside."

Years after, when Moore had left Ireland, tried to forget Ireland, and even said that he hated Ireland, a chance allusion to *The Lake* or *The Untilled Field* would set him telling of " the happy inspiration of a man returning after long years to his native land."

CHAPTER VII

IRELAND: DISENCHANTMENT

I

ONE MIGHT HAVE SUPPOSED that after renouncing his
Celtic hopes Moore would retire to the ivory tower of his
art. But the permanence of the unexpected was a feature of
his character, and the year 1903 saw him take a step which
brought him again, for a moment at least, into the limelight
of controversy. This step was the public avowal of his Protestantism. His interest in Dujardin's exegesis had set him
reading the Bible from beginning to end; there were many
things in the Old Testament which repelled him, but as
soon as he came to the Gospels he began to ask why he had
been allowed to grow up in a misunderstanding of Christianity and in ignorance of the great literary art of its
founder. And when he read St. Paul's Epistles he spoke of
an important spiritual experience. It was of a nature, he
said, which would justify him in making application for
membership of the Anglican community in Ireland; and
one evening, without consulting anyone, he wrote a letter to
the Protestant Archbishop, Dr. Peacocke, in which he said
that since he came to live in Ireland his thoughts had been
directed towards religion, and now he realised that the
purest form of religion was to be found in the Anglican community; would His Grace direct him how to become a
member of the Church of Ireland? The Archbishop was
at the seaside, and he referred Moore to a hard-worked
philanthropical clergyman, his neighbour in Ely Place, a
Dr. Gilbert Mahaffy. " I dare say," said the clergyman,
at the first interview, " you are right in finding that we
Protestants are superior in intelligence, but we have our
beliefs, Mr. Moore, and they are not so vague as yours."

They argued about texts. " I take my stand upon St. Paul ! " Moore cried. The final act in his conversion was to kneel at a table and to say the Lord's Prayer.

The scene was recounted to his friends ; everyone in Dublin heard of it. It was admitted that the Church of Ussher, Swift and Berkeley had not risen to the occasion by recognising the important place which Moore occupied in the world of letters, but sympathies in general were extended to the clergyman, as the victim of an unwarrantable flight of wit. When taxed with deliberate comedy Moore defended his sincerity; it was true he was an agnostic, but, he said, Protestantism had no limits to overstep, being but a stage in human development. He may have felt, for he was now something of a theologian, that Protestantism with its " grace " and " election " is nearer to the artist than Catholicism which must always account the man of more intelligence, of more taste, of more imagination, as nothing compared with the veriest dullard who keeps the rules. He was asked why he could not remain an agnostic or lapsed Catholic, and to that he replied that his spontaneous sympathies had always been with the natural Protestant who, unlike the agnostic Catholic, is open to " religious discussion." But the main motive of his action was a desire to dissociate himself from the Irish Catholic, and this, he argued with some reason, could only be done in Ireland by taking steps to become a Protestant: in Ireland, where the distinction embraces so much more than religion, one must be either Catholic or Protestant. " Martyn has said so and the Irish Protestant is my kin, and not the soft, peaty stuff that comes from Connaught." " But," some ventured, " your own family is Catholic." Nothing angered him more than this ; he would reply either that his family was a detestable one from the religious point of view, spiritually apathetic without a heretic in it but himself; or that the Moores were Protestants not so far back, his great-grandfather, the merchant of Alicante, having been of very doubtful Catholicism, a conformer for material reasons.

His brother tried to dissuade him from " religious discussion," and in deference to Colonel Moore's feelings he refrained for a time from writing to the newspapers. A local reviewer, however, spoke of the author of *The Untilled Field* as " himself a Catholic " and he says in *Salve* that this upset his mental balance, and he asked : " Is the shame eternal ? " But a light broke into his mind suddenly. . . . " I remembered that the welcome the priests had given Edward VII when he came to Ireland had not pleased the patriotic Gaelic League, and it occurred to me that I might get a nice revenge for the words ' himself a Catholic ' if I were to write to the *Irish Times* declaring that I had passed from the Church of Rome to the Church of Ireland, shocked beyond measure at the lack of patriotism of the Irish priests." The reason he gave at the time was a different one. He wrote on account of a statement publicly made as to his change of religion, and of which he complained, as properly a private matter, concerning only himself. The editor of the *Irish Times*, John Healy, was always indulgent towards Moore, and published his lengthy letter on 24th of October, 1903. It showed that all that was positive in his anti-catholicism rose from his Irish conscience and returned to it. " Without opening my soul like a public building," he wrote, " I must give one reason which leaves me no choice if I am to remain an Irishman but to say good-bye to Rome "—and he gave the political reason. A. E. warned him that he was courting obloquy, but for this he did not care.

2

When first he came to Ireland Moore was by way of having cut himself off entirely from English life, but he now showed signs of wishing to construct bridges for a possible return. He resumed correspondence with many of his friends in England, stopping in London for long periods on his way to and from Paris, whither he went, he said, to be regilded. He was thinking of himself when he described his priest in *The Lake*. " He didn't want to learn anything, only to admire. He was weary of argument, religious and political. It wasn't that he was indifferent to his country's welfare, but every mind requires rest, and he wished himself away in a foreign country, distracted every moment by new things. . . ."

The letters of the foreign countess grew more and more delightful. They babbled like a brook and transported their recipient where Nature murmurs her irregular rhythms. But it soon occurred to him that the lady might make herself useful to him by translating his books into German. He stood rebuked when she replied that she was " not a governess," and that abroad only hairdressers read translations. The *Confessions of A Young Man* shocked her a little, for she did not share Moore's love of the French, who had " oily hair and fussy manners." " Please be very English," she wrote, "and you will not disappoint me. Young men [in my country] when they admire something very much, a hat or a dog, a house or a waltzer, a racehorse or a lady, used to say *Das ist Piccadilly 121*. It's nonsense after all, is it not? They ought to say 12, Waterloo Place [Sir William Eden's rooms in London]. Tell me more about Sir Owen. . . ."

He gave his age, not quite accurately, as 46, and sent her his photograph; she said that she liked middle-aged men. " Don't show my letters to your wife," she added. He had thought that he might meet her in Venice or in Munich, but on a visit to Paris in the Spring of 1904 he sat down to write a letter which he thought to be tactful, excusing himself:

> The weather is beautiful and it inspires love; the delicious Aphrodite awakes me every morning. . . . I could love you Gabrielle I understand so well when you say that life is dry and empty when one hasn't a lover. . . . We are in the middle of love's season and what a joy is the divine sentiment of union. But Gabrielle I am going back to Ireland to write books. Why? I cannot answer. I often wonder; an instinct drives me. But if I were free it would be enchanting to meet you in Munich. But if I were to go I should lose my chance of writing *The Lake* and writing a comedy that tempts me. You are better than literature I know, I can see you are a dear woman. . . . Your photograph tells me all about you. I appreciate you

Gabrielle, do not judge me by my letters. There is a better side to me and I have not shown it in my letters to you. But if we were to meet, you would like me better. But if we were to meet what would the end be?

In June he spent three weeks in London, " three weeks of dinner parties, operas and assemblies." It was enough, and he was glad to return to his work. " I shall finish *The Lake* and a comedy," he wrote to " Gabrielle " from Ely Place. " The subject of the comedy is a lady who writes to an author and what comes of it. If it is ever acted in —— you must go to see it."

The plot resembled Balzac's *Modeste Mignon*. The author, with whom Gabrielle corresponds, has a secretary, a young poet, and he cannot understand why the author does not hasten to Munich to meet his correspondent. One night the matter is discussed after dinner—the author has a dinner party every Saturday. When the guests have gone the author tells his secretary the reason for his reluctance and authorises him to go to Munich and use his name.

In September we find Moore, rather surprisingly, again in the company of Mrs. Craigie. He may have met her during his season in London and spoken to her about the play which was in his mind. At all events she invited him to Steephill Castle, Isle of Wight, her father's residence, and they worked together upon the comedy of the " Coming of Gabrielle," which at first bore the title of *The Peacock's Feathers*. She was to advise, he was to write; and much of the dialogue was taken directly from " Gabrielle's " amusing letters.

23.9.04. *To Dujardin.*

The comedy will be signed by me and by her but it— the comedy—is almost entirely mine, for an almost miraculous thing has happened. I asked her [Mrs. Craigie] for a stenographer; she telegraphed that she had one. . . . I dictated the comedy, I who work with such difficulty, in three days. The lady who has plenty of talent and is a celebrated author, read the comedy and she has told me that she doesn't care to touch it. I read the first two acts this morning—she exaggerates. She is a very good business woman and has charge of all the arrangements, and in the morning she walks in the garden and on the terrace in the most delicious Watteau costumes, rose coloured silks and flowers in her hat. Her great friend is a priest. If the comedy is a success you must translate it.

He was again much taken with Mrs. Craigie, and he spoke of leaving Ireland and settling in the Isle of Wight. Twice already they had been friends, twice already they had quarrelled, and their third association ended as unfortunately as the others. Mrs. Craigie was not satisfied with the division of labour and she wanted to alter Moore's text. " I have had a sad experience with my collaborator," he wrote to Dujardin a few months later. When Dujardin next met him he asked what had happened, and Moore related in his reply some fantastic lover's quarrel. " I was walking in the Green Park," he said, " and I saw her in front of me. I was blind with rage and I ran up behind her and kicked her." At first he related this story with faint embarrassment, but when he grew accustomed to his invention, with relish. The scene in the Green Park was afterwards used in the sketch " Lui et Elles " which appeared in the 1921 edition only of *Memoirs of My Dead Life*, where a heartless woman, on whose face he detected a mocking smile, receives the assault " nearly in the centre of the backside, a little to the right," and seems highly gratified to find that she had aroused such a display of feeling. " It was inevitable, I said, part of the world's history, and I lost sight of all things but the track of my boot on the black crêpe de Chine."

Later in answer to a question by William Heinemann he wrote :

You know I suppose that I had an affair with the lady in question about a dozen years ago, more than that, 14 years ago—I think, and that she shook me off as soon as the exalted person appeared on the scene. For ten years we saw nothing of each other; about two years after her return from India she began to send me messages and after some scuffling I agreed to go to see her. We began the comedy, the three act comedy, about which we quarrelled, our last quarrel. She wanted a subject, etc. We became quite friendly for a time and one evening we sat together talking till one in the morning discussing whether the person would marry her, at that time the person's wife was very ill. When I am in London we'll talk the matter over and I will tell you everything I know.

3

His plans were many, and he proposed as soon as *The Lake* was finished to publish a sort of history of his literary life. This book did not make its appearance until long afterwards, but already, at the end of 1903, its title, *Avowals*, was chosen and some groundwork was done in the shape of a few papers which were printed in English and American periodicals. It was also in this year that he began a history of his senti-mental life, writing " Spring in London," " Flowering Normandy " and the other early chapters of *Memoirs of My Dead Life*. *Moods and Memories* they were then called, and the later name he may have owed to his happening upon an entry in the *Journal des Frères Goncourt*: " Mémoires de ma Vie Morte would be a pretty title for a book."[1] The articles were published, somewhat disconcertingly, in *Dana*, a grave magazine of independent thought, recently founded in Dublin by Eglinton. They were a free gift to a friend, and although the editor sometimes made a wry face as the contents were disclosed to him on Saturday evenings, he appreciated Moore's generosity and even suggested altera-tions which were in the right key. Eglinton had a knack of hitting on good titles, and it was he who gave the name of " Orelay " to the scene of one of the gallant episodes in the book. The last chapter was to have been called " My own Funeral," and in this instance it was Richard Best, John Eglinton's colleague at the Library, who interposed with " Resurgam."

To his brother, who retained his faith in the Gael, he

[1] May 25th, 1857, p. 189 (Charpentier, 1887).

wrote: " I hope you will try to awaken the dead, for even if they turn in their graves your success will be great . . . but you must not count on me to assist you any further. I am immersed in literature and I am more than ever convinced that I had better follow art than anything else." " Read Litledale," he advised, when he heard that the nuns were teaching one of the Colonel's children. " A priest came to see me. He seemed to be more wide-minded than you and so does Edward Martyn and so does everyone else. I meet no one in Dublin who thinks that the entire education of the country should be handed over to the religious orders except yourself. I was afraid all the bigotry was on my side . . . I always suspect myself." But not all his letters to Colonel Moore were in a quarrelsome strain.

Stackpoole called here yesterday and we were glad to see each other. I was sorry however to hear that his children are Catholics—even the little boy.[1] Evelyn was here and Toby who looks well and is going to a convent school. I am afraid this arrangement will destroy all hope of the literary tradition being continued. I enclose a cheque £50 which I hope will be of use to you. I have just read your letter—it arrived this morning. I am much obliged. It is good of you to take so much trouble but you always have been the best in the world. No kindness from you will surprise me.

In 1904 Werner Laurie brought out a new edition of *The Confessions of a Young Man*. The original text was scarcely disturbed, but the book was provided with a new preface originating in the recovery of the letter, long mislaid, which Pater had sent to Moore on first reading its contents. Being a letter of praise from " the last great English writer " it had given the *Confessions* the character of a sacred book. In the August number of the *Pall Mall Magazine* Moore dealt again with Pater and indulged the luxuriance of his imagination in an account of his personal relations with the author of

[1] De Stacpoole was a papal duke from Galway. It was likely therefore that " even the little boy " would be a Catholic.

Marius. This paper, remodelled, afterwards formed part of *Avowals.*

His special pleasure, he said, on re-reading the *Confessions*, was to find that he had thought about Pater twenty years before as he still thought of him, but he had a minor pleasure in being reminded by a certain passage of the book of his early love of France and of Protestantism. A strange twin love: the Catholic Irishman mixes more easily with the French than the Englishman or the Irishman of Protestant culture: if Moore had imbibed Anglican reticence at Eton or at Rugby he might not have fallen so easily on his feet in Paris. His temperament and mind, many continued to think, manifested the escaped Catholic rather than the natural Protestant, but in his bent towards self-realisation and self-development he was profoundly non-Catholic. The question has been discussed by a South German pastor, Weferling, in a University thesis, *Das Religiöse Gefühl bei George Moore.* Weferling knows nothing of the private occurrences of his author's life, but finds a strain of undogmatic piety and even mystical proclivities in *The Brook Kerith* and in *Evelyn Innes,* and regards the dislike of intellectualism which Moore shows as a Protestant phenomenon. There was a contradiction in Moore's nature, he concludes, and it is shown in the rivalry for his early affections between Shelley (whose pantheism is more repugnant to the Catholic mind than Pagan sensualism) and Gautier: *Gautier sein und Shelley bleiben.*

" I find," Moore now wrote, " not only my Protestant sympathies in the *Confessions* but a proud agnosticism, and an exalted individualism which in certain passages lead the reader to the sundered rocks about the cave of Zarathustra. . . ." The reference to Nietzsche is interesting, because Moore, as John Eglinton recalls for me, caught a good deal from the German " impressionist " philosopher of whom he had heard much earlier from Dujardin. I myself remember his admiration for his friend, Daniel Halévy's, *Vie de Nietzsche*; it was in this way that biography should be written, he said. Two of the most successful of his paraphrases resulted from this acquaintance, the one at the close of " Resurgam " (*Memoirs of My Dead Life*) from Nietzsche's poem of the

Eternal Return, the other in *Evelyn Innes*, where Ulick Dean
bids farewell to the opera singer (the symbol of the two ships
which have crossed paths), from Nietzsche's page on
" Stellar Friendship."

4

In 1905 it befell Moore to be appointed to the distinguished
and venerable office of High Sheriff of Mayo. " There are
two things from which one cannot escape," he wrote to
Dujardin, " death and the office of sheriff, and besides there
is a certain analogy, for if the executioner fails to put in an
appearance, the sheriff must cut off the condemned man's
head." Miss Susan Mitchell, the ballad-monger of the Irish
movement, improvised some verses to the tune of " The
Wearing of the Green."

> *Oh, then, Martyn dear, and did you hear the news*
> *that's going round ?*
> *Your old friend George will seldomer in Ely Place*
> *be found,*
> *He's left his loving neighbours, he's left his*
> *hall door green,*
> *To execute the English law in Ballaghadereen.*

His duties were to meet the judge for Assizes in Castlebar
and go to Court with him, carrying a sword, and also to
give a dinner to the judge. He stayed at Castlebar in the hotel
opposite the old tree from which " Fighting Fitzgerald "
was hanged in 1800. Tom Ruttledge, his agent, was sub-
sheriff, and so he had a friend with him to whom he could
talk in the evenings. The work was not exacting, and Moore
passed a good deal of time reading the correspondence of
Wagner and Mathilde Wesendonck.

15.7.05. *To Lord Howard de Walden.*
I am here sheriffing but the wearisome business is over
at last and I return to Dublin on Monday. I am sending
you by this post Wagner's letters to Mathilde. I cannot

find words to tell you the interest with which I read them, a book that helps you to see a little further into life than you saw before is a rare event and when I began to read Mathilde's letters to the poor afflicted soul, afflicted in the first instance by nerves, and in the second by the world's adversity, a sudden light was thrown on the intimacy and mystery of woman's love of man, a thing in itself and quite different from man's love of woman—not always but in Mathilde's case yes. She was one of the great—a word is wanting—lovers of the world, different from Héloïse, St. Teresa and the Portuguese nun. I hope to finish *The Lake* by the first of August.

Reading was never a pastime for Moore, and he would lay down any book for conversation. But he often begged his friends to give him something to read. Lord Howard de Walden induced him to take a better view of Kipling and was generally successful in pleasing him with his suggestions, as was also John Eglinton, who handed him *Don Quixote* and Rousseau's *Confessions*. " An excellent intelligence," he wrote to Lord Howard de Walden after reading a book by Lowes Dickinson, " clear, intense and penetrating, and I am glad you and he have become friends, the only real pleasures are intellectual pleasures and the keenest pleasures are derived I think from intellectual companionship rather than from books. Dickinson's book is a good one but the man should be better than the book."

In August he was in Paris, where he corrected the proofs of *The Lake* and wrote the dedicatory epistle. The book was inscribed to Dujardin as an acknowledgment of the larceny committed by its author in using *La Source du Fleuve Chrétien* for the title of the imaginary Ralph Ellis's work of exegesis, and also in memory of old friendship. The dedication gives the mood in which his new novel was conceived and written, a mood remote from the political passion which had brought him to Ireland in pursuit of the Celtic Renaissance. He is speaking of Valvins in the forest of Fontainebleau, " where our old friend Mallarmé lived . . . and where I read *The Lake* to you." " Pour expliquer la tristesse de ce beau pays parsemé de châteaux vides, hanté par le souvenir des fêtes d'autrefois, il faudrait tout un orchestre. Je l'entends d'abord sur les violons; plus tard on ajouterait d'autres instruments, des cors sans doute; mais pour rendre la tristesse de mon pauvre pays là-bas il ne faudrait pas tout cela. Je l'entends très bien sur une seule flute placée dans une île entourée des eaux d'un lac, le joueur assis sur les vagues ruines d'un réduit gallois ou bien normand. Mais, cher ami, vous êtes Normand et peut-être bien que ce sont vos ancêtres qui ont pillé mon pays; c'est un raison de plus pour que je vous offre ce roman."

The Lake is about a priest who (before the story opens) has driven a young unmarried schoolmistress from the parish because she is about to become a mother. The girl goes to London where she earns her livelihood as an author's secretary. The priest's conscience reproaches him for a harsh act; he gets into correspondence with the young woman and discovers gradually that he loves her—that she had come into his life like a fountain, shedding living water upon it, and that it was jealousy which prompted him to speak against her and not any concern for the morality of the parish. He can never see her again, and his life will drag out by the shores of the lake until he is taken away to the grave. But in one of his last letters to Rose he speaks of the liberation she has brought him in body and mind: "these are not two things but one thing." He is flying from Ireland and from the priesthood because "there is a lake in every man's heart, and he listens to its monotonous whispers year after year, more and more attentive, until at last he ungirds."

Moore believed in "good" and "bad" subjects, and, as this book has been regarded by many of his readers as the best of his novels—even placed above *Esther Waters*—it is interesting to know that he thought that he had stumbled on a "bad" subject in the priest's revolt against celibacy. He confided in Lord Howard de Walden shortly before the book came out: "It is a great misfortune to choose a bad subject; I am writing better than I used to but I cannot redeem the subject." He was also doubtful about the correspondence which formed so large a part of the book. The best critics applauded the lyricism of his Irish landscape and the anguish he put into the study of the priest hesitating on the lake shore. They found the letters less interesting, and it was on the letters that the characterisation of the girl chiefly depended. Had he failed to write natural letters out of which a girl like the spring would emerge, her hands wet with flowers ?

If finally he liked *The Lake*, it was because of the great difficulty of the telling which he had overcome: his preservation of the unity of scene. He explained (in a preface to a later edition of the book): " . . . The one vital event in the priest's life befell him before the story opens, and to keep the story in the key in which it was conceived it was necessary to recount the priest's life during the course of his walk by the shores of a lake, weaving his memories continually, without losing sight however of the long, winding mere-like lake, wooded to its shores, with hills appearing and disappearing into mist and distance. The difficulty overcome is a joy to the artist. . . . The drama passes within the priest's soul; it is tied and untied by the reflux of sentiments; and the weaving of a story out of the soul substance without ever seeking the aid of external circumstance seems to me a little triumph. It may be I heard what none other will hear . . ."

The book in its slow movement foreshadowed the work of his later period (*The Brook Kerith, Héloïse and Abélard* and *Aphrodite in Aulis*). It was the turning point in his writing, and the first of his books of which the complaint was made that he seemed to be more interested in manner than in content. He described its reception in a letter to his brother: " Some say that it is my best book, others that it is well written but dull." But *The Lake* did not merely show a great advance in Moore's choice and command of language, it marked a change of style—in Gibbon's sense of style as " the image of the mind." The image of Moore's mind had changed under the influence of his return to memories half hidden for years, and the change determined the content as well as the form of all his later work. Yeats had told him that his mind was " argumentative and abstract," and perhaps this book, which appeared to come wholly out of a mood of imaginative reverie, was a reply to this criticism. The intellectual processes of Father Gogarty are not shown, his reasons for rejecting dogma. " It seemed to me," he wrote to his brother, " that men are moved to reject dogma instinctively just as the swallows are drawn by the spring tide. Rose Leicester[1] represents the spring tide and her breath awakens Gogarty. He gets up and goes in search of life. The story is no more than a sun myth. The earth is frozen in dogma and the spring comes and warms it to life."

He did not visit Moore Hall while he was writing *The Lake*; he could summon the landscape at will to his mind's eye. But his letters to his brother were filled with questions about the history of the old castles and the islands, for he was not versed in the legendary associations of his native place, and the priest in his story was an antiquarian. The setting of the scene called up a surge of memories, and when the Colonel came to Dublin it was Moore's delight to hear him talk of childhood and of family. Unfortunately these subjects tended to provoke the religious discussion which Colonel Moore particularly wished to avoid. " I don't think," Moore would say to him, " that there was much literature to speak of in the family until agnosticism made its appearance. I was not the first agnostic; grandfather was one. But agnosticism is not so infallible a receipt for the production of good literature as Catholicism is for the production of bad."

There is no question that the religious difference, while it left Moore's relations with Martyn and Gill much as they had always been, did gradually disturb the affections of the brothers, and that Moore became very irritable under the thought that his heirs were to be Catholics. But in spite of the unhappy modification in the relationship it was decided that Colonel Moore, whose retirement from the Army was impending, should occupy Moore Hall and live there with his family as long as he wished. It was also decided to dispose of all the other Moore property under Wyndham's Land Act, which favoured landlords, and the matter of the

[1] In later editions the name was changed to Nora Glynn.

sale was put in the hands of Colonel Moore and of Ruttledge. They did not succeed in effecting the sale, and the reason in Moore's opinion was that they asked too high a price. He was no business man, but his prognostications on the subject of Irish land were shrewd enough. " Twenty-two years purchase of second term rents," he wrote to Colonel Moore on the 5th of April, 1905, " is quite sufficient, and if the landlords do not settle on these terms I assure you it is my firm conviction that within the next ten years they will lose half their properties."

5

He had now given up all thought of becoming a national character, and day after day passed quietly at Ely Place with his secretary; the days went by, every day the same as the previous day. On summer evenings he would mount his bicycle or play a little lawn tennis in his garden. He was fond of a game of lawn tennis and was quite a useful player but his style was now a little cramped by a shoulder dislocated in a fall and badly set because he refused an anæsthetic. He wore his bowler hat while on the courts, a survival of a custom from the early 'eighties which looked odd.

Casual callers at Ely Place were not encouraged; Moore defended the time which he considered consecrated to literature, but he himself paid casual visits, taking advantage when it suited his own convenience of the easy and amiable informality of Dublin life. In Dublin, where the gifted so often lack ambition, people always found time to provide him with information and with ideas, and even to write things down for him; conversation was still his method of learning, and in Dublin he learned a good deal. His day's work ended at about four, and after tea he would go for a walk, which might end up at the *Irish Times*, at the rooms of E. V. Longworth, a young barrister, at the offices of the Co-operative Society, or at the house of the Italian musician, Esposito, who was dear to him; of Martyn, more and more absorbed in politics, he now saw comparatively little. Longer expeditions brought him to Lady Ardilaun's country home at

Clontarf, to Stella's garden in Rathfarnham, to Sir Walter
Armstrong's Howth villa. He enjoyed visiting R. Y. Tyrrell,
the classical scholar, at whose house he was sure to find
clever young people to entertain him. Tyrrell and he were
indifferent to each other's attainments.

The National Library, the friendliest library in the world,
remained open till ten; it was a great blessing to Moore who
hated to be alone after dinner; there he would ask either
for John Eglinton or for Richard Best. One evening (it must
have been soon after his " conversion "), when St. Paul
occupied the chief place in his mind's eye—a thickset, hairy
man, surely (he said to himself) the real founder of Christianity—he heard from Eglinton of a book that had just come
in to the library, the views of a certain doctor on the Crucifixion. This doctor was inclined to think that Jesus might
have been taken down from the Cross in a state of suspended
animation. Moore was already aware of the theory that Jesus
had not died on the Cross, and he knew, too, that Jesus was
supposed by many to have begun life as an Essene monk.
Why, then, should there not have been a return to the
monastery? And why should not Paul, many years later,
after a day's preaching in the Palestinian hills, have knocked
at the door of that monastery? In this way could be explained what had been puzzling him ever since he read the
Epistles: Why did the Apostle never repeat any of the sayings
of Jesus, and why does he appear to have known nothing of
the life of Christ but three things—the Last Supper and
Betrayal, the Crucifixion and the Resurrection? It was the
climax of Moore's career as an exegete; in the twinkling of
an eye a story suggested itself to him. He went home and
dictated the scenario of *The Apostle*, making Paul kill Jesus,
because when Paul found Jesus alive he felt that all his
teaching was in vain.

If John Eglinton was not in his office, scripture was abandoned for that evening, and he would go on to Best for
English grammar. The conversation would turn, as so often
with Moore, on literary style and the difficulty of writing.
" But you write well, Best. Why don't you write more? I
wish I could write like you." Moore's hand would then go to

his waistcoat pocket for a slip bearing a sentence which he had found intractable during the day's work. On one occasion Best casually referred to the subjunctive mood as one that might be used in a certain predicament. " But what is the subjunctive ? " exclaimed Moore, with elevated eyebrows and shining eyes. " Give me an instance." When the usage of this moribund mood was explained to him, he cried out: " Oh, I would give *anything* to be able to use the subjunctive. If it be; if it rain; how wonderful ! But I will *always* use the subjunctive mood."

Saturday was the night on which he expected A. E. and his particular literary friends at Ely Place. He was fond of telling them the story he had in mind, and then of reading to them portions of the typewritten manuscripts or proofs. He was not a good reader, and sometimes it was difficult to give him the attention he expected and deserved, but he was ready to listen to criticism, and when he thought it good to be guided by it. F. MacCurdy Atkinson and E. V. Longworth, both lately from Trinity College and well versed in ancient and modern literature, were two of those who helped him in this way; and both of them became his affectionate and lasting friends. Oliver Gogarty, who presently took the house next to his garden, ministered to him in a stream of witty anecdotes, lampoons and limericks, combined with a marvellous memory for verse. Synge came once to his house; indeed everyone who was writing in Ireland found their way there some time or another. To the young Celticising poets, Padraic Colum and Seumas O'Sullivan, he was kind and cordial, if rather discouraging. " How well you all write," he would say. " I also wrote poetry when I was young, and some of the things in my *Pagan Poems* were considered good."

It would be wrong to think that Moore was cold-shouldered in Dublin. Although his views were publicly denounced, he encountered very little personal hostility. None of his friends were encouraged to know about the others, but he went pretty well everywhere that he wanted to go, and his social life in Ireland was more varied than has been generally supposed. He can scarcely be said to have revisited the scenes of his *Muslin* days, but he gained some acquaintance with the conservative culture of old Protestant Dublin, and was not altogether unappreciative of it. If it was proposed to invite him to a conventional house, his hostess might ask the other guests first, particularly if they were young women, whether they minded meeting Mr. George Moore. The young women did not mind, and they usually found him charming, although his reputed attitude towards any woman not positively repellent prevented them from feeling especially complimented when at the end of the evening he would ask them to come to dine with him alone very soon.

6

The last chapter of *Memoirs* was ready at the beginning of 1906, and the manuscript went at once to the publishers. Moore rightly thought that this book would have a lasting value, and he was not greatly perturbed on finding that the spirit in which he related his life in the garden of Armida did not meet with the approval of English reviewers. Memories of London, Paris, Sussex and Mayo were the substance of the volume, old memories all, except that one which became famous, " The Lovers of Orelay," an adroit description of himself as an elderly beau, on a tryst with a young woman in the South of France. Reading it, one recalls an enigmatic saying of his: " After five and twenty—certainly after thirty love adventures are no longer indiscretions but matter for literary inventions." Doris, in " The Lovers of Orelay," is seen as a museum piece, a figure remembered on canvas, rather than as a living woman. When in his later correspondence he mentioned some episode with a woman he would usually say that he was now coming home to " write an account of it for his new book."

But any account of him without reference to him as lover might as well not be told. It could be described as the centre of his being, and he would never allow others to suggest that he preferred talking of love to practising it. He spoke of the lady of Texas, whose strange story is told in a later edition of the *Memoirs*, as a real being, and so she certainly became to those who heard him tell the story so often. (A young man in America, so we are told, even claims to be the product of this episode.) Details of his adventures he has given himself, which can be read by all who wish, and Tonks' experience shows that he did not resent attempts at illustrating them. It may be that the narrative he was building up became so real to him that it became at last a part of his memory. " Half imagination, half reality " is his brother's comment; and his details must certainly be often accepted with reserve. To take the example of " Euphorion in Texas " : an American woman on a visit to Dublin was frequently with him at Ely Place, but she had not come to Dublin for the purpose which he described. He at once began talking of her to all his friends; and yet he was very much vexed when another lady, who came to tea with him one day at this time, took up a necklace which lay on the mantelpiece and said : " The lady from Texas, I presume."

In a later and elegant edition the title was extended in the eighteenth-century style and became: *Memoirs of My Dead Life of Gallantries, Meditations and Remembrances, Soliloquys and Advice to Lovers. . . . With many Miscellaneous Reflections on Virtue and Merit.* And in one of the chapters we read: " My thoughts run upon women. And why not ? On what would you have them run ? On copper-mines ? Woman is the legitimate subject of all men's thoughts. . . . We forget women for a little, while we are thinking about art, but only for a little while." It is a cry from the heart, for Moore—particularly as he grew older—was haunted by the mystery of sex; and he was happier in the company of women than in that of men, happiest of all with one woman. His views on the conduct of women were peculiar and extreme: he would not have thought to compliment woman by placing her on a moral pedestal, yet he knew the emotions of pity and chivalry, as his story " The End of Marie Pellegrin " shows: " She wore her hair as a blackbird wears its wings." The unhappy prostitute moved him to compassion, and he was even touched by the idealism of the suffragettes.

Women, even those who criticised his way of writing about

sex, liked him when they knew him; perhaps they felt that
he had understanding and was akin to them, and perhaps
they were pleased by his lack of any airs of masculine superiority. There was something feminine in his character,
though not in his mind; he wrote in the *Confessions*: " I am
feminine, perverse," and the statement was true in the sense
that he was guided by instinct and emotion rather than by
reason and reflection. " It is the kindly Moore of whom I
would speak," says the victim of one of his literary indiscretions. " I knew George Moore for twenty-five years. The
world has lost a valued man of letters who enriched
literature, but it is not of the artist I speak and not the artist
I mourn but the friend whose heart and human sympathy
I saw worthy beneath the mask of life." Did he ever alter or
seriously disturb the course of a woman's life ? Certainly, in
one case he did so, that of Miss Christian, the Englishwoman
who came to Ireland in his wake. He has given his own
account of the end of his friendship with " Stella " in a
passage in *Vale* which he could not be dissuaded from
publishing, although he was warned that it would be cen-
sured in Dublin where Stella was well known and liked. The
fact is that Miss Christian wished to marry and have children
and that after some uncomfortable debate Moore agreed that
she was right. A year after her marriage to a Dublin gentleman she died in childbirth: she had been dead many years
when *Vale* appeared.

Moore's friends in Dublin (who, as Eglinton in his *Irish
Literary Portraits* observes, knew him only as an austere and
laborious liver) listened with some amusement to the histories
of his love-affairs, told so broadly. After being thus regaled
one evening, the old painter, J. B. Yeats, the poet's father,
remarked that, "speaking as a philosopher, not as a moralist,"
he must say that Moore was a man of thoroughly bad
principles. Moore did not exactly boast, for he assumed that
other people's experience was very much the same as his
own. Some of his listeners felt perhaps as Dr. Mitford, Swift's
editor, felt, after a consideration of Vanessa's behaviour to
the Dean: " To me this is all astonishing, who never experienced the slightest voluntary offering of any female affection,

and whose timid advances have generally been received with coldness and dismissed with indifference." It finally began to be set about that his stories were quite without foundation, that when at the age of fifty-four he began to speak freely of a declining vigour he was merely admitting at last to a life-long disability. Such questions are difficult to investigate, but there is no reason to reject the substantial truth of his own account, which seems to fit such facts as can be verified and also to go some distance towards explaining a strain of pruriency which runs through his later works: an intense curiosity about the details of sexual behaviour which he turned to excellent comic advantage in *A Story Teller's Holiday* although many readers regret its occasional jarring appearance in the later romances, *The Brook Kerith*, *Héloïse and Abélard* and *Aphrodite in Aulis*. The frank naturalism of the earlier novels has quite a different effect, and could not have provoked the gibe of a hostile reviewer of *Héloïse and Abélard*: "A man with whom any pretty girl might walk safely through the deserts of Sahara. . . . Moore brings to love-affairs the noxious mind of a prude." He himself resented and resisted the imputation that the adventures he described were imaginary and wrote in 1919 to his publisher, referring to a book by John Abthorne:

Once the veracity of a biography is impugned the author's book becomes more or less discredited . . . I am prepared to go into a court of law and swear that these love affairs are facts not fictions, and that I believe that the statement that they are fictitious depreciates the value of the books. You will I hope put the matter before the writer, and explain to him that you cannot allow our joint property to be depreciated by a false statement, you will tell him also that this false statement writes me down as liar; he attacks my property and my honour and you will tell him that the passage must be withdrawn unconditionally.

It has been commonly observed that Moore's attitude in his books towards love and sex is what the English call "French," by which they mean something chilling and unromantic. It is quite true that full-blooded passion lies generally off the track of his literature and, so far as we can judge, of his personal life. The sharp disjunction of the love of the body and love of the soul expressed in a passage from *Héloïse and Abélard* and discussed by Moore in an illuminating talk with Mr. Charles Morgan (quoted in the latter's *Epitaph on George Moore*) must be held to point to such a conclusion; for all passionate lovers, however poorly they may succeed in rationalising their belief, claim to have experienced in love a subtle interpenetration of spirit and sense. For illustration we must turn to literature, and ask ourselves whether we can ever say of Shakespeare's two very different pairs of lovers Romeo and Juliet and Antony and Cleopatra: " Here the love of the soul is forgotten, and the love of the body begins."

But if we admit that Moore divided love into separate compartments, and choose to call the resultant chill " French," we must also allow that his work and his personal life show little trace of an element which all French novelists place at the very heart of sexual passion. He was almost without jealousy in his relation with women and seemed to suppose that the world in general was as free as he was. The evidence for this is to be found throughout his novels, and it ought to be enough to remind readers of the curious half-autobiographical episode of the hermit Gaucelm and the Lady Malberge in *Héloïse and Abélard* (Chap. XXII), the cordial dinner party of Evelyn Innes' two lovers, Sir Owen Asher and Ulick Dean, in *Sister Teresa*, and the meeting of Ralph Ede with his wife, years after she has deserted him for the actor Dick Lennox, in *A Mummer's Wife*.

7

Moore brought out another volume in 1906: the reprint of a delightful lecture which he delivered at the request of Sir Hugh Lane on the occasion of an exhibition of Impressionist paintings in Dublin. " Lane, you tempt me," he said. " I am the only one in Dublin who knew Manet, Monet, Sisley, Renoir, Pissarro; I knew them all at the Nouvelle Athènes."

"HOMAGE À MANET"
From the painting by Sir William Orpen

Reminiscences of the Impressionist Painters bore the imprint of a
Dublin publisher; it was no more than a pamphlet, with a
dedicatory letter to Steer, and Moore afterwards incorporated the text in *Hail and Farewell*.

" The day I received the booklet," he wrote to A. E.,
" I was dining with Steer and Tonks; MacColl, Rothenstein and others of the ' new English kin ' were dining with
Steer too; the circumstances were so fortuitous that it was
impossible not to read the preface [the address to Steer].
Everyone was delighted." He went on to Paris from London
and on his return to Ely Place he informed his circle that
Catholicism was not dying in France but dead. The fact is
that he had become a rather embarrassing guest in French
houses where there was usually a mother, or a mother-in-law,
who went to mass. In Ireland he thought of lending a hand to
Michael Davitt in the foundation of an anti-clerical newspaper. He admired the courage and resolution of the old
Land League agitator. " When Davitt calls I run to open the
door for him, the only man for whom I do that." But Davitt
died, and afterwards he saw no way of helping his country
except by writing " a sacred book." Autobiography was an
unusual form for a sacred book, but he remembered
St. Paul.

It is now that we first hear of *Hail and Farewell*, the work
which was to be the main occupation of Moore's declining
years in Ireland. The book was first conceived as a call to the
Celt to escape from priestcraft, and it took the form of a
demonstration of the incompatibility of art and dogma:

26.3.06. *To Colonel Moore.*

Kuno Meyer has been staying here, and at the end of the
week I wearied a little and had to tell him that I wanted his
room for you. He is anxious to meet you, and I have got
myself into a real quandary. Can you manage to come up
and stay a night or two or three or four and solve the
difficulty. . . . If you cannot come will you send me a
telegram saying that you are very sorry that you cannot
come till Thursday or Friday and that you will telegraph

again. I would prefer you to come of course. I have got a little job for you. You see I am writing my Farewell to Ireland. It is to be called Ave Hibernia ! Atque Vale and the theme is that Catholicism has not produced a book since the Reformation. I want to be quite fair and if you like you can supply the arguments on the other side. This will be very easy to do as it takes the form of dialogue.

The Colonel arrived; he warned his brother to be careful, as he might be sorry afterwards. It wouldn't do to say that a Catholic never painted a good picture. " But Raphael had a mistress," Moore replied, an argument which was to appear in his book. The Colonel recalls for me that he mentioned Racine, and that his brother after muttering something about "two insignificant classical dramas," settled down to listen carefully to an account of Racine's achievement and place in literature. Moore then caused the Colonel to read out some passages from Newman, and this was a success: it was conceded that the prose of the *Apologia* deserved censure. But there seemed to be so many gaps in Moore's knowledge that the Colonel on returning home drew up a few notes on the Gothic cathedrals and posted them to Ely Place. He was afraid that his brother would say in his book that the Catholic Church had made no contribution to architecture. Moore thanked him for the information in a very friendly letter.

The visit is the one which is described in *Salve*, the second volume of the Irish autobiography. It is among the " transposed " events in the trilogy, as it took place long after Moore's conversion to Protestantism, the scene with which *Salve* closes. The conversation with the Colonel starts with Literature and Dogma and goes on to family history, childhood and schooldays. It is a composite representation, touched up no doubt, of what passed at their various meetings and of the contents of their correspondence.

A repetition of what he had told the Colonel in March is found in the following letter to a correspondent much favoured in byegone days. The Marquise Clara Lanza, after a long silence, had sent him a criticism of *The Lake*. She was now a convert to Catholicism, and she had considered the novel from a Catholic standpoint. He was to refer to her later in a preface to the American edition of *Memoirs of My Dead Life*: " A lady who used to write to me on all subjects under the sun. I remember the irritation her letter caused me—my book was there to interpret or misinterpret as she pleased; added to which her ' conversion ' to Rome was an annoying piece of news. Fifteen years ago she was an intelligent and beautiful woman, if photographs do not lie. . . ."

8.12.06. *To the Marquise Clara Lanza.*

I am sorry to say that I shall not be able to feel much interest in your new book. The intellect of the world, you see, has drifted away from Catholicism; intellectually it is a desert. Since the Reformation Catholics have not produced a book. . . . That is hardly an exaggeration. Spain produced some literature that was written by Catholics—all the Italian writers since Dante (nearly all) were agnostics. Protestant Germany has produced a great literature, Catholic Germany nothing. North America Protestant, South America Catholic. How can you feel an interest in a religion that degrades the human mind? The only Catholics who produce books are all converts, for they retain something of their original liberty. Clara, Clara, Clara, for shame.

An early description of the trilogy is found in a letter to Dujardin, written in April 1907. Moore was working " like a nigger or like Balzac. Certainly my work is not worthy of Balzac and it may not be worthy of a nigger, but at all events I am writing eight hours a day and I am exhausted at the end. You know the title of my book *Hail and Farewell*. It takes the form of a novel without women. I have been so long occupied with the eternal feminine that I dwell with pleasure (in literature) upon the eternal masculine." Sometimes he preferred to call the trilogy a history. He placed events where they " composed " best,[1] but nowhere in it did he invent out of nothing.

His hope that he might share in the building up of a new and better Ireland on the basis of the language revival had been real enough. And in conversation he was pretty free with his criticisms of those who had brought him to Ireland on a wild goose chase. But, for the purposes of his book, his business was to cultivate an ironical and detached personality constructing a complex humour out of an appearance of paradoxical simplicity, and to see himself, even in the matter of his anti-Catholic passion, as others saw him, while remaining the real hero of his narrative. His experience among the Irish, even the slight wound to his pride, had sharpened his wits and given his intelligence a more incisive force. He still loved A. E. and acknowledged a debt to Irish writers. It is true that in *The Untilled Field* he was thinking more of Turgenev's way of telling a story than of the Irish way, and that the prose of *The Lake* bears no resemblance to the prose which was then being written in Ireland, either by Yeats or anyone else. But much of the artistic philosophy which underlies Moore's work from *The Lake* onwards is to be found in Yeats's critical essays of 1900 to 1906—in such a phrase as " the reveries that incline the imagination to the lasting work of literature " ; and he adapted to his own purpose that belief in spoken rhythms and a story invented for telling rather than reading which inspired so much of the work of the Anglo-Irish School.

A search for personal foibles began, and Moore made the mistake of supposing that Yeats's poetical talent was already exhausted. But he was liberal in his praise of the organiser and propagandist in Yeats, and knew him from first to last for a master spirit. " All the Irish movement rose out of Yeats and returns to Yeats . . . we have all wanted repertory theatres and art theatres and literary theatres, but these are vain words and mean nothing. Yeats knew exactly what he wanted." In the Abbey Theatre Ireland " spoke for the first time in literature " ; other Irishmen had written well before Synge, but they had done so by casting off Ireland. This

[1] As in the case of the conversations with Meyer and Colonel Moore.

work was the work of non-Catholic Irishmen, and therefore did not oblige Moore to revise his opinion of the incompatibility of literature and dogma. Indeed, the Abbey Theatre was the target of attacks from the representatives of Catholic Ireland and of the apostles of the language which Moore had hoped to save. The Gaelic League as a literary force was spent, and under its influence the schools for which *The Untilled Field* had been written were soon to have the worst text books in the world.

8

For a while he spoke as though his departure from Ireland were imminent. He returned very enthusiastic from a visit to Touraine with Lord Grimthorpe, saying that one was ten times better there than in Ireland and that it was no wonder that Balzac wrote the *Comédie Humaine*. " But what would I do with myself there ? " he asked ; and his choice if he left Dublin seemed to narrow down to a flat in Paris or a house in London. He decided to put off his removal from Ely Place until the appropriate moment, and that would evidently come when he could place his farewell to Ireland in the hands of his publishers. " It will break my heart to leave you all," he said to A. E.; but for the sake of Ireland he felt that he should issue his message as quickly as possible.

In the end he stayed in Dublin for another four years. *Hail and Farewell* developed into an elaborate work in three volumes and was put aside now and again for other tasks. A revision of *Evelyn Innes*, for instance, occupied a good part of 1907. Sometimes he felt discouraged. What could he add to art ? he asked himself, and yet he kept pushing along, finding fault with his secretary if she were half an hour late, as if it mattered. " I am crazy to see Pompeii," he wrote to Lord Howard de Walden, " and yet here I sit writing for no purpose that I can discover." In such moods he felt glad that he could turn to English friends like Lord Grimthorpe or Lady Cunard, visits to whose houses could provide " a provincial author " with the total change of scene he required.

13.8.(07). *To Lady Cunard.*

My dear Maud,

I was delighted to get your happy letter. Of course you enjoyed your season, we all enjoy what we do well and your life is a work of art. I work with ink and paper, the sculptor takes a block of marble, the painter pigments and canvas, the actor, it is true, takes himself but he has to get an author to write for him and a scene-painter to paint for him; he requires rouge and limelights—you require none of these things and the result is more astonishing. I wonder if you ever see yourself—I fancy not, you are very little spectator—I mean *que vous etes si peu spectateur.* Perhaps you would not be so wonderful if you were self-conscious. To-night I am feeling depressed and life seems a weariness. I have come in from a little walk, but it has not freshened my spirits. These fits of depression come after long periods of work. You will say why not cease to work and go somewhere for a change—this cannot be, work taken up must be finished, added to this it would be unwise to spend money now; consols are down to 80 and this slump in the money market is making the sale of land in Ireland an impossibility. The work I am engaged on will not bring me any money. Things do not look very rosy. We all have our troubles and mine are very slight compared with Lord Grimthorpe's. He has managed to pull through and to-day I see his name mentioned in the newspapers as the probable successor to Lord Sefton, who is retiring from the ministry. Your kindness in asking me to Holt in October touched me, it isn't probable that I shall be able to come, but thank you all the same. You have always been the best and truest friend. There is no one like you, Maud—no one as fascinating, no one as clever, no one as good; and every year it seems to me that I see you in a more beautiful light. But why are you going to Marienbad? People go there to be cured but of what? I can't make out, men and women. I'll write to you again. But of what shall I write—what would you like to hear.

as ever
George Moore.

On one visit to the Cunards at Market Harborough he read the lessons in Church. The incident is described in a letter to an Irish friend.

(Undated). *To Mrs. Murray Robertson.*

Here the sheep graze peacefully—nothing by the way grazes turbulently, and there is a deep valley out of which a knoll upspringeth and the light strikes the crest and the bright green spot sets off the dimness of the great hill opposite. . . . I read the lessons last Sunday and charmed by the beautiful protestant service I felt myself dissolving into prayer. If I could pass the examinations I think I should like to take orders. It is so nice to live in a protestant country away from the low papist. But you'll think me bigoted. And dear Russell, give him my love and tell him I have read four stories by Maxim Gorki which pleased me very much.

There were long walks through the fields with Lady Cunard's daughter, Nancy. He was shocked to discover that she was being taught the products of the English towns. " Nancy is going to be a young lady, and do you think that when she goes down to dinner upon the arm of a guardsman she will turn to him and say: ' What is Leeds famous for ? How many knives does Sheffield make ? ' " He loved the walks with her, and the little girl was set the task of collecting all the wild flowers, positively all; in *Sister Teresa* they were useful to him. Even on his holidays he worked. Retired behind the locked door of his room, he would write and write, and be furious if disturbed; at luncheon time the footman might succeed in conveying to him that Lady Cunard was growing impatient; he would detain the footman for half an hour to ascertain what the footman thought —about a cricket match.

Lord Howard de Walden was another friend of whose hospitality he made liberal use. When one summer he heard that Seaford House was let, he reproached his friend with being as uneconomical as God who certainly destroyed San Francisco because of the crime of Millet's *Man with the Rake.*

He was plagued, he said, by the suspicion that the real motive of the letting was to make sure that George Moore would not arrive again.

9

By the autumn of 1907 the new version of *Evelyn Innes* was approaching completion. In a letter to Dujardin Moore wrote: " Since I saw you I have revised and recomposed my novel for Hachette. The first version seems to me to be incredibly futile." The book was subsequently brought out by Fisher Unwin, but the impulse to revise had been due to an offer from Hachette's. Moore hoped for the best, but he had very little faith in translators. He felt that translators used him badly, and it gave him great pain to read the pages from the *Memoirs of My Dead Life* which were now appearing in *La Revue Bleue*. " An awful translation," he said; and writing to Dujardin in October he cited a paragraph from " The End of Marie Pellegrin."

A few days afterwards I heard in Barrès' studio that she had escaped from Russia; and that evening I went to Alphonsine's to dinner hoping to see her there. But she was not there. There was no one there except Clementine and the two stockbrokers; and I waited eagerly for news of her. I did not like to mention her name, and the dreary dinner was nearly over before her name was mentioned.

He asked his friend to compare the translation of the sentences in *La Revue Bleue* with his own translation which ran as follows:

Peu de jours plus tard on parlé (*sic*) d'elle dans l'atelier de Briot, et j'appris que Marie s'était echappée de Russie. On n'en savais plus long, et pour avoir des nouvelles plus precises j'allais le soir même chez Alphonsine esperant de l'y voir. Mais personne . . . seulement Clementine et ses deux coulissiers; et en face d'eux je quittais la conversation pour la detourner sur Marie sans que l'occasion se

presenta: le triste diner tirent a sa fin avant que son non
fut prononcé.

Where his own books were concerned Moore could not
tolerate any French but his own, and yet he was always
quite ready to admit that he did not " know " the language.
" A translator's French brings my stomach up," he was to
write some years later in *Avowals*. He was conscious of his
own unreason in this matter, but it enraged him to think of
the two versions of *Esther Waters*, one of them a collaboration
from which a hundred pages had been cut. Once he had said
that France was the country of " good translations," but
his own experience had caused him to abandon this view.
His intolerance had a high motive in the esteem in which,
abstractedly, he held a translator. " Translation," he wrote
in the *Epistle to the Cymry*, " is a more difficult art than
original writing . . . we learn to use a language better by
writing out another man's thoughts than our own; if we
write out our own we select thoughts for translation that
we can express easily." The translator seemed to him to be
the most fortunate man in the world because he was freed
from " the misery of composition " and yet might improve
on his original in verbal beauty. Moore practised in a small
way what he preached, and he would often put his regular
work aside, and think of nothing for some days but how to
put some celebrated passage from French or English writers
into an English or a French that would be exact and at the
same time distinguished.

His luck in Germany was no better, so he said. The first
German of importance with whom he had dealings was
Dr. Heilborn, a fellow contributor to *Cosmopolis*, in the late
'nineties and early nineteen hundreds. Heilborn was instrumental in making him known to some extent in German
literary circles through articles and translations. He wrote a
very laudatory review of the original *Evelyn Innes* and Moore
wanted him to translate the novel. The proposal fell through,
and Moore then turned to Max Meyerfeld, the German man
of letters to whom *The Apostle* is dedicated. An acquaintance
sprang up; Moore disclosed all his literary projects to

Meyerfeld who preserves many first editions of the English author, manuscripts of the sketches that later went into *The Untilled Field*, the six numbers of *Dana* containing the germ of *Memoirs of My Dead Life*, and a long scenario " By George Moore and John Balderston " for a dramatisation of *The Brook Kerith*. They used to meet in London and Paris and Meyerfeld shows with relish a singular snapshot of his old friend, dancing in a garden in his pyjamas, while a charming young woman, a friend of Dujardin, sits upon the grass, fully clothed and unconcerned: the converse, as it were, of Manet's celebrated *Déjeuner sur l'herbe*.[1] He supervised the German productions of *Evelyn Innes* and of *Esther Waters*, and the friendship finally broke down under the strain imposed upon it by Moore's nervous interventions. He got it into his head that the work was being badly done, and (in the case of *Esther Waters*) that there had been an interference with his text. " This German," he would say, " omitted the christening scene in his translation of *Esther Waters*." The translation (which was not Meyerfeld's) had been based on a specially revised edition sent by Moore and the German followed the English sentence by sentence. At the end of a long correspondence Moore acknowledged that he was in the wrong, but a friendly note which Meyerfeld wrote to him after the war did not lead to a resumption of the relationship.

In September 1907 he sent a short tale about an imaginary painter and two art collectors to the *Cosmopolitan*, New York, a journal to which he had been introduced by Miss Viola Rodgers, who was then working for certain American papers and had come to Dublin in search of an article from him on art. He was captivated by the vivacity and beauty of this young Californian, and began a friendship and correspondence that lasted for the rest of his life: indeed he came to have for her a feeling much warmer than friendship, especially in the years just after the war when he generally saw her on each of his visits to Paris. He was pleased to think, he said in the first of many letters, that they were fellow-contributors to the *Cosmopolitan*.

[1] See the illustration facing page 370.

14.9.07. *To Miss Viola Rodgers.*

I should like to be " sous la même couverture " allow me my little whimsical turns of thought do not stamp upon me for the little joke do not frown.

10

The new *Evelyn Innes* and its translation was the subject of a further reference in a letter to Dujardin of the 4th of January 1908.

I have been working at *Evelyn Innes* and I have rewritten the novel from top to bottom. Not a line of the original remains—yes there is the first sentence. In a few days I will send the proofs to Hachette for translation by a master-hand. What ill luck pursues me ! Orestes was pursued by the furies, I by a French more detestable than my own . . . I am sorry, dear friend, that you should be unable to read *Evelyn Innes*, because the miracle is accomplished, and I have turned an eyesore into a beautiful thing.

In 1907 the three Papal documents against Modernism had been published, and Moore was indignant when Catholic Ireland refused to share his interest in the agitations of the religious life of Europe. Dujardin wrote to ask him what the Irish thought of the great ecclesiastical drama provoked by Loisy. " They don't think about it," he replied very truly. The Bishops had scarcely considered it necessary to refer to the Encyclicals of Pius X. " A Western Tibet," cried Moore, and he remembered that his friend Eglinton, measuring the religious consciousness of a people by their capacity for heresy, had once written an essay to show that the island of saints was the one country in Europe which had never produced a religious genius. His anger was sincere, and yet he felt at times that it was contrary to common sense. His brother was at Moore Hall, and months had passed without word from him. He sat down to write.

3.3.08. *To Colonel Moore.*

It is so long since I heard from you that I hardly know how to begin a letter . . . Isn't it strange that religious prejudice—beliefs none possess, not even the saints, so they have lamented—divide brothers from their brothers and sons from their fathers. You see I except mothers and sisters; the female is not a religious animal, if she were the world would have ceased to exist long ago. But however repugnant a Protestant may be to you come to see me, my dear Maurice.

The Colonel came to Ely Place, but he had not been there many hours before George lifed up his voice to denounce the fundamental irreligiosity of the Irish race. The Colonel defended the Irish—and also preferred *Esther Waters* to the later style. He said that it was a pity that he had ever shown George their grandfather's preface to the *History of the French Revolution* (" Grandfather dreams and we hear him dream," said Moore), if his brother's later style was the result of it.

In April 1908 Moore was busy with the new *Sister Teresa*. Fisher Unwin published it in the following year along with the third version of *Evelyn Innes*. The novelty of the new editions, particularly that of the *Sister Teresa*, was substantial. The earlier *Sister Teresa* had been a quiet book of convent life, almost as quiet a book as *The Lake*. But in the 1909 edition the story was greatly lengthened by the introduction of exuberant descriptions of Edwardian society, and by new inventions such as Sir Owen Asher's hawking in North Africa, a fine piece of music and colour (some years earlier Moore had pursued this sport with Lord Howard de Walden in England), and Owen's yacht in the great storm. Owen's hatred of Catholicism has grown much more strident. " They have got her, they have got her ! But they shan't get her as long as I have a shoulder to force open a door. . . . They will get her I tell you ! those blasted ghouls, haunters of graveyards. . . ." The book had a new ending. Evelyn now decides that she has no vocation for the religious life. She leaves the convent and becomes a social worker. Owen sees her from time to time, and a platonic friendship is established —peace between old lovers, an idea dear to Moore.

The 1909 editions of the two books deserve mention because it was while he was preparing them that Moore conceived the idea, so important to his later evolution, that he had a special gift for telling a story as the ancients did. He believed that he had given classical form to a sophisticated modern psychology. " Ingres and Antiquity," he now began to say, " alone know how to simplify " ; and in sending Dujardin a copy of *Evelyn Innes* he wrote some significant sentences: " There is plenty of sentimentality in the English novel, and heaps of prudery, plenty of love even, but there is not a single love story. By a love story I mean a story of two beings who meet, love and are separated by material or spiritual events—and who are at last united in death, peace or marriage—it matters not which. That is the manner in which the ancients understood love stories, and that is what I have done, unconsciously perhaps." His satisfaction with the revisions did not however endure, and eventually it seemed to him that the original versions, the *Evelyn Innes* of 1898 and the *Sister Teresa* of 1901 were the best, or at least that all the months spent on rewriting them had brought no adequate reward. To close the history of these two books prematurely, at a subsequent date Mr. C. D. Medley, who was then acting as Moore's lawyer and had already negotiated for the release from Walter Scott of all the rights which that publisher owned in *Esther Waters*, the *Confessions* and the earlier novels, approached Fisher Unwin in the matter of *Evelyn Innes* and *Sister Teresa*. But Unwin and Moore had quarrelled violently, and Unwin therefore refused to part with these books. On his retirement from his business they became the property of Benn, who reprinted them in the " Essex Library," *Evelyn Innes* from the 1898 edition and *Sister Teresa* from that of 1909 (the reader passing from one volume to another finds a disconnected narrative). These annoyances may have contributed to Moore's decision to exclude the two novels from Heinemann's " canon."[1]

[1] After Moore's death Mr. Medley secured the release of all the rights from Benn.

11

In January and February 1909 Moore was in Paris with Blanche and Dujardin, and he read to them his " Gabrielle " comedy. Mrs. Craigie had died, and by arrangement with the executors he was now entitled to do what he could with the play. It seemed to Dujardin to have possibilities and the idea of a French adaptation was broached. But there was a drawback; a lady in Homburg with whom Moore was in correspondence and whom he called " Emily," had already been entrusted with a German translation. Now she wrote to say that she had finished the work, and Moore was in a quandary. Having interested Dujardin in his play he was dreaming of a great success on the French stage; besides he wanted to do a good turn to his old friend. So upon his return to Dublin he devised a clever letter to " Emily."

My dear Emily

I took the comedy to Paris with me, and went over it with a French author examining it microscopically. It appears that the principal scenes are well written but I left many little things undone which seemed unimportant, but which very often prevent a play from being accepted. As you have not written to me about it, I fear you have had some difficulty in getting your adaptation accepted, and this letter is to tell you that you must not be discouraged. I will send you this piece in a much more finished and attractive form in a few weeks, and I think you will have no difficulty then in getting it accepted. Meanwhile don't do anything with the play, get it back from any management you have submitted it to, for I feel sure it would not be successful if played in its present form. The revisions are really slight and to make them will not take you very long, and then you will have a play which will be both a pleasure and a profit to you.

" You must not think that a disagreeable situation is likely to arise," Moore wrote to Dujardin. " The Homburg lady may be about rehearsing her translation at this moment but it isn't likely, and it's still more unlikely that she will proceed after receiving my letter."

Later he wrote: " I am enchanted with your work, and I am sure you are on the way to making a delicious comedy. Therefore I cannot help you for the scene of the third act; another reason: I have come to the end of my tether as far as this comedy is concerned, and I can't return to it; it is a dish of which I have had too much." Nevertheless throughout the spring Dujardin was the recipient of a stream of letters bearing on the work, for Moore was inclined to suspect a threat to the literary quality of the play whenever his friend attempted to increase the effective drama of a passage. By May a certain measure of agreement had been reached: the comedy in Moore's opinion was one of the prettiest ever written, and it would be a shame if Claretie did not accept it for the Théâtre Français. Two rival versions of one scene were still in existence; " but," Moore wrote, " if you prefer yours be sure that I will be good and will not attempt to impede the performance." The Countess (Gabrielle) had been made to marry Sebastian, the secretary, supposing him to be the great man, the author of *Elizabeth Cooper*, and the scene in question was the one in which she confronts her young husband with the deception. " I have read it," Moore wrote in another letter, " to two or three people and they found it delicious. They especially liked the scene between Sebastian and the Countess—the scene of silent fury." Dujardin warned him that theatrical reality sometimes provides sad surprises .But to this Moore would never agree. " Your criticism," he replied, " probably comes from an actor."

The autobiography remained Moore's chief care. It advanced, notwithstanding his other employments, the watch over Dujardin and the preparation for a French lecture on Balzac and Shakespeare which he was to deliver in Paris the following year. At the end of June he looked forward to a holiday.

29.6.(09). *To Colonel Moore.*

I'm sorry to hear that you have not been well lately— you don't say what has been the matter with you. So one wonders. But you say that you hope you will be able to come to Dublin soon. My arrangements are to leave here on the seventh of August. I am going to stay with the Divine Vision and shall remain away a couple of months— coming back in September to finish *Hail and Farewell*. I am two-thirds through with it.

After spending the month of August in England he visited Blanche at Dieppe and then went on to Paris where he was drilled for the accent and delivery of his lecture by a retired member of the Comédie Française, Mademoiselle Richenberg, a little blonde with rather childish manners who spoke the most exquisite French. She had been for most of her stage career the *ingénue* of the Comédie Française and when Moore met her she was nearly sixty, a Baroness and still the perfect *ingénue*. It grieved him to hear that Dujardin had not succeeded in finding a producer for the play, and on his return to Dublin he besought his friends to account for the ill-success. At last one of them gave him the explanation. Davenant and Sebastian, arguments and telegrams, all had been beside the purpose; nothing could have redeemed the play from the mortal sin of its origin. " The game is up," he wrote to Dujardin in November. " . . . yesterday a woman painter—painters alone understand literature—said to me about the comedy, ' You went wrong from the start. A woman who marries by mistake the man whom she shouldn't marry is a subject for farce or for tragedy.' And we tried to write a comedy."

His fine and sober paper on Balzac and Shakespeare, now to be found in *Avowals*, was published in two numbers of *La Revue Bleue*. On the 18th of February 1910 he read it out to a distinguished audience at the Salle de l'Agriculture. The French Press gave him a pleasing character. " A novelist of talent, above all an exquisite short story writer. An Irish Catholic who has publicly turned Protestant. He hoped to scandalise but only raised a smile. He is a dear rosy baby, and very droll. He has humour and a heart of gold. . . . Was it not he who complained of the lot of a starving dog which found itself in a vegetarian restaurant ? "

12

When in the summer of 1909 Moore said that *Hail and Farewell* was three-quarters finished, he must have been alluding to a rough dictation of an outline of the work. Four years were to pass before the third volume, *Vale*, was ready for publication. After greatly extending and elaborating the scope of the autobiography, he had fallen into difficulties with the second chapter of *Ave*, where he was trying to describe his peaceful life with the Bridgers in Sussex, the days in which he was yet untroubled by a Celtic aspiration. A. E. once described to me the state of despair in which Moore brought this chapter to him. " He read me out something about a rabbit farm, which I found very dull; and as we walked round Merrion Square, I told him that he should scrap the chapter altogether and begin with Yeats and Martyn coming to Victoria Street to beguile him with an account of the Irish theatre."

After taking A. E.'s advice he saw his troubles fade: a text of *Ave* was quickly established, and by the middle of 1910 only a few features, a few pages remained to be added. He was again away in August, but he hurried back to Dublin at the beginning of September, and by the end of the month he could say that the first volume of the trilogy was ready for the printer. Heinemann wished to publish at once, and the day of departure was near, because, as Moore explained, it would be " in bad taste to remain in Dublin meeting my friends and acquaintances, my models, in the street." He was indisposed to modify any of the characterisations. T. W. Rolleston might want more back to his head and Dr. Hyde less. But if these gentlemen sat for their portraits would they complain if the painter did not in one case add a slice and in the other omit a slice ? " Max Beerbohm," he wrote to Eglinton, " has caricatured everybody ferociously; his representation of me hardly resembles a human being; I have never complained. Is this care for personal appearance confined to Dublin ? Well, I shall add five or six lines about my own personal appearance which shall be savage enough."

He did not add the lines, but Rolleston forgave him for the

sentence: " As if guessing that someone was admiring him, Rolleston looked down the table, and I saw how little back there was to his head . . . a punctured Messiah ! " In later years, both exiles in London, the twain struck up a considerable friendship, the 1920 edition of *Esther Waters* being dedicated to " An Irish Protestant like myself " who " could always love Ireland without hating England." Whenever he dined with Rolleston, Rolleston used to say: " I am putting you to sit, Moore, where you can't see the back of my head."

The " intricate windings of the story " were to lead him at last to Moore Hall. For three years Colonel Moore had been in occupation of the house, but had not received a visit from his brother, its owner. " I can see the lake with my mind's eye," Moore used to say to his secretary, " of what use to go there ? All the beautiful curves of the bay are before me, along Kiltoome and Connor Island." But he now began to speak of visiting his brother; he wanted to discuss business with him, and to be shewn the improvements which Colonel Moore had carried out during his residence. These improvements worried Moore. He had spent £600 on the house when Colonel Moore moved in, and ever since he had been reproaching himself for an act of irrationality, for he was certain that the day of the Irish gentry was over: who thought otherwise indulged in a foolish dream. And now a new gate was needed. " And is your father with you ? " he wrote to Miss Nancy Cunard. " Tell him I am writing to him for advice about a gate—a gate my brother is putting up at Moore Hall. I am leaving Ireland and shall never see the gate again (I propose to go to see it). You will ask what is the use of putting up a new entrance gate to a place which I am leaving for ever. The only answer I can make to this very sane question is that the world is full of foolish people and your affectionate friend George Moore is one of them."

In regard to Moore Hall his sentiments and instincts were always in conflict. " You may live there," he said to his brother in 1906, " but no other Moore will ever live there. I divine these things. I can't tell you how I know them, but I do know them." It annoyed him that Colonel Moore should persist in a different and more hopeful opinion; and he

wrote in *Salve*: "In the Colonel's face, so refined and melancholy, I could trace the conflict between dreams and reality,
the conflict that makes Ireland so unsuccessful." "Do you
propose," he said in another letter, " to rebuild the ruins of
ancient Ireland ? " All the same no Tory was louder than he
in his denunciation of the conduct of the Liberal chief
secretary, Mr. Birrell. There was a rumour in these years that
legislation would be introduced which would force Irish
landowners to dispose of parts even of their demesnes to
landless men. If Moore Hall was cut up in this way he would
quit Ireland forthwith, he said, and never give his country
another thought. To be Mr. Moore of Moore Hall (an old
seat of Protestant gentry) meant a good deal to him, especially as long as he remained in Ireland.

The sale of his other properties, postponed in 1905, was
now being effected. He aimed at receiving a number of
years' purchase sufficient to provide him after the repayment
of mortgages with a thousand a year: a capital sum of
£25,000; and this was, roughly speaking, the amount which
he was ultimately paid by the Land Commission. In recent
years he had been quite prosperous; a letter from his bank-
manager shows that for 1908-9, after spending £989, he
had a balance to his credit of nearly £1,000. But in 1910,
when the estate began to be sold, he was, for some technical
reason connected with the sale, left for one year rather short of
income from his properties; he complained and his brother
brought him the accounts, but he refused to look at them,
saying that he could make nothing of figures. Later on, in
conversation with Ruttledge, he was reminded that the estate
had been paying £100 a year for the education of his elder
nephew for a year or two. "And to whom is the money being
paid ? " "To Downside," Ruttledge replied. "What is
Downside ? " On being told that Downside was the well-
known public school of the Benedictines, he grew angry,
and said that such donations would injure his character, as
he had published it to all the world that he cherished the
strongest possible objections to Catholic education. To these
complaints the Colonel replied that George had sent him a
cheque for £50 when the boy was under other Catholic

teachers before going to Downside; and there for the moment the matter rested.[1]

In December 1910 news came of the serious illness of Augustus Moore in London. Moore had been on fair terms with this brother in recent years, and he was greatly agitated at the thought of the charges that might now be laid upon him, for Augustus was in poor circumstances and had a wife and son. However he was ready to help, so he told the Colonel, but he could not face the deathbed—anything but that. The Colonel went alone to London, where he found Augustus, game to the end, engaged in forming " a syndicate " to pay the expenses of an operation. The sum of £150 was raised, and George contributed, but Augustus died before the doctors could operate. Opening his *Irish Times* the next day Moore read the obituary notice in which Augustus was described as brother of the famous novelist and a member of " an old Roman Catholic family long settled in the West of Ireland." He stood aghast at this libel on the religious beliefs of his ancestors, and the next day his protest appeared in a prominent place in the *Irish Times*.

The libel has become so painful to me, and as your publication has given it fresh currency, I take this opportunity of telling that my family was Protestant until my great grandfather went to Spain. He settled in Alicante, and by successful trading amassed a fortune of three or four hundred thousand pounds. It would not have been possible for him to do this if he had remained a Protestant . . . My grandfather was a man of letters, a very cultured but unsuccessful man of letters, as he confesses himself in an enchanting little preface to his unpublished *History of the French Revolution* (the preface I intend to include in my new book). He was a disciple of Gibbon, and many passages in his published writings show him to be an agnostic. Of my father's belief I know nothing; he went to Mass on Sundays, so I suppose he was a Catholic.[2]

[1] In *Vale* the discovery is supposed to have taken place a few months later in the course of a visit to Moore Hall.

[2] But some years later he wrote that his father and he often discussed religion together.

"GEORGE MOORE, HISTORIAN": GEORGE MOORE'S GRANDFATHER
From the painting by Thomas Wyatt

The letter closed with the statement that he would have no hesitation in making it a condition of his will that his heir should carry on the Protestant traditions of the family.

13

After Augustus's funeral in London, Jimmy Glover and a few of Augustus's close friends being with him in the house, the Colonel opened a letter which had come to him from Dublin. It was from his brother, and there was nothing in it about Augustus. The Colonel glanced at the letter; he was wrought up and stumbled on the word " dwindling " which he mistook for " swindling " ; when the friends were gone he wrote a violent reply, for which he afterwards apologised.[2] He also offered to repay the money spent on his son's education, but Moore would not hear of this and tried to smooth down ruffled feelings; tempers improved, and in the following February he paid the long deferred visit to the Colonel at Moore Hall.

Mrs. Moore was a little anxious at the prospect of an exacting guest. He was sure to fuss about the coffee and good coffee was not easily come by in the West of Ireland. Castlebar was searched in vain, nothing but coffee essence was to be found, and the Colonel recalls that on the first night of the visit it was a fine healthy brew as black as ink. But at least it was not thin, and Moore was delighted. " My dear Evelyn, your coffee is wonderful, you must tell me the blend." They then spoke of Julian Moore, now rarely seen by any member of the family, but present at Augustus's funeral.

So the first evening passed; and the next day Moore inspected the famous gate and other innovations, and professed himself very much pleased with his brother's care of the place. They drove to Ballinafad, their mother's old home, where the monks now were, a gift from Llewellyn Blake, Joe Blake's brother and heir. The account of the drive in *Vale* is a composite description of several surrounding places, not all on the road they travelled. Moore insisted on

[1] " My dwindling income," Moore had written.

chatting with the monks, but only indifferent subjects were broached. Afterwards the Colonel said that it was distressing to see all the family plate in the hands of the monks, and Moore retorted that it was illogical for a Catholic to entertain such a sentiment. With that the religious wrangle recommenced, and presently Moore renewed his offer to bring up one of his nephews in the Protestant faith. Though the Colonel had been warned by Edward Martyn that the situation was serious, he could not yet believe that his brother cared a straw in what religion the boys were educated. But, having read the letter in the *Irish Times*, he pointed out that the Moore property was to have been settled on his sons (one or both) if they learned Irish, and protested that it was unfair to make new conditions. " How can you call yourself a Protestant," he asked. " Do you believe in the Bible ? " " A little," was the reply.

Moore really showed himself in quite a genial light during the stay. The boys themselves were there, and when they giggled a little and imitated his mannerisms he did not complain. But the real object of his visit, an agreement in regard to the expenses of the upkeep of the house, was rather lost sight of in theology and in the collection of material for a book in the Irish idiom. Moore took long walks in the neighbourhood, renewing his acquaintance with the old people, to one of whom, Honor Glynn, a Blake retainer, he presented an umbrella in return for the pleasant stories she told him.

In Ely Place the astonishing man, who had said that Protestants and Catholics do not mix, composed a graceful letter in French to a cousin who was a Carmelite nun ; she had implored him to burn his books and make his peace with the Church ; and in his reply he wrote : " We are the two dreamers of a family little given to dreams ; the two who have known how to make sacrifices—you for God, I for art. You tell me in your letter that you are perfectly happy, and that there is no greater happiness than to live with God and his Sacraments. I also can say that I am perfectly happy with my art ; it fills my life from one end to the other."

14

A last letter from Ely Place was written to Dujardin.

The upset [his removal from Dublin] is a serious thing for me and will occupy me for some time. The scenario of my play *The Apostle* has been published in Germany in a review; it will now appear in book form, preceded by a study of St. Paul. The study will surprise you, as you know the range of my knowledge on these subjects. I will send it to you, you will find my English too difficult, but curiosity will induce you to inform yourself of the contents.

His old friend, Frank Harris, was on the trail of the same subject—a post-Crucifixion meeting between Jesus and St. Paul—and therefore Moore left the typescript of *The Apostle*, together with the Prefatory Letter to Max Meyerfeld " On Reading the Bible for the First Time," behind him in Dublin with a publisher, having decided that it must appear immediately, even in an unfinished state. On the other hand, he took with him a dramatic version of *Esther Waters* on which he had been at work off and on for the past five years, hoping that Herbert Trench would produce it at the Haymarket. The play is first mentioned in a letter to the Colonel, written in 1906, in which Moore says that his next task will be to dramatise the famous novel for Yvette Guilbert who has for years been waiting to play the part of Esther. Later on, he had handed the material to Lennox Robinson, the Abbey Theatre dramatist, then a young man fresh from a Cork rectory, who was asked to make what he could of it. Lennox Robinson writes to me: " I had only just come to Dublin; and nothing could have been more remote from my experience than horse-racing, betting, English servants and the kind of life described in *Esther Waters*. Moore used to come round to my rooms every afternoon to see how I was going along; he was very agreeable and complimentary, and became more and more interested. Then one day he took the manuscript from me, and I did not give the matter another thought until years later. I read the book of the play and found something very familiar in the dialogue of the second act."

The late W. F. Bailey of the Land Commission gave a farewell party and invited John Eglinton, Longworth, Philip Hanson (son-in-law of Dr. Tyrrell of Trinity) and Mrs. Hanson (Deena Tyrrell), John Healy, and Susan Mitchell. His going from Ireland is described at the close of *Vale*: the morning after Bailey's party, a grey misty morning in February, saw him on his way to the boat, no trace of rancour in his heart. " It was very sad leaving those ten years of my life . . . a very different departure from the one I had long been meditating. The ideal departure should have been on an evening in May, and with the golden west behind me I should have watched from the vessel's stern the beautiful outlines of the coast and the lovely shapes of Howth. . . . I should have murmured the words of Catullus when he journeyed over land and sea to burn the body of his brother, and to fit them to my circumstance a change of a single word would have been enough: ATQUE IN PERPETUUM, MATER, AVE ATQUE VALE."

15

In London he stayed for some time at the Burlington Hotel. His literary hopes were running high : an offer reached him from America, £1,000 for twenty lectures, but it did not tempt him, and he had great pleasure in picking up the threads of his old life in London, and in explaining why he had left Ireland. " I used to think how happy he seemed," says an Irish friend of his, Mrs. Murray Robertson, who saw a good deal of him at this time, " and how well satisfied he was with himself. He would invite me to his hotel on Saturday afternoons, his secretary's half holiday, and we had many walks together. One I remember well. We were passing a house in Cheyne Walk when his eye was caught by the beauty of a tree in full bloom. I could not tell him its name. ' I must know the name,' he said, and, leaving me to stand on the pavement, he marched up the steps. A caretaker answered the bell, and the next thing I saw was the door slam in his face. The tree was a Japanese mallow, I afterwards learned.

"We engaged in many arguments. 'Dear me, dear me,' he would say when I demurred to his political and religious propositions, 'women cannot appreciate the abstract. Never, never will they rise above the concrete, you, dear Nora, least of all.' Sometimes he was so ill-tempered that I used to declare that I would never darken his door again. Then he would reproach me with neglect, and, oblivious of his last fault, charmingly beg me to dine with him. After dinner a letter to Dujardin was generally produced for my corrections. 'We can't sit still talking about nothing,' he would say.

"It was a real joy to go with him to the National Gallery, although he professed to hate museums. He laughed when I said that he should leave his Manet to the nation. I remember another day when we went to some modern exhibition together. People surged about him, and I was left alone. The Duchess of Rutland approached, and the crowd round him gave way, so that she might have G. M. to herself. When the Duchess moved on, he rejoined me and we looked at the pictures together until he espied the tall figure of Sir Edward Carson at the far end of the room. 'I must thank him for all he has done for our country,' he said, and once again he left my side. I watched Sir Edward looking down his nose, as he gravely acknowledged G. M.'s tribute. Afterwards he brought me to tea at a nearby restaurant. The place was very crowded, and we had to share a table with a mother and daughter, two very nice looking women. G. M. was assiduous in small courtesies, passing the cakes and so on, helping them on with their coats when they left. The twain were evidently much taken with this elderly gentleman who talked so interestingly and was so affable. When they had gone he turned to me and said complacently: 'I wonder what they would say if they knew who I was.' It had been one of his successful days."

CHAPTER VIII

EBURY STREET: HISTORICAL
ROMANCES

I

Moore had set Tonks and divers friends house-hunting
for him, but he disregarded their discoveries of some charming houses, saying that the addresses were not good enough,
among them a delightful small and old house overlooking
the Physic Garden of Chelsea, which he described as a
rabbit-hutch. In the end he found his own way to No. 121,
Ebury Street. He entered the house croaking and foretold
the end of his fortunate days. He could give no reason for
settling in the " long, lack-lustre " street of Ebury, except
that it formed a passage between his Bohemian friends in
Chelsea and his fashionable friends of Belgravia.

No. 121 was about the same size as the house in which he
had lived in Dublin, but he was now without a garden in
which to walk nearer than the Chelsea Hospital.

3.4.11. *To Dujardin.*

I am in London and am renting this house, or rather
this little hole in which to carry on my authorship. I have
been pretty ill, not seriously but painfully. [He had drunk
a glass of iced milk at his hotel.] The fits of indigestion
were so dreadful that I thought I was enceinte. . . . For two
days they injected morphine; I recovered, then I got ill
again. But enough of pharmacy—*Hail and Farewell.* The
first volume will appear in September.

In June he visited his friend at Le Val Changis. On his
return, when he was fully installed at No. 121, the inter-

viewers called. He spoke of his forthcoming Irish book, and showed his pictures. " No, I doubt very much if I shall buy any more. You see the walls are pretty well covered. If I had a larger house perhaps I should like to buy a Sisley. There is one I have never forgotten. Post impressionism ? Cubism ? No, one's taste forms and one can no longer see ahead. Monet used to admire Corot more than any other painter, but Corot thought that Monet should have turned his hand to something else than painting."

The dining-room, running from front to back of the house, became his usual workroom. The bow-window which he had put in to give more light was a source of great vexation. The builder had substituted a plan of his own for the one Moore had in mind, and before Moore had detected the occurrence the bow sprang from the inner screen instead of curving from the surface walls, thus revealing the partition of masonry in the wall and destroying the symmetry of the façade. Three Mark Fisher landscapes were in this room, and two portraits: one by Couture, a painting of 1850 or 1860, and one by David. He preferred the David, a French lady done just before the artist's death in Brussels. " One can tell that she was an admirable house-wife, one ate well in the house she looked after—admirable beef-steaks and omelettes, oh ! Now look at the Daubigny, what an admirable quality he gets into the sky. There is a portrait of myself by Miss Harrison, and that little Constable with the beautifully drawn hill is a nice picture—an expert with a taste for dull pictures cast a doubt upon it once." " Weren't you angry ? " " Not in the least; the expert had already been taken in by an alleged Constable. I was only sorry that he had been so stupid." " This portrait in the corner——? " " A portrait of me by Orpen, an early work. Come upstairs with me to the drawing-room and I will show you some pictures that will interest you more. The picture on the staircase is a Steer and a very good one, painted when he returned from France under the influence of Degas. Now don't you like the hanging of that wall ? Doesn't the Monet look beautiful ? " And he would continue to speak of his two Manets, his two Berthe Morisots, his Monet and his

Charles Condor in phrases almost identical with those that occur at the beginning of *Salve* when he shows A. E. around his pictures in Ely Place. " You will see a pastel by Degas as you go down the staircase. And there is an Ingres drawing; the rest are reproductions, but I thought I must have one piece of paper on which the sacred hand had rested. Here we are back in the dining-room again ! "

In the drawing-room Moore had, besides the pictures mentioned in *Salve*, a water-colour of a girl by Ford Madox Brown which he valued very highly, protecting it by curtains from the rays of the sun. This room was only used on the occasions when he gave a formal dinner-party, rare occasions, for ordinarily Moore preferred to have one person only with him at a meal. He then dispensed with ceremony and usually greeted his guest with abuse for mistaking the hour of dinner. Or if the guest came early he would at once open out with his views upon some writer, or with an account of an effort he was making to drag himself out of a quagmire of difficulties in his own work. When he went out to dinner there was generally a look of mild boredom on his face as he entered the drawing-room; perhaps this was a cover for a certain amount of shyness, which only wore off as a conversation, particularly if it involved an argument, put him at his ease.

" It hardly seems a worthy subject to bring into the life of a great writer," Tonks writes to me, " but as he so often spoke of it it may be worth while saying something on the question of food and drink. About wine I think he knew nothing, he was prepared to add water to every wine. When he gave his friends claret at dinner he thought it proper to send his maid round the table with a jug of hot water to be added to the wine. He talked so much about the shad, in French *alose*, that one lady forbade him to mention it again." The merits of the John Dory—" so much better than the dull sole "—roused him to eloquence. In Dublin he had sent letters to the *Irish Times* about another neglected fish, the red mullet.

2

The publication of *Ave* was delayed until November. I am enabled, by the kindness of Mr. Nelson Ward, to give an anecdote relative to the final proof-sheets of this book. " I was acting at the time," he says, " as Moore's legal adviser, and the following is a note I made of a conversation that took place upon the occasion of my first visit to Ebury Street :—

MOORE : I am surprised that you have made no remark about my pictures.

WARD : I have heard that you have good pictures, and I noted some of them when I came into the room, but I hardly liked to refer to them immediately on my arrival, as I came here on business, and I proposed to ask if I might examine them on leaving.

MOORE : I understand from Tonks that you are an admirer of Dickens. Have you read any of my books ?

WARD : Yes, I read *Esther Waters* many years ago.

MOORE : Don't you think that is better than anything Dickens ever wrote ?

WARD : Candidly, I don't.

MOORE : I have recently written a new book, and I have the proof-sheets of it here. It is called *Hail and Farewell*. I will read to you one of the opening paragraphs. My friends tell me that they consider it the finest piece of prose in the English language. (*Reads*) :

" And I used to go to Pump Court, sure of finding him in his high canonical chair, sheltered by a screen, reading his book, with his long clay pipe and a glass of grog in his hand."

WARD : Excuse me, but he must have had a fairly large hand to be able to hold a long clay pipe and a glass of grog in it at the same time.

MOORE : That never occurred to me, or to any of my friends. Of course, any ordinary person could call attention to it. A schoolmaster might notice it. I must alter the words. Yes, I will alter it to " with his long clay pipe in his hand and a glass of grog beside him."

WARD: No, I don't like that.

MOORE: Why not?

WARD: I do not like the rhythm. I should say, " with his glass of grog by his side." The other sounds too much like " with his martial cloak around him."

MOORE: No, " beside him " is better.

WARD: I prefer " by his side."

MOORE: I do not agree. I shall write " with his glass of grog beside him."

" I do not think he read to me the remainder of the paragraph, and I left him soon afterwards. Weeks later I happened to pick up, at my club, a copy of *Ave*. I turned to the opening paragraph and read ' his glass of grog beside him, his long clay pipe in his hand.' "[1]

The reception given to *Ave* did not satisfy him entirely. The book caught on as a piece of gossip and Moore objected, saying it was as much a novel as any book he had written, so far as the form was concerned. " I took a certain amount of experience," he said, " and tried to mould it." Later on a more lavish praise was showered on the book; in a letter to the Colonel he spoke of a slow but continuous sale, and added that he felt he was " a little nearer to the summit of Parnassus." To others, he now described himself as the first English writer of prose narrative. Tonks says: " When we spoke of Jane Austen he became a little disturbed and would say: ' She is well enough, but her field is too limited.' Fielding he thought poorly of, but unquestionably he admired Sterne, perhaps looking on *Tristram Shandy* as not being prose narrative, why I do not know."

It was useless to mention the names of Dickens and Thackeray. He had his own way of disposing of these

[1] Other sentences in the opening paragraph of *Ave* are also, perhaps, open to schoolmaster's criticism. There were still some traces of the French idiom in his writing. " At this time I was very poor; *all the hours of the day* were spent in writing *some* chapters of *Esther Waters*."

claimants. " Thackeray, the name of a butler. Thackeray, I shall want the carriage at four o'clock." Dickens was " a man called Dickens—well, if you *like* him." On one occasion a journalist mentioned Schiller to him, and he " inferred " that Schiller must be one of the authors recommended in the schools who extract vast yawns from the breast. This drew a comment from Croce in far-off Naples upon a certain British writer, who " must be considered a crank, yet is not altogether wrong in the theory of a sound of a name because the name of a celebrated man often becomes impregnated with all the impressions aroused by his work, with the judgments of admiration or disapproval which it has received, and with the greater or lesser degree of the warmth of the said judgments."[1]

To add to the satisfactions of the year Bernard Shaw recommended the play *Esther Waters* to the attention of the Stage Society. There were two performances at the Apollo Theatre.

20.11.11. *To Dujardin.*

The acting could not have been better: an excellent Esther, quiet, sensible, tactful—no genius, that is to say no stage tricks [Miss Lucy Williams played the part]; eighteen characters, a real portrait gallery with due respect paid to age, temperament and manners. It succeeded perfectly, but, as you are aware, there is no public for serious plays.

Moore wrote a charming preface to the play when it was published in book form. There they all were (he described his attendance at the rehearsals): the old butler, William Latch, Esther herself and the others, all his beloved characters in the flesh at last, all looking exactly like themselves, " and not one of them looking older than when I first knew them." The production was not a success, for, apart from the dialogue by Lennox Robinson in the second act, what was shown on the stage amounted to little more than a series of

[1] Benedetto Croce: *European Literature in the* 19*th Century.* Chapman & Hall, p. 32.

literary scenes, the dispute over the Silver Braid sweepstakes being taken almost word for word from the novel.

Nothing, however, daunted him in his dramatic endeavours, and during the next eighteen months, in the intervals when he felt free from the long labour of his Irish autobiography, he took up once more, for the Stage Society, *Elizabeth Cooper*, banishing from his mind, as far as possible, all memory of his collaborations with Mrs. Craigie and with Dujardin on the same theme, and radically altering the original conception by causing Gabrielle to see through the deception and at the same time fall in love with the secretary. One may anticipate a little by saying that the Stage Society produced the play on the 23rd of June, 1913. Moore sent his servants to see it and they came back enthusiastic, but the Press was lukewarm, and it seemed that somehow or other he had just missed writing a good fantastic comedy. If a friend had not dissuaded him Moore would have given the part of Gabrielle to an actress who was then very little known, Miss Edith Evans, whom he had admired in a Shakespearean play. Miss Evans played the part of the maid, and played it so well that it became the best part in the comedy.

3

Moore did not lose sight of the Colonel and Moore Hall after leaving Ireland, and there were acrimonious passages in the correspondence between the two brothers. Neither would confess to have been at fault, and in May 1911 the Colonel reached the decision that he did not care to stay any longer in his brother's house. He wished to educate his children abroad, but in acquainting George of his intentions he recited past grievances, the attack on his religion and the threat to disinherit the family if they did not abjure Catholicism. He added that he wished to be under no obligation to his brother in the matter of the money that had been spent on his son's education at Downside. Once again Moore replied that nothing would be gained by any attempt to repay the money, and that he had not wished his nephews to become Protestants for the sake of the money—he had wished them to be intellectually free, and this seemed to him to be within his rights.

Colonel Moore left Moore Hall a few weeks later, to settle his family in Brussels, and the lonely western mansion was closed, never to be reopened. The brothers met in London; George was interested in a life of their father on which the Colonel was engaged; and their relations took a turn for the better. They corresponded on the subject of the sale of his Ballintubber, Ashbrook, and other properties to the Congested Districts Board. The Board offered £40,000 in cash and Government stock, but attempted to impose a condition that it should be permitted to confer grazing rights in the Moore Hall demesne on the people in the vicinity. Moore was incensed, and he brought his case to the notice of the Irish Secretary, reminding Mr. Birrell that Moore Hall had been for generations an oasis of culture in Co. Mayo, and asking if it was the Government's policy to let Ireland wholly revert to the peasant. Were the encroachments made no gentleman would ever again care to occupy Moore Hall, he said; and he wrote to his brother: " To sell Moore Hall out and out, if I can get a good price, would be heart-breaking. Don't think I wish to do this, I am quite as unwilling as you are. But if I don't sell Moore Hall it will be sold in the next generation, of that I am quite sure." He did not wish to reawaken the spirit of resentment and suspicion, but being himself disillusioned he could not refrain from acid comment on his brother's political activities and beliefs. Colonel Moore spoke of a movement now on foot to persuade the Government to give better prices for Irish land: landlords were to withdraw their support from Carson and to help Mr. Asquith to pass the Home Rule Bill. " How can I help the Government to pass or defeat the Home Rule Bill ? " Moore replied. " And how are you to help the Government ? By promising not to go to Ulster and place your military knowledge at the service of Sir Edward Carson?" One thing he was determined upon: if the Board insisted on grazing rights they must buy house, garden, everything. He won his battle, and the Board not only relinquished the attempt to acquire grazing rights in his demesne, but advanced the price for the other properties by £3,000. In the upshot, after repaying all the mortgages, he realised about £30,000 from the sale to his tenants, and was left with his " dreaming house " and some five hundred acres of land about it.

In August 1912 Colonel Moore was in Brussels with his family, and Moore paid him a short visit there to offer advice and help on the subject of the biography of George Henry Moore. After that the Colonel came to London for a few weeks. The brothers continued to discuss the biography. There were differences of opinion as to the style in which it should be written, and these differences led to a renewal of the theological wrangle. " The public," Moore said, " doesn't want to read about parties in Mayo in the 'seventies, but if you must introduce politics into your story the facts should be verified by an idea : for instance, when Father brought the priest into politics, was it because he believed in organized religion, or was it because he looked upon the priest as a democratic element ? The priest is no longer a democratic element." Tempers were frayed, and one day about this time the Colonel happened to call at Ebury Street. George was out, but *Salve*, which had just been published, lay on the table. The Colonel began to read, and came upon the passages in that book which relate to himself. He noticed that Atkinson, who was also in the room, avoided conversation, and leaving the house in a very angry frame of mind, he went back to his lodgings and wrote a letter of bitter remonstrance, at which his brother expressed much surprise :

21.10.12. *Moore to Colonel Moore.*

The unexpected always happens. The chapters in which I speak of you in *Salve* were written six or seven years ago, when I began the book, and they have been hardly altered since, merely verbal alterations, no more. They were read at the time to Russell and to Magee, and they did not think that the chapters contained anything to which you would take offence; in fact Russell told me that I was placing myself in a very unsympathetic light, and that all

the sympathy would be with you. The chapters were submitted in proof to Longworth; he did not think that they
contained anything that would annoy you. I asked him
again and again if my descriptions of you could be compared with my description of Yeats, and he answered that
there was nothing to which you could legitimately take
offence. He was wrong, Yeats was not offended and you
are. Well, well, it is a tricky world and I am sorry that I
have offended you. Every precaution was taken to avoid
doing so, but you see something in the chapters which
nobody else sees ! . . . Do come and see me.

24.10.12. *Colonel Moore to Moore.*

I might object to your putting into my mouth your
versions of conversations built up merely for your own
glorification, a method of controversy so easy that you
took the strongest objection to it when employed by Archer
though he was honest enough to submit the proofs for your
correction. . . . I cannot read your description on pp. 255–6
without seeing the bitterness and personal antagonism
which underlies the whole. To take phrases:—" the
vague inconclusive eyes," " the faded empty look,"
" slouches along hands dangling out of his cuffs,"
" untidy mind," untrue, probably libellous statements
about my reasons for going to mass, etc. These are only
bits which emphasize your attitude to me; an attitude as
I said of personal animosity; the representation of feelings
which have been boiling up in your mind for the last two
or three years. . . . Butter in other places will not soften
these expressions. There is no one more sensitive as to
your personal vanity than yourself; I once sent you an
article and you chose to object to a phrase, a mild phrase
not meant to apply to you. You roared like a bull. . . .

25.10.12. *Moore to Colonel Moore.*

I can only assure you that my aim is to describe how
two brothers united in everything else found themselves
divided by an idea; and I can assure you that if I had

thought that you would have taken it to heart I should have modified the expressions to which you take exception. The " faded empty look " does not apply to you but to the portraits of Philip by Velasquez. It is true that I say that you resemble Philip, but surely this is mere whimsicality and cannot be described as personal animosity . . . Manet in the opinion of many people made me look like a figure of fun but I published his portrait of me in *Modern Painting*. . . . I swear to you that my affection for you is unchanged and will always remain unchanged.

27.10.12. *Colonel Moore to Moore.*

One cannot help thinking that if you really wanted to know if I would object it would have been as easy to show me what you had written about me as any other part of the book; and if you examine your conscience you will find that however reluctant you may or may not have been to annoy me, you were not prepared to sacrifice your little paragraphs on the altar of friendship . . . You wanted to put them beyond recall and chance the rest. This is putting the matter in the mildest possible way; you have tried to represent me as mentally contemptible and physically ridiculous so as to contrast with your own extreme cleverness. It will not make matters any better to write any more, so I will drop the subject. . . . Perhaps one day I will write your biography. Who knows ?

28.10.12. *Moore to Colonel Moore.*

A more untrue statement was never put forward than that I made you seem mentally contemptible and in the dialogue you speak as well as anyone can speak; of course you get the worst of the argument but that is inevitable— whatever may be the ultimate truth the believer must get the worst of the argument with the agnostic. In Pascal's celebrated dialogue the believer has the worst of the argument all the time . . . In the book you answer me as you answered me in life many a time, and were you endowed with all the wit of all the world you could not have answered me any better. You ask me why I did not show you those parts of my book. Because if I had heaven only knows what you might not have asked me to change—in half an hour my book would have been a wreck, and if I had shown it to Magee he would have wished many things altered, and A. E. would have revised the book from his point of view. . . . Your charge that I have made you seem physically repulsive[1] seems to me equally unfounded—that I have caricatured, yes—but I did not think anybody minded that. Max and others have caricatured me out of all human resemblance but I never objected; and passing from pictorial caricature to literary I cannot help reminding you that Yeats did not object to my portrait of him. How you could take seriously my quissical romancing about Bellini and his school I fail to understand. . . .

Don't write to me again on the painful subject of *Salve* for *six months*. By the way Walter Osborne painted your portrait and it should rebutt and repudiate and give the lie to my insinuations that you are to be discovered in the portraits by the school of Bellini. If you like I will have it photographed and it can be published in the illustrated papers.

The atmosphere was clearing, and peace might have been restored but for fresh troubles which arose out of Werner Laurie's engagement to publish the Colonel's biography: *An Irish Gentleman: George Henry Moore*. Should it not have a preface by George Moore ? Werner Laurie asked, and Moore, who thought that his brother had done the work very well, especially the racing chapters, consented to write a preface. He showed his brother what he had written; again the Colonel's indignation waxed, for it contained a statement that their father had committed suicide, and a further irritation arose over a letter from George which ridiculed a proposal to publish a photograph of the Colonel in uniform as a frontispiece of the book. Maurice Moore then left London for Galway, feeling that George could not resist

[1] " Physically *ridiculous*," were the Colonel's words.

the temptation to humiliate. He had accepted, but was little satisfied with, a compromise which they had reached in regard to the preface. Moore would not altogether omit the reference to suicide, but had written instead that he *would like to think* that the circumstances of his father's death pointed to suicide. " He died killed by his tenants, that is certain. My brother gives a letter which I would like to believe points to suicide." In Galway the Colonel met relatives who urged him to remove all shadow of doubt from the question, and, moved by their entreaties, he sent Werner Laurie a slip for inclusion in the biography to say that the words must be taken as expressing the prefacer's wishes, not the facts. Moore afterwards found this slip in his copy of the biography; he accused his brother of bad faith and of an endeavour to advertise the book by raising a fraternal controversy—an endeavour, he said, to which he must refuse to be privy. The Colonel felt that he was near the end of his patience. " The kindly, good-natured George that I knew for fifty years is dead," he replied. " Prosperity and exaltation alter certain characters." The exchange of letters grew angrier and more passionate, and when it ended the separation between the two brothers was final and complete.

4

For the rest, the year 1913 was occupied almost wholly with the completion of the trilogy. *Vale* appears to have given Moore more trouble than either of the other volumes. From certain passages the danger of libel actions loomed up, and Longworth, who combined legal knowledge with literary taste and familiarity with Moore's subject, had frequently to be consulted. One chapter, written as far back as 1909, was omitted at the request of the Irish poet, Seumas O'Sullivan, who figured in it: he enjoyed it himself, but feared that it would pain his family. A. E. let it be known that he was on the watch. " But what am I to do ? " said Moore. " If I put nothing in it is a bad compliment. If I describe his home life in the style of a Christmas card he will not like it."

17.11.13. *To E. V. Longworth.*

As usual you are right—about many things if not about all . . . The passage about Russell will, of course, be entirely re-written and I will send it to you. It is of the utmost importance not to give offence in this quarter.

The passage about the impotency I am afraid I cannot change. If it were changed it would be nothing at all . . .

At the beginning of 1914 the proofs were coming in.

20.1.14. *To E. V. Longworth.*

I am much obliged to you for the proof and for striking out the sentence which might involve me in a libel action. For years I have been looking forward to writing those chapters on Moore Hall and you do not say if I have succeeded or if I have not, whether it is the best or the worst part of the book. The reviewers will say nothing that interests me; it is your opinion and the opinion of one or two friends that I value.

The portrait of T. P. Gill in particular caused some scandal: Gill used to visit at Ely Place up to the time of Moore's departure from Ireland, and the famous chapter in *Vale* comparing him and Plunkett with Flaubert's ludicrous characters, Bouvard and Pécuchet, fell like a bolt from the blue, especially as he was still the head of a public department. It would be wrong to suppose that Moore was expressing his personal animosities, or even cynicism, in this or any other chapter of *Hail and Farewell*. He would seize upon some obvious peculiarity or weakness in his model (which aroused his delight rather than his contempt), and proceed to a remorseless elaboration for purely literary purposes. Here, for example, he is delighted by the notion of linking Plunkett and Gill together as the Irish Bouvard and Pécuchet, and enlarges upon it without bothering about the justice of the picture as a whole, satisfied that it has composed well. " A man can only have one sort of conscience," he used to say, " and mine is a literary one." But the plea (offered to his brother) that he did not hesitate to sacrifice himself as well as his neighbour to his art, is disingenuous;

he chose which of his own frailties and absurdities he would exhibit, his neighbours were not given the choice, and it may be added that he had the schoolboy's genius for divining what was most likely to tease and to humiliate.

The anti-Catholic bias of the book was not disguised, and yet the portrait of Martyn, the great Catholic, was drawn with humanity and affection. It went deeper than the characterisations of A. E. or of Horace Plunkett, brilliant captures of an external likeness both. A number of solecisms appeared in the text, and were not corrected in subsequent editions: Bossuet, "that detestable man," is spoken of as the persecutor of Madame de Genlis, who was born three years after his death. Soldiers who have served in the Peninsular wars pass through Italy on the way home. St. Augustine was only seven when the Emperor Julian died, but Moore marvels at the fact that it had never struck any-one before that they were contemporaries : "Augustine and Julian—how wonderful. Landor should have thought of the learned twain as a subject for dialogue." In a comment on the doctrine of the Mass accident becomes incident. "The substance is the same, but the incident is different. Or it may have been that the incident is the same and the sub-stance is different; one cannot ever be sure that one remembers theology correctly." The scholarly friends to whom Moore used to submit his proofs must have been napping.

5

Ties that had bound him to Ireland were being severed, but Ireland continued to play an important part in the life of his imagination, and he had in mind further Irish stories which he hoped to write. But that inspiration could not last for ever; the trilogy had been the foundation of his literary life for so long that the thought of lonely years without a subject now excited his apprehension. He had lately brought out new editions of old books, *Impressions and Opinions* and *Spring Days*, with Werner Laurie, but the revisions of early works would not be enough to occupy his old age. The early novel was better than he " thought for," but he did not want

to write a novel of that kind again. He would " dream "
life not " copy " it, and the novel of contemporary life did
not lend itself to dream. There was the life of the past, and
he still kept the scenario of *The Apostle* by him, wondering if
he would ever make something less melodramatic of his
famous invention, the meeting between St. Paul and Jesus.
On this side lay prodigious and obvious dangers of another
kind, for he was without scholarship, and his temptation,
as a Protestant controversialist, to view Biblical history too
much in the abstract would be immense. But he was willing
to face this risk, and towards the end of 1913, poor
traveller that he was, he surprised all his friends by announcing that he was about to set out for the Dead Sea, " in search
of a story or drama."

He was gone before *Vale* was published : alone, though
perhaps he would have liked a companion, for when I met
him one evening in Chelsea he suggested that I should accompany him. " I leave Marseilles by the *Macedonia* for Port
Said, bound for the land of camels and concubines," he
wrote to Dujardin on the 16th of February, 1914. " I have
ordered 50 of the first and 500 of the others." A letter to
Lord Howard de Walden shows him on board his ship.

23.2.14. P. and O.S.N.Co. S.S.
My dear Howard,
    I usually begin my letters " dear Howard " the " my "
is the cry of a despairing soul deprived of women's society
for five days and after a couple I began to wilt. My appearance is rueful, and the tedium of this voyage, of the passengers, is hard to bear. Just now a man asked me what
book I was reading and I answered *The Sentimental Journey*
and while praising the writing I mentioned that it was
pleasing to come across the celebrated phrase " God
tempers the wind to the shorn lamb." But he broke in,
" Another of Lloyd George's howlers which shows him
to know as little about sheep as pheasants ; we don't shear
lambs." Apparently Lloyd George quoted the well-known
phrase and the passenger on the *Macedonia* accepted it as
original. I rose with a sigh and went to the barber whom

I found to be more deeply read in English literature than myself. He had read *The Revolt of Islam* many times and knew Burns by heart. . . . My mistake was to leave London without a pair of breeches and my hopes are set on Port Said and the possibility of getting a pair there or a pair of riding pads. If my knees get chapped I don't know what I shall do to get the landscape into my head. It's probable that I shall write again and now dear Howard will you give your wife my affectionate regards. I hope you won't think the expression exaggerated and, in view of my blighted life, my drooping petals, will allow it to pass. After all it is the right word for if you don't think affectionately of a friend you might as well not think of him or her at all.

Always affectionately yours

George Moore.

Hail and Farewell had caused many readers to murmur " Sterne." Moore had never read a line of Sterne, so he said, and before setting out for the East he asked Edmund Gosse to lend him copies of *The Sentimental Journey* and of *Tristram Shandy*. Gosse obliged, but ever afterwards Moore insisted that he had played a little trick on him. " Gosse," he said, " used to like us to put C.B. after his name when addressing our envelopes to him. I never would. I used to scrawl disrespectful letters of the alphabet on my envelopes. He didn't seem to mind, he never referred to the matter, but what do you think ? When I opened my copy of *Tristram Shandy* on the boat, I found that he had given me an ex-purgated edition—full of blank pages, and little dots. . . . So he had his revenge."

The Sentimental Journey recalled him to antiquity, " perhaps more than any other book of the modern world." " Like a translation of some small Latin or Greek work, it read to me," he wrote many years later, "*Daphnis and Chloë* or *The Golden Ass*." And he reminded the passengers, as the ship passed through the Straits of Messina, of rugged Polyphemus peering over the cliffs and discerning Galatea in the foam. . . . He spoke of Dido weeping on the shores of the African coast.

. . . But nobody was on board who knew him or his writings, nobody who had read any book that he had read, or had seen any picture he had seen.

One friend he did make, an agreeable man who helped him in the little complications of life on board ship. It was a fortunate acquaintance, for when they reached Joppa Moore was still under his wing, observing with astonishment the miraculous ease with which arrangements were made, Asiatics propitiated and complicated problems unravelled. " The man seemed to be all-powerful and begged me to tell him what I most wanted to see. The place, I said, where the woman was taken in adultery." He never learnt that his influential protector was a member of the firm of Thomas Cook & Son.

He found his way to the Grand Hotel, Jerusalem. Within a fortnight, or less, and not without enduring what for a man of his age was considerable hardship, he had executed his design in Palestine, and was turning homewards. From Cairo, on the return journey, he wrote a number of letters to London, announcing his discovery of the Essene monastery, and giving a harrowing description of the badly made Jerusalem breeches. One of these letters was to Mrs. St. John Hutchinson, a friend whom he had lately made.

Friday
  [14.3.14]

New Khedival Hotel
    Cairo,
      Egypt.

Dear Mrs. Hutchinson,

After faring the farer returns home weary of the luminous sadnesses of the south and with a great longing for the cloudy melancholy of the north.

On arriving at Jerusalem I went away on an Arab horse whose pacing is different from anything I had experienced before, and rode to Jericho about 20 miles from Jerusalem through stony hills rising steeply out of and descending steeply into stony vallies [sic]; sometimes the hills fall asunder and reveal precipitous sides of white clay, nearly chalk; and the colour of the wilderness is a dirty white and a dirty green—the green of wild rosemary and thyme. A little grass grows here and there and the flock guided by wild shepherds nibble it as it passes. A country as naked and as savage as the psalms. A Roman road winds to the right and left along the sides of precipices, several hundred feet deep—a very unpleasant country for horse riding. At last the fair green of Jericho appeared between the hills and it was then that I learnt the beauty of green, and it brought home to me sensations of home and friends. Why the Romans came to this fearful place I have been thinking ever since we passed the ruins of a Roman outpost on the borders of the plain. But it is desert till within a mile of the town and so tired was I that the beautiful hills of Moab could not rouse me and I failed to admire that evening the long wavering rose-coloured line that the vapours rising always from the Dead Sea veil, making the beautiful scene more beautiful—no sea is as blue as the Dead sea—a poisonous chemical blue.

It was almost impossible for me to dismount; I threw myself from the horse and tottered into the house asking for a hot bath and a bottle of vinegar.[1] And these two remedies enabled me to pursue the journey next day. We crossed the Jordan, a muddy stream, and rode through some cultivated hills till we came to a village. Ten miles was my start that day. Jackals howled all night and the insects in the carpet and the insects afloat in what I suppose I must call the air made that night one that I shall not forget easily. We rode into Moab; slept at Moab and inquired for Monasteries, but there is none on the east of the Dead sea, perhaps never have been any, and so we rode back to Jericho as soon as our horses were rested. We had to spend a couple of nights in Jericho and as soon as the horses were fit to travel we rode along the coast of the Dead Sea—a long day's journey; we were in the saddle twelve hours and our horses were very tired when we arrived at our desolate destination. A town had once been there and this sulphuric spot is mentioned by Josephus as being the principal set-

[1] The hot bath and the bottle of vinegar were not forgotten; see *The Brook Kerith*, p. 20.

tlement of the Essenes. A few stone huts are all that is there now, and the few Arabs that live in them live as Beduins often on a little camel's milk. My heart misgave me as we pitched our camp and I know not how we should have returned if our muleteer had deserted or how my father endured the heat of the Dead Sea in May. He mentions in his diary that he rode from Jerusalem to Joppa in a day and that his horse was very tired at the end of the journey. His son was too tired to think about the horse or anything else that night[1]; and next day we began the return journey at daybreak. I think that I rode on in a dream, and on arriving in Jericho I felt that I should never be rested again. A century of sleep in a feather bed would not be enough. The journey from Jericho to Mar Saba is a long one, and we might have wandered off there if we had not heard that what we sought was within a couple of leagues of Jericho, in the great chasm known as the Brook of the Chariots. A path about three feet wide leads round the cliffs, sometimes passing under over-hanging rocks. Arab horses are sure-footed and they picked their way safely through the rubble unconscious of any feat. For myself I daren't look up or down. Three hundred feet up and three hundred feet down scare me, and I confess that I slipped off my horse's back and gave him to the dragoman to lead. It is in this terrifying chasm, high up between a cliff and a cliff that my monastery hangs, like an eagle's nest, and it seemed to me that the monks had slung a bridge over the chasm lower down and the green of two pepper trees refreshed the eye. Terrace after terrace, none more than a couple of yards wide testify endless patience and labour. This chasm seems to have tempted the religious-minded from the beginning for opposite the present monastery are ruins of former monasteries; and some of these are attributed to the Crusaders and some to earlier aspirations. The first thing to do was to discover if there was a way through the cliff up to the hills above, for without one this monastery would not suit my purpose. A

[1] The father was twenty-seven when he made these journeys, the son sixty-two.

difficult way it was admitted to be and a difficult way I found it; a sort of chimney in which there were broken steps and passages took us to the stony hills and stony vallies through which I remembered that Jesus once led his flocks, and tired beyond all words I lay awhile among the lilies of the field and said: " It was here that Jesus conversed with the shepherd."

In this extraordinary monastery a woman lives, a nun, and some of the monks are very handsome; and when they are not in their church they labour in the terraces that zig-zag down the cliff. A monk who found the solitude of this convent insufficient lives opposite in the ruins with a little ewe lamb that follows him like a dog.

I am ashamed to send you this rough draft of a letter but no secretary is by me to whom I can dictate so I have to send it as it is untidy as a man in a night cap before he has had his bath. But I send it to you for I think it may please you to hear from me. I don't know why I should think this but it is pleasant to think it and I direct the envelope hoping that you will give my kind regards to your husband and to all our friends.

Very sincerely yours,
George Moore.

Moore's visit to Palestine was brief; but it had served its purpose: to avoid errors in his rendering of the Holy Land, and to supply a background, no less real for being unobtrusive, for the events of his story. Long descriptive passages, local colour of the cruder sort, had never been a part of his method; and at this stage of his development he was less inclined than ever to hold up the narrative for the sake of landscape painting. But he wished to be familiar with the scene against which his actors were to move, aware that such knowledge would help him to render something that was immutable in the heart of man; man is a part of his background, and universal emotions derive from material surroundings the colour that gives them reality. Moore knew this in *The Brook Kerith*, and in *Héloïse and Abélard* his success in conjuring up the picture of a vanished world was still greater; whereas a certain unreality in his *Aphrodite in Aulis* may be ascribed to an imperfect visualisation of the scene, for Moore's scholarship was not sufficient to take the place of the traveller's eye. It is difficult for one who does not know Palestine to decide how much he owed to his brief visit and how much to the Bible, particularly the Old Testament (note his phrase above: " a country as naked and as savage as the psalms "); but his success in creating a credible background to his story cannot be denied. Incidents of shepherd life, fairs and cock-fighting may be traded to his memories of Mayo and the Sussex downs, but the appearance of these scenes in the book are hardly sufficient to justify John Freeman's comment that it is the soft green island which he remembered again and again while writing his Syrian story.

By the end of March Moore was in Paris on his way home, calling on Dujardin, who had annoyed him by producing, during his absence in Palestine, " *Clara Florise*, a comedy in three acts by George Moore " at the Comédie Royale. This was the French version of *Elizabeth Cooper* and the *Peacock's Feathers*, the last result of the collaboration which had extended over so many years. The cause of Moore's displeasure was the actress to whom his friend had given the chief part, but Dujardin had acted within his rights; *Clara Florise* was his property by a recent contract with Moore, although Moore (for reasons of a non-literary order) had put his sole name to the piece, which was later printed in Paris (copies are very rare) and deposited in Dujardin's name with the French Society of Dramatic Authors.

A packet of letters followed him from Jerusalem to the Hotel Brighton, forwarded by a friend whom he had asked to walk round to Ebury Street now and again—" as I walk round to Tonks "—to look after things in his absence.

24.3.14. *To Mrs. Murray Robertson*

It was most kind of you to send me the reviews. I have long ceased to draw conclusions from book reviews, but if I hadn't I should say that *Vale* was on the way towards a large publicity. You speak in a letter received this morning of a " virtuous howl of indignation " but it was all milk and honey you sent me; true your friend on the *Daily News* squeaked a little, a prespeterean (*sic*) you tell me he is and I add, one who is not unlikely to bring up his children Roman Catholics. But I thank him all the same for his review. You say that you have sent another batch of letters to Jerusalem, I hope they all follow me safely and run to earth here. And now about that which interests you much more, Ireland. Redmond's request that English soldiers shall be sent to Ulster reminds me of the fellow who fled from Waterford in the eleventh century to England and brought over King Henry's knights—Ireland's greatest traitor and the cause of all her woes. History repeats itself and I am certain that if force be used against Ulster that Ireland will be ruined in the twentieth as she was in the eleventh century . . . the only way to get a united Ireland is to leave out the five northern counties—a pikestaff is not plainer. But nobody can see it, no one can detach himself from his prejudices sufficiently—you my dear friend least of all.

After a few weeks in Ebury Street Moore paid a visit to Dublin, where he gathered news of the effect of *Hail and Farewell* on his Irish circle. Certain lines in *Vale*, he learned, were making Yeats reluctant to see him again. He went on to Westport to discuss business with his agent, Tom Ruttledge, and spoke much, and angrily, of his brother Maurice. Although he had but lately written in *Vale* that the payments to the Catholic school were a misunderstanding for which no one should be held to blame, he now—exasperated, perhaps, by the Colonel's refusal to take his religious convictions seriously—spoke of a deception. A direct conflict of evidence appeared which had not been forced into the light three years earlier, as to whether Moore had agreed to the payments. The Colonel said he did, and Moore denied it categorically. "What sort of a hypocrite," he exclaimed, " would I have seemed in the eyes of my co-religionists if it had not been discovered until after my death that while I was attacking Catholicism with my pen I was paying large sums of money to the Jesuits and Benedictines? I should have appeared the exemplar of all the hypocrisies outdoing Tartuffe. I should have presented a being so impossible that men would have said that nature exceeds the imagination of Molière, Fielding and Sheridan." Ruttledge might have replied—perhaps he did reply: " No, they would have said that you showed an amiable inconsistency in a desire to help your brother, even at the expense of your principles."

Later in the summer, at Ebury Street, he prepared a new edition of *The Untilled Field*, to which he was adding a preface on the vexed problem of Synge's place in modern Irish literature. " *It was just as if on purpose to make an omedaun of me* [George Moore] *that Yeats brought him over from Paris in the year 1903, though he had no English on him at the time, only the little that's heard in the National Schools. . . .*"

A faint sprinkling of the *Playboy* idiom would, he thought, improve his stories. " I have done what I could with the idiom," he wrote to a friend, " and in places I have done pretty well, but my vocabulary is exhausted . . . I enclose a preface . . . You will do me a great favour if you will translate into Irish—into very thick Irish idiom—the passage marked."

6

August 1914 and the outbreak of the War found Moore in London. At first he seemed to be very little affected, and when Tonks, one evening, told him that Namur had fallen, all he said was : " Oh, this kind of thing makes the newspapers more interesting." Tonks's face became grave, and he set about telling him what an awful thing the war was. " I think I really frightened him," he writes. But Moore reassured himself: the Navy, he declared, was safe so long as it was commanded by a man of the name of John Jellicoe—a splendid name.

Later on, during the winter, a letter to *The Times*, abjuring his friendship with Kuno Meyer, who was conducting pro-German propaganda among the Irish in America, attracted attention by its virulence even among the mass of similar polemics in which elderly men of letters were prone to indulge at this time. And yet Moore was fond of Meyer, the

German scholar in old Irish, whose portrait is among the most sympathetic in *Hail and Farewell*, though not among the most accurate. " It was from Best that I learnt he was once an excellent cricketer, and though now crippled with rheumatism, it was easy to see that he must have looked well on the cricket field in white flannels and a blue belt . . . never a fast runner, I am sure of that, therefore I place him at point. . . ." " Where *did* Moore get that story of my being a cricketer ? " asked Meyer coming into the Library. " I can't imagine," Best replied; " but stay, I remember telling him one day that I had just seen you on the pier at Bray wearing white flannel trousers."

For his refusal to cherish idealistic sentiments and hopes he earned reproaches; but as an ageing author who was not politically minded (the only politics about which he cared anything were Irish) he showed good sense in refraining from the instruction of statesmen. The new book which he was writing, the ideas which he was putting forth in new pre-faces, the revaluation of his past experiences, meant more to him than the drama in Flanders. There is hardly a mention of the War in the long correspondence with E. A. Boyd, the Irish-American critic, on which he entered about this time.

17.8.14. *To E. A. Boyd*

If it had not been for Yeats, Synge would never have written anything but board-school English. Yeats trained him through dialect, he dunged the roots, and when this was done, Synge grew and strengthened, and putting forth new shoots he wearied of the dialect and began writing in English. The Wicklow and Kerry sketches are full of good things; but it was Yeats who taught him to write; and it was Yeats who taught Lady Gregory. She had not written anything at all until she met Yeats. . . . He seems to me to be a very fine schoolmaster. I owe something to him myself and I take this opportunity of acknowledging it. He seems to me to have devised a method of testing, or to speak more plainly, he has devised literary formulæ not unlike the pictorical formulæ that Walter Sickert invented and that have ennabled countless ladies to paint gable

ends barely distinguishable from the " master's." Walter
Sickert teaches how " values " may be dispensed with—
how vermilion worked into ultra-marine will produce a
symbolic sky that harmonises with the brown roofs in
which Indian red is used largely. Ultramarine broken with
vermilion is not a sky but it stands for a sky. The drawing
can also be dispensed with by means of a photograph
which is enlarged and squared out upon the canvas.
" Quality " is necessary in oil painting, and it cannot be
dispensed with, but a sort of wholesale " quality " is
arrived at by a series of little dabs; and these dabs protect
the artist from linoleum. The London County Council pays
for all this teaching and every year a tribe of little female
Sickerts go forth all over Europe bringing back endless
gable ends. It seems to me that Yeats can do very much
the same in literature as Sickert does in painting.

In September Mr. and Mrs. St. John Hutchinson invited
him to stay at West Wittering, where Tonks also was to be
found.

1.9.14. *To Mrs. St. John Hutchinson.*
The partridges were a deliberate act of kindness and I
would ask Tonks to partake but he is as you wittily remark
in process at this moment of transfiguration. His seriousness is depressing but I am inclined to think that I would
sooner be depressed by Tonks than amused by any other
man. As to your invitation . . . I hardly know what to
answer. I spend long days alone with my cat, my hand
plunged in the silken fur, thinking how to write the first
chapters of *The Apostle.* To get the exact swing one wants
into a chapter and for the next chapter to chime in, a
sort of antiphonal music, is very difficult. If I succeed
in solving a certain musical problem may I come ?

By *The Apostle* he meant his new book to which he had
not yet given the name of *The Brook Kerith.* In October he
was with the St. John Hutchinsons at West Wittering, where
he arrived with a bad neuralgia. He spent the holiday
walking about the country in a bowler hat, which he wore

even when he went out with the guns or boating. In the evenings he " corrected " stories and a play which Mrs. Hutchinson was writing; Tonks drew caricatures of these " lessons in literature " ; and in remembrance of the visit Mrs. Hutchinson received the proofs of the new edition of *The Untilled Field* with the inscription: " These proofs are for Mary Hutchinson in return for her kindness in asking me to West Wittering when I was suffering from neuralgia, cured, thank God, by the fine air about the beautiful estuary and many happy walks through the oak wood that lines the shores."

Older friends did not forget him, and during the war and the years following, he was often asked to visit at Hill Hall in Essex where Mrs. Hunter, her daughter Mrs. Williamson, and her grandchildren, were now living. He endeared himself to the young people and to their friends, and showed a homely solicitude for all that concerned their lives. The erudition of Miss Elizabeth Williamson astonished and delighted him. " If she wed," he cried out in one of his letters to Mrs. Williamson, " she will be lost to us, to Greek and to astronomy for ever." At Hill Hall he discussed the details of his books with everyone, including the bailiff and the head keeper, from whom he learned many of the phrases about sheep and dogs, which graced the pages of *The Brook Kerith*. " Do you remember," he wrote long afterwards to Mrs. Williamson, " the evening I read you the first chapter, how you recognised its worth, and glimpsed the book to come ? "

In the summer of 1915 there was one unusually eventful week-end at Hill Hall, of which Mr. Gerald Festus Kelly, the artist, has kindly sent me an account.

When I arrived at Hill Hall in the late afternoon, Mrs. Hunter told me that George Moore was coming down for the week-end, as usual, and that Réjane was coming also, and that my French (which I spoke with great fluency in those days) was going to be useful, for with theatrical people one never quite knew . . . and George Moore was sometimes so tiresome, poor dear.

That rum, delightful man turned up just after lunch on Saturday, and was glad to see me. (I was one of his great admirers, and, I fancy, a very good audience.) All that afternoon we walked up and down the flagstones, he telling me about the book he was writing, which was to be called *The Bridge of the Horses* or *The Ford of the Horses* (I cannot remember which), and of the many good, in fact the many overwhelming reasons for that being the only possible title of the book. In August 1916 this book was published under the name of *The Brook Kerith* which shows that there was at least one alternative !

George Moore was a little disturbed when told that Réjane was coming. She obviously threatened to be a counter attraction, and that was a thing he didn't like. He said that comedians were very tiresome, and had, I think, made up his mind not to like it. All through dinner he wasn't quite in his best form. He kept referring to the fact that he thought a delightful week-end was going to be spoilt by this wretched comedienne. He cross-questioned me about the rôles I had seen her play, and showed little or no pleasure in the enthusiasm that I expressed for that lovely artist; in fact he said pettishly that he was surprised that an artist like me seemed to have such shaky taste where the theatre was concerned. I began to rub my hands in anticipation of a lovely time.

Réjane must have turned up at last on Saturday night, and it was not until lunch time on Sunday that she made her appearance. Moore had been walking about with me all the morning. I was not allowed to play tennis, but had to attend entirely to him, which I was quite delighted to do. He was in fine form, his conversation was delightful (if that was the kind of conversation one liked).

At lunch I was sitting near George Moore, and Réjane was on my other side. It was not long before hostilities commenced. We had been treated, at dinner the night before, to a long dissertation on the fact that it was indeed curious to notice that conversation with an actress could start on any subject in the world, but that within four or five sentences it comes to be about one or more of the great

plays she had acted in. And it was certainly true in this
case. Very early on in lunch Réjane began to move
stealthily towards a description of one of her magnificent
parts. George Moore was not to be outdone, and began
a long and, if I may say so, well-worn anecdote about
what precisely Manet had said to him upon perceiving that
his hair was pale yellow—a narration that was not very
new to anybody but Réjane, who listened with ill-
concealed amazement. I can believe she had no fixed idea
who this Manet was. Moore, more to annoy her than
because he could have taken any pleasure in so silly a
phrase, said that Manet had said something about
" blonde come les blés de paradis." At any rate, Réjane
muttered in my ear something like " cet homme là . . .
imbécile . . . mais vraiment un *imbécile*."

Moore was droning on about Manet, and after a few
more phrases, he mentioned some date which gave Réjane
an opening. " 1878 ! Ah ! Je rappelle cette année-là.
Je jouais . . . Je portais une telle et telle robe." Only a
snort came from Moore who continued to report how
extremely impressed Manet had been by the high light on
his hair, or the tone of his underlip, and these two went on
at it, shamelessly egged on by me, to the annoyance of
Mrs. Hunter, who was much more angry with me than
with either of them, because, she told me afterwards, I
only encouraged them. It took me quite a time to convince
her that really they were giving a most marvellous entertainment, and should be encouraged by every means
within our power to go for each other.

That lovely lunch slowly ended, and we moved away,
Réjane to lie down, and Moore to seize me convulsively by
the arm, with muttered imprecations upon " cette sacrée
comédienne." Until tea-time I listened to rambling
invective.

Réjane came down to tea and told how she had always
wanted John Sargent to do a drawing of her, and how Mrs.
Hunter had finally coaxed Sargent into promising to do
one. Réjane was delighted at the prospect. This exasperated George Moore. He pointed out, first that Réjane

was a wreck, secondly that Sargent's drawing was particularly unpleasant. Réjane called me away from him, and for some little time I danced attendance on her. She was extremely good company. Admittedly she was very anxious to talk about herself, but as she was one of my great admirations, it was by no means unpleasant. It was very amusing for me to watch George Moore prowling about, disturbed that his audience had been collared by the other side, and before we went in to dress for dinner he took me aside and said that it was scandalous that this worn-out old woman should be drawn by Sargent. He repeated at length how bad he thought Sargent's charcoal drawings were.

Some months afterwards I saw the drawing Sargent had done. He has managed, by a miracle, to see her as she had been some twenty years before, and though I have not seen the drawing for years I seem to remember that it was one of the best he ever did, rather like the Lady Randolph Churchill in character, of great simplicity, and not disfigured by a tiresome black background. It was exhibited at the Grafton Galleries, and who should I see there but George Moore. He came up to me, and said, " Have you seen that appalling drawing ? I think it is disgraceful. If he must draw her, why doesn't he draw her as she is ? "

7

" I can see you from here," Blanche wrote to him at this time. " You are sitting at one end of your table in Ebury Street. At the other end is your secretary; between you, breakfast, toast, bacon and tea. You have been working in this way every day, since August 1914, without reading a newspaper, polishing landscapes of a Pre-Raphaelite Galilee, carving images of Joseph of Arimathea, of St. Paul, of other biblical figures in which it astonishes you to find I am not greatly interested at the moment. . . . And your letter to me closes on a note of irritation; you are astonished that André Gide is translating *Typhoon* by Joseph Conrad, a *completely worthless writer*, you call him. . . . Do I dare avow to the

pleasure which I have had from *Mr. Britling Sees it Through ?*
. . . My dear friend, the Tower of Ivory dates from our
twentieth year, never forget this while you are scanning the
melodious and numerous phrases of *The Brook Kerith.*"[1]

The Brook Kerith was a long book, but it did not take more
than fourteen months to finish, and Moore afterwards
attributed the faults which he found in the first version to
his too great haste in writing it. Between times he brought
out a skilfully revised edition of his " Galway girls " book of
1886, now called *Muslin*, in the same format in which the
Irish trilogy and the new edition of *The Untilled Field* had
been issued. He wrote a preface to *Muslin*, showing through
the spy-glass of memory a young man of strange appearance
(" yellow hair and sloping shoulders ") as he tripped down
the staircase of Dublin Castle in the early morning, thinking
of the iniquity of the marriage market. The book drew a
gratifying encomium from Sir Edmund Gosse: " You must
put up with a little comment, I have read *Muslin* very carefully and with close attention. I have nothing but praise to
give it. It is young, fresh, and beautifully composed : no one
but you could have done it. The writing is always good,
sometimes exquisite. The book is full of beauty which I prize
more than any other quality, and it has evidence of rare
tact—I mean in the deliciously lovable figure of Alice. . . ."

While writing *The Brook Kerith* Moore was in constant
contact with the late T. W. Whittaker, author of several
works on neo-Platonism and a director of the Rationalist
Press Association. They had been introduced by Dujardin,
and they soon grew to be at ease with each other, in spite of
the gulf which divided their respective experiences of life.
In May, 1916, Moore was able to send several chapters of his
book to the scholar, who had little fault to find with the
general clearness of effect. " I like your friend Whittaker,"
Moore wrote to Dujardin, " he is very intelligent and a good
fellow." " You disreputable and envious mannikin," Whittaker wrote to Moore, " remember that I taught you all
you know."

Tonks helped for the scene in which Jesus, very ill and

[1] *Mes Modèles.*

badly wounded, is taken from the tomb by Joseph. Moore
wanted to know all about balsams and medicines, how long
the attributed illness was likely to last, and even the sort of
things that an old woman, looking after a very sick man,
would be likely to say. Being ignorant of much of what
people without medical training usually know, he was
exacting in his search for information, and the task which he
gave Tonks was not an easy one, since it referred to the
practice of a very distant period. Tonks was also called upon
(then and there, one day after dinner) to make a sketch of a
path winding down a hill with various places indicated to
him, the path then mounting up another hill, and beyond
these there were to be other hills. Moore found great pleasure
in the sketch, and it prompted his imagination for the delightful day's truancy of Joseph and his tutor outside Arimathea (*The Brook Kerith*, pp. 22 *seqq.*). Steer used to say that if
Moore described a landscape it seemed based upon a picture
rather than upon direct observations of Nature, and Tonks'
experience seems to have supported this view.

At the start Moore was oppressed by the feeling that he
would be able to make little or nothing of the figure of
Jesus; and, indeed, the Jesus of the Bible always remained
for him a shadow compared to the great reality of St. Paul.
His belief in the historical reality of Jesus was very slight.
Dujardin, when publishing his *Source du Fleuve Chrétien*,
followed in essentials, while modifying certain details,
Renan's view of the Gospels. When, subsequently, he
adopted the theory which sees in Jesus a myth, a spiritual
being only, Moore hesitated, for he was tempted to follow
his learned friend along the new road; as early as 1914 he
had said to Dujardin that " after a pretty close study of the
gospels " he was assured that Jesus " never existed on this
earth," and that were he a younger man he would sacrifice
his imagination of the meeting with Paul and write quite a
different story on the basis of the " mythical " theory.
Always, however, Dujardin refused to regard Moore as a
serious exegete, and was certain that in the end everything
would be sacrificed to story and description.

Now, on a last analysis, it was Moore's opinion that his

book was built round the personality of the character to whom he gave the name of Jesus, St. Paul having been displaced from the position which he had occupied in the scenario of *The Apostle*.

20.3.16. *To John Eglinton.*

My intention regarding Jesus does not seem to transpire. I did not wish him to fall into a sort of mental coma for fifteen years. My idea is that a man who believed implicitly that his father would send down angels to lift him from the cross would on waking from the swoon, find himself unable to live unless he put the past clean out of his mind and fixed his thoughts in the present. In a word, to save his mind Jesus feels that he must not use it. . . . I find on page 325 : " He had given himself up to the service of his flock with profit to himself. . . ." On the next page, 326, I read : " He sat wondering how he could think so quietly of things he had put out of his mind. . . ." I was afraid to make a more explicit statement for if we explain overmuch we become trite and insipid.

10.5.16. *To John Eglinton.*

Many thanks for the proofs and for the statement that the new pages are successful; I owe them to your criticism —many thanks.

If you hold that Jesus was divine and all he said was therefore eternal truth, your position is unassailable, but if you admit that Jesus was a human being, whose mind was liable to grow or decay, you must admit too Jesus's criticism of his turbulent youth; and if you admit that he did not die on the cross and threw himself into the present, shutting out from his thoughts the past—and the future (I look upon his time of shepherding as a time of hibernation) you must admit that it is reasonable to suppose that his mind must have progressed through Pantheism to the verge of Buddhism. You understand Buddhism, I don't, and that was my luck, for if I had understood Buddhism I might have been tempted to attribute some of its doctrines to Jesus, whereas I had to invent a doctrine for him, and I invented that whether we seek a corruptible or an incorruptible crown the end is the same—desire of heavenly things leading to sin just as much as desire of earthly things. You are a better metaphysician than I am and can probe the doctrine. For the moment it seems to me satisfactory. I wonder what Russell would think of it, and I wonder what you think of it.

I think on the whole I have done better with Jesus than with Paul. Paul is an historical, Jesus a legendary character. Paul painted his own portrait and did it so thoroughly that he left me very little to add.

I am tempted to add the enclosed paragraph. It will cost money to add it, but Paul's vision of his death in Spain at the end of his speech to the Essenes ennobles him, exalts him and I have just managed to insinuate that he did not care to listen to Peter and John's babblings about Jesus, that he liked to listen far more to the Jesus locked in his own heart. A splendid subject for an essay this would be for you, dear Magee, but the exigencies of prose narrative only allowed a hint. If I had followed out this thought my narrative would have dropped into an essay.

8

The publication was fixed for the late summer of 1916, two editions being arranged for, one of 250 signed copies. Werner Laurie was the publisher, for William Heinemann did not care to associate himself with a biblical subject by George Moore. While the book was being printed, Moore visited his agent, Tom Ruttledge, at Westport. On his way to the west he stopped in Dublin, where he saw Best, Eglinton, A. E., Gogarty, and, viewing the havoc of the recent insurrection, formed impressions which found a place in his next book, *A Story-Teller's Holiday*. Best was walking down the street with him one day when a lady, with whom his acquaintance was only slight, bore down upon him to say that since reading his denunciation of Kuno Meyer she had forgiven him for all his other writings. He stared at her in blank astonishment, and turning to Best when she had gone, he asked irritably: " What the devil was that woman talking about ? " Already he regretted having joined in the hue-and-cry after the German scholar; and when Meyer died a few years later he wrote to Best:

I have just laid down Kuno Meyer's collection of ancient Irish poetry, and feel that I must write to you about it, for it is so marvellous. I would that this letter were going to him, for I did not appreciate him or his learning when he sent the book to me—not enough. Learning ! There was much more in him than learning, I felt there was, I suspected but I did not realise his worth. We all appreciate when it is too late. How I hate the war that took him from us and I despise myself for not having understood him better. It is all too sad for words . . . and I will write no more, for what I am writing will harrow you.

During his stay in Dublin he interested himself in a little book, meant for inclusion in an " Irishman of the Day " series, upon which Miss Susan Mitchell, a charming poetess, had been for some time engaged. Moore gave Miss Mitchell to understand that she might write as freely about him as she liked, take any liberties she would, advising her, no doubt, in the same sense as he advised E. A. Boyd, who was also minded to write on him at this time. " Well, I am part of life like Yeats and Lady Gregory, and you have as much right to sketch me as I had to sketch them, and if your book have any value, its value will depend on how much of yourself you put into it. . . . All Gautier is in his sonnet to the tulip. . . . *Moi, je suis la tulipe, une fleur de Hollande.* You know the rest. Whilst writing about me, write about yourself, I am only a pretext."

" But yours," said Moore to Boyd, " will be a man's book." Perhaps he did not expect great things from Miss Mitchell, but when the little book appeared he was really very angry. The biographer had approached her subject in too facetious a spirit and seemed to regard Dublin's opinion as the last word on Moore. But the injury that most rankled was Miss Mitchell's neglect of all that he had said on the subject of the instinctive and far-off origins of his Protestantism. " The little Catholic boy of that name," she wrote, " who went to Confession—of course as a literary man he would deny the Catholic George Moore." A. E. thought the book very clever, and his steadfast defence of Miss Mitchell was the cause of some discord. There must be, Moore now thought, some malice in the shaggy friend, a benevolent malice no doubt, but the discovery jarred with his conception of a model mystic, and very soon he became sure that A. E. had instigated many of the offending passages.

The troubles in Ireland preyed on him, and he had dreams of Moore Hall going up in flames. One night of the autumn, at Ebury Street, roused by a fetch light, he flung himself across the hearthrug and broke his wrist in the fall.

28.8.16. *To Miss Viola Rodgers.*

A dream woke me up suddenly; the light shining on the brass of the bedstead deceived me and thinking the bed-clothes were on fire I threw myself forward to extinguish the imaginary flame and fell headlong from the bed across the hearthrug sustaining a pretty severe shock and breaking my wrist very badly.

He had intended to go to France, but the broken wrist prevented him. Miss Rodgers, whom he had recently seen in London, was on a journey to America, and he wrote to her sadly in September: " When I meet you again I shall be even more elderly than I am to-day, and less capable of enjoying your wit and your winning presence. . . . There is nothing for it but to continue the Collected Edition, a prosaic fact that must be accepted. And it is well to continue my task unintermittently for in a few years the literary sap will have gone out of me: how very sad life is, and how very vain. We go through life accomplishing nothing of any importance. Even the war will accomplish nothing."

When Miss Rodgers returned to Paris, he proposed to accompany her—in the middle of the war !—on a journey through France and Italy.

9

Orders for *The Brook Kerith* came in so rapidly that the publisher was obliged to increase the size of the ordinary but highly priced edition. The Press notices made a mixed showing. " The first part of the book, which deals with the youth and manhood of Joseph of Arimathea, is a fine piece of writing," said the *Saturday Review*. " In scheme, treatment and style, it is reminiscent of *Marius*. Here we have the same dream-struck youth, pensive, mystic and wistful, with a hieratic scrupulosity that disposes him from the start to religious life. . . . Mr. Moore is singularly indifferent to public opinion. He writes under an inner compulsion to please himself." But the *Saturday Review*, like the *Nation*, could make little or nothing of the drawing of Jesus. The reviewer for *The Times Literary Supplement* seemed to draw a line between artistic and other criticism by fixing attention on the sub-title of the book : A Syrian Story. There was no question, he said, of making a comparison between *The Brook Kerith* and the " lives " of Jesus, whether written by believers or unbelievers. The reader might, if he wished, give different names to all the characters in Moore's book, but Moore in using the biblical names was guiltless of offence against tact and good manners, since his Jesus was evidently meant to personify an ideal of moral beauty, and gave no impression of a satire upon belief.

But how in speaking of *The Brook Kerith* shall one draw the line between æsthetic and other criticism ? No doubt it is right that the Jesus of Moore's fancy having survived crucifixion should greatly change and develop; but criticism must vary, according as one regards *The Brook Kerith* with Humbert Wolfe and John Freeman as a retelling of the greatest story in the world, or as a " Syrian story " having no more than a nominal link with the Gospels. Some admirers of the book have shown an excess of zeal in saying, first that it conveys a fresh revelation of " the man behind the Gospels," and then rebuking for æsthetic irrelevance those who object that they find in Moore's book no such revelation. " It is a tribute to the eternal freshness of the life of Jesus

Christ that this restatement in mere human terms should contain so much of beauty and so much of truth," says John Freeman, who elsewhere speaks of " a simple imagination," and implies that the credibility of the restatement is a matter of no moment. In the controversy which followed upon the publication Moore himself did not seek to have it thus both ways, for he laid stress upon the worth of *The Brook Kerith* as an imaginative reconstruction of the origins of Christianity, and recapitulated proudly the steps in his career as an exegete. He would not allow that his shepherd mystic was incompatible with the Jesus of the Gospels. . . . " So you think I should have made a *clever* Jesus," he said to A. E. at the end of a long argument. But what, after all, is the Jesus of the second part of *The Brook Kerith*, the Jesus who goes back to his lambs and believes in not flying in the face of Providence ? Certainly not the " Protestant Jesus " whom (in a letter to John Eglinton) he claimed to have depicted. Rather, perhaps, the type of a Catholic monk doing penance for the sins of an arrogant youth devoted to Communist agitation.

The style was the outcome of enormous labour: Moore believed that gold was there, but placed very deep, so he trained himself to dig very deep. His writing aimed at continuity and suggested to the reader the movement of a stream, not in flood, but a stream in summer, with certain varieties of speed and kinds of flow but never violent. . . . " We talked many times of this stream of ideas," says Tonks, " and he never seemed to disagree with my way of seeing it." It was Moore's opinion that painters judged his books more correctly than writers; his contemporaries in authorship showed little friendliness towards his Syrian story. Frank Harris snorted across the Atlantic at the scholarship. Bernard Shaw complained of the monotony: " I read about thirty pages of *The Brook Kerith*. It then began to dawn on me that there was no mortal reason why Moore should not keep going on like that for fifty thousand pages, or fifty million for that matter. . . . " But the book found many eager admirers among the younger generation, and there began to be formed that ardent little group of literary men, such as John Freeman, Humbert Wolfe, Charles Morgan and David Garnett, who looked to Moore as a master of English prose, and prepared the way for his later position as an unofficial and rather impish Grand Old Man of Literature.

10

The new book was taking shape in his mind : *A Story-Teller's Holiday*. It was in part another autobiography, and in the opening Moore is seen setting out for Ireland, staying a short while in Dublin among his friends, and then proceeding to Westport, where, in Tom Ruttledge's park, under beech trees by an old mill, he and a fictitious fern-gatherer, Alec, vie with each other as shanachies. Before beginning this new work in earnest he undertook (in the last months of 1916) the republication of *A Modern Lover*, changing the title to *Lewis Seymour and Some Women*. He found that *A Modern Lover* was so full of nonsense that it resisted ordinary revision; but he had a soft corner in his heart for the earliest of his stories, and so he composed a new novel exhibiting the latest evolution of his style and written round the original anecdote which he still deemed to be excellent—" invented by the folk behind me, developed by the artist in front of them." " The copy," he wrote to E. A. Boyd, " has gone to Brentano. I think you will enjoy it, I will not say appreciate it or esteem it, but you will enjoy it." In the new treatment of the anecdote Lewis's exploitation of women was treated in a spirit of frivolity which would have appalled the reviewers who, in 1883, had dealt so kindly with *A Modern Lover*. The book gave pause as late as 1917, and before Eglinton whose comments were " bitter as the weather," Moore defended himself by declaring that, after having mixed in " the great hurly burly in England and France," he could vouch for it that, outside of the daily work, the one interest and occupation of men and women was sex. Even the evangelical was interested in sex and availed himself and herself of the white slave traffic as a subject for conversation. Either the Sunday paper did not reach Terenure, or his " dear Magee " was " as unreasonable as a Roman Catholic."

Letters to Best, the Irish scholar, and to James Stephens, the Irish poet, shed an interesting light on the history of *A Story-Teller's Holiday*, Moore's chief task in 1917. They show that in his care for detail and the right setting he retained more than a trace of his naturalistic training. In February 1917 he was finishing the seventh century love-story of Liadin and Curithir which had been long known to him in Kuno Meyer's beautiful translation. " As soon as I hear from you," he wrote to Best, " I shall begin ' The Nuns of Crith Gaille.' A holy man arrives from France, and before beginning it I should like to avail myself of your erudition. Have you ever come across a description of a convent or community . . . in your readings among the ancient texts? . . . Can you give me a name for the young monk? He would land where ? Waterford or Dublin? and would make his way across Ireland to the county of Mayo ? Have you met with any description of the journey or of similar journeys in your readings that I could work into my narrative ? "

There was another story which he knew from publications of the Irish Texts Society. It was called " The Madness of Suibhne Geilt," and it told how a tenth-century king lost his reason from the horror of a battle and turned into a wild man of the woods until he was at last shriven and made sane.

9.4.17. *To Richard Best.*

The story of the madman fills me with despair, so wonderful it is, so much beyond the reach of the modern story-teller. Upon this story a case might be made out that Shakespeare was an Irishman, else he could not have written *King Lear* and could not have known this story unless he was possessed of an intimate knowledge of the Irish language, the story not having been translated in his time. . . . But the abridged version does not satisfy me. I want the full text (O'Kiefe's) and am willing to pay for it.

He got his stories ready made, but under his treatment they wore the air of spontaneous inventions. By May 1917 he had brought the first three to paper in rough form, and

the draft was sent to James Stephens in Dublin. " I think,"
he wrote, " that if you will correct my mistakes and sprinkle
the idiom over the story working it in here and there, now
and again, whenever you get a chance, crossing out any of
my sentences you like if the omission will help you in your
editing, you will have accomplished the end I have in view."

In July he was again in Ireland. One night he dined with
the Bests who were struck by his excellent spirits. He gave
the theme: pure poetry, " poetry about things," an unmade
anthology which had been in his mind since 1912: everyone
at Best's table was invited to give examples of poetry un-
enlightened by thought. After dinner his host put an album
of reproductions of great pictures into his hands, which
beguiled him for hours; he left saying that he had never spent
a happier evening. The next day, at the house of his musical
friend, Dr. Esposito, Cadorna was his theme, " a wonderful
name "; and he kept repeating the word with evident
satisfaction which increased when Best suddenly informed
him that the name might be explained through Celtic as
" Battle thundering." So many other generals had been sent
home one by one, whereas Cadorna seemed immune from
the ebb and flow of opinion. It was within a few weeks of
Caporetto, and perhaps Moore never regained his confidence
in his theory of the sound of a name after this disaster.

Best demurred to " Thou didst lead " in *The Brook Kerith*.
" Thou leddest " would be better, he thought. " But why ? "
said Moore, hesitant; and seeking a further opinion he was
glad to meet Mr. Osborne Bergin, the Celtic scholar, at a
party given by John Eglinton at Terenure. " You are a
grammarian, tell me," he said. But Bergin would not be
drawn, it being his opinion that the function of a grammarian was not to make rules but to deduce them from
practice. " Oh, now you bore me, Bergin ! " he cried
plaintively. " I have as much right to bore you, Mr. Moore,
as you have to bore me." Bergin, nettled, gave signs that he
did not intend to address another word to Moore that day.
There was an awkward pause, and John Eglinton remembered that he had to send off a telegram. Happily the subject
of R. L. Stevenson was broached by another of the guests—

a lucky hit, because it happened that Moore had just been making magnanimous amends to that charming author in his preface to *Lewis Seymour*. The same guest had read but one of Moore's books, but he spoke of the pleasure which *Modern Painting* had given him; again he found favour, the question of the republication of *Modern Painting* being under consideration at this moment. " It could not be bettered," said Moore. " It could not be bettered." At teatime, someone referring to the War, Moore was again moved to express his confidence in Cadorna. Tongues were loosened, and Moore looked down the table at the scholar who still maintained a stubborn silence: " Now that the conversation has become general," he said very pleasantly, " perhaps Bergin will join in."

At the Ruttledges his genial mood persisted. The family took very little notice of him, but he did not resent this in the least and was perfectly happy taking the dogs for walks in the woods. One hot day he joined in a game of tennis, playing not at all badly, said the critical girls, and wonderfully for a man in his sixty-sixth year—in a fine suit of tussore silk pyjamas. At any hour of the day he was apt to stroll into one of the girls' rooms, wearing a puzzled look: for he had, he explained, lost his way downstairs.

The unhappy misunderstanding with the Colonel persisted. One day during his visit to Dublin the two brothers met on the stairs of A. E.'s office. They passed each other without a word, and it was the last time they were to come face to face. Both of the Colonel's sons were at the War; the younger of them, Ulick, when on leave in London, had called at Ebury Street. His uncle was out at the time but on hearing of the visit wrote to the young man, reminding him that he was not on speaking terms with his father " and never shall be again." " You may say," he continued, " that if we were to meet it would not be to discuss religious questions . . . but the fact remains that I despise Roman Catholics and one cannot change oneself. But Protestant or Roman Catholic whichever you may be, you are certainly a brave fellow who has done the right thing. . . . So you are going out again, your wound being healed. Bravo."

It is evident that his grievance against his brother had become very much aggravated in his mind, and that he was now fully determined upon disinheriting not only the Colonel but the Colonel's family. Lately he had shown some interest in Peter, Augustus's only son. "After my father's death in 1911," Mr. Peter Moore writes to me, "whenever I might be in London, George Moore used frequently to invite me to his house. Shortly before the War broke out I took a little flat in Paris, and I remember that I thought to please my uncle by sending him a description of a beautiful girl with whom I had fallen in love and of my first hearing of Wagner's *Ring*. My uncle replied with a letter saying that he 'gathered' I was leading a pleasant life—'keeping a woman and listening to operas . . .' He hoped my money would last but I must expect nothing from him. However, when the War broke out and I asked his help to get me into the Army (I had short sight) we saw each other again, and he took a good deal of trouble for me, writing to Lord Howard de Walden, etc."

11

On his return to London Moore continued his *Story-Teller's Holiday*. Remembering the success of the sketch for *The Brook Kerith* he asked Tonks to make another drawing for him on which he could base his description of the Garden of Eden for one of the chapters. "The idea interested me and I was glad," Tonks writes, "to do what he asked. I was then stationed at Aldershot with the R.A.M.C., and I used to amuse myself in the evenings in my lodgings by carrying out the design, which was much more elaborately done than the sketch of the descending path for *The Brook Kerith*. When I sent my design to Moore I expected to get a letter of warm thanks, but no acknowledgment came. Some time after I asked him if he had received the design; all that he said was that he had, but that it was no use to him. Another instance of his childish egotism: he liked the first drawing because he could use it, the second he could not use, and therefore it did not exist for him. Moore indeed had the divine selfishness of the artist."

He was presently to find that " The Garden of Eden " did not fit into his book, and that instead of trying to make an impersonal narrative of it he must bring back Alec Trusselby from his drinking bout and relate the story to him in the first person. " The Garden of Eden " in its new form reached Stephens in August. " You will read my intention," Moore wrote, " to relate it in the language of Alec Trusselby. You will also notice that towards the end of the story I drop into what we will call for convenience sake, English."

Stephens was to strengthen the idiom; the work done by him amounted almost to a collaboration, although not all his emendations and proposals were adopted. That Stephens succeeded in saving the story from every likeness to Voltaire that the ingenious might discover, was Moore's first opinion; but by the end of the month the story was thrown once more into the melting pot, and was being redictated at the rate of two or three thousand words a day. " If it ever finds its way into print," Moore wrote to Stephens, " you will meet a new acquaintance in whom you will recognise an old friend."

On his last visit to Dublin he had given Best a copy of *The Brook Kerith*, asking him to read it through and mark the passages that might be revised. Best now sent him a list of about sixty faults of style. " Here and in America," Moore replied, " *The Brook Kerith* was received as one of the most beautifully written books of modern times. I never thought it was; it was written too quickly. . . . But I had no idea that so many faults could be discovered in it. Your list seems to have been compiled by John Horne Tooke; his spirit seems to have awakened in you again. I am sure that all your suggestions are arguable, and I am sure that you have pointed out a great many errors that might be corrected."

The list proved useful to Moore when he summoned up courage to look through the pages. In one place a Galilean peasant had asked if a certain man had " business capacity "; he changed the expression to " fit for trade." There had been three re-issues of the original edition of 1916, and now Moore began to prepare the revision which Heinemann published in 1921.

But why, he often asked himself, must he persist in the writing of books? The world would be no wiser or better whether he finished *A Story-Teller's Holiday* or left it unfinished.

5.10.17. *To Mrs. Williamson.*

. . . But there it is, I couldn't help finishing it, and, as I say, was prevented thereby from writing to tell you how much I enjoyed my last visit to Hill Hall. Of all my visits the last was the pleasantest. I got a telegram yesterday from your mother asking me to come down by the one o'clock train, but I couldn't come, and was sorry I couldn't come. The air raid will begin next week and I think of that fortunate woman who sleeps alone in a cottage in a wood and is not contented with her lot. I wonder if the exchange were open to us if she would swap beds with me. Her cottage seems to me an ideal place to sleep in.

Tonks called yester evening and we went for a walk, he is excellent company, and the company of one whom one knows completely is a great pleasure. Friendships are best in the first months and in the last years; the middle period is not so good.

The old fighter in him was roused when an attempt, obscure enough, was made to interdict *The Brook Kerith* under the blasphemy laws. It failed, but no sooner was this case off his hands than he was involved in what he described as " one of the strangest libel actions that ever befell a man." " A large industry," he wrote to the secretary of the Authors' Society, " and the writing of fiction depends upon my winning the action."

. . . *A Modern Lover* was published 34 years ago and the principal character is one Lewis Seymour a painter who lives upon women—on his mistress' money and he afterwards becomes an academician through his wife's influence.

I rewrote this book but did not change the name, the character or the profession of Lewis Seymour. Lewis Seymour is the same in both books and now a man called Louis N. Seymour has brought an action for libel. If the book entitled *Lewis Seymour and Some Women* is a libel, *A Modern Lover* is a libel, but when the libel was first published the plaintiff was four years old. Question can you libel an infant? *A Modern Lover* has been in circulation for 34 years except for a small period while Walter Scott's rights or lack of rights were being debated; as soon as the point was settled I re-wrote the book but so far as Louis N. Seymour is concerned the books are identical, one is better written than the other but the substance is the same. A second question therefore arises : Can Louis N. Seymour bring an action against Walter Scott?

You will see that if Louis N. Seymour wins his action the writing of fiction will have to be discontinued and all the past will be jeopardised for if a man can bring an action and win it against the publishing of a book bearing his name thirty-four years after publication a man can bring an action against a publisher for re-printing an eighteenth century book. All the Tom Jones can issue writs.

I need not labour the point you will see at once that this is a matter in which your Society is concerned—You should stand in with me and get the benefit of the advertisement.

Sir George Lewis advised that Moore should brief Sir William Jowitt, who was already his friend, and Moore did not omit to supply the eminent Counsel with " nice points to bring out in cross examination."

We shall meet to-morrow at the Law Courts. Lewis sent me a telegram yesterday and this morning I received a letter from him. All the same the case is not down for hearing in the *Telegraph*.

I hope that you and Mr. Williams will not forget that

there are *two or three Louis Seymours in the London Directory*.
Are these too to bring action against Heinemanns ? Is Mr.
Bentham and Mrs. Bentham to bring actions ? Is Gwynne
Lloyd to bring an action and Lady Helen Trevor ? In the
days when the book was written there was no Lady Helen
Trevor. Today there is. But according to my learned
friend opposite the fact that she came into being after the
publication of the book does not matter, and I should like
to point out that the present suit is an indictment against
nearly all literature—only prayer books will escape; any
book in which a character acts contrary to the laws given
unto Moses on Mount Sinai is liable to an action for libel.
Shakespeare, even the Bible will not be immune ! Any
man called Abraham can bring an action against the
publishers of the revised version. . . .

Moore found it " more than unpleasant to have to explain
artistic questions to a magistrate at Bow Street in the middle
of a crowd of policemen and attorneys." He won the case
(*Times* Law Reports, Nov. 23rd 1917) despite the pathetic
evidence of the plaintiff that he had been made a butt for
soldiers' jokes in Flanders where he used to receive post-
cards saying, " What price the girls ? "

" The times are strenuous and difficult," Moore wrote to
Mr. St. John Hutchinson. " Our paths are interrupted at
every moment by new obstacles. There was the Seymour v.
Heinemann case, and Heinemann says that the clause in the
agreement makes me liable for costs. . . . I have also just
heard that my tenantry have started cattle driving in my
domain. Liberal government has turned Ireland into a new
Russia."

12

About this time Moore made a discovery which served
him very well. Knowing that he was never likely to become
a popular writer and repeat the success of *Evelyn Innes* or
Esther Waters, but that he could count on a certain public, it
occurred to him that he should bring out his books in future

at a high price, in limited editions. This marked his separation from modern literature, he said (" books are now being sent round with the morning's milk up to standard ")—a *volte-face* on the part of a man who claimed to have saved English fiction in the 'eighties by cheap publication. *A Story-Teller's Holiday* was the first of these limited editions, which it pleased Moore to issue under the sign of Cumann Seaneolais na h'Eireann (Society for Irish Folklore), but no such society has ever existed. From now on each of Moore's books brought him in about £2,000; but although he became as he grew older more and more careful of his expenditure, perhaps the least of his motives was the desire of gain. " A strange charge," he said, " to bring against a man who in a long life has never aimed at popular success." His pride, as John Freeman has pointed out, now extended to the outward form of a book, and he came to demand the same conscience in the type-founding, type-setting and paper-making of a book as he himself showed in the writing. The dignified privacy of publication harmonised well with the aristocratical pose, as of some survivor from the eighteenth century, which he now adopted in life, not indeed among old friends but to newcomers in his acquaintance, and so successfully that upon his death one of the obituarists referred to his possession of beautiful manners.

Whilst Moore was finishing *A Story-Teller's Holiday* he more than once expressed the opinion that he might never wish to write another book. " Your lot," he said to Stephens, " sitting in the great rooms of the National Gallery giving orders about the hanging and dusting of pictures, is a happier one than mine. But the last illusion of great minds is belief in the happiness of others." When *A Story-Teller's Holiday* appeared he spoke of it as his " despised book "; yet the stories put into Alec Trusselby's mouth rank among his most successful achievements in simple narrative; the racy vigour of the Anglo-Irish idiom and the richness of the comic detail approach the best of Synge; while the grave beauty of Moore's own stories, together with the perfect balance of the meditative prologue and epilogue, gives the whole work a unique place among his writings.

14.2.18. To James Stephens.

I am fairly tired out with composition and am determined not to write any more, if ever. My secretary is leaving me, and this will be an excuse for reading and going to see my friends, any friends who will receive me. I wish I could find some employment like yours in a museum, something that would dissipate the day for me. I have written enough—I feel it all over me that I have written enough.

Avowals, however, still awaited completion, and perhaps his mind was already straying to an imaginative reconstruction of the story of Héloïse. He also spoke of a drastic revision of *Modern Painting*, and of a new *Memoirs of My Dead Life*.

18.2.18. To Miss Viola Rodgers.

How much pleasanter the book [*Memoirs of My Dead Life*] would be if you were one of the memories related in it. If I had not been timid when we met in Dublin for the first time! . . . If you were here I could help you to link up your story—that is my speciality, my gift if I have one, the power to link up a story. All English stories are badly linked together, so badly that they seem to me like heaps of old clothes, the sleeves of one gown sewed on to another . . . The power to mould a tale isn't a great gift but it is a useful one.

Modern Painting was to be "moulded." It would now open, he said, with an account of the Pre-Raphaelite movement, to be related as " a story with incidental descriptions of pictures," for he had come to loathe the essay form. Two years before he had written a very good " conversation," " The Dusk of the Gods," for the *Atlantic Monthly*, with J. F. Balderston, now a frequent visitor to Ebury Street, as his interlocutor. Now followed a criticism of art and morality, another dialogue, in which Mr. Balderston also figured. " I think," Moore wrote on its publication to E. A. Boyd, " that I have exhausted the subject . . . My address to the jury pleases me, and I think I ' floor ' the imaginary judge on a neat legal point," and this dialogue, as it took its place in *Avowals*, may be regarded as Moore's final version of the early pamphlet, *Literature at Nurse*.

Another subject upon which he had meditated as long and as painfully as Censorship was English fiction; and he intended to start *Avowals* by demonstrating the deficiencies of English prose narrative to Edmund Gosse. Gosse took precautions.

21.3.18.

My dear Moore,

There is one point which I must emphasize without delay. You say that I am to be " announced by the servant," and to be introduced into your study, and immediately to ask you " to give some account of the work " you are " engaged upon." In other words you present me to your readers as a *journalist* come to interview you for some newspaper ! ! This I absolutely refuse to allow you to do.

You must not start by giving yourself *le beau rôle* and making me venal and ridiculous. You must treat me as well as yourself, and I insist on the place chosen being a neutral one. We can be walking together somewhere out of doors, wherever you like. And you can represent me as mainly desirous to hear your views, not anxious to put forward my own. But I cannot allow you to put me in the degrading and subaltern position which you propose in your letter to-day. The thing will be great fun if you will only do it properly: but you start with the idea of humiliating your interlocutor, and I won't allow it. Come out in the open and be a hero.

Ever sincerely yours
Edmund Gosse.

We might be walking together in Regent's Park, in the garden opposite the house.

How DARE you propose that I should " apologise for interrupting you in your work ? " Damn your infernal cheek.

E. G.

Don't think I am opposed to the scheme: it will be very amusing but you must behave like a little gentleman, or else I won't play with you.

E. G. *bis*.

" I chaffed you with too heavy a hand," Gosse wrote a few days later. " . . . But you will not take it too seriously, for you know how much I admire you, and how vivid an interest I take in all the movements of your unique imagination." Gosse was right, however: it was Moore's dear ambition to play a trick on this close and lifelong friend whom he suspected of being as partial to the society of bishops as to his own. One indiscreet invention of his mind, concerning an elderly author and a lady, he longed especially to put into Gosse's mouth. " He won't see it until I put it into print. And then he won't scold me for long, because he is too fond of me." " But did Gosse tell the story ? " " No, but he might have."

The depression of the winter passed away, and 1918 was a busy enough year for Moore. His health remained excellent; he dined out in London a good deal, and still liked to pay visits to country houses, particularly to Sir William Geary at Oxon Hoath in Kent and to Mrs. Hunter in Essex. Once while he was staying with Sir William Geary a beautiful woman asked him of what he had been thinking as he walked on the terrace. " Of writing," he replied; " and since I have been here I have devised three stories."

Moore had told Stephens that he now intended to " read," and he did partially carry out this resolve by enquiring into contemporary appreciations and into what was happening around him. On Arnold Bennett his views were more accommodating than they were on other writers who had " arrived." It is uncertain how much we should attribute this to his amazement at Bennett's facility and his personal liking for the man and how much to real admiration of the work. That he had been flattered when Bennett acknowledged his literary indebtedness to *A Mummer's Wife* is certain. " An astonishing fellow," Moore would say, " who sits down regularly at his writing-table, calls the maid, asks her to bring his paper, the finest quality, his box of water-colours with which he decorates the title page, and a glass of water. Then he starts writing and goes ahead without pause, and without altering a single comma . . . Not an erasure."

There were also some of the younger men whom he was to approve: Mr. Charles Morgan (*Portrait in a Mirror*) and David Garnett (*Lady into Fox*), for example, but the later D. H. Lawrence seemed to him to be but vapour and shadow. He appreciated *Sons and Lovers* and parts of *The White Peacock*. Lawrence wrote to him when he could find no publisher for a philosophical work as to an author who had also suffered from the timidities of English taste, but he was urged by Moore in reply to " return to his dahlias," the " description of human persons " and to eschew vague sensual abstractions. " I would like you," Moore added, " to keep the classes separate. . . . It is possible that miners may retire into corners while their mothers are laying the table for supper, to discuss Shelley's poetry and Bernhardt. But it does not seem wise to introduce these incongruities into English prose narrative."

Obviously Moore could not approve an attitude towards sex which is without either poetry or irony, the solemn attitude of a man of the people. Moore wanted to preserve decency for the sake of indecency, whereas Lawrence would have abolished both.

An interesting event of the year was the appearance of the edition of his early novel, *A Mummer's Wife*, in the form in which it now has its place in the collected edition. Most of the revision of this book had been devoted to the removal of *clichés* and clumsiness, and there was little evidence of an attempt to clothe the old Naturalistic framework of the story in the new style of subjective reverie. A few trite phrases and essays at jocularity were inadvertently allowed to stand : a landlady is referred to as " the worthy woman " ; Kate's baby is a " puling pulp " ; and Montgomery at the piano is said (by the author, not by one of the characters) to be " spanking away at the dominoes." But such infelicities and obscurities disturb the atmosphere of the tale less than an occasional half-hearted attempt at the later manner. On the verge of her elopement with Dick, Kate Ede is terrified of missing the train. " ' Dick, dear, do make haste. . . .' ' We've plenty of time,' he answered, and she read in his face the desire for another plate of crumpets." The dedication to Robert Ross is interesting. " The wandering life of the mummers gives an old-world, adventurous air to the book, reminding you of *The Golden Ass*—a book I read last year." Moore is anxious to show that his realism has been from the beginning of the romantic rather than the naturalistic sort.

13

At the end of July, the dialogues with Gosse being completed, Moore went once again to Ireland. But the Sinn Fein or pacificist sympathies of A. E. and of the group about A. E. increased his sense of alienation from his native country. In order that his own views should not be misinterpreted, he drove, as soon as he arrived in Dublin, to the Phœnix Park and inscribed his name in Lord French's visitors' book at the Viceregal Lodge. The action was reported to Mrs. Hunter.

His Excellency is in Belfast and probably will not see it. All the same I am glad I did it, for [to] do so is to confirm my sanity in a country where there are many madmen. I called yesterday to view some old glass and was shown some pieces, my attention being suddenly distracted from them by the news that my dealer was a subscriber to *A Story-Teller's Holiday*; and I learn from him that there was no falling-off, a matter in which I am deeply interested at the moment for though reviews do not teach one how to write they tell whether a book is likely to be appreciated or despised. My art dealer was the first I met who had read the book.

As the war drew to its close a simple admiration of the Allies laid hold of him. As Foch advanced he lost his head entirely and abandoned all æsthetic principles. "America," he wrote to Miss Viola Rodgers, " has behaved splendidly. She is playing the part of Greece in the modern world, and who would have believed that the old heroism was possible in modern life ? The Germans seem to be more barbarous than they were when Cæsar overcame them. Foch seems to have all the genius of Cæsar, and the Germans may decide to bring the war to an end this year and we may let them do so which will be a pity for they should not escape from seeing their own country ravaged, and it will be a sore day if peace be signed without our having a cathedral or two to our credit."

The political idealists excited him to disdainful paradox. " Horace Plunkett is at work again," he told Longworth on his return to London. " He has a new scheme of voting which will turn Ireland into a western Russia." If the Germans failed to adopt " voting " and English and Irish ideas of what constituted a day's work, they would, he feared, rob the Allies of the fruits of victory. " ' Dear Edward ' says that he isn't sure the Germans wouldn't be a blessing in Ireland. On his face I could read the picture that his fancy summoned up. The Irish sitting on the walls and smoking pipes and playing cards while the Germans ' developed ' the country. It doesn't occur to him to ask for whom. Wonderful indeed is Edward."

He now openly confessed to a moral conservatism, although in a way that was peculiarly his own, for he was always himself and nothing but himself. A young girl was being criticised in his presence for her unconventionality. His comment was that " no man thinks the worse of a girl for not being a virgin, but she must behave." But indeed his general views on the prospects of humanity had undergone little change since the date of the *Confessions*: " Education ! Progress ! How stupid it all is. How stupid." The opinion has not changed, but the expression is different. We no longer hear " a bawl from a low artists' café "; the tone is that of an urbane man who takes the general happiness into consideration, and when there are elections does not fail to record his vote on the right side. " Of one thing I am sure," he wrote, " my own county of Mayo is drearier for landlords and people alike in the twentieth century than it was in the first half of the nineteenth."

While he was in Ireland he paid his usual visit to the Ruttledges, saying before he left for the west that he would not, when at Westport, make the journey—eighteen miles—from there to Moore Hall, because he could see Moore Hall with the eyes of memory, the best eyes of all. But it is said in Mayo that, on one afternoon of this July, a car was seen to arrive on the lake side below the Georgian mansion. It stopped at the boat shelter, and an elderly gentleman alighted who was believed by some labourers on the place to be Mr. George Moore. The gentleman did not climb the slope. After a long look across the lake and up to the house he stepped back into his car, which then drove away in the Westport direction.

Ruttledge had called his attention to the woods around Moore Hall (timber was fetching a big price during the War), and the incident furnished him with a pretext for the " voyage to childhood " which brings *A Story-Teller's Holiday* to its enchanting close. Ruttledge was cast for the rôle of the tempter.

But even if you succeed in preserving Moore Hall unchanged for a few years . . . Moore Hall will certainly fall into ruin. As soon as you have gone the trees will be felled, and the lead taken from the roof. . . . It is true . . .; time overtakes the most enduring monuments, but men continue to build. . . . Why then should it be very foolish of me to dream of Moore Hall as a hostel for parsons and curates when I am among the gone ? The Irish Protestant Church is very dear to me, and Moore Hall might serve as a token of my admiration of a Protestantism that has given to Ireland all our great men and our Anglo-Irish literature. . . . The past tells us whence we have come and what we are, and it was well that I refused to allow the trees to be felled, for sitting by my fireside in Ebury Street I should hear the strokes of the axe in my imagination as plainly as if I were living in Moore Hall, and the ghosts of the felled trees would gather about my arm-chair in Ebury Street.

His race was " scattered, broken and in exile "—the race of the Protestant ascendancy in Ireland, to which he now claimed that his family, down even to his father, had belonged. The Colonel had lost his second son in France; the elder, Maurice (nicknamed Rory), called upon his uncle soon after the Armistice. Moore asked him to narrate his campaigns to him at dinner and to stay the night. " I cannot call to mind a finer young man," he afterwards wrote to his sister-in-law whom he wished to exclude from his conflict with her husband, because she was a Protestant. " He seems to me altogether admirable, physically as well as mentally. I did not ask him what his religious beliefs were but in telling me the superstitions of the North American Indians he revealed his truly Catholic soul. . . . His father would never allow me to see him while he was a child; now it is too late to save him and I am writing to you to tell you that I have suffered too much from Catholicism to wish to meet Catholics. . . ."

It is again made clear that it was essentially Irish Catholicism which provoked him. In London several of his friends were Catholics, and although he was always abusing their religion to them, he was quite happy in their company. And towards women on this question he was more lenient. He was never able to take the religious interests of women seriously, and in his new book he made Héloïse believe in Heaven only because Abélard believed.

14

The rest of the year was spent in dreaming *Héloïse and Abélard*. The subject baffled him when he first examined its possibilities. The letters did not show Abélard in a pleasant light, and he complained: " If I finish my book at Abélard's confession to Héloïse of the calamity that has befallen him and his request that she shall take the veil and that he shall become a priest, I could get a certain shape, but I don't care for dramatic situations." And there was another difficulty: the passing of the story among more or less civilised people in conditions of life which he would be compelled to investigate. *The Brook Kerith* passed in conditions which have remained permanent—among fishermen and shepherds and monks who live in caves. The discouragement was considerable, but he kept turning the story over in his mind, and by the autumn of 1918 he seems to have felt that he could surmount the difficulties.

Two years he thought the book would take him, perhaps three. It took him nearly three, and its history, like that of *A Story-Teller's Holiday*, can be largely traced in his correspondence. Every day he dictated fifteen hundred or two thousand words of what he called " rigmarole." It was a new system, a strange one, but it worked, and he kept to it from now on. Had his eye fallen upon the results of the day's dictation he would have stopped to revise; but his secretary was instructed to keep the type from him, and the dictation familiarised him with his subject and enabled him to " write " it better later on. In an undated letter to Mrs. Williamson he gave an account of his new method:

> My life passes by in loneliness and composition. I see hardly anybody, nobody for long but my secretary. . . . *Héloïse and Abélard* is the theme of my dictations; and these are continued without interruptions and are locked away in a closet as soon as transcribed for my plan is to proceed with scarcely more knowledge of the furrow behind me than the ox. I am told that the dictations read very pleasantly lapsing occasionally into rigmarole which is inevitable; I am not credulous but the story seems to shape itself easily and well. I recognise good material in it and ask myself if I shall be able to write it adequately when the year of writing comes to pass. I write to you about *Héloïse and Abélard* because I have nothing else to write about and am regretful that I cannot write about life in general as well as you do, if I could I would.

" If I could only realise it," he told the same correspondent in October, " I think it would be as good a story and as beautiful as any story I know, and yet unlike any. But I fear it—the beginning especially."

28.12.18. *To Mrs. Crawford.*

Will you ask for a book—the book of a French architect whose name I cannot even attempt to spell, a double-barrelled name, the first name beginning with a V. the second is simpler it is merely Duc; and after glancing through this admirable and useful author's pages will you try to arrive at a reasonable conclusion regarding the number of rooms in Canon Fulbert's house in the rue des Chantres . . . I hope to begin the " writing " to-morrow and Héloïse comes home in the second chapter and that is why I am praying that it may be your need to go to the London library.

" Moore will not study," wrote Frank Harris, " and cannot read authorities; yet he is industrious in his own way. His method of writing is laborious in the extreme. Before beginning he makes a scenario, divided into chapters, then he writes the book hastily chapter by chapter, putting in all his chief ideas; finally he goes over the whole book, re-writing it as carefully as he can."

As in the case of *The Brook Kerith*, so with *Héloïse and Abélard* Moore invoked the aid of friends and acquaintances who were specialists in departments of knowledge with which he had no familiarity. Some notes from T. W. Whittaker survive. Héloïse (Whittaker suggests) might reflect that the ancients knew there was more to discover " and why with her lover should not the time have now come ? " Moore sets the scholar at work upon researches concerning the depravity of the clergy in 1200. These researches are not very fruitful; on the other hand, Whittaker supplies justification for the turning of Abélard into a troubadour. Moore wishes to bring a reference to John Scotus Erigena into his narrative; and the scholar reassures him by saying that Abélard's rationalising the Gospels in relating Virgil to St. John is also to be found in the Irish metaphysician. Whittaker sends him a suggestion for the line which Héloïse's soliloquy might take: " This new dialectician transforms everything. We had been told that, according to the ancients Porphyry and Boethius, genus and species are real things.

The particular things we see could not exist without them. If there was not humanity there could not be men and women. Without rationality there would be no recurring thing. . . ."

In this way Moore provided himself with explanations of the significance of the great mediæval controversy between Nominalists and Realists, Abélard's part in which brought him into conflict with the Church. Explanations from a text-book would have been useless to him. He acquired what he wanted to know by means of conversation or correspondence, and in both cases his teacher's information had to be conveyed to him in relation to some specific scene in his book. But having finished with him Whittaker said that he had found an excellent pupil in Moore; and indeed the clarity and colloquial simplicity of the philosophical disputations were not the least of the many excellencies of *Héloïse and Abélard*. He looked to Mrs. Crawford for the architectural details of his book and for the costumes.

1.7.19. *To Mrs. Crawford.*

I am afraid that you are treating me with very little consideration. I asked you to help me with a work of art and I find to my great regret that almost anything is accepted as being more important. I asked you to give me some help and mentioned that it would be paid for. . . . But of course a Catholic girl had to come down for the week-end. Do you think you are treating me quite fairly. I am sure that you do not.

18.7.19. *To Mrs. Crawford.*

The two nuns with Héloïse walk round the convent and the nuns explain to Héloïse the changes that have been made in the convent and in the grounds about the convent. . . . I cannot write this scene for I do not see the convent and its grounds as clearly as you do. The nuns show Héloïse around as a house-agent might. . . .

24.7.19. *To Mrs. Crawford.*

As I know you to be entirely trustworthy I know that you are working out a plan of the convent for me. It is

very kind of you and I am sure you are doing it excellently
well. But I doubt if this convent will ever be as good as
the *Evelyn Innes* convent. . . .

" This new adventure," Moore wrote to Best in September,
" is even wilder than *The Brook Kerith*." He had just revised
The Brook Kerith for a Tauchnitz edition. " These small
corrections are due to you. It was last night that I took out
your lists and it was not till last night that I began to appreciate the skill of your analysis. I did not really know that
scholarship could go so far. I have availed myself of nearly
all your suggestions and I am more obliged to you than I
can say."

A delay had occurred in the publication of *Avowals* owing
to the difficulty of finding suitable paper. When it did
appear it was, he said, " a book full of printer's blunders
and mine." He was ready to rewrite his books on the proofs,
but he could not correct proofs, and looking forward to a
final edition of *The Brook Kerith* he remarked in a letter
that he would wish Best to read the proofs if he would
accept a fee. Best offered to do the work as a labour of love,
but got no reply.

It was rarely that John Eglinton gave his work unreserved
praise, but an article by this critic in the *Irish Statesman*
described *Avowals* as " the most delightful of all Moore's
books."

12.11.19 *To John Eglinton.*

I should have written to thank you before for your
article, if all my present life was not being spent on the
narrative of Héloïse and Abélard; everything is put aside
for that story which will probably bring me disappointment in the end for such is the way of all writing.

The only fault I find with your article is that you do
not write at the bottom of it—to be continued—for you
will make a book of these articles which are all, or nearly
all, very good. . . . I thought Yeats' poem extremely
beautiful and am glad that I was published in the same
number. To read even one stanza of this poem brings the

conviction that one touch of real poetry is enough to
redeem us from the endless poetasters who interrupt
our path in love.

The poem referred to was Yeats's *Prayer for my Daughter*.
Moore now realised that he had been deceived into thinking
that Yeats's poetical impulse had died soon after youth.
" Why does Yeats never come to see me ? " he used to
complain during the later years in Ebury Street.

15

The work progressed, and by March 1920 he had written
Abélard's lecture on faith and reason, which, heard by
Héloïse in the cloister, causes her to lose herself, body and
soul. " My audacity causes me a thrill," he wrote to Mrs.
Crawford " . . . I showed Abélard's lecture to Whittaker last
night and he said he could not have imagined it possible to
do it as well."

There followed a visit to Brittany and Touraine in pursuit
of the romance of the learned lovers. He wrote to Mrs.
Crawford from Tours :

I walked around the old fortress of Le Pallet with
Monsieur le Curé who knew all about Héloïse and Abélard.
The Musée des Beaux Arts would have delighted you—
the sculpture of the 12, 13, 14 centuries—la serenité triste
de la vierge d'Amiens et la tristesse mondiale du roi
Salomon. I shall never forget the casts, casts that reproduce
the originals exactly. But if I were to tell all I should be here
until the day after to-morrow. I had intended to leave by
the 3.30 but on arriving at the station I learnt that it did
not stop at Blois. The hotel made a mistake and I start
at seven by an omnibus train and arrive at Blois at nine.
But you must not think that this is why I am writing to
you.

I wrote asking you to come and see me but you did not
come. I return to London in nine or ten days, my memory
stored with memories of the Loire and a more precise

image of Abélard before me. I lie in bed in the morning
and lose myself in dreams, seeing Abélard and Héloïse and
hearing them talking and suddenly I fall to wondering
if I shall get all this dreaming down on paper—if I shall
see the proofs. . . .

On his return from France he told an anecdote of two
American sailors whom he had met while travelling to
Nantes. He met them again at a Duval restaurant in Paris;
knowing that they could speak no French he went over to
their table and ordered food for them, sitting down with
them. They said they were going to England the next day.
" So am I ? " said Moore. " To learn English ? " they asked.
Moore couldn't understand what they meant by that until
they explained that they had never heard a cultivated
Englishman speak English. In telling the story he added:
" I didn't tell them I was Irish: that would have befogged
their minds. They really thought I was French."
As he had been unable to call on Dujardin at Le Val
Changis, he compensated his learned friend by sending him
some lines on a favourite fish.

> *La chair est bonne de l'alose,*
> *Plus fine que celle du bar,*
> *Mais la Seine est loin et je n'ose*
> *Abandonner Pierre Abélard.*

He took great pains with the French verses, which after
much revision and many consultations with Dujardin and
Mrs. Crawford, he published in the *Fortnightly Review* and
later included in *Conversations in Ebury Street* (p. 170). On subsequent visits to Le Val Changis he would call at Dujardin's
fishmonger and recite the piece, gathering around him a
delighted crowd. Here, as in England and in Ireland, he was
on excellent terms with the common people, and on his walks
about the forest he used to stop the nursemaids and work-
people and engage them in pleasant, even intimate conversation. They all loved " ce Mister Moore."
His letters continued to show him at work on the medieval

romance, but in 1920 he brought out *Esther Waters* with an epistle dedicatory to T. W. Rolleston, a former Dublin friend, now in London—one of the victims of *Hail and Farewell*, by whom he was forgiven. There were a good many improvements in the writing.

23.7.20. *To Mrs. Crawford.*

Dear, dear Nia,

I haven't seen you for a long time. Last night I discovered among some old papers that your admiration for Sister Josiane was quite legitimate for you found the name yourself and established her as librarian. Will you supply me with a name for Sister Marie Coeur de Marie. I should like to look out some names with you at the London Library. However this may be come to tea or lunch next week

as ever

George Moore

August was made pleasant by a visit to Lord Howard de Walden at Chirk Castle, Denbighshire, and he wrote letters from there to Mrs. Crawford and to John Eglinton.

23.8.20. *To Mrs. Crawford.*

I gather that so far *Héloïse and Abélard* does not fall below my *general* standard. I hope I am not misinterpreting your letter. To your strictures I reply that it was open to me to leave out the trouvères. I chose to include them for without their presence the story would have been thin and narrow and colourless (in my opinion) . . . and having introduced them I was bound to reintroduce them and the court of love with which they were associated. I may have done this badly of course. Jean Guiscard is done from Pierre Vidal a troubadour and such an incredible being that I made him drunk. The story of his wolves and the finding of Arthur I thought excellently well invented . . . I am glad you like *Esther Waters*. I like it myself and look upon the book as a great blow from the shoulder comparable to Georges Carpentier's blows. But

had I to choose between it and *The Lake* (the revised *Lake*)
I should be embarrassed. You wouldn't but I think you
will understand what I mean when you receive the book.

The weather is very cold and I am returning to London
at the end of this week and hope you will come to luncheon
soon after. I am very much obliged to you for reading the
proofs of *Héloïse and Abélard*. You picked out the bits I like
myself and I think you will like the nuns. . . .

Many critics besides Mrs. Crawford have felt that the tale of
the lovers was somewhat lost sight of in the descriptions of the
Courts of Love which followed upon the flight of Abélard
and Héloïse from Paris. The drama of the book began at
Tours, and the forest journeyings were considered as a sort
of interlude.

28.8.20. *To John Eglinton.*

I suppose that the excessive use of dialogue and monologue stole upon me unawares, and was caused by an
innate dread of speaking directly of the twelfth century.
One of the last chapters begins " The winter began early
in 1127," or words to that effect, and I remember experi-
encing a certain reluctance in writing the phrase. I shall
keep my eye on the text and try to escape now and again
into the " past indefinite." I have already thanked you
for having saved me from a too specific statement of
the philosophy of the period, and I think I have told you
that the cut cost me £6 15.

Moore read some Morris prose while at Chirk Castle, and
felt at the end, he said, like someone who has been poisoned.
" But oh ! that I knew the language as well as ' Topsy '," he
confided to John Eglinton. " ' Topsy ' seems to be able to
write the language spontaneously. All the same, nobody ever
did, and nobody ever will read the stories he wrote in it
except perhaps W. B. Yeats. Lang knew the English language
almost as well as Morris and in his lovely translation of
Theocritus we come upon more than a hint of Morris. . . .
If I knew the English language as well as either of these two
writers, or as well as you do, I could skip joyfully to my grave."

But for Morris's verse he had always a profound admiration. " The poem I sent you," he wrote in 1921 to Miss Nancy Cunard, " is very beautiful, one of the most beautiful things in English poetry. I am sending you to day the volume from which it was taken, *The Defence of Guinevere and Other Poems*, by William Morris, the most perfect first volume of poems ever published by any man. . . . Morris is our only improvisatore, perhaps the only great improvisatore that ever lived. He could go to his study and write five hundred lines of *The Earthly Paradise* and return quite cheerful and happy, as if nothing extraordinary had happened; and these five hundred lines were never casual—every one was perfect. *The Defence of Guinevere* is one of the most beautiful poems in the language. The *Tomb of Arthur* I like better, perhaps, but every poem is good, especially *The Blue Closet*; that is a darling poem. Read it, Nancy, and admire the perfect craftmanship of everything in the volume."

This eulogy occurs in one of a long series of letters addressed to Lady Cunard's daughter, whose schoolroom he used to invade at Holt, now grown into a young woman with an active interest in literature and the arts. A close bond of sympathy developed between them; Moore delighted in the company of his young friend, and when she was away he would pour out by letter a constant stream of affectionate advice and comment.

Many years ago a poet said to me and his words have often been with me: If you go out and amuse yourself when you can't write your art life will waste into nothingness. An artist's life is in this like an acrobat's, he must exercise his craft daily, when inspiration is by him and when it is afar. He must not wait for inspiration, he must continue to call it down to him always and at last it will answer him—I should have said be always by him. You have received the second story. I think it contains the core of a poem but if you do not continue to write vainly the subject will never become familiar. It is only by vain writing that the subject becomes us. . . . My difficulty is always with the first two or three chapters, most people, with the last; and the explanation of this is that I always write with the end in view, almost gluttonously, like the child at the cake during dinner.

You are journeying with gusto, I perceive, making new acquaintances and picking up last year's. How delightful ! Your letter stirs my longing always incipient, sometimes very active, for speech with you and sight of you. But you would not be content to journey with me—I should become wearisome at the end of the week, despite the hill villages, their pictures and spires.

I found myself not long ago at a party, an enchanting party, a music party, and not having heard a note for many months the music fell like dew on a thirsting flower. I'd like to tell you about the songs that pleased me and my appreciations, but you would like to hear what I am doing.

Nancy, if you would hear the Muse you must prepare silent hours for her and not be disappointed if she breaks the appointment you have made with her.

To receive the Muse as it is her due to be received you must have an apartment. You must dine in and alone very often. You see that I am prescribing . . .

You know I have set my heart on your reading *Paradise Lost* not for pleasure but for profit and you have not read a line of Milton; yet you expect to write blank verse. Ah, if you had an apartment how easy everything would be. I could come to you for dinner and discussion and the reading of *Paradise Lost*.

Monsieur Gillet has written a long piece about my life in *La Revue des Deux Mondes*, October 15th, [1923] in which he describes my life as being a series of impulses. I could tell him of another life still more impulsive and restless.

16

The remainder of 1920 was spent with *Héloïse and Abélard*. One event of importance, outside of literature, befell him during its course. In July he had a new cook-house-keeper,

Clara Warville: her admirable conduct of his domestic economy added much to the ease and comfort of his declining years. She stayed with him until the end; and I am much indebted to her for her picturesque account (which will be found in a later chapter) of Moore's last ten years, an account which might well have pleased him more than many solemn literary tributes. " A very kind and comfortable woman," he said to Mrs. Williamson, " who I hope will remain with me until the end of the chapter." He had a new parlour-maid also. She was a Catholic which was " vexatious but not so vexatious in servants as elsewhere. Indeed, I often wonder where we should get our servants if the Catholic Church were to cease to exist suddenly."

" My life," he wrote to Mrs. Williamson at the New Year, " has dropped into writing, and I can see nothing in front of me except correcting the proofs of *Héloïse and Abélard.* But I shall be very glad to get a letter from you for the sake of the beautiful literary style and the warm heart behind the style, which to some extent accounts for the style. I hear that Tonks was staying at Hill Hall, I am glad for he is good Christmas company and if one is that one is seasonable all the year round." At Hill Hall himself a few days later, he wrote from there to Miss Viola Rodgers, to tell how tired he was after passing the last proofs. He would return to London, he said, to write some trifle, but chiefly to meditate on a long holiday from literature in France, for if he did not go to France he would soon be unable to speak or read or write French.

At the end of February he was in Paris, searching for his friend, who had an apartment in the Palais Royal and shortly afterwards acquired a lovely country house in the valley of the Juine.

28.2.21. *To Miss Viola Rodgers.*

I asked you if your hotel was near the gare de Lyons because I didn't know where it was but when I read it was in the avenue Montaigne near the Rond Point I began to count the chesnut trees in my imagination. . . .

While he was staying with Dujardin that spring Miss Rodgers spent a day with him. " How pleasant it was sitting by you," he wrote after she had left, " and how pleasant it is to recall the seat, the light coming and going and the birds singing in all the branches."

In July he went to stay near Miss Nancy Cunard at Dieppe. Some pretty notes to Miss Rodgers followed the visit.

6.8.21.

My dearest, I have been away in Dieppe living in the prettiest of inns—an inn of unimportant rooms, mere beds, a summer inn that expresses itself in a large orchard sloping down to a winding river along whose low banks the tables are ranged—a brown river that the willows and poplars follow with a fidelity that sets me thinking of thy vagrancy. The waiters hurry through the apple boughs with plates and dishes of excellent food.

17.8.21.

. . . I have others in my head " the end of Don Juan " but I need not enumerate. Dearest Viola it will be a great pleasure to see you again. I have never met so sweet a woman and there are times even in the midst of all this writing when my heart is full of you.

18.8.21.

If you come to London you will show me some photographs. If An open house awaits you and a loving heart as you well know yet you write if Would that the monosyllable had been when

23.8.21.

. . . During my walk I indulged myself in the hope that I might see you in London but you wander farther and farther and now you are in Vienna. If we wedded your wandering instinct would come upon you and I'd find myself alone, soon too soon.

31.8.21.

The picture postcard you sent me interested me vastly for I did not know that Breughel was nearly so great a man—the composition, the vision if I may use the cant word of to-day, is wonderful. The herding of the beeves in the wild autumnal landscape we should have admired together.

17

After *Héloïse and Abélard* came more revision of old books. At the beginning of 1921 a Moore Hall edition of the *Memoirs of My Dead Life* was being prepared by Heinemann, and Moore was greatly pleased with Philip Telden's work in rearranging and redrawing an old engraving of the house in Mayo for the title page. Next came *The Lake*, an addition to Heinemann's black edition (uniform with the original edition of the trilogy, the new *Esther Waters*, *Muslin*, etc.), with the preface in which Moore attributed the common and feebler parts of his work to Amico Moorini. The text was changed very considerably by the introduction into it of those various devices first applied in *Hail and Farewell*, which produce the effect of something written by ear, or of oral narrative, with its continuous action. There is action even when Father Gogarty soliloquises; his thoughts are not described, he is shown thinking :

" He goes as a dream goes," Father Oliver said, and a few minutes afterwards he was sitting alone by his turf fire, asking himself in what dreams differed from reality. For like a dream Father O'Grady had come, and he had gone, never to return. " But does anything return ? " he asked himself, and he looked round the room, wondering why the chairs and tables did not speak to him, and why life was not different to what it was.

At that moment he caught sight of a newspaper upon his table. " *Illustrated England*," he muttered to himself; and he fell to wondering how it had come into the house. " Father O'Grady must have left it," he said, and began to unroll the paper. But while unrolling it he stopped. Half his mind was still away, and he sat for fully ten minutes lost in sad sensations.

His play *Elizabeth Cooper*, once again rewritten under the name of *The Coming of Gabrielle*, was scheduled for production in the autumn of 1921, and its author drawn once more into " the theatrical whirlpool, the infernal vortex."

13.10.21. *To Miss Nancy Cunard.*

Playfair tried to keep me away from rehearsal till I began to suspect him, so one day I turned into the theatre at eleven o'clock, seated myself in the stalls, and awaited events. Playfair said I was a naughty child to come before I was sent for, but that all the same he was glad to see me, to which I answered that we didn't seem to be altogether agreed as to the cast. The rehearsal began, and it was very much like the rehearsal described in a volume entitled *Ave*.

They were not agreed; and after a feverish interlude of " arguments and telegrams " the project was dropped.

Towards the end of the year Moore was at work on a new story, " Hugh Monfert," a name appropriate to the young man, a lover of the Middle Ages, who imagines himself as a knight riding to the lists, and, of all, practising chastity. Hugh has been brought up by his mother in the harshest aspects of Catholicism, intensely lonely. The tale—a long short story—has an unexpected dénouement: Hugh's marriage with the sister of a friend and the annulment of the marriage upon his realisation that he was " attracted to Beatrice not for herself but for the likeness to her brother." " Hugh Monfert " recalled the far-off days of *A Mere Accident* and of " John Norton " in *Celibates*; it was a third attempt to interpret, and build up a story round Edward Martyn, imagined outside his Irish environment. " We never come to the end of dear Edward," Moore used to say; and in inviting Mrs. Crawford's interest he wrote: " I would like to interpret the influence of Catholicism . . . I often succeed best in interpreting things distant and alien."

Like *Avowals* and *A Story-Teller's Holiday*, *Héloïse and Abélard* came out first in a limited edition; later on, when it was published in a more accessible form, the general body of readers preferred it to *The Brook Kerith*, and perhaps Moore himself came in the end to agree with them. They found the setting more attractive, the inventions more felicitous, and the treatment more varied. " Moore gave us about this time," says Tonks, " an amusing instance of his innocent admiration for his own work, but no doubt he had thought over the matter as a judge might, carefully working up to his final judgment. At one of our Saturday evenings in the Vale he began talking of the rarity of the epic in English literature. As a form it was not for us. ' There are three English epics,' he said: ' *Paradise Lost* and *The Brook Kerith*.' " What was the other ? asked Tonks. The other was *Héloïse and Abélard*.

In the last ten years of his life Moore worked at writing with the same kind of energy that Michael Angelo worked at sculpture, and it is only fair to say again that often the same sense of failure came over him. He might hold judicially that *The Brook Kerith* and *Héloïse* were two out of the three English epics, but it did not follow that he was fully satisfied with either book. In the case of *Héloïse* he felt, as soon as the book had been published, that his intentions had neither been fully achieved nor understood. " So few," he was saying a year later to Mr. Barrett H. Clark, " bother to analyse the book carefully. It would have been very easy to discuss the form, compare my treatment of it with others' treatment of similar themes, and so on, yet apparently no one ever thought of that. The book is modern both in spirit and mood. I am now going through it again, cutting out everything that could remind the reader of a search for the archaic, yet preserving nothing that is distinctively modern. I aim at making the style a kind of composite of modern and eighteenth-century English."

CHAPTER IX

EBURY STREET: CONVERSATIONS

I

EVERY YEAR now Moore paid visits to Paris where he had still many friends, some of them his oldest friends, some freshly made: Madame Duclaux and her sister Miss Mabel Robinson, the Halévys, Aristide Marie, Dujardin, Miss Viola Rodgers, René Boylesve, Paul Valéry, Edmond Jaloux, and the young G. Jean-Aubry, his interlocutor in one of the *Conversations in Ebury Street*, whose acquaintance he had made in London during the war. Jean-Aubry it was who suggested that the *Memoirs of My Dead Life* should be published in French, and the Moore Hall (1921) edition of the book was prepared to serve as the text for the French translator. The usual difficulties arose: Moore disapproved of points in the translation, and while he was in Paris in May 1921 he had to call upon Daniel Halévy and Jaloux to correct it. The book appeared first in a number of Halévy's famous *Cahiers Verts*, with a woodcut illustration of Moore Hall as seen from the lake; and then in Bernard Grasset's edition, without the " Lovers of Orelay." He descended on Grasset's office to protest, and found that no one knew his name. " I was embarrassed," he said, " when I had to tell them that I enjoyed some little reputation in my own country. But before I had left the office I received a pat on the back and was told that I appeared to be an intelligent person anyhow."

Moore never reached as large a body of French readers as did some of his contemporaries, nor did his works ever appear in French in a collected edition. And in his later years he had the discomfort of watching the conquest of intellectual Paris by *Ulysses* and *Lady Chatterley's Lover*. France was the best of Moore's life, or so it seemed to him, and yet he was now outdistanced by Lawrence who disliked France with a Waterloo-like ferocity. But *Memoirs of My Dead Life* was received with much sympathy and a certain gratitude towards its author for his love of France at the time of her deepest humiliation; no Frenchman would ever have written of the " *delightful* seventies." The publication gave rise to two excellent studies of Moore: one by Daniel Halévy in *La Revue de Paris* for the 15th of October, 1922, and another by Louis Gillet in *La Revue des Deux Mondes* for October 1923. What mattered to Moore, what he loved to dwell upon in his talk, was not modern France, nor the new developments of her art and literature, but the France of his youth, the France which he had built into the artistic fabric of his life.

Blanche he now saw but seldom and rather coldly. Their theoretical differences on the relation of life to art could not be overcome, and moreover Moore, who had always regarded himself as Blanche's sponsor in England, was vexed by the warm friendship which had sprung up between Blanche and Henry James. But Blanche continued to admire Moore's work, and to marvel from a distance at his extraordinary character, both affectionate and self-centred, a disposition, he used to say, that did not render one's friends happy, but explained in some degree the admirable results which Moore reached in old age, his paradoxical progress in writing.

2

It was now his opinion that there was a much more interesting and intense artistic life in London than in Paris. But in Boylesve and in Paul Valéry he felt vital presences through whom he was able to capture something of the spirit of the charmed past; and Madame Duclaux has told us that when Boylesve died he grieved: " That delightful man, I wish I had met him sooner." Although he often spoke of ending his days as a writer where he had begun them, he did not seek out some contemporary Nouvelle Athènes, where the talk might be of Gertrude Stein or of

Joyce, of Proust or of Lawrence; he seemed to prefer the
company of Academicians and the editors of grave reviews.
It is rather strange that he was not decorated by the French
Government, but if he felt any disappointment at the over-
sight he never showed it.

Madame Duclaux feels sure that he never seriously considered settling again in France. But if one met him by
chance in Paris he was as likely as not engaged in a hunt
for some apartment to exchange, he said, for Ebury, " be
cause I cannot die in Ebury, Ebury is not worthy of my
death." One year he put an agent to great trouble, asking
for a house in the forest, near Dujardin. The agent showed
him various houses, but he rejected all, explaining when he
came to the last: " *Monsieur, il faut que vous connaissez le sujet
du roman que j'écris.*" Jean-Aubry described to him the
character of various provincial towns. Moore liked the sound
of Amboise and Beauvais; " but," Jean-Aubry asked him,
" how would you pass your time, as you neither fish nor
garden ? " " My dear friend, I am thinking of learning
French," he replied. At one time he was desirous of
being accepted as a lodger by Miss Viola Rodgers. " I have
often thought of asking you to take me in as a lodger. Why
not ? I am old enough. You like my chatter and you never
come to London and I dare not go to a town in which sleep
is impossible everywhere except in an apartment overlooking
the gardens of the Palais Royal." . . . " I am sorry you can't
have me as a lodger in your apartment, living there alone
will not be the same as living there with you. . . . I should
like to go for a trip. I should like to visit the pretty towns in
France, but I never seem to see anything but Paris and
Fontainebleau."

But on his visits to France Dujardin was still the great
stand-by, and at his hospitable table Moore sometimes met
young journalists and others who wished to discuss recent
tendencies in the French novel. He was not unequal to the
challenge: he had read the first four volumes of Romain
Rolland's *Jean Christophe*, and thought them very good, but
was not moved to read more. " After all the length of a work
must be determined by weighing the interest and importance

of the subject matter. *War and Peace* is a long book because
war and peace are long things: the *Iliad* and the *Odyssey*
are precisely the right length. In any event I prefer Homer
to Rolland, because the Greek poet does not moralise."
He had read some of Proust; thought him clever, but without a sense of artistic selection. Here however he displayed a
sudden modesty: " Doubtless my judgment is at fault, or
my taste, for I am not in sympathy with Proust's generation;
and I imagine I cannot as an artist appeal to the intellectual
sympathies of this generation . . . I present only the spectacle
of an elderly gentleman speaking his mind."

The two old comrades still scolded each other, still made
it up. As late as 1922 one of Moore's visits to Le Val Changis
concluded by his saying that never, never would he come
again. " It is too wearisome. Dujardin seems to go out of his
way to meet the disagreeable things which I spend my life
in trying to avoid. I declare I don't think he can be happy
unless he is in trouble." Moore caused a cab to be called,
but it did not come, and the trunk was taken to the station
in a barrow, himself alongside on foot, trying to keep the
trunk from falling into the muddy street. Arriving in Paris
he drove to Foyot's where he had last stayed, but his room
was gone and the house full. So he curled up on one of the
little wooden benches in the courtyard, and not till six in the
morning could they arrange a bed for him in one of the
servants' rooms. " My God, how I slept," he said the next
day. " I didn't wake up till one this afternoon. I can still
feel those slats on the bench that dug into my back. And I
can't put on my shoe: my heel got infected at Dujardin's. . . .
I think it must have been a mosquito bite. I have paid my
last visit to Le Val Changis." But reconciliation followed,
and before the year was out Moore was writing (for *Conversations in Ebury Street*) an affectionate passage on those aspects
of Dujardin's management of life which were apt to disturb
the convenience of his guest. He even went—with misgivings
—to see a play by a friend of Dujardin. " She wrote a book
of reminiscences," he remarked apprehensively, " and one
anecdote was six hundred pages long. What are we to
expect of her play ? " But the play exceeded expectations,

for " only once in a generation," said Moore, " is it permitted to any mortal to write a play like that. I shall write
to Dujardin just what I think of it, and tell him that France
has lost a good concierge."

3

This episode and much talk and incident which give a
vivid picture of Moore in Paris in his seventieth year are preserved in the unpublished notes of Mr. Barrett H. Clark,
from which he has kindly allowed me to draw extensively,
both here and elsewhere in my narrative.

" I had carried on a sporadic correspondence with him,"
he writes, " between 1914 and 1919 from America, and just
after Christmas 1921 my wife and I left home and settled
in Paris. In February I wrote to Moore in London saying
that I hoped to see him there later in the year. A few days
later a uniformed footman from the Hotel Brighton appeared
at our door, and delivered a message asking me to dine that
evening. Moore was at a desk in the writing room when
word was sent of my arrival. He made a somewhat dramatic
entrance—with just the touch of a flourish. He was dressed
in blue serge, with a soft grey shirt and loose collar. The
most noticeable things about him are his pure white silky
hair and flowing white moustache. He looks much younger
than when I saw him in 1914. Dreamy light blue eyes ; drooping shoulders ; long arms, soft hands with tapering fingers.

" With few preliminaries we walk out into the street . . .
we walk on, a long way, through narrow by-streets to the
Boulevards, all the way to the Boulevard Montmartre, and
turn a little way up the Rue d'Hauteville. What restaurant ?
I forget the name, but I think a famous old place, well known
to Moore. He was a little nervous as we came in. . . . I had
tried to pilot him between hurrying buses, but that wasn't
easy : he clung tight to his closed umbrella, held under one
arm, and as he talked, gesticulated with the other. But he
calmed down, and ordered dinner in the old-fashioned manner, asking advice of the waiter and the *patron*. ' But what in
the name of Heaven are these *Coquilles St. Jacques* ? ' It was

rather a long evening, but later on Moore gathered momentum. A great deal of what he said, and the way he said it, can be read in his books, for Moore certainly repeats himself. . . . We rambled far and wide, for he brings a subject to an abrupt close the second it ceases to interest him . . .

" Speaking of Donnay's *Amants* he was reminded of his own *Coming of Gabrielle*, and Nigel Playfair's recent wish to produce it, but his eyes were dull when I said that both the writing and the sentiments in *Amants* reminded me a little of the early Moore. He went on to say that he hoped to dramatise *The Brook Kerith*; and *The Brook Kerith* caused him to snort at St. John Ervine's remark that his Syrian story had been conceived from three different standpoints. We then started to talk about the dramatised version of *Esther Waters*, and I told Moore I thought he should revise it. He begged me to try my hand upon the work. ' Read it again, think the matter over, and when I am back in Paris in a few weeks you will be able to tell me what you can do.' He had begun the meal by showing some interest in the food as it was brought in, but now that he was talking about his books he looked up wonderingly and a little irritated every time the waiter uncovered a dish or asked a question. He was well launched in a discussion of *Impressions and Opinions*, and for ten minutes he left his food untouched. So did I. ' I cannot understand how I could write such horrible stuff as I did in some of those essays. Most of the papers are very poor.'

" I ventured to say that I was amazed to perceive how dispassionately Moore could look upon his own work, and that he and Jules Lemaître seemed to have, to an extraordinary degree, the ability to regard every book, their own and others, as though they had never before heard it mentioned. ' How do you account for that ? ' The blue eyes focussed on me, seriously, almost accusingly. ' About the other man you mentioned I can't say, but speaking for myself, I'd say it was because I was never educated, I educated myself; I am still learning. I suppose that's it.' He was in fact just as bitterly critical of his own work as he was of the work of his contemporaries, except that he does look upon some of his own work as good. ' I see just what I have done, the good

and the bad. I have perspective too. I happened to come
upon the scene at the right moment. I was present at the
beginning of an important artistic and literary rebirth. I
came to France, I wrote the first serious novels in English.
I invented adultery, which didn't exist in the English novel
till I began writing. . . .' The waiter came to ask a question.
' For God's sake, now what is that ? Where was I when the
waiter came ? Oh yes. If I had been born at another time
I might have become a writer, but what I wrote would have
been without point or meaning. . . . No, I don't think I shall
lecture in America. I have many good American friends, but
I am afraid I shall not like your country. You Americans
tell me so. But I did sign a contract with Pond, to deliver a
series of lectures. Among other things I had to promise I
would travel alone. Probably the agent was afraid I would
take some woman with me.'

" We must have been at the table for at least three hours
and I remember the feel of the drizzle as we walked away
from the restaurant that night. We paused after a moment
by the entrance to the Passage des Panoramas, and Moore
pointed with his umbrella down the arcade towards the
room on the second floor where he had lived for many
months during the seventies. I suggested when we reached
the hotel that since it was past midnight he might want to
go to bed. ' Bed ? Why suggest that ? Are you bored ? Let us
sit here in the writing-room, and let us talk about Pater. Do
you smoke cigars ? No. No matter. Sit down. Do you know
Vernon Lee's work ? Never mind. Not long ago she came to
see me, I don't remember why. Maybe it was to tell me she
liked *The Brook Kerith*. The name of Pater was mentioned by
me or by her, I forget, and I said that the poorest page in
Pater is better than the best page I ever wrote. Vernon Lee
reflected for a moment on that, and then, with a smile,
answered that it might well be so, that it was almost true.
I liked her frankness, for she spoke the truth.' He turned to
me. ' You are, my young friend, too young to appreciate
Pater; I am myself. I sometimes think I am only beginning
to appreciate him. Pater wrote better than I write because
he had a finer mind than I have. You can't write beyond

your mind. True there is what may seem to some people a certain monotony in Pater, and he has no humour, but it is so very easy to be facetious (that's one of the things that's wrong with Bennett) and I have great difficulty in cutting out the smart sentences and humorous passages from my own work. Pater knew better than that. He knew what was right and what was futile and frivolous.'

" He then wondered what effect dictation would ultimately have on literature, and remarked that he found it easy to dictate, especially the first draft. He gets his ideas down in this way, in order to be able to know what to use and what to discard. He cannot dictate as a rule even a paragraph that will stand as a final version. Many of his pages have been gone over and revised twenty times at the very least. And now reverting to Pater he repeated as though to himself, ' You can't write beyond your mind. Pater knew that, and he had a great mind. . . . But tell me, you have come so recently from America, how do you account for this American reform mania ? Good God, you are always trying to make your people behave. It's so absurd, isn't it ? ' Prohibition and literary censorship in particular aroused his anger. ' It's all the fault of that damned *Mayflower*,' he said.

" I soon made another move to get up and leave, but Moore was irritated; he was just beginning to warm up. I settled myself comfortably in my chair and listened. Curiously enough, Moore often hesitates for the right word, and not infrequently gets it wrong. He feels for a word, and unless he is sure of it, appears deliberately to mispronounce it as though showing his contempt. For instance, he was speaking of an editor who commissioned him to write an article on the decay of the English language. The viewpoint suggested was that of the close relationship between France and England geographically. ' The contig—contiguity,' Moore started, and somehow couldn't master the word contiguity. No wonder he marvelled at Arnold Bennett's facility. He even marvelled at mine, since I gave him the word he was trying to twist his tongue round; and he began to speak of my project to write a series of articles on the Paris of Balzac and the Paris of George Moore."

Later in the month Moore took Clark to the Louvre, where he wished to see some recent acquisitions. On the way he asked his companion what he had been writing, and Clark said: "An article on Adolphe Appia." "Appia? Appia? Why Appia? However, it is possible to write a good article. I hope yours will be good. Is it?"

Without waiting for Clark's answer, he reverted to a conversation of the other night on the blasting effects of modern education. "Everyone thinks he must needs write a novel or paint a picture, and the result of all this activity is a mess of hopeless mediocrity. My friends tell me the system is faulty. But I tell them it must always and necessarily be faulty; the idea itself is wrong. . . ."

The Louvre acquisitions were not particularly striking. Moore liked a Berthe Morisot portrait which reminded Clark of Manet. "There was a painter," said Moore. "The paint seemed to leap to his canvas. I used to think Corot was a great painter. I am off him now. Now I much prefer Rousseau, for Rousseau goes to the root of things, to nature herself, while Corot is trying to improve on nature." Ingres, as always, inspired Moore's admiration. The *Renan* did not seem as good to him as it had done years ago, but he paused in front of the *Apotheosis of Homer*. "You don't like it? But we agree on Manet at any rate. Look at the *Olympia*. This nude is alive; the flesh lives. When Manet paints nudes they have meaning. Most painters just take it into their heads to paint nudes." Much more followed on the subject, but two small Diazes drew Moore away from Manet; and he then said that he had had enough of the Frenchmen, and went in search of the Rembrandt portraits. Of them he said nothing, but looked only, and then passed to the Rubens, observing that he liked only the small sketches with their drawing and subtle colour. They stopped in another room to look at a couple of Fromentins: "A fine painter; as fine as a man can be who is not a great painter; his writings are beautiful, but somewhat dull. And now we have enough of art. Two hours at a time are quite sufficient. You speak of Conrad. Oh, a very bad writer. You like some of his books? Dear, dear! You pain me. No, I have not read *Victory*, and in spite of your advice I will not read it. Have I told you my epigram on Hardy ? ' George Eliot's miscarriage ! ' "

Spring came, and Moore returned to Paris intent upon the *Esther Waters* collaboration with Clark: he had taken a dislike to the Hotel Brighton, and asked his collaborator to engage rooms for him at Cayre's Hotel in the Rue du Bac. In the end he drove to Foyot's instead of to Cayre's and joining Mr. and Mrs. Barrett Clark at the Deux Magots for luncheon next day, he explained: " It's a long story; Lady Cunard's daughter, Nancy, got me a room at Foyot's. As I wrote to you I was afraid Foyot's was going to be too noisy, but when I arrived I drove there first, intending to go on to Cayre's. But in my room there was a large bouquet of forget-me-nots. I am a sentimental old man. The hotel is dreadfully expensive, especially the food. That's why I didn't ask you there to breakfast. And now let's change the subject and speak of our play."

A few evenings later, Moore told the Barrett Clarks how he had recently been amusing himself by copying out lengthy passages from *The Return of the Native* for his friend St. John Hutchinson who persisted in admiring Hardy. " He cannot write at all, and his machine-made plots are just absurd. Look at the way he drags in those trivial and unessential episodes merely in order to make use of the moonlight. I recall that absurd scene in *Tess of the*—er—that *Tess* book, where the man (what's his name ?) carries Tess over the plain at night. Moonlight, of course." When he had finished with Hardy, and had invented a scandalous anecdote about Watts-Dunton, James Joyce entered the restaurant, and sitting down, looked at Moore out of one eye, the other being covered with a black patch. Moore stared at him, and then enquired in a stage whisper if " that " was Joyce, and how he made his living.

He was now tired and wishing to move, but at the door of Foyot's he detained his companions, saying, " I want to say what great pleasure you have both given me. And besides you have given me help. I should never have done that revising of *Esther Waters* but for you. This is not flattery, I am a poor hand at that; did I ever tell you about A——?

No ? Well, he once asked me to dinner, or to what I supposed would be dinner. I enjoy good food, and I like to have enough of it, but he served tiny *coquilles* of chicken, a little cheese and coffee. I was disgusted, and I can assure you that I was in an evil humour. In the library, however, A—— offered me a cigar, but I was afraid it would make me sick; so I told him bluntly that I didn't smoke before dinner. I got up, walked out of his house and went elsewhere for something to eat." With a little movement of his head Moore turned squarely about and waved his hand without looking round.

It was agreed before parting that Barrett Clark should arrange for the placing of *Esther Waters* in America, and that the play, if produced there, should be signed jointly. All smiles, Moore saw Clark off from the railway station : " We shall soon be as rich as Carpentier," he said. Shortly after his return to England, however, he rewrote the third act, and so remodelled the fourth that it amounted to a new act. He sent the MS. to Clark. " I glanced over it," says Clark, " and found that though the third act was rewritten, eight or nine pages of my dialogue were retained verbatim. I thought the new end of the play absurd, but I sent a pleasant little answer. . . ." It was then arranged that the managers should choose between the two versions, with a division of the profits in the case of either of them being produced. " If the American manager prefers your version to mine by all means let him have it," Moore wrote in June; but all his efforts were directed towards persuading Clark to with-draw this version, which must now, he said, be regarded as Clark's adaptation, not as a collaboration, and signed by Clark alone; and when in September the Dramatic Theatre Guild rejected their joint version he complained of an infringed agreement, saying that his adaptation should have been submitted in the first instance, and that he had seen at once that it was impossible for Clark to collaborate on so English a play. " I am surprised at your unwisdom," he added. Finally Moore got back the second version from Clark, and gave it to an agent; to save Moore's feelings from being hurt, Clark was still to accept half the proceeds of any production in America, but he must destroy the original version. These suggestions were refused, and Clark prepared a statement defending himself against a charge of having infringed their agreement, but he allowed the collaboration to repose in the bottom drawer of his desk while Moore's version went the rounds.

This was the last of Moore's many attempts at dramatic collaborations, all of which in one way or another came to grief. There is a passage in his short story " Hugh Monfert " which artlessly shows his conception of the ideal collaboration : Percy Knight is asked to tell " how he and his sister had achieved the difficult task of writing together. She showed me what she had written, Percy answered, and I altered it. Didn't you quarrel over the alterations ? We did sometimes : but in the end Beatrice saw that she was wrong."

4

At this time Moore never tired of talking of the edition of his works which Horace Liveright projected for America. It was to be called the Carra Edition. " Liveright wants me to reprint *Flowers of Passion* and *Pagan Poems*, and *Mike Fletcher*. I will not give in. The Carra set will include only the work by which I wish to be remembered; *Evelyn Innes* and *Sister Teresa* and *Mike Fletcher* are not to be resuscitated. *Celibates* is full of bad things. I am rewriting it for him. *Literature at Nurse?* An early trifle, the essence of which I have incorporated into the " Address to the Jury " in *Avowals*, a book in which there is much to be rewritten. *Hail and Farewell* shall stand as it is, and people seem to like *Héloïse*, but after all isn't there more stuff, more *nature*, in *A Mummer's Wife?* That book was observed with the naked eye. It was vilely written, but you will have noticed how much better the revised edition is. *A Mummer's Wife* will have its place among the Carra books.

" Arthur Symons said *Impressions and Opinions* was your best book." " Oh, horrible stuff ! Yet I shall keep the ' Degas ' and ' Mummer Worship,' but the ' Degas ' shall go into the new *Modern Painting*. *Vain Fortune* I might revise if I could lay hold of the Scribner edition of the book. I like *Spring Days*, but the public didn't. *Mike Fletcher*—don't speak of that awful book. I hope no one will find a copy." He himself once found a copy, and handed it to Mr. C. D. Medley, with this inscription: " I have read few books that I like better than *Spring Days* and no book that I dislike more than *Mike Fletcher*. It would be too difficult to say which is the worst—the composition or the writing. A detestable book ! "

No doubt about *A Story-Teller's Holiday*—every author must have one " joyous " book to his name. *The Brook Kerith* had been lately revised (1921) : it would need further attention. " I did shocking things in it. There are entire passages in the original edition that make my blood run cold. *Memoirs of My Dead Life* ? You will like this in the new edition. The book was originally made up of a few stray articles and stories. I have now tried to give it some sort of artistic direction, and you will be amused with the new frontispiece, a coloured photograph of myself at the age of five."

Before coming to Paris in 1922 Moore had finished his book of short stories, *In Single Strictness*, and this was published in America by Boni and Liveright, and by Heinemann in London, before the end of the year. To Barrett Clark he spoke much about the stories and read him an " advertisement," just ready, of two hundred words, all one sentence, it seemed, explaining that the temperaments of the people in the stories were so closely related that the book could be looked upon as a single narration divided into five chapters. " It's clear, isn't it ? If a long sentence is clear, it is as good as a short sentence—or better ! Better, I say." The five stories were all highly wrought examples of the later manner, that continuous active movement, which Moore called pure narrative, the extreme reaction against apostrophic fiction. " Hugh Monfert " and " Henrietta Marr " were revisions of two of the stories in *Celibates* ; and the other three, the more sympathetic of these studies of ineffective and of withdrawn lives, " Wilfrid Holmes," " Priscilla and Emily Lofft " and " Sarah Gwynn," were new subjects. The young man in " Wilfred Holmes," when asked to produce the accompaniments of his opera, has to confess that the accompaniments are unwritten, nothing but the top line. It has seemed to him that he may gain a footing in musical journalism by joining in a correspondence which a newspaper has started on the subject of bird songs.

To this felicitous invention was attached a little history which went back to the days when Moore, still living in Dublin, had heard a blackbird whistle a tune in John Eglinton's garden. Eglinton was invited to remember. " I hope you have not forgotten that bird. If you have your forgetfulness is inexcusable, for I spoke to you about him not once but twenty times, and I have often thought of him and can recall at this moment my astonishment, for to hear a bird whistle five or six notes correctly is a ghostly experience, like hearing a parrot talk. I can remember the shape of the little tune—a perfect lilt it was—but fifteen years ago are a long while and so much passes through my head that I remember nothing except the book I am engaged upon and the things that concern it. I can't remember the notes of the tune, but I remember the shape." And while he was writing " Wilfrid Holmes," the *Daily Mail* opened a correspondence on the subject of bird songs, and he would have told the readers of the *Daily Mail* of his experience in Eglinton's garden if it had not been for his " almost insurmountable " dislike of writing letters to the paper. Later on, when he was in quest of a commonplace theme to illustrate Wilfrid's musical powers he did not know where to find it until he heard a party of revellers in a French train singing the melody which is transcribed in the last pages of the story.

It was not very long before he took a dislike to " Hugh Monfert "; " like a damp squib, it seems to me," he was presently saying to John Eglinton. But " Wilfrid Holmes " and the other stories were, he thought, as good as anything of their kind that he knew: Eglinton appears to have characterised them as " dim," and he retorted: " It may be that you have not been at pains to compare these stories with other psychological stories. There are not many psychological stories in the English language, but Tourgenieff has been translated, and I ask you to say, hand on your heart, that you thought of ' Sarah Gwynn ' in connection with Tourgenieff and came to the conclusion that Tourgenieff would have done more with the subject than I did."

5

Many country houses in Ireland were being burned during the winter of 1922–3, and a day seldom passed when Moore's imagination did not show him Moore Hall blazing among its woods, casting up a fierce light over the tranquil lake, lighting up the old ruins on the water. On the night of the first of February 1923, the Republican army, or a party of young men under that name, arrived at Moore Hall and after rousing Reilly, the steward, and bidding him make himself scarce they set the house on fire. The rascals thought it decent that they should first take some church vestments out of the house which had come from Spain, and these they left on the carriage-drive, but nothing else escaped destruction; only smoking walls remained when dawn came.

Moore said to me a few months later: " I knew it would happen. I told Garvin. I went to his office and said: ' If you allow a man called Gwynn[1] to refer week after week to my brother, the Colonel, my house will certainly be burned'"; the sense of this remark being that Colonel Moore was a Senator of the Free State and the Republican army was under orders to burn the houses of Senators. Sir Horace Plunkett's house was destroyed, ostensibly for the same reason; and when Sir Horace, after his long years of service to Ireland, came to England to end his days, Moore felt a bond of sympathy, and said that the appreciation of Plunkett in *Hail and Farewell* was inadequate, as indeed it was. But the motive for the burning of Moore Hall, as for the burning of many other country houses, was probably agrarian rather than political, the hope being entertained that, with the owners unable or unwilling to rebuild, division of the demesne lands (long ago prophesied by Moore) would be a speedy consequence of the incendiarism.

[1] Mr. Stephen Gwynn was Irish correspondent of the *Observer*.

Reilly sent his employer a detailed account of the outrage, and the account was so excellently done that Moore published it in the *Morning Post* with the alteration of one word (débris) only; the next day he sent his steward a cheque for twelve guineas. It was to Reilly, an intelligent and critical admirer of his writings, that he owed the preservation of the portrait of his grandfather, the possession that he cared most about at Moore Hall: a few months earlier his steward had observed that a bad spot caused by damp was appearing in the canvas; and Moore hearing of it directed that the picture should be taken from its frame and handed to Ruttledge to bring to London. It arrived at Ebury Street the day before the burning; and henceforth the distinguished old gentleman with the slightly tossed hair and chocolate coloured coat hung in a recess on the landing where Moore would often stop to gaze at him as he came down in the morning. He liked to think that it was a Wilkie, but in the Dublin National Gallery, where the charming portrait now hangs, it is attributed to Thomas Wyatt.

Moore's writings had animated the shores of Lough Carra with his presence and Moore Hall was become in recent years a place of pilgrimage for literary wayfarers in the West of Ireland. We have his letter to Mrs. Robinson Jeffers, the wife of the American poet, written a month or two before the burning; she had been " near to visiting Moore Hall," and her story drew his mind back, he said, to " years long past over. . . . A number of pictures rose up before me: your carriage driving through the gates, the winding avenue and myself on the steps waiting to receive you." Moore would rather almost anything had happened than this destruction but to his friends who condoled with him on the loss of his dreaming house he said: " Ireland is not a gentleman's country." A long letter to John Eglinton not only expressed his immediate pain and anger against Ireland, but also contained an interesting analysis of the intellectual relation between himself and the old friend who was so often his uncompromising critic.

16.8.23. *To John Eglinton.*

We are friends, but we are not reader and writer. We are friends because we are both animated by a dislike of the Irish character and papistry. No country is so foreign to me as Ireland, but I am not sure if this last sentence represents you. I think it does; you will never be at home in Ireland, and since the burning of my house I don't think I shall ever be able to bring myself to set foot in Ireland again. Wherefore I hope that you will come to England and that I shall spend some more evenings with you and renew a friendship that was laid many years ago and build again upon it. Our dislike of Ireland is a sufficiently broad basis for us to rear a noble fane of friendship; dislike of Ireland is deep enough in us, strong enough, close enough, intimate enough, for us to be able to scorn our literary differences. So convinced am I of this that I write without hesitation that you are without æsthetics and I [with] little else. These last words will perhaps seem to you hard to bear, but they are true and as they must be borne it would be well to recognise the fact and to bear it cheerfully. Perhaps you will understand me better if I say that you have only thought yourself out of dogma, but I was born outside it. . . .

We are not reader and writer, but something better, we are friends, and our friendship is built upon such a basis that your misunderstandings of my writings do not hurt me; indeed I like your misunderstandings, for they are yourself, and intensely yourself, a self which I would not change if I could, since it won my affection long ago and holds it still.

Having come forward with an explanation of your very perverse mind, or what seems to me your perverse mind, a mind that I once compared to a lonely hawthorn tree standing on a hillock, full of thorns and some blossoms, I hasten to repudiate the explanations that slipped from me. We are not reader and writer [not] because you did not compare one of my stories with one of Tourgenieff's. We are divided for much deeper reasons. We come from a different heredity, and circumstance in your

case favoured the Puritan seed. We were born, it is true, in
Ireland, but my cradle was rocked in the Nouvelle
Athènes.

Soon after this John Eglinton bade Dublin farewell,
reducing still further the number of friends remaining to
Moore on Irish soil. Longworth, Atkinson and Rolleston
now lived in London; and although A. E. and Martyn
remained in Ireland, neither of them now counted for much
in Moore's life. The detachment had been gradual; as late
as 1917 A. E. was still designated by Moore as his literary
executor. But a grievance, A. E's alleged collaboration
with Miss Mitchell in her book, had magnified itself as the
years passed. There was no open break, and A. E. used to
call upon his former admirer on the rare occasions when he
was in London. " A. E. has just been here " Moore once told
a friend. " After listening to his views on America for half
an hour, I said to him, 'Now A. E. what about a little chat?'"
Light polished conversation of the kind practised at Ebury
Street was one of the gifts with which the fairies had forgotten to supply the Irish mystic.

When *Hail and Farewell* was published Edward Martyn
said that he would not read the book because he wished to
remain friends with the author, but neither had now any
wish for the other's company, Martyn being wrapped up
in the preparation for death and Moore finding that an old
joke was wearing rather thin. A touch of rancour, however,
appears in a passage from an unpublished manuscript by
Martyn which Mr. Denis Gwynn has quoted in his *Edward
Martyn and the Irish Revival*: " Mr. George Augustus
Moore by constituting himself my Boswell has obtained a
certain notoriety of mean vanity like his prototype." When
Martyn died in 1923, Moore found that the two forgotten
plays *The Heather Field* and *Maeve* had been bequeathed to
him, a flash of humour on which he made no comment;
but he showed some emotion when he heard that, by another
direction of the will, Martyn's body was to be handed for
dissection to medical students and then buried in a pauper's
grave side by side with the unclaimed workhouse dead.

6

Between June and December in 1923, Moore published
two articles in the *Fortnightly*, both preparations for *Conversations in Ebury Street: Sunt Lacrimae Rerum*, a reverie of childhood, and another of his dialogues, " George Moore and
Granville-Barker." He had a continual preoccupation with
the theatre, and took a lively interest in the Phoenix Society
of which his old friend Lady Cunard was President. " My
admiration for this warm-hearted courageous woman
compels me," he told Granville-Barker, " to praise her
whenever her name is mentioned." At a performance of
Love for Love given by the Society he saw Athene Seyler:
" in a masterpiece easily the greatest comedy actress I have
ever seen." Miss Seyler played in his *Coming of Gabrielle*
when it was given during the summer for three matinées
at the St. James's Theatre. Her acting was greatly admired;
the play itself received trifling, if agreeable, notices from the
critics during the same week in which the newspapers were
filled with elaborate descriptions of the life and work of
Thomas Hardy, the Prince of Wales having just taken tea
with the author of *Tess* at Max Gate.

20.7.23. To Mrs. St. John Hutchinson.

Your pretty article is as pretty as one of your gowns,
flounced and garlanded. Thank you for sending it. I
was disappointed and dejected till I saw my comedy. I
saw it yesterday and it seemed to me one of the prettiest
comedies ever written. I cannot imagine anything better.
The press seemed to think differently but the journalists
will not quench so pretty a comedy and *The Coming of
Gabrielle* will add one more to the long list of mistakes.
It would seem that the press is never right. The articles
would not have mattered; it only needed half a dozen
performances for the comedy to collect an audience but
Faber is a sick man and must get a long rest. Athene was
even more wonderful than I thought she would be. Have
you been to the St. James ?

The plot had been changed once again since the last version of *Elizabeth Cooper*. The curtain now descended upon the foreign Countess, as the three weeks bride of Dayne, making an appointment in Venice with the great novelist. " A lollypop, but a very pleasant one," was his own description of the play.

His displeasure with Ireland did not prevent him from choosing that country for the scene of his new historical romance, *Ulick and Soracha*, and he was soon on the trail of some authority on the medieval period, whose knowledge he could use. Best recommended him to Professor Edmund Curtis, a young historian of Trinity College, Dublin, who had lately brought out *A History of Medieval Ireland*, but Moore found this book rather stiff reading. " The events are so numerous," he wrote to Curtis, " that I am sometimes a little blinded by the detail. You say on p. 131 : On May 25th, 1315, Edward Bruce landed, etc., but after the fall of Carrickfergus you seem to me to drop the story of the Bruces and tell the story of Richard de Burgo and other stories. On page 237 we return to Robert Bruce. Of course the story I am thinking of writing was not in your mind when you wrote your history. . . ."

History, it was clear, did not possess the " melodic line." Moore's interest in the period arose out of a desire to write a story about Castle Carra and his lake, and these places, he knew, had legendary associations with the Bruce invasion of Ireland. " It may hap that I may see you in Ireland," he was saying to Best in November, " a country I never intended to see again; but so vexatious and embarrassing is the river Shannon to me that I may have to go over to explore. . . . What a dreadful place, according to Mr. Curtis, Ireland was in the fourteenth century, the Scotch-Irish coming over, Bruce and company, ravaging, burning, destroying, creating famine everywhere they went. . . ."

10.2.23. *To E. C. Curtis.*

I am much obliged for your letter, which gives me nearly all the information I need. When you suggested

Ballintubber I smiled, for indeed I required no information about Ballintubber which was once my property.

For the romantic ride in search of a nun, 70 or 100 miles are necessary, and I wish you would suggest a convent in Westmeath. I cannot do with less than a two day's ride. The hero's name is definitely fixed, Ulick de Burgo. His valet's name is Teague O'Dorachy, an admirable name, and I am obliged to you for calling to my remembrance some characteristics of the race.

On his next visit to England Edmund Curtis was invited to dine at Ebury Street, "so that we may settle various questions over a good cigar, and you can tell me how you learned that difficult language Irish." Not having known Moore in his Dublin days, Curtis, whose interests centred in Ireland and the Irish language, felt a little shy of the great London author; and it was therefore agreeable to find that Moore still preserved his curiosity about the Gaelic past. To defend the language against the charge that, like the race, its promise was better than its performance, Curtis quoted a lovely eighteenth century poem, the title of which is (in Irish) "I am stretched upon your Tomb." The theme is that of a young man who spends every night lying upon his sweetheart's grave to the wonder of the people and the wrath of the clergy. Being much pleased with the music of the Irish and the skilful internal rhyming, Moore caused his guest to repeat several of the verses and to translate one of them:

> *Do you remember that night when you and I were*
> *alone together*
> *Under the foot of the thorn tree,*
> *With the night shedding its dews upon us?*
> *A hundred praises to Jesus*
> *That we committed no sin there,*
> *And that the crown of your virginity*
> *Is like a pillar of fire before you.*

When Curtis had finished reading he looked up, and saw that his listener's eyes were bright with unshed tears.

On another evening Moore spoke with delight of the story called " The Madness of Suibhne Geilt," and showing Curtis a favourite page, he asked him—thinking perhaps to put his guest's scholarship to the test—whether that kind of Irish (middle Irish) was very different from the modern. When Curtis replied that it was, he put one hand over the Irish Texts Society's translation, and asked him to translate from the original. It seemed that Moore recognised in the old Irish story tellers his own kin; but he complained that modern Irishmen lacked courage in all fields, except perhaps the military. " You should be writing the story of the Bruces," he said. " Ah, you Irish have no courage." The Irish language led to religion by way of the Bible, which, as both agreed, went excellently into Irish, until St. Paul was reached. Moore gave his reasons: the rest of the Bible is folklore, but with Paul, the intellectual, we ascend sharply into metaphysics. " Paul speaks," Curtis observed, " of the Last Supper as one who already accepts transubstantia-tion." From this Moore dissented, and continuing, he expounded the view that neither in the Gospels nor in the Epistles is any statement of the divinity of Jesus to be found. He seemed to be in a vein of contrariness and derision; but upon Curtis's quoting the text, " the true light which lighteth every man that cometh into the world," he allowed that such indeed was Paul's belief, and explained it as " that which was born with every man," the " something " that every man brings with him into the world: an unexpected concession from one who was reputed to be a philosophical materialist.

7

In 1923 Moore published *The Apostle*, a play founded not on the 1911 sketch of that name but on *The Brook Kerith*; there was one new invention, a scene with Priscilla, Aquila, Timothy and others at Cæsarea, ending effectively with the departure of Paul for Rome, watched by his dear friends. The text came out in a limited edition, Moore's only publica-tion in 1923, but besides beginning *Ulick and Soracha* he pre-pared several books for publication in the following year:

Conversations in Ebury Street and *The Pastoral Loves of Daphnis and Chloë* (also limited editions with Heinemann), a revised *Avowals*, and *Pure Poetry*. The new *Avowals* was the first of his books to be published in the form with the mottled covers which was afterwards adopted for the Uniform English edition of his works. He now began to choose the books which were to be allowed into this edition—his " canon "—some of the volumes which he was permitting into the American " Carra " edition being excluded. The Carra edition, twenty volumes by Boni and Liveright for subscribers only was completed in 1924; it contained four works which did not find their way into the " canon ": *Lewis Seymour and Some Women, Spring Days, Evelyn Innes* and *Sister Teresa*. *Impressions and Opinions* was rejected; but some essays from this book were preserved as an Appendix to the *Confessions of a Young Man*: " Le Revers d'un Grand Homme," " Mummer Worship," and " An Eighteenth Century Actress." The early paper on Balzac was rewritten, without the use of much new material, to suit the style of the *Conversations*; but the " Degas " of which Moore had spoken favourably to Barrett Clark was discarded.

He was pleased to receive the homage of young admirers, especially when they were young women of an attractive appearance. He would reply to their enthusiastic letters without condescension, interest himself in their personal affairs, even accept the rôle of a sort of pagan Father Confessor. His abundant sympathy was in fact, only a part of his intense curiosity: like Mdlle de Scudéry in Ste. Beuve's portrait he might have said: " I have lady friends who have been in love for me, and they have taught me to speak of it." Invitations to tea (or more rarely to lunch) would follow and sometimes an odd sort of intimacy would ensue, half exciting and half pathetic, the yawning gulf of the generations bridged by a flimsy structure of hero-worship on the one side and a not wholly sublimated sensuality on the other.

A clever eager-spirited girl who wrote to express her admiration of his work remembers the first invitation to tea which followed on their early correspondence. " My youthful imagination had not pictured a great author as a rotund old gentleman, not very tall, with a somewhat florid complexion, white hands which hovered over the tea table, and a great liking for hot buttered muffins. The famous drawing-room seemed to me to be Victorian and a little stuffy. I had never in my life conversed with so old a person, and I soon found that a gulf divided us. He was of the nineteenth century, I of the twentieth. I looked forward to what was to come, and he backwards, always to France and his life there. He stopped short at Turgenev and Manet, and cared for few of the modern authors whose names I tentatively mentioned. He would not discuss politics, and expressed but little sympathy with my regret at having missed a University education. His own education only began after it had ostensibly finished, he assured me, when he left England and went to France to study painting. He seemed to forget that the world was not composed of geniuses who can only develop their gifts by escaping from the common mould. I could not help being surprised by what seemed to me a reactionary outlook in one whom I had regarded as an apostle of freedom and a breaker of idols. Perhaps I had forgotten that his first novel was published in 1883."

Sometime later, on her way through London, she received an invitation to lunch. " During the meal he seemed a little distrait. I exerted myself to the utmost, but I could not find a topic which would interest him. Afterwards, in the drawing-room, he brought out a manuscript. It was part of *Ulick and Soracha*. ' Tell me,' he said, ' how this passage sounds to you ': whereupon he read in his pleasant Irish voice, beating out the rhythm with his hand, a piece of what seemed to me perfect English prose. I could not criticise so lovely a creation. But it seemed to me that in his eagerness to achieve perfection he had forgotten I was but an unknown literary aspirant, who could only appreciate the work of a master, not tear it to pieces. ' I shall have to rewrite all this,' he said sadly, ' it won't do, it won't do.' He kept on appealing eagerly, even pathetically, for my judgment on this word or that. When he spoke of his own work I found in him none of the vanity with which he has been charged."

Towards the end of 1923 *Ulick and Soracha* was laid aside that he might fulfil an engagement hastily entered into with his publishers: the translation of *Daphnis and Chloe*. We see him at his new task in letters which Lord Howard de Walden and Mrs. St. John Hutchinson received from him in the following April.

To Lord Howard de Walden.

I appreciated physically and mentally your gift of a fine salmon—the finest perhaps—at least as fine as any that I have eaten. If you are back in town I'd like to see you. I am translating *Daphnis and Chloë*, which I think is the beautifullest story in the world; there is too much kissing in it, and in this you will agree with me. I am using an old french translation principally and sometimes find myself stopped by a simple phrase. I cannot put English on this. " Or, parmi tels jeux enfantins amour leur voulut donner du souci." *Souci* is a difficult word and if I can I'd like to keep the phrase in its naked simplest. " In the midst of their childish games Love thought how he might put care upon them." Lumpy ! " Into their childish games Love thought how he might interject a care." Horrid ! The next sentence begins " In the neighbourhood there was a she-wolf, etc." Or, " Whilst they played childish games Love thought how he might worry them," how he might worry or tease them. " Love fell to thinking how he might tease them," " fret their lives with care, and in the neighbourhood there was, etc." " Love fell to thinking how he might tease them "—too pretty for the Greek, but mayhap I shall have to adopt it. Care seems unmanageable. I can't get the " leur voulut donner du souci," can you ? As it is too cold for water-colour painting you might try. I bet you can solve the riddle.[1]

To Mrs. St. John Hutchinson.

To day I finished the third book. One more remains to be done into English so you see I am a hermit. I had a

[1] In the book the sentence ran : But whilst they played Eros wrought trouble for them.

Greek scholar here the night before last but he was of little or no help, our points of view being opposed. After a long wrangle he rose and went to fetch a book he had brought with him and began to read a frightful farrago by an Oxford scholar called Jebb. I bore with it as long as I could, and at last cried: " But what you are reading is not English but a medley of Greek and English." He turned a plaintive nose in the air and answered " Perhaps you are right but I know Plato so well that I cannot detach myself." These scholars learn one language for the purpose, so it would seem, of dishonouring another. I have heard of Jowett, but who is Jebb ?

Many others besides T. W. Whittaker were called upon to speak of the Greek text with Moore, including Miss Mary Somerville from Oxford, who helped him also with other books and revisions, notably with *Ulick and Soracha*. She met him through Gosse who, half in fun, said he was not a proper acquaintance for her, adding however, that if she wished to learn how to develop a story she must go to school with Moore. Moore was told that he must behave—that on the very slightest complaints from the young woman he would suffer the direst penalties, be forbidden the house at Regent's Park, and so on.

He was more than ready to let people think that he was working direct from the Greek, and was incensed with Gosse who lured him into acknowledging his lack of Greek one Sunday afternoon at a tea party, after he had been talking of the book. Mostly he used the French translation of Paul Louis Courier, at first construing the French literally, then turning the result into his own English; if obscurities were encountered he turned to the old English translation by George Thornley. Miss Somerville has recalled for me one fantastic interlude, a wrangle about the position of the pool, πρὸ τοῦ ἄντρου. Moore shuffled nervously to and fro; where was he to place it, there, where the small table stood in the back drawing-room, or there, in the centre-piece of the Aubusson carpet? The sunlight suddenly falling on the centre-piece of the carpet decided the matter.

The remaining publication of 1924 was the beautiful Nonesuch *Pure Poetry*; the anthology which he had long meditated.

16.3.24. *To Miss Nancy Cunard.*

When you were a little girl I used to talk to you about an anthology of pure poetry but you were too young to understand objective poetry, and now the anthology is completed. Would that we had searched out the lovely flowers together but we cannot go searching for poetry whilst a sea is between us. I propose to cross the sea in May and to spend a month near Fontainebleau. Shall I see you or are you going to spend the month of June in London? The romantic story has been draughted in several dictations and only requires going over with the pen; and the title of the story for the moment is " The Rape of Saraha " (rape used in the original sense of *enlèvement*). But I am not satisfied. " Ulick and Saraka " is more reticent and I like reticence.

My love to your mother to whom I'd write if there was any chance of getting a letter.

The selection of pieces was discussed with John Freeman and Walter de la Mare in a dialogue which appears both in *Conversations* and as part of the introductory essay to the anthology. The rest of the essay consisted of a soliloquy on æsthetics, poetry and painting. It seems clear that Moore intended the book to be a work of scientific criticism, for he founds the notion of pure poetry on the uncertain ground of a distinction between the world of things which is " permanent " and ideas which are " ourselves " and ever changing: " We must stem the desolating tide of subjectivity." It is rather an over-simplified definition of the objective faculty to regard it as solely directed towards " things " —the sun, flowers, etc.—and in effect Moore's choice seems to have been really governed by a middle-aged distaste for what is metaphorically called philosophical poetry. But there are charming and characteristic touches in the essay, and it is a pity that he could not find a place for it in his collected works. The anthology itself begins with Skelton and closes with the famous spring chorus from *Atalanta in Calydon*, and contains all the obvious lyrics from Shakespeare, much Coleridge, Keats, Tennyson, Morris and Poe: no Wordsworth and less Herrick than one would expect. If he included nothing of the modern school it may have been from a diffidence to which, among his younger friends, he sometimes confessed. " I see now," he wrote to Miss Cunard, " that to be intimate with you I must study free verse else resign my post as critic of your verse and an exponent of your talent, and so I propose to read some of Eliot's verses with you when you come to London in 10 days or a fortnight. You shall be guide."

In May he went to Paris, having arranged to see Miss Rodgers and to put up at her hotel, but learned from the concierge that she had just gone away for a month. He " returned through the gardens bewildered and unhappy. . . . You knew I was coming to Paris to see you and that I had been working eight hours a day to free myself from Liveright for your sake. I have written three books inspired by a single hope, one I sent you, the others will be published in the autumn. I am free and you left Paris the night before I arrived." The episode was somehow accounted for, and Miss Rodgers offered him her Palais Royal apartment when she went to America. " But are we to be always a thousand miles apart ? " he wrote to her.

Very rightly he was pleased with *Conversations in Ebury Street*. " It is a gay book," he said in another of his letters to Miss Rodgers, " like a blackbird. I hop and I run, I cock my tail and I break into song."

By the autumn *Daphnis and Chloë* was ready. He had come to this work, as he put it later, trembling and frightened; but it was not long before it seemed to him that he was writing his most musical prose. With *Daphnis and Chloë* he proved by experience his theory that the translator of a masterpiece could enjoy all the pleasure of creative work and escape all its pain.

31.8.24. *To Miss Mary Somerville.*

. . . I am going to Gosse's tonight but shall not bring him the page proof of *Daphnis and Chloë* though I am more in love than ever with my translation. It seems to me to be the only thing worth doing that I have been able to do. I have redeemed the loveliest of stories from bad greek and bad english. To do so much is to have done something but that something does not seem much on this gloomy day in Ebury Street. Moreover one little sentence flylike troubles me and I wish you were here to help me to catch a lovely english equivalent. But if you were here you would hark back to scientific translation. Even Pater believed in exact following ' with no variation in structure, of word after word as the pencil follows a drawing under tracing paper.' But only a draughtsman can trace and the uninstructed would not know *what* to trace nor *how* to trace and only an artist can draw a line. The animal does not recognize a picture of his master, and a savage who had never seen a drawing of a man would not recognize that a drawing of a man was intended to represent a man. The savages and the animals know nothing of Nature for they have not art, in other words, and briefly, art created nature. I did not put all this into my preface for I did not want to repudiate the authority of Pater too violently which was perhaps wrong of me. We *translate* always into terms agreed upon ; sometimes the terms are good sometimes bad but in both cases we *translate* i.e. we recreate.

8

He suffered a great loss in the death of Tom Ruttledge whom he had designed to make his principal heir—" my oldest and dearest friend," Ruttledge is called in the inscription of a presentation copy of *A Story-Teller's Holiday.* Very few links with the old days in Mayo now remained. Common friends tried to mend the breach between George Moore and his brother ; and just before Ruttledge's death Colonel Moore himself sought conciliation.

December 24th, 1924.

My dear George,

Some months ago I passed the age of 70, and surely if ever, the time has come to survey the many years in the wake and to plot out the few that remain, so that they at least may be spent in happy quietude of mind and heart. You may remember that Tiresias said to Ulisses when he travelled to the land of the shades, " Your life shall ebb away very gently when you are full of years and peace of mind, and your people shall bless you." What more can the old desire when the passions that torture are gone and the loves remain in memories that are sweet.

The old, unlike the young, can gain peace by taking it, and I have resolved to hold it whether my people bless me or not. To attain the blessing one must abolish enmity, therefore I clear my conscience and say to you—the only person as far as I am aware with whom I have any quarrel, I forgive you any injury by word or deed you may have done me and I am sorry for any word or deed by which I may have caused you pain.

Yours affectionately,
Maurice Moore.

January 5th, 1925.

My dear Evelyn,

My brother has written me a letter saying that he will forgive me anything I may have done him if I will forgive him any wrong he may have done me. I have never done him any wrong, my conscience is quite clear, and as the past cannot be undone, there can never be any real forgiveness. This letter is not an attempt to enlist your sympathies, nor do I wish to enlist the sympathies of your son Maurice whom I liked very much when he came to see me at the end of the war. He wrote me a somewhat flamboyant letter about the burning of Moore Hall which I have not answered for the simple reason that I could not compose an answer that satisfied me. He is in America with his Aunt your sister and seems to be a resolute hard-working lad. I often think of the things he told me about the war, and every word he said endears me to him.

Affectionately yours,

George Moore.

In other members of his family Moore now seemed to have little or no interest. None of them came to his house. Yet he had not been ungenerous to his relatives in the past, and towards one of them at least he still showed solicitude of a practical kind.

After Ruttledge's death Moore entrusted a great part of his affairs to Mr. C. D. Medley, with whom also he struck up a lively friendship. One useful friend in Mayo he retained in the person of Mr. John Garvey, a lawyer with an important practice in that county, who during Ruttledge's illness handled his claims for compensation in the matter of the burning of Moore Hall. Moores and Garveys had been neighbours and landlords in the old times, and Moore took a great fancy to Mr. Garvey when some years previously they renewed acquaintance in Westport. A presentation copy of *Daphnis and Chloë* led Mr. Garvey, a member of the Irish Synod, to raise some objections to the book on the score of morality. Moore's reply is a pleasing example both of the respect he could show towards those who held sincere opinions and of his continuing desire to explain himself to those outside literary and artistic circles as well as to those within them. Mr. Garvey had expressed a wish that he would write something that would elevate humanity.

I think my answers will hush your scruples.

I know of no book that everybody can read. Books are written for different perceptions and different minds. . . . *Daphnis and Chloë* is a book for the few, and be sure that its beauty will keep it out of the hands of the vulgar. . . . *Daphnis and Chloë* was written seventeen hundred years ago and for seventeen hundred years the greatest minds in all countries have looked upon this tale as one of the most beautiful ever written. Amongst these was Amyot, a pious French bishop, who was the first translator of the tale;

another was Goethe considered to be one of the greatest
minds that has ever lived in this world. . . . Indeed it is
no exaggeration to say that every knee of consequence
has been bowed before *Daphnis and Chloë* for seventeen
hundred years, and I do not think that a book, a picture,
or a temple, that men have thought about and loved and
reverenced for seventeen hundred years can be reproved
with justice by any man living now. Anything that man's
thoughts have turned to during the course of the ages,
any oracle around which men's voices have hushed,
contains something in it of eternal worth, something that
cannot die and will return in different ages again and
again; and *Daphnis and Chloë* is one of these eternal
recurrences.[1]

The indelicacy of the subject shocks you, but is it more
indelicate than any great work ? Is it more indelicate than
Shakespeare and the Elizabethan dramatists ? I do not
think so. And I am certain it isn't more indelicate than
the Bible; do you remember *Chronicles* ?

I would remind you that Humanity has continued to go
its way through the ages always the same, never better,
never worse, taking to its bosom the artist who writes
about Humanity for Humanity without troubling to
point out which is the right road and which is the wrong
and casting out the preacher as a bore and a humbug.
You write in your letter that you are sure I will resent
your advice. I do not resent it; I beg you to believe that.
And my opinion of you is so high that I feel certain you
will appreciate my answer to your strictures.

9

The rewritten *Héloïse* came out in 1925 as the second
volume of the uniform edition, and *Hail and Farewell*
appeared in the same year as a member of the limited
edition for subscribers, divided into two volumes instead
of three and with a new preface " Art without the Artist."
Moore had worked on *Ulick and Soracha* through the winter

[1] An adaptation of a passage from Pater.

of 1924-5, and in a letter to John Garvey he described the
' new draft ' with enthusiasm. " It was all simple to me
except the beginning, and I began the story fifty times and
these fifty beginnings often brought my secretary to the
verge of tears. She has now confessed her tears—not very
long ago, for it is not so very long ago that this capricious
and intractable story ceased to kick and plunge and became
tractable, a perfect palfrey always looking round to see if
I am near and turning her left side for me to mount her."

In May he was in Paris, very happy about his book,
and very eager, as I myself remember, to discourse upon it
and upon the subject of the Bruces in Ireland. He was still
in search of someone who would undertake a history of the
Bruces: if neither Curtis nor Lord Howard de Walden
would do it why should not I ? It was the finest subject in
the world, and if he had been a younger man he would
have made it his own. He was asking himself—and the same
question is raised by Ulick in the story—why the Celts had
failed to dominate the British isles, as they might easily have
done, if Welsh, Irish and Scots had combined under Bruce
to break the Plantagenet power. The fact that such speculations could interest him shows that he still felt the Celtic
call; and it is worthy of mention that he wished at this time
to contribute an article in praise of the Irish language to a
Dublin magazine. Professor Curtis discouraged him, for he
thought that thirty years after the original adventure his
reappearance in this sphere would be past a joke.

To Mr. Vincent O'Sullivan, who met him on this visit
after an interval of many years, he seemed to have become
very British: *un vieux monsieur, très respectable* a French newspaper called him, rather to his displeasure. " He was
coming," says Mr. O'Sullivan, " from some entertainment
where he had found the Abbé Henri Bremond, recently
elected to the Academy, and the Abbé Mugnier, a wit and
much desired guest at dinner parties. Moore was ready as
usual to talk of his latest book, and one of the abbés asked
to see it. ' I will send it to you with great pleasure,' he
replied, ' but I ought to warn you that it contains some
passages that are perhaps unfitted——!' ' Bien sûr, bien sûr!'

murmured the abbé blandly. To Moore, who had no doubt
formed his notion of Catholic priests from what he had seen
in Ireland, this first contact with the liberal and highly
cultivated clergy of France was astonishing ' Those Abbés !
Never shall I forget them. *Bien sûr, Bien sûr !* ' "

" I had come recently from Prague," Mr. O'Sullivan
continues, " and I had bought a hat there—a hat, I may say,
which would have aroused no notice in any Continental
city, and which Moore in his unregenerate days would have
passed easily enough. But now with eyes trained to St.
James's Street he was rather shocked. ' That is a very odd-
looking hat you have,' was all that he said directly on the
subject. But the hat pervaded his talk. Whenever he wanted
to draw a comparison he took it either from my hat or from
the very English-looking bowler which lay on his knees.
Not long did he let me forget my hat, whether the topic was
religion, the English novelist, the French poets, his own
latest book, or Edgar Allan Poe. In this last conversation I
was ever to have with him it was no longer a temperate
admiration for Poe that he showed, but enthusiasm. He
provoked me to some objections, and the dispute waxed hot,
for I was far enough by this time from the awe of my young
days. I did not see why I should be bullied into silence
because George Moore had laid down the law. If I had
realised his age I should have been more respectful, but I
never thought of him as an old man."

The house in Fontainebleau had been closed or let, so
there was an end (as he expressed it in a letter which Miss
Somerville has shown me) of " the forest, the terrace, the
shelving swards so often written about and the poets who
used to collect there to talk about Mallarmé from dewy
morning to evening, *albe et rose*."

Moore wrote a sonnet of farewell which exposed him to
" many invitations from countesses with literary tastes."
Gosse did not like the sonnet; but " many countesses read it,
and some few transcribed it in their albums." The octave
was as follows:

> *Adieu, Val Changis, à jamais !*
> *Forêt, pelouse, et la terrasse*

GEORGE MOORE IN DUJARDIN'S GARDEN

Ou j'ai vu groupé tout Parnasse
Depuis vingt ans au mois de Mai.
Nous ne reverrons désormais
La nymphe de si bonne face
Qui pose le pied avec grace
Malgrè mon très mauvais français.

But in spite of this defection Paris agreed with him so well that he began again to regret that he was not more often there, and even suggested to Miss Cunard an interchange of houses ; yet another collaboration which came to nothing.

August 20th 1925.

Dearest Nancy,

When I was your age a french writer said to me : you are missing your chances of becoming an english writer by living in France. On looking back I cannot avoid the conclusion that I should not have done as well as I have done if I had not returned to England. We must live a great deal in the country we address. Now what do you think of this ; well, you can live in my house in Ebury Street for six months of the year and let me live for six months in your flat ? A very simple arrangement. You will pay my servants and I'll pay yours. The arrangement from a literary point of view will be highly beneficial.

Always dearest yours affectionately
George Moore.

10

The award for the destruction of Moore Hall amounted to a little over £7000. Moore was pleased, for he could never have sold the intact mansion for that sum. Nevertheless, he continued to cherish the opinion that he would be lucky if his days did not end in the workhouse, and he chose to describe the £7000 as something that had been saved from the wreck of his fortunes. " I am distraught," he wrote to John Garvey. " The difficulty of investing the money is very great. . . . What do you think of Conversion $3\frac{1}{2}$. . . .

I always hear it is better to spread out one's money. Africans are well reported. Can you throw any light on these perillous questions?" And he was inconsolable, when in the act of stamping a letter he tore a five centime stamp. " Oh, my Lord ! Look what I've done ! " To Mrs. Crawford and other friends he declared quite seriously that need would compel him to lecture in America, and to guard against the perils of Communism he kept an account in three London banks. On the other hand, he never spared expenses over his books; his endless proof corrections must have cost him a small fortune, and he was very conscientious in persuading his less opulent friends who helped him in his writing to accept generous payment for their trouble.

8.12.25. *To John Garvey*.

I was glad to get your letter, for I often think what a pleasant thing it would be to start from Dublin to pay you a visit at Loughlinstown House. I am glad to hear that *Hail and Farewell* amuses you. It will hardly fail to amuse you, and as you read on you will find that the narrative is enriched at every moment by new and often unexpected matters. . . .

I enclose a cutting from the *Daily Mail* and from this you will learn that the compensation I received for the burning of Moore Hall will have to be augmented by 10 per cent.

Ulick and Soracha was ready in the summer of 1926 after an unexpected delay, caused in the first instance by the preparation of a text of *The Brook Kerith* for an illustrated edition, and in the second by further rewritings. As Mr. Charles Morgan has explained in his *Epitaph on George Moore*, he would redictate from his first rapid draft, after having revised it to some extent with his pen, sometimes using this draft for no more than a sentence or two and handing his secretary, who was often distracted by his driftings to and fro, what was in effect a new draft unconnected with the old: the process was repeated again and again in the case of *Ulick and Soracha*. In one of the early copies there was a wonderful elaboration of the rock-blasting incident in the account of the De Burgo stronghold on Lough Carra. The physicist, Mr. F. C. Turner, was called in to throw light on some researches which Miss Somerville, at Moore's instance, had undertaken into fourteenth century pumping. Moore wanted to spray cider from a distance upon the heated rocks in the moat. He could not grasp the problems of physics involved in turning the entrails of a bull into a hosepipe, and he was with difficulty dissuaded from adopting the expedient of making the soldiers hoist the barrels of cider into a fir tree in order to obtain the necessary pressure. Moore, it seemed to Miss Somerville, identified himself with his characters, and she believed him when he told her that while writing certain passages of *Sister Teresa* he used to feel as if he were himself a nun. His characters were not criticised and annotated in advance; and in the scene in question from his Irish story Bridget's talk with the soldiers showed his own irritable and stubborn incomprehension when confronted with the laws of physics.

There were many lovely episodes in the final version: in a letter to Best about the book he pointed in particular to the meeting between Ulick and his father after Ulick's return to Ireland. " Tolstoi," he observed, " would have written this scene exceedingly well. My scene is just a little better than my contemporaries would have written it." The work was destined to add a second volume to *A Story-Teller's Holiday* when this took its place three years later in the uniform edition. It took the shape of a further conversation with the Westport fern gatherer, the love story and travels of the Norman knight being related by Moore and the end of Tadgh O'Dorachy, a sort of coda, coming from Alec Trusselby.

21.7.26. *To John Garvey.*

I should have written to you before to thank you for the efforts you are making to save enough money out of the wreck of my fortunes to enable me to live to the end of the chapter in comfort; but a crazy piece of work—the preparation of the text of *The Brook Kerith* for an illustrated edition—has kept me grinding away. It would take too long to explain the wearisomeness of these days. . . .

Ulick and Soracha seems to be well received and the faults in the book that vex me do not appear to be perceived by others. There will be some things in it you will regret and some things you will like, but I don't think you will like the book as well as *Héloïse and Abélard*.

I was disappointed that you did not come on to London when you were in Nottingham, within three hours of Ebury Street. It was worth your while to cross the sea and travel many miles to see a cricket match, and not worth your while to travel three hours to London.

1.8.26. *To John Garvey.*

You have worked wonders and provided me with a feeling most pleasurable to me—gratitude. I was always your friend instinctively from the first and I remember the day when we discussed St. Paul in Tom Ruttledge's garden. I don't think I have seen you since and that carries me on to the cricket match which you came to see and which I hoped would bring you to London. . . . But we shall meet again for I shall go over to Ireland to see you; I cannot say when, but I shall go; and the journey will not be long delayed.

Ulick and Soracha has been well received and is spoken of as one of my best books. But there is sorrow everywhere—sorrow that I have come to the end of my stories mayhap, and sorrow that your gout spoilt the cricket match for you and prevented you incidentally from coming to see me, and sorrow too that gout may keep you out of your business. A man is never well without his business. Remain in it as long as you can despite your investments. I have some valuable pictures and am thinking of selling them and putting the money into American Liberty Bonds, which I suppose is the safest investment.

He had some "lovely subjects" in his head : one concerned a young sculptor who sees two girls swimming across a strait and then admiring themselves on the bank, in this way providing inspiration for a statue of Aphrodite. This was afterwards an episode in the last of Moore's novels *Aphrodite in Aulis*. About this time he revised *Peronnik the Fool*, a short romance, developed from a hint in *Héloïse and Abélard*, which had first appeared two years before in the Carra edition, and was ultimately reprinted with *Daphnis and Chloë* in the Uniform English edition.

II

The revisions of old books continued, generally but not always to their advantage. Moore's early autobiography should certainly have been left untouched as it had gushed in all its immaturity from the unconscious in 1886, the spontaneous reflection of a period and a mood. But a new edition now came out, showing the changes which had been made in the book since the 1904 issue. Though not extensive they were not confined to points of style and grammar, and some of them exemplify in an odd way Moore's tendency to see his work outside space and time. He could not, for instance, forbear from substituting " to talk to us, the legitimate children of the nineteenth century, of proofs that we ought to believe in the Catholic God," for " to talk to us . . . of logical proof of the existence of God."

For some time past he had been in search of an illustrator. Tonks did not want to help him in this way because he felt sure that his attempts would end in trouble, as they did. He made a number of illustrations for " The Lovers of Orelay " and when they were done Moore said they would not suit because the longest measurement must correspond to the height of the book. Tonks then introduced him to a young student from the Slade School, who seemed to be the very man he wanted. Rex Whistler was hardly known at that time, but when Tonks saw him at the beginning of a term at the Slade School he at once recognised his very considerable gifts and remarkable inventive faculty. He was certain he would make Moore's book, just as Tenniel made *Alice in Wonderland*.

Whistler showed Moore some of his sketch-books, but Moore could see nothing in rough sketches, and wanted Whistler to bring elaborated drawings for the book. Whistler brought the finished drawings, but as they seemed to reveal something in the book hidden to Moore, he said that he must have others, and finally Whistler, much disappointed, gave up the attempt. The story of the illustrations for *The Brook Kerith* is a very different one. Moore discovered Stephen Gooden for himself, and informed Tonks one evening that the right man had appeared. " Oh, I remember Gooden," Tonks said, " I knew him as a student at the Slade School where he did some very good drawings, besides this I lately came upon certain fresh illustrations of his which surprised and pleased me; in fact, when I first saw them, being engravings, I did not associate them with a student of the Slade School." It displeased Moore to hear that Tonks had known Gooden for so long; he wanted to think of the artist as his own discovery. When the great question of the engravings for *The Brook Kerith* came up, Tonks learnt from Gooden that he had become an engraver by practising with the engraving tools of a relation, and to some purpose, for he was now as good a copper-engraver as could be found. At first all went well between Moore and Gooden and an engraving as a frontispiece for *Ulick and Soracha* was accepted after some criticism. But in the matter of *The Brook Kerith* Gooden showed a proper desire that his own interests should be respected and made a businesslike arrangement that he should produce so many illustrations. Moore then, as one could have foretold, began to criticise the designs and said disagreeable things about them. Gooden was not in the least disconcerted, and continued with the work and gradually Tonks noticed that as Moore received the proofs he became more and more inclined to praise them, until finally he became Gooden's most devoted admirer.

12

A very able man, whom Moore now saw frequently, was the late G. Leverton Harris, an M.P. who had held office in

"THE CONVERSATION THEN TURNED ON TONKS"

From a water-colour by Henry Tonks

Left to right: George Moore, Henry Tonks, L. A. Harrison, P. W. Steer, Nelson Ward

the Government during the war. Moore established a great
friendship with both Leverton Harris and his wife. Leverton
Harris, when over fifty, discovered that he had a considerable
gift for painting, with the result that he became a student at
the Slade School: Tonks introduced Moore to him with some
trepidation, and Moore met someone who could out-talk
him. Almost up to the end of his life, he was generally glad
to meet new people, when he was advised beforehand, but
liking did not always follow upon meeting, and during an
evening he would often change from an amiable man into a
morose and silent one because someone had entered the
room, thereby destroying the flow of a conversation in which
he was deeply interested. But if his host talked on, regardless
of his presence, and by chance hit on a subject that revealed
the new-comer as a man who knew a good deal about a
subject of interest to him, Moore would at once join in the
conversation as if nothing had happened. Once Tonks and a
number of his friends were dining at the house of L. A.
Harrison in Cheyne Walk; Moore sat on the right hand of
his host. All went very well and he was in good form until
Harrison reminded Nelson Ward about a series of caricatures
by Tonks which were to be shown to the guests. Nelson Ward
then produced the caricatures, laying them on the table, and
as was perfectly natural they were looked at and commented
on by everybody; in other words the conversation then
turned on Tonks. This was too much for Moore, who pushed
his chair back from the table and sat gazing into vacancy
exactly like a sulky child. He never knew of it, but Tonks
made a somewhat elaborate illustration of the scene.

Tonks' Saturday evenings at the *Vale*, Gosse's Sunday
suppers and an occasional good concert were now his chief
pleasures. Long train journeys into the country caused him
no discomfort and he used to descend from time to time upon
John Eglinton in north Wales, and upon the Granville-
Barkers in Devonshire. He usually came home from these
expeditions sooner than his servants expected, but the reason
was the desire to continue his writing, not an old man's wish
for his fire-side. A difficulty arose with English men of
letters whom he knew: most of them were friends of Thomas

Hardy, and it was uncomfortable to meet Hardy after having been in Moore's company, as Hardy showed that he knew very well what Moore had been talking about. After having had his fling at the Wessex novels in *Conversations in Ebury Street*, Moore might have left the subject alone, but he could not do so: the Wessex novels replaced Catholicism as his favourite object of attack.

" Intellectually," Tonks writes, " Moore developed, he was learning to the end, but he was still as incapable as a child of four of grasping that there are other individuals who can make themselves unpleasant if he does not learn to curb his temper and his desires and to keep his feelings to a certain extent to himself. The world was his. Yet to learn to live alone is essential to those who wish to gather something of the mysteries of life; be he scholar, writer or artist he must develop something of the divine selfishness; this quality Moore certainly had, but he might have shocked fewer people if he had learned to make his selfishness less obvious."

For a long time he avoided the subject of the disabilities of old age, but gradually he seemed to mind less when Tonks or Steer spoke of it, until he became so interested in his condition of impotency that he would talk at length about it. He lamented the state, but as a philosopher he felt it right to give his friends the benefit of his experiences, and his life as a lover still seemed to be the centre of his being. His artist friends used to warn him that in the free use of forbidden words he was now slipping behind; it amused him to be told this: at least he had shown the way. When writing his story of the Greek sculptor, *Aphrodite in Aulis*, he was always asking what he should call that part of the human form known to anatomists as the gluteal region; there was the obvious and familiar word " bottom " of course, or " buttock," or he might have included it as belonging to the general term " flanks," a word he was fond of using though he was never able to say exactly where the flanks began or ended; none of these would do and he finally decided on " rump," which seemed a rough word to describe the chief charms of Venus Callipyge.

Nearly everyone who tried to paint a portrait of him

suffered considerably. He was generally pleased to pose and the first sitting used to go off well, but as the work progressed he grew more and more displeased and would hardly look at it. Steer gave him a portrait which he had painted of him, but no one who came to Ebury Street was given a chance of seeing it. After Moore's death Tonks asked Clara where the portrait was, and she said that one day on going to find Moore in a kind of box-room at the top of the house she saw him hard at work rubbing the paint off the portrait and afterwards cutting the canvas with a knife: an act of vandalism which greatly distressed Steer when he heard of it.

CHAPTER X

EBURY STREET: THE END

I

AT THE END OF HIS LIFE, however difficult his friends
may often have found him, there was an excuse ready to
hand, if he had wished to give an excuse. Moore was a
suffering man, often a grievously suffering man. His splendid
health had begun to be troubled; he complained of difficulties during micturition, but neglected for too long to
take medical advice, waiting, indeed, until the pain had
become unendurable. At last he was fortunate enough to
fall into the hands of Sir John Thomson-Walker, certainly
the most distinguished of surgeons in that branch of work,
who did all in his power to make life endurable for him.
Not only was Sir John a great surgeon, but he soon became
a sincere friend of Moore, and it is to him that *Aphrodite in
Aulis,* the last of Moore's finished works, is dedicated.

Moore had at first no idea that this book would develop
as it did. The incident, already mentioned, of the bathers
was what first attracted him, but after a while he said that
he should begin earlier (the beginnings were always his
problem) with Rhesos's (the young sculptor's) father setting
out from Athens to Aulis, and in this way Kebren gradually
became the central figure in a story of Greek family life and
the swimming episode only one of various inventions and
incidents. *Aphrodite in Aulis* is set in the fifth century B.C.,
but Moore said afterwards that " small gentry " poisoned
the book, a remark to be elucidated by recalling that at the
close of the eighties, while he lived with the Bridgers at
Shoreham, he had planned a modern novel on the subject
of old people watching their children grow up and go out
into the world.

Contrary to his usual custom, Moore preserved in the case of *Aphrodite* a large number of documents relating to the work on hand : letters from John Eglinton, T. W. Whittaker, E. V. Longworth, Roderick Enthoven (the architect), S. C. Atchley of the British Legation in Athens, sketches of his own for various passages, and so on. In March 1927 he was searching for good names for his characters, and many of those which he adopted were provided for him by John Eglinton : Kebren, Earine, Thrasillos and Rhesos for the two brothers, *Rhesos and Thrasillos* being the title which he gave the book at first. On an introduction from Mr. John Penoyre of the Hellenic Society, he began, in May 1927, to write to the late Mr. Shirley Atchley. The swim was still the central episode.

I would prefer the two young girls to swim the strait than to cross it by the bridge—*une bien plus jolie entrée en matière*, and my hope is that you will write : " at certain hours of the day, between ebb and flow, there is little or no tide." The girls come over to bathe, and it will be kind of you to mention that there is a pretty cove on the mainland that might tempt them over, the " pretty cove " is of no consequence; though it does not exist to-day it might have existed 440 B.C. My name : George Moore, is fairly well known in the world of letters—you may have heard of *Esther Waters, The Brook Kerith, Héloïse and Abélard.*

In a further letter to Mr. Atchley he said :

The young sculptor, who is lying among the rosemary hoping that Aphrodite will appear and instruct him in the statue he is minded to carve of her, will catch sight of the maidens admiring each other's figures, and they, being uncertain which is the better, call him to decide the point. I need hardly say that this is not the whole of my story but merely an incident in the story, and of course I shall be able to write it a great deal better if I know exactly the possibilities of swimming from one shore to the other ... I am sorry to trouble you with questions, but you have invited me to do so, and if you would care to read any book of mine I shall be only too pleased to send it to you. I have written better than *Esther Waters*. Would you like a copy of *Héloïse and Abélard*?

At the end of June, he was able to post a typescript to John Eglinton, which showed the arrival of his rhapsodist Kebren at Aulis and his discourse to the household of Otanes, the shipbuilder, on the origin of the *Iliad* in Helen's beauty as a religious idea, Kebren saying that many beautiful episodes in the fall of Troy were rejected by the framer of the *Iliad* and—Moore's own voice—that there is more eyesight in the blind Homer than in any other poet.

25.6.27. *To John Eglinton.*

I think that in the revision I shall limit the lecture to two things : first, how the *Iliad* came to be written. From that there seems to be no escape, any more than there is an escape ir an introduction to a book from stating when the writer flourished. In painting a full face the artist must put two eyes; from the two eyes there is no escape. After the account of how the *Iliad* came to be written I think I shall go on, as in the text, to Helen. Cebren can break down at any point, and he had better break down when he has said all that he has to say about Helen . . . In the next chapter he will remember with some bitterness all that he omitted to say overnight. . . . He is sure that if he hadn't been overcome by fatigue and had made plain that all Greek art, literature, sculpture and architecture, was derivative of Helen (that is to say, the *Iliad*) Otanes would certainly have invited him to stay a few more days in his house. . . . The beginnings of every story try me to the utmost, and it is the beginnings of stories that will end by preventing me from writing any more . . .

The opening continued to trouble him. " The ends of stories," he wrote to S. C. Atchley, " have no difficulties for me : the end leads me as a magnet leads."

Mr. Atchley affected some concern for the reputation of the bathers: " Your young ladies would probably be less likely to be seen if they took their bath to the north." But in a series of letters he supplied voluminous and useful details concerning the width and current of the Euripos and, later, still fuller descriptions of the scenery along the road between Athens and Aulis. After assimilating the information, Moore sent a draft of the opening chapter to Atchley, who commented upon it minutely. That he should have occupied so much of his time and the time of his correspondent with the business is an instance of his thoroughness, for the whole episode of the journey is told in six and a half pages of the book.

The year did not pass without the usual revisions, the most important of them ending in the republication of the book of short stories, *In Single Strictness*, under the title, *Celibate Lives*. The text varied from the original by the substitution of the tale " Albert Nobbs " (from *A Story-Teller's Holiday*) for " Hugh Monfert." It was not one of Moore's most popular books; again his gifts as a short story writer failed to receive their due acknowledgment. The reviewers neglected *Celibate Lives*, but he was too bewitched with his Greek story to have time to complain. Strolling with D. S. MacColl across Hampstead Heath, on an afternoon of the autumn, he was told that his sculptor was very much post-Phidian, but about this he did not care. During their walk Moore surprised his companion by observing: " You write much better than I do." " I relieved his mind," says MacColl, " by criticising my own book, *Nineteenth Century Art*, which he thereupon urged me to revise. Afterwards I sent him a copy."

—.9.27. *To D. S. MacColl.*

My belief in your literature was declining but the magnificent book you sent me has revived it and I hasten (it was only to-day that I cut the string) to congratulate you. My afternoon has gone by very pleasantly reading your beautiful descriptions of the pictures that I have thought about since I began to be æsthetic. . . . I do not share all your opinions. Poor Burne-Jones presents a forlorn spectacle. But Lady Lilith looks well enough. There was a painter in Rossetti ruined by a certain faculty for writing verse. . . . When you have an evening to spare come to dinner or shall I have to wait until you move from the hill to the plain ? I cannot close this letter without one more compliment. You have written one first-rate book and one first-rate book is enough.

In November he had put on paper a sort of text for *Aphrodite* up to the last chapter, and was preparing *Hail and Farewell* and the *Memoirs of My Dead Life* for their appearance in the Uniform edition of his works. (The trilogy was not, however, published in this form until 1933.) In the final edition of the *Memoirs* he omitted " Lui et Elles," apparently on literary rather than on personal grounds, bringing the " Elizabeth " of this story (and of *Vale*) into the first of the sketches " Spring in London," where also there was an interesting example of one of his constant devices to obtain smoothness and continuity in his prose. The general habit of authors is naturally to give a new thought a new sentence ; Moore would insinuate a fresh idea in the last clause of a sentence, restate it after the full stop, and so bind it close to the next movement of his thought.

Park Lane dips in a narrow and old-fashioned way as it enters Piccadilly. Piccadilly has not yet grown vulgar, only a little modern, a little out of keeping with the beauty of the Green Park, of that beautiful dell, about whose mounds I should like to see a comedy of the Restoration acted.

I used to stand here at this very spot, twenty years ago, to watch the moonlight between the trees, and the shadows of the trees floating over that beautiful dell ; I used to think of Wycherley's comedy, *Love in St. James's Park*, and I think of it still. In those days the Argyle Rooms, Kate Hamilton's in Panton Street, and the Café de la Régence were the fashion. . . .

So we read in the previous editions; but now:

Here is Piccadilly, and forgetful of Elizabeth and of catching cold I stand at gaze, thinking that Piccadilly has not yet grown vulgar, only a little modern, a little out of keeping with the beauty of the Green Park, remembering that it was my wont to linger here some twenty years ago, watching the moonlight between the trees with the shadows of the trees floating over that beautiful dell, thinking of Wycherley's comedy, *Love in St. James's Park*. I think of it still, and how in the days agone the Argyle Rooms, Kate Hamilton's in Panton Street, and the Café de la Régence were the fashion.

Here we observe, in its smallest manifestation, Moore's ceaseless care for the flow of his writing; what he did with the sentence he did also with the paragraph, the episode, indeed with the whole story. We reach the great moments as though round the bend of a river: however astonished and moved we may be, the stream is unruffled. In *The Brook Kerith*, which had followed *Celibate Lives* into the Uniform edition, there were many changes, mostly directed towards this continuity. Moore's paragraphs, already longer than those of most authors, become still longer, and the story proceeds more than ever by its own impetus. He perceived that the first edition contained clumsy or colourless pieces of writing, which he cut out altogether: for example, such things as this sentence in the description of Mathias's discourse to the Essenes :

He was willing, however, to conclude that his manner of treating the Scriptures was not approved by the entire community, but in view of his learning, the proselytes were not admitted to his lectures—one of the innovations of the President who, in spite of all, remained one of his supporters.

During all this time he was feeling very miserable, and could not be cheered by the news from Gosse that the Prince of Wales had entered a bookshop and bought three of his books. He spoke of a month in Paris: " I shall not allow the Continental to entrap me," he wrote to Miss Rodgers. " I shall come straight to you, and we will play at Darby and Joan." But by the beginning of 1928 he doubted if he would ever be able to accept an invitation again.

His own doctor and a surgeon dwelt on the gravity of his condition, and he fixed up a few matters that were on his conscience.

4.2.28. *To E. V. Longworth.*

Your remarks enabled me to remove from the *Memoirs* many little indulgences which would fret the ear and the eye of the æsthetic reader. I am now sending you pages 113–176. The first pages of " The Lovers of Orelay " were included in the last signature, and have been returned to the printer. I am not very well at present and would like to get this pretty trivial book off my hands. *A Story-Teller's Holiday* needs more correction and is worthier of it.

Other letters show him in negotiation with the Land Commission, which was about to take over Moore Hall and the land adjoining, the last few hundred acres of his Mayo property. The demesne was repurchased from the Commission by Colonel Moore, in the hope that it might be preserved in the family; it has lately been sold for the price of the woods to a timber merchant.

2

On the 7th of February he called on Sir John Thomson-Walker, who has kindly furnished me with an account of the visit :

It was in the late afternoon at a time that I spent with my secretary, struggling with a heavy correspondence. I had gone through the hall to look for a paper and found an elderly gentleman arguing with my butler and insisting in loud tones that he must see me at once. I did not know who he was but he was evidently a very obstinate

person and the quickest way, in the end, would be to
see him. I learned that he had just consulted a surgeon
who told him that he had only fourteen days to live and
that immediate operation was necessary. With this the
patient did not agree and he arrived at my door to follow
the first advice of his doctor. He was seriously ill, suffering
from a form of diabetes and from an enlargement of the
prostate gland.

I told him how seriously I regarded his condition and
said that immediate operation was out of the question.
He should enter a nursing home without delay and remain
under treatment for some time before any operation could
be attempted.

Then began an argument that I was later to recognise
as the preliminary to any arrangements that ran contrary
to his views. He was no worse than he had been for
months past except for the effect of the knowledge I had
imparted and the shock that the previous surgeon had
given him; he had a book in his mind that must be written
whatever the risk, and, moreover, if he had the book in
skeleton he could work at it during the long days of
convalescence which I had led him to expect. He would
require two months to do it.

A week convinced Moore that he was unfit to write anything, but it did not lessen his independence. On the 14th
he entered a luxuriously equipped nursing home. There
was a cab-rank below his window and as the theatres and
concert halls emptied there was some bustle and talk in the
street. In his wrath Moore rose and toured the corridors in
his nightshirt, summoning the nurses and matron to remove
him to some other room, the best, at the back of the house.
His surgeon, he swore, would never allow his patients to be
so tortured. It was like trying to sleep between the rails in
Waterloo Station at the height of the holiday season. When
Sir John arrived the next morning the exhausted matron
explained the situation and prepared him for trouble. " Is
it true," Moore asked, " that Isidore de Lara slept in the
room I occupied last night ? " " It is true." " And he made

no complaint ? " " None." " Ah ! " said Moore, " de Lara suffers from a strange disease, unknown to medical science: the name of the disease is ' The Garden of Sleep.' Forty years ago he composed that air and for forty long years it has been circulating in his brain, torturing him and banishing sleep. The noise of that street drove for a few brief hours the jangle of his song from his brain and he had peace and slept."

Many friends visited him and he dictated letters to his secretary.

20.2.28. *To Mr. and Mrs. St. John Hutchinson.*

My dear Friends

You have sent me the flowers that I love most of all, anenomes, and I would try to put my appreciation of these flowers into words if I were not lying in a Nursing Home. Many thanks. I hope to be well in a month and to be dining with you or you with me.

Always affectionately yours
George Moore

A few days later another brief note arrived " for Jack and Mary Hutchinson." It ran: " *Anenomes.* The petals scan the weary hours while George Moore dreams of his friends."

29.2.28. *To Sir Edmund Gosse.*

I tried three or four subjects of conversation, but nothing seemed to interest you, and you left in what seemed to me like a great hurry just as I was going to tell you about my literary project of five articles, French landscapes, with a French book in each.

I can see you perched quite comfortably sitting on the bridge at Chinon, turning over the leaves of a purchase made in the '80's or the '90's, and I can see you—oh, what nice days those would be, seen through a drift of your prose: the early mornings, the starts; the luncheons, the omelettes, the dinner in a new town, and always a new book to say something about ! I raise my hand against Victor Hugo, Baudelaire and Villon; they are too far away and the world is weary of them; and I clamour for an article on the poet who hanged himself—this time a literary article, very little about the Gustave Doré alley and some nice touches about the landscape round Ermenonville. There are, of course, many others.

You have often given me a hint. Why shouldn't I give you one? As soon as you are well come to see me, and we'll improvise the five articles together. I am as agile as an Italian greyhound going through hoops at improvisation! Do come; we shall have such fun.

1.3.28. *To Lady Cunard.*

My dear Maud,

This letter is to confirm all I said to you last night: that if I should die before you, most of my property will come to you. But the part of my property that will interest you will be my books, and to keep them in publication, properly advertised, and printed, you will need an editor, and I am sure that you will never find one who will be able to assist you as well as my old friend, W. K. Magee. I shall leave him £200 or so for the task, which is a light one, and of course if you should absorb more of his time than at first seems necessary, you will know how to reward him.

The first job of work he will undertake will be the publication of part of my correspondence with Dujardin. He will translate the letters from French into English, and he'll write a Memoir. He knew me in Ireland when I came over as a sort of troubadour to help the Irish to do the very thing they didn't want to do, which was to retain their own language. Those were days of storm and stress that he'll be able to tell the story of from a different point of view from the one adopted by me in *Hail and Farewell*; and then he'll be able to say a great many things to the right and to the left which will interest many readers. *The Brook Kerith* for instance, has never been prefaced properly as yet. I have written for it lines of introduction, but *The Brook Kerith*, as it is the only epical narrative in the English language, deserves a preface of, shall we say, ten or fifteen pages, and nobody will be able to write these pages better than Magee. And there are a hundred other things which I needn't worry my head about now.

Magee will be passing through London in a few days, and I wish you would write to him at:—

The Arlington, Exeter Park, Central Gardens, Bournemouth, asking him to come to see you on the subject. It would be well worth while that you should meet and have a few words together.

Always affectionately yours

George Moore.

His condition was worse than was anticipated; there was a high percentage of poison in his blood. Always he talked of his books, even when he was desperately ill with uræmia; and he gave to his surgeon a copy of *Héloïse*, with this inscription on the flyleaf:

To Sir John Thomson-Walker.

We have a tryst for the eating of a dinner in the summer at The Ship, Greenwich, and my regret is that our tryst is not at Meung where Héloïse and Abélard breakfasted on an excellent piece of shad in the 12th century.

Shad is unknown to you and it would have been a pleasure to me to have initiated you into its delicacies.

But all good fortune may not happen.

George Moore, March 26th, 1928.

When he might not talk of his books he became very restless. Tonks was Sir John's great support, for he knew Moore so well that he could understand, and to some extent, control his whims and fancies; his surgical knowledge made full discussion easy and profitable.

E. V. Longworth was called in because it was on Moore's mind that all his remaining strength should go into the completion of *Aphrodite*, and that his new edition of *A Story-Teller's Holiday* might therefore have to go without a preface. Longworth promised a preface to his old friend, a figure pitifully shrunk beneath the red dressing-gown, whose voice, however, bore no trace of sickness when he spoke of his work. Then he was cheered by pleasant accounts of the production (1 April, 1928) at the Arts Theatre of his little Shakespearean conceit, *The Making of An Immortal*, the plot of which had been handed to him so many years ago by that generous man, A. E. The play was notably well cast, with Malcolm Keen as Burbage, Charles Laughton as Ben Jonson, Leslie Faber as Bacon, Charles Carson as Shakespeare, Brian Glennie as the boy-Juliet Prenny Lister, Sybil Thorndike as Queen Elizabeth, and Edmund Gwenn, Edward Chapman and D. Hay Petrie in smaller parts. Robert Atkins produced, Sir Thomas Beecham, in the unusual rôle of a composer, supplied a little incidental music, and there was a distinguished audience. . . . " To read the play had been charming,"[1] wrote the critic of *The Times*, " full of humorous sketches of character, decorated with a luminous fancy, enriched with a prose which, even in its lightest lines, belongs to Moore and none other. How would it be in performance ? . . . The play is not at its best till it is brought on the stage."

By the 4th of April, Moore was well enough to face an anæsthetic and the suprapubic tube was introduced, a form of drainage which would place him in a safe position in regard to the obstruction and could be continued indefinitely without greatly curtailing his activities. When he improved he chafed under confinement; he craved to have the obstruction removed at once, a proceeding which would have been fatal to him. On the 18th of April, Sir John Thomson-Walker wrote to a doctor friend who enquired whether the patient would be fit to pay visits:

He is not fit to stay with friends at the present time as he has not yet been launched on his own . . . and, of course, he is very casual about all these mundane matters. He will probably return to Ebury Street about the end of this week . . .

We are all very fond of George Moore but he has led us a fine dance.

[1] *The Making of An Immortal* was published by Edwin Rudge in 1927.

3

Moore left the Home on the 21st of April, 1928, and returned to the charge of his medical attendant, Dr. Comerford. A male nurse had to be provided to help him, for he was quite unable to deal with any mechanical device, however simple. He could enjoy fair comfort and dine out, but it was not easy for him to stay with friends. While he rested he felt very much as he was to make Otanes, the old man in *Aphrodite*, feel after he had been near to death.

It seems that I was very near to death, Kebren. Loxias saved thy life, Otanes, and he thinks the recovery will endure. I was dying easily, without pain, Otanes continued, and—And regret being picked out of the grave ? I cannot tell, Kebren, whether I am glad or sorry. But of this I am sure: that on the approach of death we apprehend with a clearer understanding than before what life is and what death is. . . . It is the fear of death that separates us from the animals, whether for good or evil I know not; but lying on my bed speechless, deprived of will, liberated from the sensual chain, I saw further into things and the meaning beyond things, their sadness and their joy, than I had ever done before.

Soon after his release from the Home he sought health at the seaside, visiting John Eglinton at Bournemouth, chatting to him a great deal about the past, for John Eglinton at this time was designated his official biographer. On his return to London he was surprisingly well but complained that he could not work. He laid *Aphrodite* aside, and before resuming it he prepared *Ulick and Soracha* and a new story, " Dinoll and Crede," for inclusion in the two-volume edition of *A Story-Teller's Holiday*. Though he groaned over the loss of " my one gift, such as it is," the day was not long enough for all that he was doing in the way of prefaces and revising; he kept as close a watch as ever on his literary position, interesting himself particularly in the selection of his letters to Dujardin, which were about to be published in America.

Dujardin thought these should be published, exactly as they had been written, in French, but Moore insisted on John Eglinton's beautiful translation.

17.5.28. *To Dujardin.*

Je suis bien aise que Jean Aubry ait alle vous voir et vous ait tout raconté. C'est l'abondance des matières, comme disent les journaux, qui m'avait empêché de vous écrire. Je ne pouvais pas me résigner à vous tout raconter—ma maladie, l'operation mineure, l'operation majeure qui m'attend et la pièce que je n'ai pas vue, et les babillage ! le garçon qui chanta aussi bien que Melba et qui joua un fragment de Juliette comme Rachel l'aurait joué. Heureusement débarrasse de toutes ces corvées (toutes choses trop souvent répétées est corvée) je puis vous dire pour vous égayer qu'un choix a été fait dans les deuxcents cinquante lettres et que les élues ont été traduites en anglais et que le livre avec une introduction écrite par un de mes amis en Irlande, recontera l'arrivée du trouvère attardé—trouvère j'etais dans ces années ou bien un Don Quischotte qui désirait l'irréalisable, le renaissance d'une langue mourante, et qui boudait les Irlandais qui ne voulaient pas abandonner leur Catholicisme. Bien sûr je ne suis pas renseigné sur la qualité de la traduction des lettres, ni sur l'esprit qu'on a mis dans la preface, trop vieux littérateur je le suis pour y mettre le nez. Il y a autres choses que je voudrais raconter mais je les garderai inédites que lorsque nous nous trouverons à table le café, des bons et des gros cigarres fumant, mais pour ces bons moments il faut attendre la grande opération. Je ne puis aller à Paris avec un cathéter dans le ventre et la nécessité matinale d'un lavage. Les jardins de Chanzy existent-ils encore ? Et vous souvenez-vous, en vous promenant dans les allées qui serpentent, de l'ami absent ?

Later in the year he was able to go to Paris, where the Halévys, Dujardin, Madame Duclaux and her sister saw him. He had business also with Miss Cunard, who was bringing out a new edition of *Peronnik* with the Eure Press.

12.7.28. To Miss Nancy Cunard.

I like very much the proof of *Peronnik the Fool* that arrived to-day. . . . I will write you in a day or two about coming over to see you. I have just come upon a packet of love letters you used to write me when you were a child [of] ten or a dozen years. They are delightful as the first flush of morning.

11.9.28. To Miss Nancy Cunard.

If you wish to make certain of selling the whole edition quickly you have only to write a preface, and the subject of the preface should be Holt. I wish you would turn past times over in your mind; spend an evening or two with the subject, and perchance it may flash into your mind in literary form. . . . Of course, a preface of the kind that I suggest would cause that cheerless soul, T. S. Eliot, to frown, but personal literature, as I have often impressed upon you, is the only literature for the age it is written and for the age that follows. . . .

It seems a pity that I should not have been all this while living in your lovely house, which I long to see almost as much as I long to see you. I shall not be happy till I am there, walking round the little domain with you and hearing about the printing. But when will this be, Nancy? You cannot help me and I cannot help myself, and a visitor has just come in and I have to leave off talking to you.

The progress he made with his Greek story was far from satisfying him, and he worked at the book during the greater part of 1929, writing a charming dedication to Sir John Thomson-Walker on its completion in November. To some extent the work was delayed by a renewed attempt to dramatise the second part of *The Brook Kerith*, a subject on which he had been in communication with Mr. Lionel Barton, the manager of the Arts Theatre, since April of the previous year. This play, afterwards named *The Passing of the Essenes*, was described as: " Three acts without any change of scene. All men." " I feel," he had written to

Barton during the summer of 1928, " that by continuing this book [*Aphrodite*] I am missing a chance of a performance of *The Brook Kerith*. A chance. There should be no chance about it, and that is the reason I am writing to you. If it were definitely settled that you would give me a performance in October I would put aside *Aphrodite* to write Jesus and Paul." His continuous correspondence with John Eglinton, whom he visited twice at Bournemouth during the course of 1929, dealt with *Aphrodite*, the translation of the Dujardin letters, Barton's visits to Ebury Street, and the performance of *The Making of An Immortal* by the " Illyrian Pastoral Players " at Beckenham.

4

Always he entertained a hope that it would be possible to perform the major operation. " By the way," he wrote to Miss Rodgers in March 1930, " why don't you come to London for my operation. The weather is favourable. I don't know why you stay away." In May he went to 129 Wimpole Street, but after tests were taken it was clear that he could not be operated upon with safety.

12.5.30. *To Lionel Barton.*

My mind is now settled, and I shall go into the nursing home feeling sure that you will have a success with the play. Those who have read it think it one of the best things, if not the best thing, I have done—Charles Morgan, yourself, Mr. Evans and a friend on whose judgment I rely.

On the return to his house he was like a child asking for a treat in his pathetic eagerness to ensure the production of *The Passing of the Essenes*. At the same time he took the greatest pains to perfect the work, and used all his influence to obtain distinguished actors. " It would be wonderful if you could get Forbes Robertson—he would bring a personality into the part [Jesus] which would raise it making it as interesting as Paul," he wrote to Barton. " I spent many hours with him," Mr. Barton says, " discussing the construction, dialogue, etc., and he was most meticulous as to every comma. Many a time I would receive a scene from him in the morning ' completed '—as he would call it—and by the afternoon a revised one would arrive, with a request that I would take tea with him and further discuss it. A most thorough man." Ian Fleming was given the part of Jesus, H. R. Hignett that of Hazael, the aged President of the Essenes, and John Laurie was the Paul. Gustav Holst wrote a plain song chant for the Essenes; and, though a busy man, offered to compose a prelude for small orchestra, but Moore thought " that the play might be better without any introductory music. . . . If Holst wants to write a little prelude you might humour him if you like."

The date was fixed for the first of October; but Moore was not present at the performance, for he accepted an invitation to Miss Rodgers's country house at Lardy: " I shall not wait for the production, I prefer you by far." Lardy lies southwest of Paris in the valley of the Juine, and Miss Rodgers's manor house and guest-house were amongst the prettiest things he had seen in his life. There was a footman to attend to him, and a highly recommended doctor, M. Ferrier, lived near by: he sent the doctor a copy of one of his books in advance. On the night of the performance in London, he read *The Passing of the Essenes* aloud to Miss Rodgers and to one or two of her friends.

While he awaited news of the play's reception he showed great nervousness. But the news was good. A small but genuine success in the theatre had come his way at last; and the writing was sufficiently distinguished to bring *The Passing of the Essenes* into his collected edition. When the English newspapers arrived at Lardy he was overcome: a note written on Lardy paper to Miss Rodgers reveals the previous tension of his spirit. " You who are so sympathetic will understand. I staked my all on a single throw of the dice, and hardly knew what I was saying when I bade you goodnight. I am feeling better . . . ' the fever called liking is over at last.' "

This was his last visit to France. " He was an invalid," Miss Rodgers writes, " but his mind was remarkably clear and his interest in life and the things about him was most acute. I knew him from red hair—pink to white. A gorgeous Irishman, the most Catholic of Catholics I always thought him, but with a faith older than Christianity. George Moore belonged to the spring; his impulsiveness, his curiosity, his great egotism—so young a characteristic—everything indicated that in his case the calendar was a crime."

15.10.30. *To Miss Viola Rodgers.*

I enclose a cheque for fifteen hundred francs, the sum you lent me, and I believe all accounts are now settled except the one marked gratitude. The gratitude account never can be settled; I shall always remember your kindness to me. Clara and Ebury Street are the same. . . . And there is another thing I would ask you to do. The admirable Arthur [Miss Rodgers's footman] said that nothing would give him such pleasure as to receive a book from me, and when you are in Paris, and of all when you are in the rue Castiglione, you might buy a copy of *Mémoires de ma Vie Morte* and send it to me. I will write his name in it and forward to Lardy in the hope that it will ultimately reach its destination and rejoice Arthur's heart. One must not judge Arthur by oneself; he is three-and-twenty, and when I was that age, and Zola and Goncourt sent me their books, it seemed to me that I walked among the clouds, which I did.

Six performances of *The Passing of the Essenes* had been announced, but so many people wished to see the play that the run was prolonged. With some misgivings Moore went to the Arts Theatre after all.

29.10.30 *To Miss Viola Rodgers.*

It will be many days before I recover from the odious memory. The poor play did not come out as it should have come out, and what pleasure is it to me that other people liked it? I wanted to like it and I didn't. The uninspired actors were between me and it all the time.

I have received the copy you sent me of *Memoirs of My Dead Life*. I will sign it to morrow and forward it to the young man whose attendance upon me whilst I was in your house amounted to devotion, or very nearly. . . .

Despite ill-luck, dearest Viola, I spent a visit with you that I look back upon with pleasure. A very different memory it is from my memory of my play.

5

Aphrodite in Aulis was published by Heinemann in a very handsome limited edition. It was another book written to please——

> *A young girl in the indolence of her youth*
> *Or an old man upon a winter's night,*

to quote Yeats's definition of his own ends, more applicable perhaps to those of Moore. *Aphrodite* was scarcely out when Moore began to labour upon it again with a view to seeing it take its place in the Uniform edition before he died. He did not like the ending. " The end of the story," he told Sir John Thomson-Walker, " should be triumphant,—triumphantly glad or triumphantly sorrowful, and the writing of *The Passing of the Essenes* prevented me from seeking as eagerly as I would have done in other circumstances for a triumphant end. . . ."

" He went on suffering and writing," says Sir William Geary. " He was advised to rest, but he declared that he must go on and correct his books, for to him each book might be bettered. In one of the books he gave me, he wrote : ' To one who knows a good book,' in another : ' In memory of what you said to me : You deserve to succeed for you work so hard.' . . . His great dictionary lay beside him, and he never wearied in the search for the exact phrase. Sometimes I would use some strange words, as " pinnock " or " grolier," which he knew not, and he was as pleased as a child finding sixpence. I told him the story of the Venus Callipyge and it entered his great book. His was no hasty writing. I have regarded his type-script, and its continuous correction ; his aim was to attain, not perfection, for he was modest withal, but his very best."

Moore's old age had not been " peace," but work which continued at an accelerated pace. Why, he would sometimes ask himself, did he not go out and enjoy himself like other people ? He might have spoken, with Carducci, of the " penal servitude of composition " and of a soul which was " weary of writing." " Out of the inner emptiness," he avowed in an unpublished manuscript, the preface to a projected edition of his correspondence with " Gabrielle," " comes the remembrance that I have never read the books I sacrifice my life to write. . . . I missed a great deal certainly. If I appealed to Yeats (the wisest man in Ireland) he would say : We must yield a little to gain a great deal. But what have I gained ? All those books, twenty or twenty-five volumes—it doesn't matter which. It is what I would have got in return that matters. . . ." He knew of course that he gained liberty by renouncing it, and yet there may have been a paradox at the core of his being : this man, who saw everything in relation to literature, never gave his friends, or perhaps even himself, the impression of being inescapably a man of letters, and from time to time he might say things that revealed not only the unscholarly man but the country squire amused at the eccentricities of men of genius. When Gosse told him (in *Avowals*) that Swinburne three times read the whole of Dickens aloud to Watts-Dunton, Moore replied : " Those two old men led an extraordinary life in the Putney villa reading to each other."

Again it is curious that Moore the artist should have wanted, as Mr. Desmond MacCarthy says, a disrespectful biographer, whereas Moore the man wanted a romantic one : he was " extraordinarily anxious to be commemorated as a man," John Eglinton tells us. He always encouraged any proposal to write about him. Indeed he scarcely realised how fortunate he was in the studies of his work and personality that appeared in his lifetime, by Freeman, Geraint Goodwin and Humbert Wolfe, and he continued to crave for a common notoriety. " Of course if I had a moor in Scotland or a yacht——! " It came about—perhaps he did not hear of it—that he was read in the conservative atmosphere of the English public school. A young Haileybury master tells me that " whenever the boys are on the History of the Middle Ages, they find *Héloïse and Abélard*: I have never known a boy not to read it to the end, and the articulate ones talk of it and want to know more of his books."

On the other hand, he may well have cherished a small grievance against the academic and political authorities. He was nearly eighty; for over twenty years his eminence, if not his supremacy, in English letters had been widely acknowledged; the Prime Minister was a great admirer of his work; the Prince of Wales bought his books. Yet no single distinction had come to him : while his contemporaries (and as it seemed to him his inferiors) received knighthoods, O.M.'s, honorary degrees, freedoms of the city, he remained simply Mr. George Moore of Ebury Street, Pimlico. It was perhaps a greater distinction, and no doubt he sometimes knew this; at other times however (for he was the most human of men) he felt ill-used and cold-shouldered by the great world. His excitement therefore when in 1930 he was summoned to an audience with the Prince of Wales was great. Alas, it was a little too great, for when he had dressed himself in his best and set off down Ebury Street, his nose began to bleed. For a time he hoped that the flow might be stanched and disaster averted; he returned to his house, but all Clara's ministrations availed him nothing : it bled and bled. There was nothing to be done but to telephone to Lady Cunard, who had helped to bring about the Royal gesture, to ask her to explain and to hope that the invitation would be renewed.

The invitation was renewed, and this time Moore reached Marlborough House safely, a presentation copy of *The Brook Kerith* under his arm : he never seemed quite certain in his later years whether he regarded this book or *Héloïse and Abélard* as his masterpiece. The interview must have passed off admirably, for afterwards Moore always spoke with the greatest reverence of the Prince. He made his way back to Ebury Street glowing with satisfaction, until a sudden thought put an end to his happiness. What demon could have caused him to choose *The Brook Kerith* ? The King had just recovered from a long and serious illness, and the prayers of all his people had been answered. To leave with his son a book which denied the divinity of Jesus ! . . . " I have lost the O.M. ! " he cried : " I have lost the O.M. ! "

Sir John Thomson-Walker continued to see Moore at irregular intervals, sometimes professionally, but usually the professional part was a transparent excuse. Sometimes he was completely taken aback by a temperament as sensitive as an Æolian harp to the faintest breath, as on the occasion, after a dinner party at Ebury Street, when Moore wrote to him to say that he had been very badly treated, having been completely excluded from conversation in his own house. It is true that Moore had been unusually silent during the meal, but Tonks and Sir John had made every effort to draw him into the conversation. Tonks came to Sir John's house in some distress : his long friendship with Moore seemed to be really endangered. They talked it over and Tonks wrote a generous letter to Moore, which he followed by a call; all was well again.

Moore was very anxious that Sir John should write an account of his own life. " Not," he said, " a list of the notable people you have met, but a real piece of literature. I will stand behind you. There is always some friend behind the author to help by criticism. Remember I advised Gosse about his *Father and Son*." Some of Sir John's personal experiences fascinated him. One of them had a " strange beauty," but might only be told under a complete disguise, so that there could be no recognition of persons; and in debating this question Moore said that anything could be written or read without offence provided that it was rightly told, the language fine and the touch sufficiently delicate, adding however that there was one episode in his own life that he had always failed to write. For examples of style he recommended R. L. Stevenson's *Travels with a Donkey* and Defoe's *Robinson Crusoe*. They spoke of revisions, and Sir John (who was not then acquainted with Moore's method) hazarded the opinion that the first version with only minor changes, was always the best; he quoted the very slightly corrected manuscript of certain authors to prove his contention. Moore agreed in regard to these authors—no amount of revision would make them worth reading.

In this way Sir John came to know Moore very well. He was attracted by the wonderful fighting spirit of the man and by his " curious simplicity," while Moore " adored " (the word is Tonks's) his new friend for his sympathy and reliability. Sometimes Moore would arrive at 96, Harley Street in an excited state, and begin to denounce the medical profession in general and, by inference, Sir John in particular. He would continue until a smile broke over his listener's face; and then he would say: " I knew I could make you laugh." Thus when Sir John himself fell ill, he found a great difficulty in passing the patient on to another surgeon. One surgeon, chosen for his tact as well as his skill, was dismissed by Moore in a wounding letter. Sir John visited Moore who deeply regretted the manner of the letter, but doctors and other surgeons continued to follow one another with disturbing frequency. From time to time the question of a major operation arose but on each occasion a full examination showed that the danger was too great.

6

In spite of his disability Moore continued to fulfil social and other engagements and to miss very little that was likely to interest him.

2.11.30. *To Ernest Longworth.*

Tomorrow, Thursday, a small part of my afternoon will be spent in admiration of Ethel Sands' pictures, but I shall be in Ebury Street about four o'clock. . . . I look forward to going for a little walk with you. . . . With kind regards to Sir Horace Plunkett, with whom I had a long talk the other day on matters which we will discuss . . . [Longworth had become Plunkett's private secretary].

But in January 1931 a chill sent him again to a Home. Here he rejected the excellent food that was brought to him, and the doctors had to send him back to Ebury Street, accompanied by a lady nurse who stayed with him for a short

"THE RED DRESSING-GOWN"
From a pastel by Henry Tonks

while. The first evening that he was back in his house he said, after dinner, to Clara: " You have saved me from death by starvation."

2.1.31. *To Lord Howard de Walden.*

I would have written to you and been to see you long ago if I had not been stricken down by illness, bladder trouble, a chill caught at Birmingham. I hope to be out of this Nursing Home and back at work soon. The word " work " is pathetic. There is very little work more for me to do, but what there is I will finish up when I leave.

He had however found an ending more illuminating and more essential to the character of Rhesos than the alfresco love-making of the first version of *Aphrodite*: "The ideal end," he wrote to Mr. Atchley, " an end that outends all other ends. . . . I walked out of my house and round Belgrave Square, and roared out the new end to my secretary when I returned (who took it down in shorthand as quickly as I could speak it) in desperate fear that I should die."

He was greatly cheered by eulogistic reviews from America, and by a pretty compliment from Athens. The editor of *Hestis* thought of publishing a Greek translation of *Aphrodite*. " It is hard to imagine, anybody," he wrote to Mr. Atchley, " who can read modern Greek and is interested in Greece not wishing to read *Aphrodite in Aulis* now that the real end has been discovered." There was a pernicious fashion —he supposed that it had even reached Greece—for " novels of enormous length, with murders and calamities of all sorts thrown together " ; but the reaction was due, and it should favour quiet stories in the style of *Aphrodite in Aulis*. Unfortunately the editor of *Hestis* decided against publishing the translation. A deeper disappointment was his inability to make " a little tour of France." The little drive with Miss Rodgers to Troyes would never come to pass.

12.2.31. *To Miss Viola Rodgers.*

. . . It is not probable that I shall ever be cured, or be able to travel about, or be anything like the man whom

you have honoured with your consideration, your friendship, dare I say your love ? I think I may, for many years.
Things have gone against us always, but who knows ? It
may be that in a month my tidings will be better ones.

10.4.31. *To Miss Viola Rodgers.*

Before this letter reaches you, you will have read my
melancholy epistle telling you of the almost insuperable
difficulties against my going to France and thereby
realising my long desired dream of a little tour with you,
but this morning I remembered your footman, that
charming young man who looked after me while I was at
Lardy.

Would you like to take him on the tour with us ? He
could look after everything, take the tickets, look after the
luggage, etc.

In August 1931 he went to stay with Sir James Barrie in
Scotland. The Castle was full of visitors, and among them
he was delighted to meet Miss Quiller Couch, the daughter
of " Q ," an acquaintance of the nineties, the eulogist of
Esther Waters. In speaking to her of her father's interest in
Shakespeare he mentioned his own play *The Making of An
Immortal*. " I hope," he wrote to Longworth upon his return
to London, " I shall have an opportunity of talking to you
about Barrie, who is the most interesting and communicative
man I have met. He gave me a book which he had printed
for private circulation. Only fifty copies were printed,
heaven knows why. A more charming book I have never
read and it is a stand-by in my present dilemma. I have
certainly lost for the moment any literary aptitude which I
had and am very unhappy." After this he thought that he
would like to make the acquaintance of Rudyard Kipling.
He spoke to C. D. Medley and others about arranging a
meeting, but it was felt that it would be better for both that
this should not come about.

But he made a few new friends in these last years, and they
often found him an entrancing companion. Much valued

among them was Mrs. Belloc Lowndes, with whom he had
many interests in common, some of them centring in French
literature. She had known him slightly over many years, and
was now touched by his evident desire to be befriended;
owing to his secretive and inveigling habit of not mixing
people he often gave the impression of complete isolation.
Of those who had died he missed Gosse and Ruttledge most.
" I would give up all my successes," he said to Colonel
Ruttledge, " for a sight of your father's face once more."
And he wrote to Philip Gosse: " I often think of you
and of your father, your house, your mother and your
sisters. I shall never forget that house in Hanover Terrace. Your father would have liked me to write his life. . . .
He would have liked an appreciation from someone who
loved him and whom he loved, I am afraid I can never do
this. . . ."

There were callers at Ebury Street; Mr. H. S. Ede, Sir
Evan Charteris, Mrs. Crawford, Humbert Wolfe, and Mr.
Charles Morgan, now his intended biographer, very patient
and attentive, whose understanding of his artistic life
delighted Moore. He spoke of this new and refreshing friend
to John Eglinton. " Morgan thinks no end of me," he would
say ; " oh, he is doing me a lot of good." When he could take
his little afternoon walks he still passed doors at which he
cared to knock—the Chelsea house of Miss Ethel Sands, an
artist whose work he much admired, was one of his favourite
stopping-places. If he was often childishly unreasonable,
particularly with those whom he had known longest, he
nevertheless showed great courage on the whole, and might
be found in his dining-room, too ill to write, and yet quite
calm and ready to talk on subjects which really interested
him. But the things, more caustic than ever, that he said
about established authors did not conduce to the enlargement of the circle of his acquaintance. Now and again some
young writer would come to Ebury Street, either in curiosity
or in reverence. If the visitor was of a reverent disposition
Moore would, as likely as not, repel him by levelling some
cruel quip at another object of his reverence. Yet he increas-
ingly complained of loneliness, and he was lonely; a sad echo

of his loneliness is to be found in the description of Otanes in *Aphrodite*: " when he had exhausted his memories of Homer he sought refuge in memories of his youth, and when these failed him he asked why nobody came to his door, as if it were decreed in Olympus that he should die without looking at his daughter's face again."

22.10.31. *To Miss Viola Rodgers.*

I would have written to you long ago if there had been any hope of my coming over to drive with you to Troyes, a place I shall never see now, for there is no hope of my being able to travel. But you should be able to travel one of these days, and nobody will be more welcomed by me than you. . . .

17.2.32. *To Miss Viola Rodgers.*

I am unhappy constantly, but to tell you why would take too long, far too long, and I should probably not convince you that there was any reason for my unhappiness. One of the reasons is that I cannot get away to France. . . . You did not come to London and I am wearing out my life thinking of you and of Paris and Lardy. . . .

If he could but have reached Miss Rodgers's holding in the midst of the fields and woods, he would have been out of sight of the distressing and perpetual struggle that " goes on here as to whose novel sells in the greatest numbers."

7

On the occasion of his eightieth birthday, it was proposed by Sir Alec Martin, Mr. Wilson Steer, Mr. Charles Morgan, Professor Tonks, Mr. Humbert Wolfe and a few others to publish in *The Times* a message of homage and congratulations, composed by Morgan and signed by admirers of Moore's work and by his friends.

TO GEORGE MOORE ON HIS EIGHTIETH BIRTHDAY,
24th February, 1932.

AVE. Feeling that a more public gift would be distasteful
to you, and that your place as a master of English letters
is already so greatly established that any formal recognition from private persons would be presumptuous in those
that offered it, we, a few of your friends, send you this
message of congratulation on your eightieth birthday,
claiming to represent therein neither the general homage
that is your due nor the honour that is yours wherever art
is honoured, but our personal friendship and our gratitude
to an artist who, since he came to London from Paris many
years ago, has not ceased to labour with a single mind in
the perfecting of his craft, who has written in *Daphnis and
Chloë* a flawless translation, in *Esther Waters* a tale that
marks a period in our literature, in *Hail and Farewell* an
autobiography that has rank with Rousseau's, in *Héloïse
and Abélard* a philosophical romance of supreme beauty,
and in *The Brook Kerith* a prose epic unique in the English
language. The uses of that language have been changed
by your influence, as though in an ancient music you had
discovered new melodies and rhythms that shall be in the
air when young men in future time have stories to tell.
You have taught narrative to flow again and anecdote to
illumine it as the sun a stream. You have persuaded words
and invention to sing new songs together that would have
been heard, as those of an equal, by the masters upon
whom the tradition of our literature relies, and on your
eightieth birthday your pen is still unfailing in your hand.
For these reasons we salute you, and for our friendship's
sake. SALVE.

Owing to Moore's attitude towards so many of his distinguished contemporaries, it would not have been possible to
make the memorial wholly representative of English literature and art. But the message was an unusual distinction;
and of those still living among whom his lot had been cast
there were not many who refused their signatures, difficult

friend and fellow worker though he had always been.

Richard Best, who happened to be over from Ireland, bought some violets for him and took them to his door at ten o'clock on his birthday morning. " You must come in," said Clara, " Mr. Moore is at breakfast, you are to dine this week, and Mr. Moore forgets which evening." " But why doesn't he come in ? " came a voice from the dining-room. Best's gift was the first of the day, and lifting the bunch to his nostrils Moore related the story of Landor's exclamation when he flung a stupid valet out of the window into a bed of violets : " I forgot the violets." He had been to a concert, and they had played Ravel, for which he did not care, and Beethoven : " in Beethoven's symphonies the second violins always play the same note." While Best was questioning this, there was a knock at the door, and a telegram was brought in. " But what is this ? A telegram ! Open it, Best. . . . I had such a nice telegram from the Prince of Wales. Oh ! I can't tell you what I think of the Prince. The great work he is doing," and he went on to describe how he met the Heir Apparent the day before at an exhibition of old walnut furniture in Sir Philip Sassoon's house in Park Lane. " Now I must get to my writing." " Surely not on your birthday ? " " Yes, even on my birthday. Till Friday then."

On Friday at dinner Moore read out his letter to *The Times*. Best found a sentence which he could criticise, and Moore, after demurring at first, said : " You're perfectly right, Best." " At about ten," says Best, " he asked me if I ever took a walk after dinner. I gathered that he hoped a walk would help him to sleep, and we went out together, he with the letter in his hand. He clung to my arm in the traffic, but near Buckingham Palace saw a pillar-box across the road ; I offered to post his letter, but he insisted on crossing again to post it with his own hand. At Jermyn Street he said that he would go home. I would have seen him home, but he said ' no,' and I think it was because he felt sleep coming upon him, and wished to rest his mind. ' Goodnight, goodnight,' he cried, turning away suddenly without shaking hands, and I saw him for the last time, a retreating figure."

Moore's pleased reply to a " more outspoken approval "

of his writings than had yet appeared was published in *The Times* on the 1st of March.

I have thought a great deal within the last few days of the pleasure it would be to me to spend three or four weeks writing letters to old friends and to those whose interest in my books has helped me to overcome many difficulties. But there is a reason why I should not indulge myself in correspondence and it is one that my readers will appreciate, for they are all true lovers of literature, knowing from instinct and experience that the thread of a story is easily broken and that characters grow dim if they are allowed to lie dormant in the imagination. I feel sure, therefore, that my friends and the signatories to the memorial would forego the pleasure of receiving letters of thanks if, by so doing, they would help me to write my book, which I trust they will like.

8

The last story he was writing was about a nun in a convent near Hampstead. She is out on an errand of mercy and accidentally meets the man she once loved but who had married someone else. He is again free when they meet, and the nun is willing to join him and to tour the Continent with him in search of masterpieces. The man proposes to found a Gallery. " Has Canterbury a Gallery ? " Moore wrote to MacColl, who advised against setting up another collection in England. Sorrento was then chosen as the site, and Moore invited Mr. Osbert Sitwell to Ebury Street to tell him how the land lay.

In May 1932 he paid the visit to Philip Gosse which the latter has described with illuminating detail in the *London Mercury* of March 1933. Philip Gosse lived fifteen miles from Brighton, near to Shoreham, in the country Moore knew so well in the period of his intimacy with the Bridger family. Gosse asked him before he came whether he would like to meet Galsworthy, who was his neighbour, and he replied that he would not.

In June he was again working at his new novel, *Madeleine de Lisle.*

22.6.32. *To D. S. MacColl.*

Your letter is a help though not exactly the help you anticipated. You will remember that I showed you a picture by Bellini mentioning the immeasureable superiority to the vague aspirations of Rossetti. You told me there were two pictures and that it was never fully decided which was the original and which was the replica. Both, I suppose, are in Vienna. . . . If you answer this letter will you give me the names of the Bellini brothers. . . .

The Giovanni Bellini was the " Venus " of the Belvedere, and a long summer evening went by as Moore and MacColl talked of the story and the pictures. A few days later Moore was again in Hampstead on what was to be the last of his Sunday visits to the MacColls. He wandered first to their old house, and characteristically found a nursemaid there to conduct him up the hill. Afterwards he would not refrain from walking by the Heath to the tube, but at the White Stone Pond he was so obviously exhausted that MacColl called a taxi for him. " I spent a pleasant hour with you and returned to Ebury Street rejuvenated," Moore wrote the next day. " You're a fortunate man to live with a charming wife on the heights of Hampstead."

He had seemed much better in the early months of 1932, but after the turn of the year he complained of sciatica, and writing to John Eglinton on the 4th of July he said that he could now only sleep in an armchair. He was reluctant to put *Madeleine de Lisle* aside, he had written 214 pages—but he asked John Eglinton to expect him at Bournemouth during the month. There was the usual difficulty in finding lodgings for him. He would not go to an expensive hotel, and two or three of the landladies with whom he had stayed on previous visits to Bournemouth were reluctant to receive him again. In the house which John Eglinton found for him in July 1932 he started badly, for on being shown around he walked up to one of the pictures and turned it to the wall.

The picture was a work in the style of Rossetti and had been painted by the owner of the house. Afterwards he made great friends with this lady, who used to read to him out of Mrs. Hunter's bible which he always carried with him on a journey. One day she found him in tears and he said that he wished he had met her sooner. She tried to comfort him: " But although you are not married, Mr. Moore, you must have many friends." She was a devout woman, and on hearing that she went to Church twice on Sunday, Moore said that it would be all right—that he had an engagement that evening. When Sunday came he wandered out forlornly to eat a lonely dinner at some big hotel.

18.7.32. *To Miss Viola Rodgers.*

I wish you would come to England; you used to come; how was it you got out of the habit ? . . . I think of you often and myself as an ugly dog that you are fond of, sitting at the feet of his mistress.

18.7.32. *To Mrs. St. John Hutchinson.*

There is nothing I should like so much as to dine with you and Hutchie, but I must go to you in comparative health and I cannot tell at this moment how I shall feel the day after tomorrow.

6.8.32. *To Mrs. Crawford.*

I've not written to you before on account of illness and the book I am writing, and what is the use of writing unless I ask you to come and see me. We are now at the end of the week and if you would like to come here to tea or dinner, as you please, I shall be delighted to see you. . . . Can you remember a description of a tea gown you wore in '72 and the accompanying garments. Search your memory please.[1]

9

One of the last portraits that was painted of Moore was by Tonks, who was much struck by seeing him seated in his

[1] It seems that his memory was confused, and that he was thinking of an older friend, Madame Duclaux.

dining-room in a bright red dressing gown, and thinking instantly, what a splendid costume for a man of letters ! wished to express him in pastel. Moore seemed to like the suggestion, and soon after the sanction was given work upon the portrait was begun. What was interesting in the surroundings of the model was the room lighted at both ends, the window near which the model sat lighting strongly the side of his head, the face being less illuminated by the window at the other end of the room. " As the sittings went on," says Tonks, " I noticed that on dull days the face was too dark so I threw some light on to the face by means of a mirror placed on a table near by. Later on, he became exasperated and finally told me that a red dressing gown was not the proper covering in which to depict a man of letters, or words to that effect. Also that it was impossible to paint a face in a false light. The pastel was never finished, and after a heated ten minutes in my studio I told him I would never during his life time publicly show it. I have hopes that it will finally reach the National Portrait Gallery.

" The last time I was foolish enough to try to paint my friend was when Orpen expressed a desire to have a picture by me. I decided to depict a scene at one of the Saturday nights which had become almost a regular Moore institution in my studio. I collected in my mind those who seemed most in keeping with the spirit of the meetings and then made many experiments in arranging them so as to make a good composition. Moore was the centre of the group well in the foreground. Steer was seated on a sofa fast asleep as he very often was when the conversation failed to interest him. The head of St. John Hutchinson just appeared above that of Moore. Mrs. Hutchinson was seated by the fire gazing intently at the principal figure and I placed myself standing up resting an arm upon the mantelpiece also fixing my attention on Moore. In order to reduce the number of sittings, I who had so often seen him seated of an evening in the well known chair had worked on him from memory and occasionally from a model. And so the pose was well established on the canvas and I was able to make good progress with the portrait when I first began to paint from

"SATURDAY EVENING AT THE VALE"
From the painting by Henry Tonks
Left to right: George Moore, St. John Hutchinson, P. W. Steer, Henry Tonks, Mrs. St. John Hutchinson

him. At the end of the first sitting he looked at it and seemed not displeased, but when he next came, I suppose he had been thinking about it, for he came straight up to my picture and told me it was impossible to paint the portrait of a man without showing the eyes; the eyes, he said, were the windows of the soul. It was in vain that I told him it was also impossible to show a man reading as he was the proofs of one of his works without at the same time showing the eyes partly covered as they would naturally be by the eyelids; the abuse continued until I in turn became roused and told him much that he would never have heard if I had not been in this abnormal state. He then sat down with great difficulty, and I took up my brushes. He came several times after this, but would never look at the picture, which I had reason afterwards to know he detested."

10

Eventually Moore succeeded in dictating a complete first version of *Madeleine de Lisle* to his secretary. In this version the man died suddenly and Madeleine returned to the convent where she too died some years later and was buried in the grounds. Miss Kingdon spent a Sunday morning at No. 121 typing out her notes, so that he could read the last chapter in the afternoon. When she arrived next morning the whole story was in the waste paper basket. However, he tried again and even despatched Miss Kingdon to Highgate to seek an accurate description of the long hill where the two nuns walk in the first chapter and also of the house in Pond Square where Madeleine meets her lover for the first time since she has become a nun. He rewrote the first chapter, which he thought very good, but then he said that he had lost his talent and was afraid that Miss Kingdon would soon have to be looking for other employment. But he kept *Madeleine de Lisle* by him almost to the end, and wanted to hear from Longworth about a canal connecting the Garonne with the Mediterranean for a voyage of his lovers: not as information but as something plausible. Had he finished the book it would have been dedicated to Miss Viola Rodgers.

In the late October of 1932, in a conversation with Mrs. Belloc Lowndes, he expressed a great longing to get out of London. She offered to take him to Oxford for two- or three days. He eagerly assented; but although she was not aware how ill he was, she felt a certain misgiving, and telephoned to his valued friend, Mr. Medley. Mr. Medley expressed a good deal of anxiety, while agreeing that Moore would feel deeply disappointed were the plan to be abandoned. Mrs. Belloc Lowndes suggested that it would be an easier journey to Brighton, and that Brighton would give him a greater change of air and scene. He was, however, very indignant at so Cockney a suggestion.

25th October, 1932.

My dear Marie,

I have little time to write letters, but let me say at once, before I begin my task with Mona, that at Oxford there is a museum, and an interesting one, and there are churches, and interesting ones, and we shall meet interesting people. In Brighton there is nothing. Oxford is good enough for me, and I hope for you.

Always affectionately yours,

George Moore.

It was therefore arranged that the visit to Oxford should take place. Mr. Medley, with great kindness and delicacy, said he would go and stay with a sister who lived in Oxford, so that he might be at hand should George Moore be taken suddenly ill. The start was made on the morning of October 27th, and Moore appeared to enjoy every moment of the long motor drive. But during the three days of their stay in Oxford, he did not once leave the hotel, and he refused several invitations, including one from Mr. and Mrs. Masefield. He spent the whole of each day, from ten in the morning, when he came into their sitting-room, till ten at night, in talking to his friend. During these hours he went over a great part of his life, dwelling, especially, on the time he had lived in Paris. He described also at considerable length, the genesis of each of his books, saying that in his opinion *The Untilled Field* contained his best work. Although it was fine weather for most of the time, he refused to take even a short drive though, strangely enough, he suggested accompanying Mrs. Belloc Lowndes to church. This suggestion she rejected, as she was aware how he regarded, and habitually spoke of, her religion.

Their journey back to London was very different from their journey to Oxford. Moore was obviously in great pain and discomfort for much of the time, and, as they approached London, his friend grew very anxious indeed. This was the only time in her friendship with him when she felt his mind at all give way. For he spoke as if he were afraid there would be no one to look after him when he reached his house: and that although she assured him, many times, that she had telephoned and made every arrangement for his comfort. When they reached Ebury Street, she went in to see that everything was quite comfortable, and found, as she had felt certain would be the case, that his two devoted servants had got everything ready for him.

" I have been ill, very ill," he wrote to Philip Gosse on the 1st of November. . . . But come by all means and bring your charming wife with you, and she will talk to you when words desert me."

The next time Mrs. Belloc Lowndes saw him he seemed well, and was talking of paying a visit to Lord Howard de Walden in Wales. But she was glad when she heard that this had been postponed. She herself had to go to America, and they had a sad parting, although nothing in his appearance or manner made her suppose that the end was near.

II

Moore continued to go out as often as his condition allowed him, but he did not again leave London. " He still came to see me on Saturday nights," Tonks writes. " To look at except for his entirely white hair he still had the complexion and I am almost tempted to say the look of a baby and one with curious greeny blue eyes. He was more abstemious than ever; one cigar after dinner, to be lighted with great care was enough for him. He was always ready to talk about the books he was writing and how he proposed to develop them. This fondness for telling others the stages in a story seemed an essential part of his method which he continued using to the last days of his life; he lived so much in himself that it was as natural to him as it would have been for a busy wife to give an account of her day's events to her husband on his return from his work. Talking remained his real recreation, he never learned to be fond of reading, but to Pater and Landor he remained faithful to the last. Not very long before his death he told me that he would not open Balzac again."

A priest came to see him in Ebury Street in the hope that he might be recalled to the old faith. He entered into amicable argument with the priest without however accepting his views. A letter which he had written in the *Times Literary Supplement* (30th of October, 1930), afterwards used as a preface to the second edition of *The Passing of the Essenes*, disclosed his continued interest in " religious discussion " : he expressed a hope that his views on the Gospels would turn many away from conventional interpretations of Christianity. " Jesus spoke for all kinds and conditions of men, and his words were meant to be everlasting, and for them to be everlasting they must be reborn in every individual consciousness." The implications of such a sentence as this can hardly be reconciled with categorical statements which Moore made in conversation, as when he told Goodwin that he considered life to be " an accident," and John Eglinton that he admitted no transcendent element in human experience. It may have seemed to some readers of his preface that Moore had his tongue in his cheek and was seeking to attract the attention of those who would not ordinarily be his readers. Certainly he sometimes led even the orthodox to believe that his case was not hopeless. A correspondent from Indianopolis, " very anxious that God might use some poor word of mine to overcome his disbelief," wrote to Moore after reading *The Brook Kerith* to criticise his denial of the death of Jesus on the Cross. Moore's reply though brief was serious:

I would like to remind you that Jesus, in the three
Synoptic Gospels, makes it plain to the young questioner
(Luke xviii. 19) that he does not lay claim to the god-
head. " Why dost thou call me good ? " he asked the
young man in Matthew, Mark and Luke, "none is good but
God." This cannot be explained away, for if he were God
past, present and future would be as one and he would
have foreseen the heresies he would promulgate by the
words quoted. The text that caused me to reject Jesus's
death on the Cross occurs in Luke, Chapter xxvi. " The
disciples are gathered together."

We need not assume insincerity in such letters, for in
different company and in response to different stimuli
Moore, like many others, would instinctively adopt different
positions with the object of drawing out his interlocutor and
finding out what he really thought. To Sir John Thomson-
Walker he said that he must recognise a supreme being, the
creator and guide of the universe, but further than that he
could not go.

His interest in religion, genuine enough, was psychological
and historical rather than doctrinal and speculative. " When
I told him," Sir William Geary writes, " a theory of the Last
Supper derived from Fraser's *Golden Bough*, that our Lord's
intention was to make the participants ' akin,' he asked the
explanation. The Apostles, as I said, were of course Semites,
and it is an ancient Semitic custom that by taking bread and
salt together, one becomes as it were one of the Family.
Further, there was and is a custom of blood brotherhood,
whereby each party drinks a drop of blood taken from the
other ; later to avoid the pain and inconvenience of blooding,
a cup of dark wine drunk together ceremoniously was taken
as constituting blood brotherhood. George Moore, while ridi-
culing the literalness of the Irish priest saying ' I can make
God,' said that the theory of Kinship in the Last Supper
was a beautiful and most reverent theory to explain the Last
Supper. He was a student of the New Testament and I have
never heard him say blasphemy."

To Geraint Goodwin he said : " If God had to send His

only Son down to patch up the boggle He Himself had already made, then one can believe anything." Orthodox Christianity was not only mythology but mythology without speculative significance. It is doubtful whether he was most himself in the negative irreligious criticism, regarded by the metaphysically minded as somewhat superficial, to which Catholicism provoked him, or in his occasional declarations that Protestantism is too completely a religion of the spirit to be ever adopted by mankind. The sure thing is that he found no contradiction between a naturalistic account of the world and the main life of his creative imagination. " The nothingness of our lives and the length of the sleep out of which we came, and the still greater length of the sleep which will fall upon us " filled him with wonder, it was the source, he said, whence all great poetry flows.

His last will (he made many wills) was dated the 31st of October, 1930, and by it he bequeathed the rights in his books to C. D. Medley, who " understands my literature, likes my books and has for many years advised me on all questions relating to them. I wish him to deal with my books according to his wit and judgement and to make what arrangements he thinks best in his discretion, and as regards the proceeds I wish him to retain these in memory of his old friend." To Lady Cunard he left all his pictures and furniture with a few exceptions, notably his grandfather's portrait which he bequeathed to the National Gallery, Dublin. Charles Morgan was to write his biography: for three years he had been working at the task with Moore's active co-operation.[1] A deep affection was recalled by the gift of £5000 for division amongst Ruttledge's children. There were other bequests: £250 to St. Peter's Hospital, £1000 each to his secretary and his housekeeper and £500 each to a number of his older friends. The residue of his estate, subject to an annuity to his brother, Julian, was left to his sister, Mrs. Kilkelly and to his nephew, Peter Moore, Augustus Moore's son.

---

[1] Personal reasons, which he gives in his *Epitaph on George Moore*, unhappily prevented Mr. Morgan from completing the biography which he had under-taken.

The net personality was £68,000, and the portion of it available for his residuary legatees represented roughly his unearned and inherited fortune. Thus, apart from the exclusion of Colonel Maurice Moore and his family from all benefits, he could scarcely have made a more normal will. It was strange that he should have ignored the Colonel. Those who spoke to him in his last years of his brother did not have the impression that he bore ill-will, and the Colonel would not have been the only Roman Catholic to benefit by his dispositions. Perhaps he did not wish to take a course which might be interpreted as an acknowledgment that he could be held in any way to blame for their conflict.

12

These letters from Ebury Street give us a glimpse of him in the last months.

30.11.32. *To Mrs. St. John Hutchinson.*

Many thanks for the book, which I shall forward to Heinemann, and he will send it to the printer to have it set up. Harrap is printing an edition with three illustrations, and Gooden has done three illustrations which are marvellous. When you come on Thursday I will show you a drawing of a magnificent cock which is as fine an engraving as was ever done in England.[1] Forgive me writing through a secretary, but I am so tired that I could not put pen on paper to thank you for the book and for the pheasant.

22.12.32. *To John Eglinton.*

I did not answer your kind letter for I was too unhappy, and am still unhappy, or distressed, if distressed expresses more accurately the mournful state a man lives in who has been robbed of his single gift. I don't seem able to accomplish the little book I had sketched out entitled *A*

---

[1] For *Peronnik The Fool.* " Will my luck give me a publisher when I am among the gone who will ask Gooden to do four, five or six pictures for my *Daphnis and Chloë*? Should such a thing happen I doubt not that God will open my ears to hear the crowing of the cock " (*A Communication to My Friends*).

Communication to My Friends, telling the story of how writing was forced upon me and the persecution I have undergone for forty years and which is just ended, leaving me a wreck.

Writing forced upon me ! So that after all it was not instinct, not " echo-augury," not guiding Providence which condemned him to the penal servitude of composition, but his mother's foolishness in putting the Irish property into the mismanaging hands of poor Joe Blake.

29.12.32. *To S. C. Atchley.*

I am crammed with work and am just going down with my secretary to have a nice cup of tea, as we say in this country. You will be glad to hear that *Aphrodite in Aulis* was not a failure. The sale was slow at first, but it has not done so badly. I gather that quite a number of people liked it— there are nice people in it, and it is prettily written.

On the 30th of December he wrote his last letter to Miss Rodgers.

Dearest Viola,

I was glad to hear from you. I think of you constantly, for you have been a good friend to me. The past was pleasant but I am afraid there is no returning to it. It is very probable that I shall never see you again, for I do not seem to recover from my infirmity. You know all about it, the tube and the stoppages that occur and the leakages. I was in your house at Lardy and you took me to the surgeon at—— I cannot think of the name of the town at the moment.

I hope to write to the Fayants to thank Mr. Fayant for the cigars and Mrs. Fayant for the roses she sent me, but I don't suppose I shall ever see them again. They have been good affectionate friends and if circumstances had been different I should have come to think of them almost as I think of you, Viola that is to say with much affection.

This is the best letter that I can write through a secretary. I am waiting for a surgeon. Good bye, dear friend.

I do not press you to tell me why you never come to England.

Always affectionately yours

George Moore.

With a secretary who was called in on the 3rd of January, 1933, he worked once more over the first part of *A Communication to My Friends*. The passages were those in which he describes his search for a publisher for *A Modern Lover* and his recall to Ireland by Joe Blake. He dictated most of them at least six times over, generally making extensive alterations in the construction and order of the sentences; and he begged the young lady to make haste. He was very ill at the time though sitting up fully dressed, and he said more than once that he knew he would die before the book was finished. Once or twice when he had polished a phrase he said: " Now isn't that beautiful English ? " and smiled like a delighted child. " Have you read *Esther Waters* ? " he asked, " my best book. Now *that* is perfect English."

Though to his great and obvious distress, his brain was no longer always working clearly, yet the detail and anecdote of the unfinished *Communication* are as beguiling as anything he ever wrote. He even contrived to sound a new note in the scenes which revolve round the Gaiety Bar and the dingy offices of his first publishers, scenes in which the familiar meditative flow is quickened by some of the vigour of his early realistic novels. No sign of illness, or of failing power, is to be discerned except in some disturbance of chronology. Naturally he is less bound than ever to the tyranny of the fact, and even plausibility sometimes becomes immaterial, as in the description of the young Moore discoursing to Zola on the beauty and austerity of Landor.

G. W. Bishop, the dramatic critic, saw him not much more than a fortnight before his death and found him looking much better than usual. Moore admired a tie his visitor was wearing, and Mr. Bishop went to the shop where it was purchased, and was fortunate enough to get a similar tie. Moore thanked him. " You devised a delightful surprise," he wrote; " on looking into the glass I felt I was much

improved in appearance by the tie you sent me."[1] In this
last fortnight he accepted an invitation to dinner with the
Prime Minister, Mr. Ramsay MacDonald, but could not
fulfil the engagement when the day came, the 17th of
January, the last day on which he was able to do any work.
Tonks and two or three friends called to enquire, and were
alarmed to hear that he was spending the nights in an arm
chair in his dining-room, under the devoted care of his
housekeeper, without having seen a doctor. They called
in a male nurse, warned a doctor and installed a telephone;
the invalid was persuaded to his bedroom, regretting nothing
except that *Madeleine de Lisle* and *A Communication to My
Friends* remained unfinished. Sir John Thomson-Walker
came, and found the expected uræmic symptoms. They had
occurred before, but to a less degree, during the inflam-
matory attacks to which he was subject. On the 20th of
January he woke from heavy sleep and found Sir John
beside him. He turned to him with a smile and they talked
for five or ten minutes about the projected trip to The Ship
at Greenwich where they would have the much discussed
fish dinner. But they must wait until the weather was
warmer, said Moore. He dozed off again, very peacefully,
and at 5.45 a.m. the next morning, the nurse only being
present, he died.

13

On the day following Colonel Moore, who had been kept
informed of the course of the illness, came to Ebury Street
to see the brother from whom he had been so long estranged.
When Clara told him that a few hours before he died Moore
was moving his hand to attract her attention, and seemed
very urgent, Colonel Moore believed that it was the old
affection returning and filling his brother's mind. Julian
Moore called, and startled the servants by his resemblance
to their late master, but Mrs. Kilkelly, seeing her brother
in his coffin, said she would not have known him, so much
had he altered; he wore on his little finger the ring which

[1] *Sunday Times*, February 22nd, 1933.

she had given him on his twenty-first birthday. A mask was made of his face, now beautiful in its restraint and repose. The cast was given to the National Gallery. To respect a wish which he had expressed ever since his mother's death, arrangements for cremation were made, the ceremony being fixed for the twenty-fifth at Golder's Green. A few of Moore's closest friends, chiefly artists, attended. These sat at the back of the Church, separated by a gap (intended for representatives of society and literature who did not come), from the front row which was occupied on the one side of the aisle by members of the family and on the other by the Prime Minister and Mr. Augustus John. The rites were performed by Canon Douglas, an Anglican clergyman whom Moore had known in his last years, but modifications in the usual service were made which respected the fact that he was of no orthodoxy. Prayers were offered for the repose of the dead man's soul, but all references to more specifically Christian dogmas, such as " the sure and certain hope of immortality," were omitted.

" Get my ashes when I die," Moore had once said to Reilly, the steward at Moore Hall, " take them out on the lake and scatter them, but make sure that the wind is blowing in the right direction." There were no instructions in his will, but it seemed appropriate to bring his ashes home for burial on an island in the midst of the lake which he had so often celebrated, and the Colonel had a vase copied from an urn of the bronze age in the Dublin Museum and a hollow cut for its reception in the stony ground of Castle Island opposite the woods of Kiltoome, a mile across the lake from Moore Hall. When everything was at last ready it was late spring, and no trace of winter lingered in the thorns and rowans of the lake islands and the great beeches on the shore. The packing case containing the urn and the ashes reached the little town of Balla on the twenty-sixth of May.

The next day was soft and cloudless, as lovely as that other Mayo day on which George Moore had arrived home to learn of his mother's death. A small party of his friends— Mrs. Crawford and Mr. Medley from London, a few from Dublin and Mayo—and a young Donegal farmer with the splendid name of Ignatius MacHugh, drove over to the shores of the lake; as the first carriage passed through the gateway into the demesne the Colonel pointed out to Best and Mrs. Crawford the tree in which his brother used to hide from the lessons of Father James Browne. Two boats, the first having an engine, awaited the party on the yellow strand below the slope on which Moore Hall was built. A few Civic Guards (lest any demonstration should be attempted against pagan burial in holy Ireland) and a journalist or two swelled the little crowd, and at first a gentle confusion prevailed while the boats were filling. But order was restored by the Colonel's military decision, and the two boatloads started off, leaving Gogarty to row Mrs. Kilkelly and himself to the island. It was hot, he says, and it seemed a very long way, but the beauty of the day and the yellow-green of the lake would not be forgotten.

On the island Best read the words written by A. E. to be spoken over the urn. " If his ashes have any sentience they will feel at home here, for the colours of Carra Lake remained in his memory when many of his other affections had passed. It is possible the artist's love of earth, rock, water and sky is an act of worship. It is possible that faithfulness to art is an acceptable service. That worship, that service were his. If any would condemn him for creed of theirs he had assailed, let them be certain first that they laboured for their ideals as faithfully as he did for his."

As the workmen closed the hollow over with cement and raised a rough cairn above it, the afternoon wore away. It took a long time. Everything was as deliberate and unpunctual as the current of one of his own stories, and the watchers had time and to spare to admire the level shores of the lake, the blue ridge of Partry rising in the west, the great woods standing unchanged around the house, and the shell of the old house itself, gone with the old life.

CHAPTER XI

AN ACCOUNT OF GEORGE MOORE'S LAST YEARS

By his Cook and Housekeeper
CLARA WARVILLE

It WAS JULY 20TH, 1920 that I entered Mr. George Moore's house at 121 Ebury Street, S.W.1. as Cook General. At the time of my arrival he was without a house-parlour-maid, but informed me that he was going to stay with Mrs. Mary Hunter at Hill Hall Epping in two days' time, July 22nd, and that would give me a chance to look around, as he would return to Ebury Street early Monday morning in time to start work with Miss Kingdon his secretary who was a charming young lady. I was very fond of her. Mr. Moore knew that I had a widowed mother and suggested that I might have her sleep at Ebury Street while he was away, for which I was agreeable being strange myself in a large house. We finally got suited with a house-parlourmaid after I had been there three weeks and soon settled down, never dawning on me at the time that I should have stayed as long as I did under his roof. He often went to Hill Hall for the week-end, but he was sorry when Mrs. Mary Hunter had to give up Hill Hall as I think he rather liked going there, and another place he used to like to go and stay at was with Sir Nevill Geary at Oxon Hoath, Tonbridge, Kent. He used to go to France and stay at the Hotel Continental once a year up to about the year 1927; if he went for three weeks he would return in about ten days with an excuse that the workmen were making too much noise, that it was impossible for him to do any writing, so he nearly always returned to an upside down house, for we always did the spring-cleaning while he was in France, as that was the longest time he was out of the house. He said he did not mind seeing the house unfinished, but of course it was not fair to us. One year he told Mabel to pack enough clothes, etc., to last for six weeks. He had not been away a week when a telegram arrived saying he was returning the next day. Every carpet was up, ready to go to be cleaned, when he arrived. Mabel said, " You can't stop here." He said he would telegraph to Sir Nevill Geary and ask him if he could put him up for a week, which he did; we had to hurry up the carpet-beaters, but the house was not cleaned properly, but that was not our fault. The secretary always had her holiday when he went to France. Mrs. Crawford was a frequent visitor to Ebury Street, Mr. Moore would write his letters in English, and she would copy them in French for him to send to his French friends in France. Mr. Whittaker at one time used to dine very often, and help him with a book called *Ulick and Soracha*,[1] Mr. Magee who lived at Bournemouth used to read through a lot of Mr. Moore's work, he used to send him a parcel to look over and alter any mistakes. Mr. Moore told me that Mr. Magee was very clever and knew at once how a book should read. He stayed at Ebury Street, each time for two nights, and Mr. Moore turned his top writing room into a bedroom, as there was no spare room here for visitors.

Mr. David Garnett used to visit Mr. Moore very often and stay to luncheon, also Mr. Geraint Goodwin came several Sundays to tea, at the time he was writing the book called *Conversations with George Moore*. He called to see him a few months before Mr. Moore passed away, he had been abroad, and heard that he was very ill. When I opened the front door I did not recognise him, he saw me looking very hard at him, and he said, " Don't you know who I am ? " and I said, " No, sir." And he said, " I am Mr. Goodwin." Then I knew the voice, as I had let him in a good many times. He was growing a beard which made him look more like 60 than 30 years of age. After he was gone, Mr. Moore said, " No wonder you did not know him."

[1] *Daphnis and Chloë*, I think.—J. M. H.

GEORGE MOORE: THE LAST PASSPORT PHOTOGRAPH

Mr. Charles Evans from Heinemanns used to lunch very often at one time, that was because he wanted to talk to him about his books being published, he also had the late Mr. John Freeman and Mr. De la Mare to dinner. Dr. Gogarty and Mr. Bodkin came very often; also Mr. Geoffrey Ruttledge, whose father, Mr. Tom Ruttledge, was Mr. Moore's agent for Moore Hall in Ireland before it was burnt to the ground. Only his grandfather's oil painting was saved. It arrived at Ebury Street the night before Moore Hall was burnt down. Mr. Moore had the painting hanging up in a recess on the first landing at Ebury Street; he was very proud of it, and I often used to see him gazing at it when he was coming down stairs.

Mr. Moore was very upset when he read in the paper about Mrs. Benjamin Guinness having passed away. He visited her in London a few weeks before his operation, and was praising up her canaries, of which she had a good many; about two days after he left the nursing home and returned to Ebury Street, her chauffeur brought a canary in a cage as a present for Mr. Moore. At first he was very pleased with it, and called it Chow, because one of his notes sounded like chow. Soon after, the bird started to sing one note, more like a squeak, and of course it was sent down to the kitchen; he would not have the bird upstairs in the dining-room again. I must admit that a squeak is not very pleasant to hear, especially when one is not feeling very well.

I remember Mr. Moore telling me that if he ever got held up with his book, which sometimes did happen, he would walk all round Belgrave Square, and nearly always what he wanted to write would come to him. He asked me if I thought it was a mile all round the square. I said as I had never been round it I could not say, he thought it was.

Mr. Bodkin always called on Mr. Moore whenever he came to London; sometimes Mr. Moore was engaged when he called, so I had a card handed to me to give to Mr. Moore with the address where he was staying, and would I tell him that he had called to pay Mr. Moore his respects. Sometimes he would ask Mr. Bodkin to dinner, or to call in after dinner for a chat. Mr. Moore often used to go and see Lady Ward at

5 Wilbraham Place, Sloane Square, after the secretary had gone; one evening on the way to see her he slipped nearly opposite our house by the pub. Miss Fenn, who lives at 102 Ebury Street, where he fell, helped to pick him up and asked if he had hurt himself, he said, " No." And she told him his overcoat was very dusty. She quite thought he would come back home to have his coat brushed. No, he went on, but the maid must have noticed it when she let him in, as he returned with a clean coat.

One day, Mr. Beverley Nichols was asked to luncheon. They had an omelette to start with, and it must have been stone cold when they were eating it, as I was waiting for the parlour maid to take up the cutlets. I said, " What a long time they have been over their omelette," and she said, " Why, they are only just eating it." She said that Mr. Moore was so busy talking to his guest that he failed to see what was waiting to be served in front of him.

Mr. Moore could not bear to see it raining, if he was work-ing in the dining-room on the ground floor, he would ask one of us to draw the blinds. One day they were never drawn back, and one of our neighbours, whom I knew quite well, passed a remark about it a few days later, and said, " I thought some one had passed away," and I said, " No, Mr. Moore was waiting for the rain to pass away."

One Sunday afternoon, when the parlourmaid was out, I looked into the dining-room to see if the fire wanted making up. As I thought Mr. Moore was asleep in his armchair, I put the coal on very carefully, one piece at a time, so as not to wake him up. I was tip-toeing out of the room, and just as I got to the door he said, " I wasn't asleep, I was only meditat-ing and remembering about my work for the secretary to-morrow."

When I first went to live with Mr. Moore in 1920, he used to go to Sir Edmund Gosse's house to supper every fortnight. I think he looked forward to that evening, as he always seemed in good spirits before he went. It was on Sunday evenings. Of course he never went again after Sir Edmund passed away, although Mr. Gosse asked him several times, but he always refused.

Up to the time of his operation, April 4th, 1928, Mr. Moore always looked forward on Saturday evenings to spend a couple of hours with Professor Tonks. Dinner must not be late those evenings; very often he would call downstairs to know if I could let him have dinner before 7.30, it pleased him if I could. We had one parlourmaid named Irene Tyrrell; but he called her Deena because he knew some one in Ireland called Deena Tyrrell; he was very fond of finding fault with the maids in front of his friends which made them feel very uncomfortable. He used to like Jean Aubry, who lived in France, to pay him visits when he came to London. He said it helped him to keep in with his French. We always had great difficulty about his friends, he was only at home to anyone who had got an appointment. Very often a very old friend would call, and we would have to give the message that we were told to give, so when they were gone, he would say, " Who was that ? " We would give him the name, and he would say, " I want to see that young man or young lady," and we would have to go after them and bring them back. There was a very large Persian cat which had a ginger fur coat called Sarky that lived at 111 Ebury Street, the house of Mr. Noel Coward's father. Mr. Moore was very fond of the cat, and often brought it in and gave it some milk, and said his hair used to be the same colour as the cat's fur before it turned white. I noticed his moustache had a tint of auburn in it, but he hated dogs. The street musicians and Mr. Moore were not on friendly terms; if any musician was playing near his house he would be after them, and tell them to go much further up the road. Most of them took no notice of what he said, so he went round the corner to Gerald Road police station, and came back with a policeman, and when nearly up to them, they would move away, with the policeman doing a grin. One lady that used to call, her name was Mrs. Ada Leverson, who was very deaf, he gave us orders that when she called again to say that he was out. He had something else to do besides shouting in her ear. What she wanted was an ear trumpet.

Mr. Moore was very fond of a fish called bass, which he could never get at any of the small fish shops, so he asked me

to go to the Army and Navy Stores, and ask if they ever had
bass to sell. They said, yes they did have it sometimes, but
no one seemed to ask for it, so I had to leave word to tell them
that whenever they had a bass would they send it on to him,
and he would pay on delivery. True, it was a very nice-
flavoured fish, and was nice even when cold with mayonnaise
sauce. Mr. Moore said it was eaten a great deal in France.
Several of his friends used to send him salmon when in season,
but he preferred salmon trout, as he said it was not so rich
as salmon. I was a long time before I could do a French
omelette to suit him; in the end he had to go to a small hotel
in Buckingham Palace Road, and ask the French chef to
show me. After I had seen it done I soon got to do it all right
for him. The chef soon earned 5s., for it only took about five
minutes to prepare and make. Very often he would crave for
a fish that was not in season.

A year or two after I went to live with Mr. Moore, I was
out one morning when a man called selling chickens. Mr.
Moore happened to see him ringing the front door bell, so he
went himself and answered it, as the parlourmaid was upstairs. He remembered that he had Mr. Whittaker coming to
dinner with him that evening, and thought he would have a
chicken from the man. Of course they always look nice, and
they truss them up to make them appear larger than they
are. I remembered it was the day the Lord Mayor of Cork
died when I cooked it. Mr. Moore could not set his teeth
in it, but Mr. Whittaker ate every bit, and Mr. Moore said he
must have had some very strong teeth, and he joked about
the chicken and said it must have been on hunger-strike too.
Glad I had nothing to do with it. There was hardly any meat
on it.

An Expensive View

I saw a piece in the paper a few years ago and the title is
just above. It read that Mr. George Moore and Dr. Oliver
Gogarty were travelling in a train and were going through
Ireland when Mr. Moore said, " Oh, Oliver, I would give
£10 for five minutes of that lovely view." As quick as thought
Dr. Oliver jumped up and pulled the communication cord,

and said, "There you are Moore, I have got it for you for half price." Mr. Moore paid up like a man.

I think I told you that Mr. Moore was very fond of cats. We had a black one, very knowing; we called him Nigger because he was all black. One day he was on one of Mr. Moore's arm chairs in the dining-room. He brushed it off; the cat never went up on the chair again; but one day Mr. Moore was laying back in his arm chair, eyes closed, meditating, when he heard paper rustling, he turned his head towards where the sound came from, and saw Nigger standing on his hind legs, pulling the newspaper on to the floor to lie on. He left it there, and rang the bell for me to see what he had done. Mr. Moore was saying what a lot of sense some animals had. The Duchess of Marlborough used to visit Mr. Moore a lot at one time.

One day, H. S. Ede, Esq., from the National Gallery, Millbank came to tea and fell in love with the tea-pot. Mr. Moore said he would give it to him, but told him at the time that the bottom of the tea-pot had been very much riveted, and that it had started to leak again. Mr. Ede knew that Lady Cunard was having nearly everything, I don't know if he ever asked her for it. Mr. George Moore was always very pleased when Mr. and Mrs. St. John Hutchinson called to see him, and no wonder, for Mr. St. John always had a pleasant smile and a pleasing voice whenever he called to see him, enough to cheer any one who was not well; he ought to have been a doctor. He always reminded me of Dr. Beaumont Comerford who used to attend Mr. Moore when I first went to live at Ebury Street. I never knew why he gave him up. Mr. Moore used to like Lady Diana Abdy to call and see him, she was very good at painting and very often would bring some of her pictures along for Mr. Moore to see, and he would give her some advice; one of her paintings he liked very much, and she gave it to him, and he had it framed.

Mr. Moore was very much upset when Mr. Leverton Harris passed away; he was not very old, and when Mrs. Leverton Harris called on Mr. Moore after the funeral,

Mr. Moore asked her if she would give him something in remembrance of her husband. Next day she brought a rather nicely shaped brass can that he used to have his shaving water in. He thanked her, but said he would rather have had a small piece of china from her drawing-room, a figure of some kind. Next day, Mrs. Harris returned with a nice ornament called the shepherdess. He was very pleased with that. It was a lovely figure, so of course he was for sending the water-can back, but she said No, she wished him to keep it, so he used it every day till he was unable to.

Mr. Moore often used to tell me that he had walked all over the house in the middle of the night, as he thought he heard some one outside his bedroom door. One night a picture that hung outside his bedroom door fell down and smashed the glass and went rolling down the stairs. He thought they were in that night, till he went on the landing and saw what had *really* happened; a good thing he did not go down the stairs, as he never wore slippers, always walked about in his bare feet, and he was sure to have got some splintered glass in his feet if he had gone down the stairs.

Whenever Mr. Moore had anyone coming to dinner he always used to come downstairs to the wine cellar to get out some claret about five minutes before dinner time. He was very fond of looking in the kitchen and asking me several questions about the food. I must have answered him very sharply one evening, and he told me about it the next day. So I said, " Well, sir, you have always told me never to interrupt you when you were busy dictating to the secretary; well, it is the same with cooks, especially just as dinner is about to be served; they don't like being interrupted. It takes their mind from their cooking, and is apt to spoil something." He quite understood, and promised not to go in the kitchen again when I was busy.

Imagine my surprise one Saturday morning, at 5.45 a.m., to hear a taxi stop outside our front door, and a man's voice saying, " I don't suppose anyone will be up at this hour, as you have said that you have not let anyone know that you are expected," and to hear Mr. Moore answer, " No, I don't expect they will, but this bell rings at the top of the house." I was up early that morning, hurrying, as was usual, to set the house ready for him on arrival. We did not expect him till the Monday, and as I was working in the front hall, I did not keep him waiting. They both looked surprised at not being kept waiting. My first words were: " Well, sir, you might have let me know that you were arriving so early in the morning. Just look at the place, not straight simply because you always come back before you are due." I must have spoken very crossly to him when I let him in, because after the taxi man was gone, he said: " A nice little tale the taxi man will have to tell his wife when he goes home to breakfast, at the beautiful reception I received after return- ing home." I said, " I can't help that, I didn't know what I was saying or doing at seeing you at that hour in the morning unexpected." The doctor had told him that a week at a nursing home at Hampstead would do him a lot of good when he had no appetite; so he fixed Mr. Moore up, and made arrangements for him to stay there for a week. He went on the Saturday, and as soon as he arrived he would not let the nurses do anything for him, if it had not been Sunday the next day he would have returned, but arrived Monday morning, soon after 9 a.m. He was always very annoyed should Mrs. Hunter call on him with feathers in her hat. He gave us strict orders not to let her in should she call the next time with feathers in her hat; we were to say he was out. It used to be very unpleasant for us when he would say " Not at home " to anybody ; and very often one of his friends would call, and when told " Not at home," would say, " Could I come in and write a note ? " We could not say " No, you can't," and Mr. Moore was nearly always in the dining-room, so we could not ask them in there, so we had to ask them upstairs in the drawing-room, expecting every minute to hear him call out, " Who was that that called ? " before they left the house; all very confusing to us and to his friends after telling us to say he was out.

He went into another nursing home in Wimpole Street, and I am sure the nurses were glad when he returned home, for they said it did not matter what they took him in the way of food, he turned against it before he tasted it. As the nurse told me that nothing can be eaten, even if it has not been touched, after it has been in any bedroom, there was a great deal of food wasted. I had to take a special dish that he used to have sometimes for breakfast, called " eggs on the plate " with little bits of bacon round the eggs. I was to see the cook, and tell her how he liked it, but I was glad she was out when I called, so I left the message how it was done with another maid. When he returned home, he said he had been starved. That was wrong, for they tried every way to please him, and the nurse told me that they had got an excellent cook there. The night he arrived home I gave him one of his favourite soups, a French soup called " pot au feu," also some fried filleted sole with Hollandaise sauce. He did not want any sweet, but said after dinner that I had saved his life. I did not understand what he meant by that, so I said, " In what way ? " and he said, " By giving me something that I could eat." But towards the end I had great difficulty in getting him to take nourishment; he did not know what he wanted, and what I thought he might like was met with disapproval.

CHAPTER XII

THE ACHIEVEMENT OF
GEORGE MOORE

By DESMOND SHAWE-TAYLOR

IN ATTEMPTING to trace the development of George
Moore as an artist I have with a few exceptions confined
myself to the consideration of those works which he himself
admitted to what he called the " canon " of his Uniform
edition; partly for reasons of space, partly because the
rejected books have been discussed in their chronological
position in the present biography, and partly because Moore's
powers of self-criticism were so nice that few would question
the wisdom of his final choice. For similar reasons it seemed
better to avoid a detailed treatment of the famous revisions
and " re-orchestrations," interesting though they often are.
So much excellent criticism has already appeared of Moore's
style and his technical achievement in prose narrative that
there is some danger of our concentrating overmuch on the
surface of his art, forgetting that a fine style, even so conscious a style as that of Moore, must, if it is to hold our
interest, be no more than the perfect and inevitable expression of an individual mind. Moore's personality and the
style in which it is so exactly mirrored are alike in being
unmistakably his own, and it was not until he had created—
out of the void, it seemed to his friends—the George Moore
known to the world that his prose could attain to its full
maturity.

I

The Uniform edition of the works of George Moore consists of twenty volumes, and the most remarkable fact about

it is that only four of them were written before his fiftieth
year. Of these four three are selected from the ten early
novels which are roughly classified as naturalistic or realistic.
That the selection is the right one no one who has looked
into the rejected novels will doubt. *A Modern Lover* was from
the first an artistic failure, though of an unusual sort, and its
vulgarity was not redeemed when Moore rewrote it in 1917
as *Lewis Seymour and Some Women*; the incidental felicities of
Spring Days and *Vain Fortune* were lost in an uncertain wandering narrative; as for *Mike Fletcher*, you mentioned it to its
author in later years at your peril. In contrast to these, the
clear portraiture and firm outline of *A Mummer's Wife* leap
to the eye, and the unity of *Muslin* is only less evident because
it is that of a social group and not of an individual. The
acknowledged masterpiece of his realistic period is of course
Esther Waters, which after forty years still makes a profound
impression by the unsentimental sincerity of its pathos and
its rich delineation of servants' hall, racing stable and public
house life. Such figures as the seedy professional tipsters,
Stack, Ketley and Journeyman, may even have seemed
prophetic of another Dickens, paler but more austere.

But George Moore was already ambitious of an art more
subtle than that of the realistic novel, and he made no
attempt to repeat the enormous success of *Esther Waters*.
At first he thought that the heightened sensibility which he
desired could be attained by building his story around a set
of rich people and artists who devote all their energy to music
and love affairs, and the result of this unhappy notion was
Evelyn Innes, the story of an opera singer and an æsthetic
baronet. There is nothing in the least dull about *Evelyn Innes*
—whatever his faults Moore was seldom dull—but the
veracity and interest of the musical background disappear
amid an almost Ouida-like snobbishness. Sir Owen Asher
is altogether too much of a swell, delightful though it is to
see him " leaning against the door-post, a half-cynical, half-
kindly smile floating through his gold moustache," or order-
ing dinner in Paris: " there is a *parfait*—that comes before
the *soufflé*, of course." If some of the earlier novels were
marred by a lack of unity, *Evelyn Innes* and *Sister Teresa*

proceed out of a false romanticism. Here indeed was the triumph of the flashy, unregenerate Moore, the Amico Moorini of the preface to *The Lake* whom Mr. Charles Morgan in his discerning *Epitaph on George Moore* perceives to have been a perpetual thorn in the artist's side. He does not quote one of the most striking of all instances of the rebellion of Amico Moorini, a long and entirely new passage in the second edition (1909) of *Sister Teresa* in which Asher and his friend Harding stroll through the gay crowds of Piccadilly and Bond Street, " a delirium of feathers, skirts, and pink ankles," discussing fashionable adulteries (" two or three ladies were mentioned whose *liaisons* reached a couple of hundred "), and only stopping to order cigars (by the thousand) and trousers (" Every suit of clothes I have, Harding, costs me fifty pounds "). The glamour and gusto of this scene is intoxicating; but that it should have been written in the middle of *Hail and Farewell* passes belief. Small wonder that his friends were blinded so long to the new Moore that was beginning to emerge.

Some critics of Moore who knew him intimately in the nineties or in his Dublin period (Yeats and John Eglinton, for example) have found it difficult to believe that great works of the imagination could be produced by the man they knew—amusing, imperfectly educated, a bit of a card, likeable but infuriating. The younger men who read the later works first and met him when the legend of Ebury Street was already established, had no such difficulty: they saw Moore as Moore had come to see himself, a priest of letters with an unusually picturesque and unusually pro-tracted nonage. Only thus can we account for the suggestions of his older critics that he never wrote better books than the best of his early novels. Their very real merits should not lead us to that assertion; they are good books, few of their period have worn so well, but they add nothing essential to English literature; if Moore had died at the age of fifty we should remember him as an interesting minor novelist who had written a single masterpiece in *Esther Waters*, and in *Confessions of a Young Man* a crude but vital account of the æstheticism of a modish young Irishman in the Paris of the seventies. We cannot think in this way of the author of *Hail and Farewell, Celibate Lives* and *Héloïse and Abélard*.

The two disappointing novels of society and convent life were behind him, and his life, whether he knew it or not, was at a turning point. If he had lived on in England he would probably have continued to write successful novels; a lucky choice of subject might even have thrown up a second *Esther Waters*. But such a prospect did not satisfy him, and he was full of vague literary ambitions which he discussed in the Temple with his old friend Edward Martyn; and in his company he met Arthur Symons and W. B. Yeats. Everybody talked a great deal, and he was delighted: he loved talking, and there seemed to be a new æstheticism in the air; his Irish friends reminded him of what he had almost forgotten—that he was Irish, and they needed him to rehearse their theatrical ventures. Why did he not join them and return to Ireland? He hesitated; then England embarked upon the hateful Boer war and he hesitated no longer.

The invitation, whatever his reasons for accepting it, came at an opportune moment. Already he had revolted against the extreme naturalism of Zola: *Evelyn Innes* and *Sister Teresa* are full of stumbling attempts at philosophy and poetry, but their popular success did not blind him for long to their shallowness. He had reached in his art a sort of dead end: a change of air was desirable. He cannot have guessed how much more profound a change was to come about when he moved to Dublin, for never was the Horatian tag *cælum non animum mutat qui trans mare currit* more completely refuted.

2

It is not easy to disentangle the influences which turned Moore to a wholly new ideal of composition: influences of which he was partly conscious, partly unconscious. It has been said that the mature artist owed everything to Ireland, and if in saying Ireland we include the personal influence of Yeats and A. E. there is much truth in the claim, for before long he began to feel an interest in the rhythm of his writing and the shape of his stories which was quite new to him. The speech of Dublin is commonly more melodious and more flowing than the speech of London; and in Yeats he was brought into close contact with a poet whose prose was as musical as his verse, a mind steeped in the traditional stories of Ireland which he loved to recite over the fire. The legends, the wayward talk, the fabulous gossip of Dublin were as stimulating to Moore as the Nouvelle Athènes: they gave a fresh direction to his talent. He listened, he warmed his spirit before the glow of A. E., and presently he began to discover in himself not only a gift for anecdote but a personality as alive to its own absurdities as to the absurdities of others. This is the double springhead from which all his future work was to flow: on the one hand his love of a rhythmical, anecdotal story-telling, quite unlike the plot-construction of the typical English novelist, which led him after many years to the twin peaks of " his little range," *The Brook Kerith* and *Héloïse and Abélard*; on the other hand that progressive realisation and revelation of his extra-ordinary self which gave us first *Memoirs of My Dead Life*, then the Irish trilogy, and finally the two volumes of dis-cursive literary criticism and table-talk, *Avowals* and *Conver-sations in Ebury Street*.

He now began to develop the conception of what he called " the melodic line," narrative not only shaped from the beginning towards an inevitable end but allowing on the way none of the personal intervention of the author that has always been a bane of English fiction, nor the abrupt transi-tions from description to dialogue or thought-stream whose avoidance is a continual problem of the novelist's art. The technical triumph which he achieved in this respect has been analysed by Mr. Charles Morgan in his *Epitaph,* and he gives earlier in the same volume a description of that method of dictating and re-dictating from what he called " rigma-role " by which Moore built up the fabric of his later work. One may wonder whether part of the famous discovery that novels had forgotten their origin in oral narrative may not have been due to the fact that about this time he acquired his first secretary and found that his thoughts flowed more easily in dictation than in silent composition. Whenever he made a discovery for himself (and he took nothing on trust) he always wished to make it into a rule of universal application; and it was not long before he was wondering why everyone did not adopt the melodic continuity of tale-telling which suited his own talent to perfection. (But not necessarily the talents of others: though the metaphor he chose was a musical one, it never occurred to him to reflect how far Palestrina or Bach or his beloved Wagner had travelled from the melodic line of folk-song or of plain chant.) Mr. Morgan thinks that his simplification of prose narrative will have a great influence on novelists of the future. It may be so; though so far there has been little evidence of it except in Mr. Morgan's own work and in the stories of Mr. David Garnett. It seems rather that his novels will remain, like those of Peacock, a little outside the main stream of English fiction, though they may well serve as permanent models of great and untiring craftsmanship. One thing Ireland had no need to teach him—the need of endless labour if the ideals of artistic integrity were to be realised. Here indeed Moore was the master, Dublin the disciple: " he taught us all the value of hard work," said Douglas Hyde.

The first evidence of the new Moore was seen in *The Untilled Field*, that volume of short stories which in simplicity, humour and perfection of outline have inevitably recalled Turgenev's *Tales of a Sportsman*. In all his work there is nothing more satisfying than two or three of these stories: " The Window," " Almsgiving," " The Wedding Gown." Furthermore, they are pure Ireland, showing a real understanding of the national character and a feeling for the national idiom quite free from the occasional artificiality of Lady Gregory's Kiltartan. In *The Lake*, a short novel only prevented by its length from inclusion with the other stories, there is less of the Irish people but more of the Irish landscape. This novel has been highly praised: unexpectedly by Mr. Yeats, for it is the beginning of that smooth narrative style for which he professes so much contempt in his *Dramatis Personæ*. It has descriptive passages of great beauty, and, in the opening pages, a vivid glimpse of the schoolmistress heroine Nora Glynn (" she hopped over the style as if she enjoyed the little jump into the road.") But she soon vanishes from our sight and the greater part of the book consists of long letters to and from Father Gogarty, interspersed with his meditations along the shores of the lake. So intoxicated was Moore with his discovery of the imaginative reverie that he did not sufficiently differentiate the priest's musings from his own: often Father Gogarty is nearly absorbed in the personality of his creator, and the background of the priest's daily life is so lightly sketched in that we are left with the somewhat irritating impression that he had nothing to do all day but to dream of Nora Glynn and the forms of the mountains across the lake.

Moore must have perceived that for the moment at any rate his dreams and reflections would play with greater advantage around his own experience than that of any imaginary character, and his next book was *Memoirs of My Dead Life*. He afterwards came to dislike the first version of the *Memoirs*, and rewrote it extensively, but it must have been immediately obvious what an advance he had made into new territory. The best sketches in the volume—the charming impressionism of " Spring in London " and " Flowering Normandy," the flawless narrative of " The End of Marie Pellegrin " (Turgenev again), the comedy of " The Lovers of Orelay "—all these are not only delightful in themselves but they prepare the way for the various triumphs of the trilogy.

Hail and Farewell, which many critics hold to be its author's greatest work, seems likely to retain a permanent interest which will outlive the interest of its subject-matter—has indeed already partly outlived it: even at the time of its appearance all but the greatest figures of the Irish literary renaissance must have been obscure to English readers, and with every year they grow more obscure. Such changes seem to leave the stature of the book undiminished: *Hail and Farewell* is one of the world's great autobiographies, though it is unlike any other. Three long volumes of this unique blend of novel and reminiscence, with no more unity of theme than lay in the personality of the narrator and in the

singleminded aim (how differently fulfilled !) of all the
conspirators who planned to rescue the Irish Cinderella from
her rags, contain scarcely a flaw or an irrelevancy. An
enormous mass of disparate material went to their making:
memories of childhood in Mayo, of France, of Sussex, a visit
to Bayreuth, intimate conversations with women, arguments
about the Boer War with artists in London, with everybody
about everything in Ireland—all these are mingled with
those early struggles of the Irish movement which appear to
be the theme of the book. How could unity be imposed on
such material, generally presented not in recollection, but
vividly, at first hand ? It might have seemed impossible, but
the sense of form was now so strong in Moore that the shape
of the whole work came to him, he says, in a week of inspiration: the rough outline from which he never strayed,
beginning in the Temple and ending with the visit to Moore
Hall. The outline is of a singular perfection; but it may not
be until a second or third reading that we pereceive it, so
vivid and so brilliant is the detail. A great deal of the art of
Hail and Farewell is the art of transition: never were joins
more ingeniously made, and John Eglinton acutely likens
the work to a series of galleries opening on one another.
Such smoothness is more than a technical triumph, it is
proof of the writer's perfect grasp of his subject.

The first thing however that strikes the reader of the trilogy
is the verve of its humour, the skill of the character sketches,
the unforgettable phrases; for who forgets the vision of Yeats
in the woods of Coole, " a tall black figure standing at the
edge of the lake, wearing a cloak which fell in straight folds
to his knees, looking like a great umbrella forgotten by some
picnic party " ? Moore had acquired an uncanny knack for
painting not only externals but character, his portraits being
by no means the travesties they are frequently supposed to
be; and the greatest of all the portraits is that of Edward
Martyn. The uncouth lovable bulk of the man becomes with
every appearance a little more real, until we reach the
wonderful chapter in *Vale* which paints for us the shabby
rooms above the tobacconist in Lincoln Place where " dear
Edward " spent his evenings reading by the light of candles

in the tin candelabra of his own design, " lying on the little sofa sheltered from draughts by a screen, a shawl about his shoulders. . . . I looked round the rooms and they seemed part of himself. The old green wall-paper on which he pins reproductions of the Italian masters, and I longed to peep once more into the bare bedroom into which he goes to fetch bottles of Apollinaris." In the end we know Edward Martyn much as we know Dr. Johnson in the pages of Boswell, and Moore's book shares another characteristic of the great *Life* in that one may open it anywhere and read a few pages with delight. Though Moore would probably have disliked the idea, I have often thought that a cheap edition should be brought out in a single volume, with an index of proper names.

3

After *Hail and Farewell* there could be no turning back, no dealing in the small change of literature. The trilogy, if it did not reach so large a public as the most successful of his novels, won over the discerning few, and those who had reserved judgment over the Irish stories and the *Memoirs* capitulated: something new and delightful had enriched English literature. The volume of essays which he had meditated would hardly do, the vein of reminiscence and confession was for the moment exhausted, contemporary English life seemed to offer a somewhat flat, colourless field for the narrative powers which he now felt within him. Like Milton, he would attempt something which the world should not willingly let die; he would attempt a prose epic.

The religious controversies in which he had embroiled himself in Ireland led him to read the Bible, and discussion of the Gospels with John Eglinton caused the notion to flash into his mind of a meeting between Paul and Jesus—a Jesus who had swooned but not died upon the cross. Fearing that so tempting an idea might be pillaged, he published in 1911 a scenario for a play on the subject—a sketch of little value to us now but for the brilliant *Prefatory Letter On Reading the Bible for the First Time* which unfortunately finds no place in the Uniform Edition, though it might with advantage have been included in the slender volume which contains *The Passing of the Essenes*, his final dramatic version of the Paul–Jesus theme. For a time his ideas on the subject still held to the form of drama; then, fortunately for the world, he began to see a long leisurely narrative mounting quietly to its great climax, a strange variant of the classical recognition scene. In anything that concerned his work Moore was always intensely serious, but never had his preparations been so thorough as now they were. He plunged deeply into biblical controversy, and, the least adventurous of travellers, undertook a journey to Palestine and arduous explorations in the hills across the Jordan where his Essene monastery must lie. In 1916 *The Brook Kerith*, his " Syrian story," as he modestly described it, appeared, and five years later it was followed by *Héloïse and Abélard*. On these two works his ultimate fame as a novelist must rest.

They have, in addition to characteristics which no one can miss, the quality, rare in English prose, of being fully conscious works of art: they are as carefully calculated in every sentence as is *Paradise Lost* in every line. England has always preferred the genius of wilful prodigality of the type of Shakespeare or Dickens to the genius which seeks expression in a classical firmness of outline: Milton and Dryden are accepted rather than loved (Dr. Johnson remarked that no man ever wished *Paradise Lost* longer than it is), while so perfect an exemplar of the classical spirit as Landor receives a rather perfunctory homage. Perhaps it is partly for this reason that Moore has been often accused of a mannered artificiality, or alternatively of a false simplicity; for in spite of his kinship with the Impressionists and Symbolists of Paris on the one hand, on the other with the romanticism of the nineties and the Celtic revival, he revealed in his mature works a genius which is, in many aspects, of a classical order. This unscholarly man, without Latin or Greek, turned instinctively at the end of his life to Longus and the Periclean age; not idly did he once remark " I am without learning, as the ancients were, but I have the eyes of the ancients, I think." We think of Moore often, as is natural, as the man of picturesque origin, the eccentric combination of country

squire and self-revealing artist. Such romantic aspects of the
man catch the eye, as he intended they should; we forget the
other side of the picture: the classical refusal to allow emotion
to break the mould of his art, the ability to see the end in the
beginning, the constant striving after perfection of form, the
sparkling clarity of description, the restraint of such great
scenes as the awakening of Jesus in the home of Joseph of
Arimathea, or the confronting of Paul with the shepherd
Jesus, or the meeting after nine years of Héloïse and Abélard.
What opportunities offered here for rhetoric, for spectacular
flights of writing. And as we read how clearly we feel the
beat of emotion beneath the calm surface.

It is a classical care for construction rather than a romantic
picturesqueness which lends such force to certain episodes in
Moore's stories; the parts derive their value from their
relationship to the whole. Early in *The Brook Kerith* the young
Joseph, musing on the death of his grandmother, fancies
that a tomb cut out of the rock would be preferable to a grave
in the earth, and speculates for a little on the most desirable
site. In an instant Nicodemus appears, and the current of the
story moves on, but the seemingly casual episode has made
the profound effect which it owes to its perfect placing.

Plot in the conventional sense there is little; rather a
story-telling that is oral and Eastern in the directness of its
tread, as it were a two-dimensional narrative without the
multiplicity of planes, the psychological analysis, the variety
of simultaneous interest to which we are accustomed in
Western fiction. Each person, each beast, each landscape
engages in passing the story-teller's whole interest and attention, and only his strong sense of design prevents the books
from becoming merely episodic. The chatter of the Breton
servant Madelon, the visit of the gleemen to the convent at
Argenteuil, the enchanting child Astrolabe (a fellow to
Shakespeare's Mamilius)—all fall into place without dis-
tracting the interest from the central theme; yet they are
seen to exist on the same plane as the dialogues of the lovers
themselves. An extraordinary achievement of the shaping
imagination, which we may appreciate the more honestly in
confessing that *Héloïse and Abélard* does in fact contain one

digression which, although Abélard plays in it a principal
part, we feel to be out of tone and too long: I mean the
episode of the Courts of Love.

It is a solitary flaw in a great book which one should be
wary of beginning to praise, it is so difficult to stop. The
unscholarly Moore gives (at least to an unscholarly reader) a
wonderfully complete picture of medieval Paris, " a city of a
thousand cries projecting its grey profile into the sunset; a
multitude of towers and spires and thronging roofs above
streets so narrow that they were already in twilight ": the
pleasant assemblies, the peaked gables and jutting storeys of
its houses, the terrible winter cold; wolf-hunts clamouring
along the snowy streets, students loitering on the bridges—all
the details that his patient friends ferreted out in libraries
warmed into life by his glowing imagination. Tired of the
complexity of modern fiction, we return with an ever fresh
delight to that ride of the lovers from Paris to Orléans
through the spring forests; the world was never so young
since Chaucer. That such a mood should have been recovered
in the twentieth century seems a miracle, and it may be that
an author whose mind had been disciplined in logic and
grammar and philosophy could not have recovered it. Moore
gained quite as much as he lost from his lack of systematic
education. His distaste for abstract speculation, due, as Mr.
Morgan points out, not to incapacity but to boredom, did
no hurt to his tale of the learned lovers, for he mastered
enough Nominalism and Realism to paint in the scholastic
background to Whittaker's admiration.

In *The Brook Kerith* we are more conscious of such limita-
tions, conscious that the writer is no metaphysician, that he
has little sense of the mystical element in religion. Many
readers have felt an inadequacy in the portrait of Jesus, a
vague kindliness in the later scenes rather than the wisdom
born of a profound spiritual experience. To say that Moore
falls short here is perhaps to say no more than that he is not a
Dante, a Vaughan, a Crashaw. On the earthly plane, the
gradual clearing of the brain of Jesus is beautifully suggested,
its slow return from stupor to thought reminding the reader
of another pastoral healing of the mind—that of Don

Quixote. The gentle charm of Joseph of Arimathea and the
fierce energy of Paul light up the beginning and the end of
the book, the contrast heightening our impression of having
travelled an immense distance when at last we take leave of
Paul in Rome. Though we may qualify the verdict of
Mr. Humbert Wolfe who sees in *The Brook Kerith* " possibly
the greatest prose book, except the Bible, in the English
tongue," and though we deplore a single incongruity in the
semi-comic episode of the dissenting Essenes who experi-
mented in marriage, the book holds us by an extraordinary
fascination of theme and treatment.

The prose of both these romances and of the later works
generally has the grave leisurely flow of a great river, as
adequate to the simplest facts of the story as to its emotional
climax. It is obvious that in this smoothness there lies the
danger of monotony, and Moore's work is not always free of
that fault. But when Mr. Yeats roundly declares that " charm
and rhythm had been denied him," and quotes with approval
an anonymous " Dublin critic " who compared his sentences
to " ribbons of tooth-paste squeezed out of a tube," we rub
our eyes in amazement, wondering how such words can be
applied to any one of a hundred paragraphs in *Héloïse and
Abélard*, let us say to that one which at the very end of the
book describes the lovers' second ride from Paris, very
different from the first :

At noon the sky was blue, the sun was shining; larks
rose wet-winged from the fields singing, and in a little
while (four hours later), the day was declining, and riding
through the dusk they saw great companies of rooks
flopping home through the sky, making for some rooky
woods about a nobleman's castle. The birds came in
thousands, and then there was a lull, a talking, a great
shuffling of the branches, as the pilgrims rode beneath
them. Again the sky was filled with rooks; at every opening
of the trees they caught sight of late-comers, and in the
blue gloom of the wintry evening, in the hour that is not
day nor night, the bats zigzagged round byre and barn

flying almost in the faces of the travellers, casting shadows on the moonlit road and then disappearing in the mist.

4

Ulick and Soracha, which appeared in 1926, is a further essay in the style of historical romance, but the setting of thirteenth century Ireland and the story itself interest fewer readers, and the book is most notable for the Sancho Panza-like figure of Ulick's servant Tadgh O'Dorachy, a lovable little man whose wanderings across Ireland with his goose Maria are related with sympathy and humour. The tale, which considered separately seemed a little slight, fitted admirably however into the second edition of *A Story-Teller's Holiday*, that collection of old Celtic legends which first appeared in 1918, one of the least known but most remarkable of Moore's books (the inhabitants of Ireland are forbidden to read it). The exchange of stories between himself and Alec Trusselby, the imaginary Mayo fern-gatherer, is framed to perfection by Moore's account of a return visit to Ireland after the insurrection of Easter Week, as humorous and perceptive as anything he ever wrote. The dry bones of medieval Irish life he found in old volumes in the National Library, whose editors would have been amazed and shocked at the lusty flesh in which he clothed their garnered legends —flesh as plump and as riotous as may be seen in a canvas of Rubens. It was indeed, as he called it, " a joyous book," and the partiality for sexual detail and bawdy words, which sometimes offends in the serious romances, here finds a natural place in the rich humour of the telling. The real earthy tang of Moore's Anglo-Irish, which (however much it may owe to Stephens' help) never receives the praise it deserves, fills and enriches the whole book.

One of the tales in the first edition of *A Story-Teller's Holiday*, " Albert Nobbs," the story of a woman disguised as a waiter which though founded on fact defeats credulity by the invention of a second disguised girl, was afterwards transferred to *Celibate Lives* to fill the gap caused by the removal of " Hugh Monfert " from the studies of celibacy.

" Albert Nobbs " loses much by the change of environment: the absurdity of the two disguises, which passed well enough in the Boccaccian atmosphere of *A Story-Teller's Holiday*, shows glaringly in the distilled realism of *Celibate Lives*. Yet one cannot regret the disappearance of " Hugh Monfert," although this long story has found admirers, and Mr. Morgan devotes some eulogistic pages to it in his *Epitaph*. He seems unaware that Moore not only suppressed the story, but actually denounced it, in the preface to *Celibate Lives*, as lacking the melodic line; and I hope that my own dissatisfaction with " Hugh Monfert " is not coloured by knowledge of that august diapproval. Not until near the end does the story acquire a real momentum: much of the early dialogue is of a really startling flatness (" Dr. Knight . . . asked her if the chattering bird they had just seen flying through the wood was a hen pheasant, and she answered no, that it was a yaffle") ; one stretch of conversation is repeated almost *verbatim* two pages after its first appearance; nor is the author much happier when he sends his two young men off on a mad scamper, in the manner of Mr. Hilaire Belloc, across the countryside: they discuss architectural remains (but far less amusingly than Moore and Martyn in *Ave*), put up at pubs, and encounter an eccentric Welsh doctor who breaks the line of the story altogether.

It would be unprofitable to draw attention to the weaknesses of " Hugh Monfert " if they did not offer so complete a contrast to the rounded perfection of the remaining four stories. The shortest is perhaps the best, " Wilfred Holmes," a little masterpiece which in twenty pages reveals the pathos and the comedy of a whole life, so adroitly blended that at the end we cannot say whether the story is sad or merry. More humanity transpires through the marble surface of Moore's prose than is often acknowledged, more sometimes than we realise ourselves as we read. Not until the last page of " Henrietta Marr " do we understand that in this revelation of the soul of a shallow woman no touch has been wasted. And the art that can build up an entire personality without any display of psychological analysis can also sketch in a minor character with a brief certainty which every writer must envy: the eccentric old lady, Mrs. Marr, lives in the single phrase which tells how she would scandalise her correct son by " talking with the butler after dinner of the cedars of Lebanon." The cedars of Lebanon ! One might ransack the encyclopædia without hitting on a subject so apt.

5

But reference books were never much in his line. Wishing to throw light on some æsthetic problem, the innocent Freeman asks (in *Conversations in Ebury Street*) : " Have you an encyclopædia ? " It was as though one were to ask a hunting squire whether he had bagged any foxes. " An encyclopædia in this house ! No ! " and in that reply we may discover both the strength and the weakness of Moore's literary criticism: that it is entirely self-reliant. For what they are worth, his opinions are his own, and there may be some significance in his choice of the conversation as the best medium for their expression.

In spite of the success of his early *Impressions and Opinions* Moore never cared to resume the essay form, and when in 1919 he found that a life-time of desultory but lynx-eyed reading and ceaseless æstheticising over the fire had accumulated enough prejudices and ideas to form a new volume of criticism, he cast it almost wholly into the form of dialogue (" a form in which criticism can be conducted more agreeably than in the essay "). No doubt his reasons were various: admiration for the very different dialogues of his master, Landor, the success of the conversation in *Hail and Farewell*, apprehension of the comic possibilities of banter with such a monument of literary respectability as Sir Edmund Gosse; above all a desire to discover in himself—or to create (in George Moore it amounted to the same thing) —further aspects of the quizzical eighteenth-century " man of taste " who begins to emerge in the trilogy. And perhaps, after all, there is also to be found in the choice a kind of modesty in this least modest of men. He was aware that many of his opinions were heretical, and based on a scanty scholarship. The essay was altogether too solemn a pulpit for views which might proceed with the greatest imaginable propriety *viva voce* from the mouth of George Moore, Esquire, of Moore Hall.

Whatever his reasons, the results which we possess in the two complementary volumes, *Avowals* and *Conversations in Ebury Street*, wholly justify his decision. Apart altogether from their critical value they possess a unifying charm of manner which makes it difficult for the reader to lay down either volume, however scandalised he may be by some of the literary judgments they contain. Moore could see very little in Tolstoy, scarcely anything in Dickens or Trollope; he maintained in all seriousness that Anne Brontë was a greater artist than either of her sisters, calling her *Agnes Gray* " the most perfect prose narrative in English literature." At times he almost seems to resemble the old lady in Proust to whom " the genius of certain great artists was completely unintelligible . . .; all she could do was to make delicate fun of them and to express her incomprehension in a graceful and witty form. But this wit and grace, at the point to which she carried them, became themselves—on another plane, and even although they were employed to belittle the noblest masterpieces—true artistic qualities." But this is far from being the whole truth about Moore's criticism. He was, it should be admitted, the least catholic of critics; and yet he could display upon occasion (as in the admirable discussion of Kipling in *Conversations*) the most unexpected comprehension of an alien art. Moreover, all his criticism derives genuine value from two factors, one general and the other relevant only to his criticism of the novel, particularly of the English novel.

He approached the work of his predecessors and contemporaries in English fiction as an artist determined to expose, by precept as well as by his own practice, certain glaring faults. He perceived that the great English novelists, despite all their inventive genius, had (with rare exceptions) scarcely a trace of discipline, unity, artistic direction: all those classic qualities which he found most perfectly exemplified in the stories of Turgenev, " shapely as a Greek vase." So exasperated was he by the English " lack of seriousness," the author's constant stepping out of his frame to address the reader, that he missed the great qualities which redeem many æsthetic lapses in English fiction : the tenderness, the humour, above all the abundant life—that sprawling reality which not all the sentimentality of Dickens, the respectability of Thackeray, the vicarage morality of Trollope can quench. But if George Moore, like all reformers, turned a blind eye on the virtues of a tradition which disgusted him, that does not invalidate his artistic ideals; English fiction was indeed guilty of the æsthetic shapelessness of which he accused it, and it is impossible after assimilating his point of view to re-read the classics of the eighteenth and nineteenth centuries without a sharpened critical sense.

The other element which gives value to Moore's critical work is akin to the self-reliance which spurned encyclopædias : an absolute integrity and originality of outlook, and an ability to observe what everyone else had missed. In *Ave* he tells of the astonishment with which he heard his laundress's explanation of Christ's apparent laxity in the matter of the woman taken in adultery : " You see, sir, he was only a bachelor." " You are quite right, Mrs. Millar, only no one ever thought of it before." Something of Mrs. Millar's simple-minded perspicacity is to be found all through Moore's critical writing. The prefatory letter, *On Reading the Bible for the First Time*, is full of this quality; and when, in the dialogue which preceeds *Daphnis and Chloë*, the scholar, Whittaker, speaks of Longus, the Greek author, Moore instantly remarks " Longus is a Latin name." So it is, and the fact is not, as it happens, very significant; but how many people notice it at all ? His talk about books is always flashing into a sudden illuminating phrase which could have come from no one else. Every reader of *Vale* remembers the words in which he confesses his inability to re-read *Tom Jones*: " Professors of English declare it to be England's finest novel, but I remembered it merely as a very empty work written in a breezy manner."

A few years later his knowledge of the book is revealed as being far from superficial. He criticises it in some detail, allowing only the reality of Squire Western, but with the

reservation that the character is so obvious that Fielding
could hardly miss him: " he is hardly more worthy of
criticism than Rowlandson." Gosse is quick to see advantage in the analogy: " But you admire Rowlandson." How
penetrating is Moore's reply: " Yes, I admire Rowlandson
until somebody speaks of Goya." Penetrating rather than
profound his criticism inclines to be; and yet he was capable
of this admirable dictum: " The true artist is neither esoteric
nor commonplace; he captures the world with broad human
sympathies, and woos and wins his fellows with his craft."
A fine maxim, the implications of which he did not always
follow out in his practice; he might have been a great critic
if he could have discovered the human sympathy as clearly
as he could assess the craftsmanship in his subject. His
criticism is not great; it is original, stimulating, beguiling,
sometimes perverse, never dull.

6

When in his last delightful fragment of autobiography,
A Communication to My Friends, the old George Moore looked
back over the long tale of his books, he confessed that none
of them gave him so much pleasure as his translation of
Daphnis and Chloë. He undertook the task at a moment when
he felt a drying-up of the springs of original inspiration,
and the freshness and charm of the Greek story captivated
him at once. The pretty invention of incident must have
recalled to him certain aspects of his own talent, and he did
not scruple to transpose sentences and invent explanations
even in the austere presence of Whittaker, as though the
story were his own. Of course he had no Greek, and the
" translation " was accomplished by way of Courier's
French; nevertheless, the graceful, flowing Greek is more
nearly echoed in Moore's prose than in any other. Even the
famous Thornley translation of 1657, though always vivid,
is sometimes clumsy, whereas Moore's runs, as he himself
put it, " like silk off the reel." The difference between the
two, and the extent to which Moore's version suffers from

inaccuracy and omission, may be judged from the following passage which I give first in the original, then in Thornley (close enough to be used as a construe), and lastly in Moore.

Ἐξέκαε δὲ αὐτοὺς καὶ ἡ ὥρα τοῦ ἔτους. ἦρος ἦν ἤδη τέλος καὶ θέρους ἀρχὴ καὶ πάντα ἐν ἀκμῇ, δένδρα ἐν καρποῖς, πεδία ἐν ληίοις· ἡδεῖα μὲν τεττίγων ἠχή, γλυκεῖα δὲ ὀπώρας ὀδμή, τερπνὴ δὲ ποιμνίων βληχή. εἴκασεν ἄν τις καὶ τοὺς ποταμοὺς ᾄδειν ἤρεμα ῥέοντας, καὶ τοὺς ἀνέμους συρίττειν ταῖς πίτυσιν ἐμπνέοντας, καὶ τὰ μῆλα ἐρῶντα πίπτειν χαμαὶ, καὶ τὸν ἥλιον φιλόκαλον ὄντα πάντας ἀποδύειν.

(*Thornley*) Now beside this, the season of the year inflamed and burnt them. For now the cooler spring was ended and the summer was come on, and all things were got to their highest flourishing, the trees with their fruits, the fields with standing corn. Sweet then was the singing of the grasshoppers, sweet was the odour of the fruits, and not unpleasant the very bleating of the sheep. A man would have thought that the very rivers, by their gentle gliding away, did sing; and that the softer gales of wind did play and whistle on the pines; that the apples, as languishing with love, fell down upon the ground; and that the Sun, as a lover of beauty unveiled, did strive to undress and turn the rurals all naked.

(*Moore*) The sun-heat inflamed them the more, for the year was now passing out of the cool of the spring into the beginning of summer, when all is in sap, when the trees begin to show their fruits and when the corn is in ear, when the voice of the cicala is heard in the branches, when the bleating of the yoes tells of the richness of the fields, and the perfumed air is delightful to breathe. The streams seem asleep, so silently do they flow, the winds seem like organs and flutes, so sweetly do they sigh through the branches of the pines; the apples are raped from the branches by the sun, their lover.

The greater softness and warmth of atmosphere in Moore's version are evident; sometimes he is neater (" all is in sap "

is very happy for πάντα ἐν ἀκμῇ); and very little seems
to be lost in the freedom. Do the streams sleep instead of
singing because Moore liked it better, or did Courier's text
have εὕδειν for ᾄδειν? I don't know, but I am certain that
the satyr of Ebury Street would never, had he realised it,
have omitted the pretty conceit at the end by which the
sun is made " to strip all naked, as if enamoured of their
beauty." (πάντας, which probably here includes both
sexes, is masculine in form, but Moore would not have
hesitated to render it as a feminine.) Such small idiosyn-
crasies and changes do not greatly matter; in this version
the spirit, if not the letter, of *Daphnis and Chloë* has found
perfect utterance in the English tongue.

The fascination exercised over Moore by the late Greek
pastoralism of Longus led him to choose, for the background
of his last complete novel, Greece of the fifth century B.C.,
the age which more than any other could have satisfied his
desire for a harmonious background to daily living, endless
talk of art and literature (though to the philosophising he
would have turned a deaf ear), and the most varied artistic
activity carried on in the full blaze of public life. Though
prudence or modesty prevented him from setting the scene
in Athens itself, the intellectual stir of Athenian life is always
felt at the periphery of his Bœotian tale, beckoning Rhesos
and Thrasillos, his young sculptor and architect, much as
Paris had beckoned the young Moore in the seventies, leading him at last to the Nouvelle Athènes that was the beginning of everything. He regarded Bœotia as a sort of Grecian
Mayo, delighting in its country scenes and people as he had
in the Irish life of *The Lake* and *The Untilled Field*. Most of
the detail in *Aphrodite in Aulis* is vivid and delightful, but
the book as a whole makes an undoubted effect of weakening power, for none of the characters (except perhaps
Biote) possesses the old firmness of outline, and the story
resembles some of the early novels in showing no clear
unity of subject: it is not so much that the movement is
slow as that it meanders, and sometimes loses sight of the
sea altogether. It is, in fact, an old man's book, relying
partly on familiar devices of technique to carry the narrative

over dull stretches; not many artists can in their eighth decade, like the miraculous Verdi, tighten the structure and refine the texture of their art. Much of *Aphrodite* can only appeal to the fervent admirer of Moore, though for him it derives an additional and rather pathetic interest from the many personal allusions (the illness of Phidias, the loneliness of the old Otanes) which in the strength of his maturity he would have abjured.

Only for a few pages does the narrative lie in Athens, but at the last, greatly daring, inviting not only the comparison with antiquity but the comparison (for Moore no less severe) with Landor, he nerved himself to the composition of a set conversation-piece between the great Athenians, bringing to the dedication of temple and statue at Aulis Sophocles, Euripides, Aristophanes and Phidias. His success is complete, no less in the solemnity with which (through the eyes of Rhesos) the tragedians and the sculptor are presented: " our thoughts model us; Sophocles and Euripides look out of their tragedies, Phidias out of his sculpture: the same dignity, the same candour, the same sweetness, the same eternity," than in the brilliant sketch of Aristophanes, " the marvellous boy," in reproof of whose levity Sophocles asks: " How old art thou, Aristophanes ? " getting for reply, " Thou shouldst be able to tell my age, master, by my words. If they are wise, I am young; if they are foolish, I am old." Who would have thought that the unscholarly Moore would know the Aristophanic tag from *The Frogs*, ληκύθιον ἀπώλεσεν (" lost his little oil-can ") ? Every classical scholar remembers it, but few could have turned it to more effective use. The humble cobbler, Thyonicus, has just read his " Bœotian hexameters."

Modesty is very winning, said Sophocles. Like courage, Aristophanes replied, and surprised at the interruption Sophocles continued: A treacherous smile played about thy lips whilst Thyonicus read his verses. A smile is enough for halting hexameters ! the boy answered. A kind word is never out of place, said Euripides, even when hexameters limp. Thou hast brought thy little oilcan,

master. And thou the vinegar, Aristophanes ! Didst come
to Bœotia to sprinkle it ? Why should I come to Bœotia
to sprinkle vinegar ? What then is thy errand ? asked
Sophocles. I came in search of a comedy. . . .

And so we come to the fantastic sketch of the imaginary
Aristophanic comedy, *The Apes*, just the sort of thing which
might have served that brilliant improviser as a scenario.
The whole episode is astonishing: just when we suppose
that we have come to the end of George Moore, something
totally fresh springs, fully armed like Athene, from that
singular and incalculable head.

7

The world is a little out of sympathy with George Moore
to-day. He represents a period too recent to have come
round into fashion again; in another fifty years his world
and his ideas will be so alien to readers that, instead of
reacting against them, they will without difficulty assume
the historical sense which enables us to enjoy the flower of
past epochs without subscribing to their modes of thought
and life. In the meantime, his admirers are, I suspect,
mostly to be found among the middle-aged. It is not surprising that the younger generation, swinging from the
depths of denial and frustration to the somewhat bleak
heights of political aspiration, should in either mood resent
that sense of spiritual and æsthetic security which enabled
Moore to devote hours of loving " re-orchestration " to the
telling of some trivial episode in his own life, to consider
personal peculiarities and the fate of idealistic movements
dispassionately and amusingly (yet without any redeeming
suggestion of universal futility), and to make a jest or a
connoisseur's pastime of physical love, that dark Laurentian
mystery which the twentieth century has so solemnly
explored. In nothing does Moore appeal less to the moderns
than in his treatment of sex, which has in contemporary
literature taken the place of the Victorians' Duty as an
object of serious endeavour. And yet to find in " The Lovers

of Orelay " a shallow passion is hardly more appropriate
than to deplore the amorous flippancies of Millamant and
Mirabell. When we consider the world's art, it seems as
though there were no view of life and love which may not
form the basis of a masterpiece, provided that the mysterious
processes of artistic digestion are complete. Earlier in this
essay I have indicated one or two passages in Moore's
books where material shows itself imperfectly assimilated
into the texture; but they are rare.

The contemplation of his work as a whole induces a feeling of completeness which is due not merely to the care with
which each individual book is shaped and polished, but to
the impression that here for once is an artist who has fully
explored and expressed his genius, who has realised the
whole extent of his spiritual demesne, cultivating every
acre of his own soil without once venturing across the walls
into alien land. Those relentless walls alone limit the extent
of his achievement, and that he was fully aware of their
existence there is ample evidence. Comparing once his
own work with that of Walter Pater, he said: " No man can
write beyond his own mind, and Pater had a finer mind
than mine," and in one of his prefaces he lets slip the phrase,
admirable in its instinctive modesty, " before I reached my
natural limits as a writer." If we had not these explicit
statements, we might have guessed that he knew the extent
of his powers by the total absence of pretentious speculation
in his work, the constant exhilarating touch of the visible
world which he understood and relished so keenly.

He used to talk, not very happily, of the " æsthetic
novel," and I suppose he is commonly regarded as an
æsthetic novelist. The phrase hardly indicates the peculiar
nature of his position. There have been many artists who
" dwell in an ivory tower "—which means in effect that
they deny those aspects of life which they cannot, or will not,
accommodate to a preconceived ideal of beauty. The
peculiarity of Moore lay in the fact that from *his* ivory tower
he was able to survey all that is essential in human experience. It was not only his early training in the school of Zola
that led him to exclude nothing, it was a temperament

naturally interested in every aspect of life which could be
felt in terms of a personal emotion—a kind of temperament
more often represented in poetry than in prose. Accepting
Pater's doctrine that sensation is the touchstone of value,
but caring nothing for Pater's philosophical speculations, he
nevertheless cast his net more widely and communicated a
more direct enjoyment of life than the master whom he
always revered. Though no mystic, Moore was capable
(passages in *Héloïse* prove it) of that sensation of being at the
heart of things, of thinking and feeling indivisibly, which can
fill a small boy with pagan ecstasy as he lies in the long
grass on a summer day. He never ceased to wonder at the
universal mysteries of life and death, the passage of time, the
unknown or pathetic destinies of man. He had the sense of
marvelling pity which could have penned the speech of the
87-year-old Firs at the end of *The Cherry Orchard*: " Life has
slipped by as though I hadn't lived."

Moore's comprehension of life was instinctive rather than
intellectual, and the shape that it assumes in his books
justifies us in saying that the cast of his mind was predomin-
antly impressionistic. It was a mind that reached profundity
neither in the metaphysical apprehension that makes saints
or philosophers or great poets, nor in the vast understanding
of humanity that endows the supreme dramatists and
novelists with the creative gift of a god. Moore's insight was
keen, his curiosity unfailing, his sympathy deep, but they
were not of that order. He resembled rather an observant old
gentleman who takes a 'bus ride into the remotest suburbs
and slums of humanity, seeing all and rejecting nothing, but
clutching tightly in a benevolent palm his return ticket. That
ticket, whose possession shut him out from the company of
Balzac or Tolstoy, guaranteed his return not only to Ebury
Street, but to the centre of all things—to the core of George
Moore.

Such an art, however perfect of its kind, is not likely to
win a general allegiance, and cannot claim admission to the
ranks of universal masterpieces. If the works of George
Moore are destined for any kind of immortality (a purely
relative term when applied to literature) it will be of a

different sort. He possesses to-day a small circle of readers who find the keenest delight in his books; and it is probable that for many years and for many generations to come his small public will persist, growing a little and dwindling a little as literary fashion dictates: the sort of public which to-day reads Landor or Sterne or Jeremy Taylor.

The man George Moore was an eccentric, and, since the man and the artist are one and the same being, it is not surprising that, for all the classical shapeliness and technical certainty of his work, the mind therein revealed should belong to the great family of English eccentrics, a literary tradition as fascinating in its variety as the more sober procession of the centre. " Central " literature is honoured by Matthew Arnold and applauded by the world, but the appeal of the eccentrics, even of the greatest, is largely a matter of personal sympathy, and never more so than when humour is in question. It is as difficult to explain our sympathies in the matter of humour as to account for our choice of friends, and though Moore is not precisely a humorous writer, much of his quality must be escaping us if his mischievous charm does not constantly provoke an indulgent smile. Everyone (except their victims) appreciates the sallies in *Hail and Farewell*, but even more personal to Moore is such a mixture of absurdity, urbanity and beauty as the end of his letter to Scott Moncrieff, prefixed to the latter's translation of the Letters of Abélard and Héloïse. (I quote the passage at length both because it is typical of much of his humour and because it is so little known.) Scott Moncrieff had dedicated his book " To my friend, George Moore, who has made these dry bones live "; and Moore wrote of his perplexity whether he should build his story around Abélard or Héloïse. Other men, he says, are visited by their Muses in the woods or by the riverside; his seeks him in his bath, and there he puts his question to her:

Shall I tell Abélard, with Héloïse for a companion, or Héloïse, with Abélard for a companion ? I know not how to choose between the two stories; both entice me; either seems a losing, yet a choice must be made. As my Muse did not answer, I began to run the two stories over in my mind, and when I stepped out of the bath she was no longer sitting on the mahogany rim; and eighteen months were spent writing the book that pleases you—tormented all the time by reminiscences of Abélard on the banks of the Arduzon and in the monastery built on the rocks round which the Atlantic surges, never certain which was the better story, Héloïse and Abélard, or Abélard and Héloïse. Every time I bathe I swear to you, my dear Moncrieff, that I beseech audience of my Muse. Once and once only it seemed to me that I heard a mocking voice speaking out of a cloud, and the words were: " Nothing forbids thee to write both stories, but I would have thee refrain from . . ." Her last words were so shocking that I dare not repeat them. Lean your ear to me, Moncrieff, and I'll whisper them. " I would have thee refrain from the double event ! " she said. " But the language of the Turf is not that of Parnassus," I cried, and fell to thinking that I may have dozed in the warm water and mingled the voice of the Muse with the dripping of the tap.

If this passage, slight as it is, strikes a reader as merely trivial, it is safe to say that the quintessence of George Moore is not for him. If, on the other hand, he is beguiled and delighted by the sensation of an epicure who has discovered a new dish, then he will find in those friendly volumes of conversation and portraits and reminiscence a permanent refreshment of the spirit. I cannot think of his beautiful novels as belonging to the main stream of English fiction, or of *Avowals*, with Mr. Morgan, as " a landmark in English criticism." The demesne of George Moore, like Moore Hall itself, lies well off the main road. You must turn aside; it is as far afield as Burton's curious hermitage or the sombre castle of Sir Thomas Browne. But when you have at last found Moore Hall and made friends with its owner, you will be royally, if a little eccentrically, entertained. You are free of the house, no family secret, no personal intimacy is withheld; but you must remember, in your turn, that certain ideas are not discussed, certain names never mentioned. After dinner, when you have admired the humanity and realism of the early daguerreotype portraits, and the soft tints of the miniatures " done to the life," your host will light the lamps of his imagination and lead you along the corridors to admire his grand historical tapestries; and very fine they are in colour and composition. But the culminating moment of the visit comes rather when the cigars are drawing nicely before the fire, and the guest is regaled with a stream of diverting talk, ranging easily over persons, pictures, ideas, memories and books, grouping tne whole world into a pleasantly formal composition around a figure in the centre, charming, voluble and decidedly odd, who is George Moore himself.

APPENDIX I

LETTERS TO MR. PHILIP GOSSE

THESE LETTERS to Mr. Philip Gosse show how fond Moore was of animals and how he hated cruelty towards them. He egged Mr. Gosse on to writing an article and chose the title of it, " The World on Trust," which appeared in the *London Mercury*, May 1924. Moore was not a professed humanitarian, but he revolted against anything that was out of nature, and although at one time he rode to hounds and was a good shot he came to think that, as he put it in *Conversations in Ebury Street*, we only hold the world on lease and should hand it on to the next generation as we found it.

6th January 1922.
121, Ebury Street
London, S.W.1

Dear Mr. Philip Gosse

I have read your article and think very well of it, my only criticism being that it would gain very much if it were filled out with comment. For instance, in yesterday's *Daily Mail* there was an account of some abominable furriers who put a wire muzzle upon a fox and had him hunted through the streets of New York by a lot of boys in order to advertise their business. The unfortunate animal cowered in every hiding-place it could find, was driven out again, and finally had its leg broken by a motor-car. I am glad to say that the miscreants are going to be prosecuted by the N.S.P.C.A. Now the question comes on reading this how far the men who do these things to animals are aware of the enormity of their offence. They are without imagination, and cannot foresee the panic of fear that this poor animal must have suffered. In fact they live on a very much lower plane of sensibility than we do.

This anecdote would lead up very nicely, with comments, to the story of the pony which you tell. Now that is another instance of a lack of imagination. The people were well-to-do; they lived in a villa; they had bedrooms and a bathroom, stables and coach-house behind, and yet they think it quite natural to send their faithful servant to Belgium to be worked to death and then eaten. And to this horrible, unforgettable obtuseness of mind they add a sickly sentimentality: they would like to keep a hoof as a memento. The soul of an honest man revolts, and he sickens at the thought that he is of the same kin as people who do this. He would like to live like the man on the desert island who saw such terrible things done by men during four or five years that he preferred to live alone for ever.

When you speak of the man who shot hundreds, perhaps thousands of birds in the hope of giving his collection to Eastbourne, and was gratified (when the authorities built him a new wing for it) at the interest the children showed, the interest being merely a gaping wonder and a remark " Lawk ! that fellow would do for my straw "[1], I am minded of Erostratus who burnt the Temple of Diana so that his name might be remembered. And thousands of beautiful birds are shot to make a schoolgirl gape ! The vanity of man is a singular thing, the desire to be remembered, no matter how, so long as he is remembered.

The small amount of morality that every human animal is capable of, gives us pause, and we remember that the Anglo-Saxon is just capable of sexual morality and that's about all. He wouldn't like anybody to know after his death that he was unfaithful to his wife; any other morality he is incapable of appreciating.

These lines will give you, perhaps the key to what I mean. Of course, you can supply many more on your own account, and then I think the article will be excellently well done. To return to my first criticism, it is a little lean.

Very sincerely yours
George Moore

[1] i.e. hat.

7th January 1922.   121, Ebury Street
                                     London, S.W.1

Dear Philip Gosse,

I did not say all I had to say in my letter to you yesterday. I think that a better title for the article would be
" The World on Trust " and I am writing now to say that
it isn't necessary to give many instances of cruelty. The
article deals generally with the subject, presupposing that
everybody knows that arms of precision have reached such
a state that it is quite possible for unthinking men to destroy
a great part of the wild birds and all the wild animals.

I enclose the copy of a private letter that I have just
written to the *Daily Mail* (you will find the article
alluded to among this week's publications, I cannot tell
you what day). The destruction of the badger in England
is only a small part of the thing; what it is proposed
to do is not to give up the world to the next generation as
we found it, but to destroy the old world. There will be no
naturalists among the generations that follow us because
there will be no Nature. There will be nothing but horses
to draw, if horses survive. I suppose there will be sheep
and bullocks, because people will always eat fresh meat,
and there will be poultry of various sorts, but that's about
all. Have we got a right to do this ? You and I think we
have not, and that is the part of your article which can
be developed to any extent. I think I would keep the
story about the fox, and the story about the pony, for
they lend themselves to some moralising. The man who
killed all the birds, hoping to be remembered by gaping
schoolchildren, also lends itself to moralising. The other
things will come in occasionally, the whales and the
chimpanzees. Now the chimpanzees lend themselves to
moralising. How are they being exterminated ? Large
parties go into the bush and discover a female chim-
panzee with a baby in her arms; she defends her baby
and is killed, and the baby is taken to Europe, forced to
smoke cigars and drink brandy, and is whipped daily for
about three years in order to put money into the pockets
of his owners. I saw one of these unfortunate animals in

Paris and can tell you about him. But an evocation of the poor mother in the African forest defending her young against a score of natives armed with spears, will stir the public. There is no use accumulating examples, because you will never be able to reach the end of them; they occur every day, one more horrible than the other.

Sincerely yours
George Moore

7th January 1922.   121, Ebury Street
London, S.W.1

Dear Mr McLeod.

I was shocked to read in the *Daily Mail* this week an article written in a tone of approval regarding the odious cruelty of badger-baiting. Why not publish another article approving of bear-baiting and bull-fighting? I am sure many readers were as much shocked as myself and I include among them Lord Northcliffe, who would never have let this article pass if he were in England. His tour seems to be an extraordinary success. He telegraphed his Christmas greetings to me, and I am writing this week to congratulate him. Is there any chance of our seeing him before next summer?

Truly yours
George Moore

28th March 1922.   121, Ebury Street
London, S.W.1

Dear Philip Gosse,

For a long time past the *Daily Mail* has been telling stories of the slaughter of wild animals. Apparently this newspaper is of the opinion that the sooner wild animals are got rid of the better. I would call your attention to the issue of to-day. The extermination of the badger, advocated some months ago, is again in evidence, how the poor beast is dug out, how the dam and her cubs are killed, etc. In another part of the paper advice is given to boys bird-nesting. I thought that nobody wished boys to destroy birds' eggs, but apparently I am wrong, for the most explicit directions are given. And in still another part of the paper some regret is expressed because the Board of Trade is determined to get rid of the American squirrel, for it destroys our native squirrels. I suppose the inference would be denied, but that is the inference I draw from the paragraph in question. However, you will see for yourself. I think that the attention of the Society for the Preservation of Wild Animals should be drawn to it. I would do so myself, but I don't know the address of the Society, and besides I think it would come better from you.

You wrote the article that we spoke about, but you didn't make it long enough, so I hear. I wonder if I could help you ?

Sincerely yours
George Moore.

APPENDIX II

THE WORKS OF GEORGE MOORE:
A SHORT BIBLIOGRAPHY

1874(?) WORLDLINESS: A Comedy in Three Acts. (London: ?)

1878   FLOWERS OF PASSION: Poems. (London: Provost & Co.)

1879   MARTIN LUTHER: A Tragedy in Five Acts. (London: Remington & Co.)

1881   PAGAN POEMS. (London: Newman & Co.)

1883   A MODERN LOVER: Novel. (London: Tinsley Brothers.)

1885   A MUMMER'S WIFE: Novel. (London: Vizetelly & Co.)

1885   LITERATURE AT NURSE: Pamphlet. (London: Vizetelly & Co.)

1886   A DRAMA IN MUSLIN: Novel. (London: Vizetelly & Co.)

1887   A MERE ACCIDENT: Novel. (London: Vizetelly & Co.)

1887   PARNELL AND HIS ISLAND: Sketches. (London: Swan Sonnenschein.)

1888   CONFESSIONS OF A YOUNG MAN: Autobiography. (London: Swan Sonnenschein.)

1888   SPRING DAYS: Novel. (London: Vizetelly & Co.)

1889   MIKE FLETCHER: Novel. (London: Ward & Downey.)

1891   IMPRESSIONS AND OPINIONS: Essays. (London: David Nutt.)

1892   VAIN FORTUNE: Novel. (London: Henry & Co.)

1893   MODERN PAINTING: Essays. (London: Walter Scott.)

1893   THE STRIKE AT ARLINGFORD: A Play in Three Acts. (London: Walter Scott.)

1894   ESTHER WATERS: Novel. (London: Walter Scott.)

1895   CELIBATES: Three Short Stories. (London: Walter Scott.)

1895   THE ROYAL ACADEMY 1895: Criticism. (London: *New Budget* Office.)

1898   EVELYN INNES: Novel. (London: T. Fisher Unwin.)

1900   THE BENDING OF THE BOUGH: A Comedy in Five Acts. (London: T. Fisher Unwin.)

1901   SISTER TERESA: Novel. (London: T. Fisher Unwin.)

1903   THE UNTILLED FIELD: Short Stories. (London: T. Fisher Unwin.) Published in Irish by Sealy, Bryers & Walker, Dublin, in 1902.

1905   THE LAKE: Novel. (London: Heinemann.)

1906   REMINISCENCES OF THE IMPRESSIONIST PAINTERS. (Dublin: Maunsel & Co.)

1906   MEMOIRS OF MY DEAD LIFE: Autobiography. (London: Heinemann.)

1911   "HAIL AND FAREWELL!": AVE: Autobiography. (London: Heinemann.)

1911   THE APOSTLE: A Drama in Three Acts. (Dublin: Maunsel & Co.)

1912   "HAIL AND FAREWELL!": SALVE: Autobiography. (London: Heinemann.)

1913   ESTHER WATERS: A Play in Five Acts. (London: Heinemann.)

1913   ELIZABETH COOPER: A Comedy in Three Acts. (Dublin and London: Maunsel & Co.)

1914   "HAIL AND FAREWELL!": VALE: Autobiography. (London: Heinemann.)

1915   MUSLIN: Novel. Revision of *A Drama in Muslin*. (London: Heinemann.)

1916   THE BROOK KERITH: A Syrian Story. (London: T. Werner Laurie.)

1917   LEWIS SEYMOUR AND SOME WOMEN: Novel. Revision of *A Modern Lover*. (London: Heinemann.)

1918   A STORY-TELLER'S HOLIDAY. Limited Edition. (London: Society for Irish Folk-lore.)

HHL*

1919 AVOWALS: Criticism. Limited Edition. (London: Society for Irish Folk-lore.)

1920 ESTHER WATERS: Revision of the Novel. Limited Edition. (London: Society for Irish Folk-lore.)

1920 THE COMING OF GABRIELLE: A Comedy in Three Acts. Limited Edition. (London: Society for Irish Folk-lore.)

1921 HÉLOÏSE AND ABÉLARD: Novel. Limited Edition. (London: Society for Irish Folk-lore.)

1921 FRAGMENTS FROM HÉLOÏSE AND ABÉLARD: Additions and Corrections. Limited Edition. (London: Society for Irish Folk-lore.)

1921 MEMOIRS OF MY DEAD LIFE: " Moore Hall " Edition. (London: Heinemann.)

1921 THE LAKE: Revised Edition. (London: Heinemann.)

1922 IN SINGLE STRICTNESS: Short Stories. Limited Edition. (London: Heinemann.)

1923 THE APOSTLE: Revision of the Drama. Limited Edition. (London: Heinemann.)

1924 AVOWALS. Uniform Edition. (London: Heinemann.)

1924 CONVERSATIONS IN EBURY STREET: Criticism. Limited Edition. (London: Heinemann.)

1924 PURE POETRY: An Anthology. Limited Edition. (London: Nonesuch Press.)

1924 PERONNIK THE FOOL: Short Story. (New York: Boni & Liveright.)

1924 THE PASTORAL LOVES OF DAPHNIS AND CHLOË: Translation. Limited Edition. (London: Heinemann.)

1925 HÉLOÏSE AND ABÉLARD. Uniform Edition. (London: Heinemann.)

1925 " HAIL AND FAREWELL ! " Limited Edition in Two Volumes. (London: Heinemann.)

1926 CONFESSIONS OF A YOUNG MAN: Revised Edition. (London: Heinemann.)

1926 PERONNIK THE FOOL. New Limited Edition. (New York: W. E. Rudge.)

1926   ULICK AND SORACHA: Novel. Limited Edition. (London: Nonesuch Press.)

1926   THE UNTILLED FIELD: Revised Edition. (London: Heinemann.)

1927   THE MAKING OF AN IMMORTAL: A Comedy in One Act. (New York: Bowling Green Press.)

1927   CELIBATE LIVES: Revised from *In Single Strictness* for the Uniform Edition. (London: Heinemann.)

1927   THE BROOK KERITH: Revised for the Uniform Edition. (London: Heinemann.)

1928   MEMOIRS OF MY DEAD LIFE: Revised for the Uniform Edition. (London: Heinemann.)

1928   A STORY-TELLER'S HOLIDAY: Revised Edition in Two Volumes, including *Ulick and Soracha*. Uniform Edition. (London: Heinemann.)

1928   PERONNIK THE FOOL: Revised Limited Edition. (Eure, France: The Hours Press.)

1929   LETTERS FROM GEORGE MOORE TO ÉDOUARD DUJARDIN, 1886–1922. Translated by John Eglinton. (New York: Crosby Gaige.)

1929   THE BROOK KERITH: Limited Edition, with engravings by Stephen Gooden. (London: Heinemann.)

1930   CONVERSATIONS IN EBURY STREET. Uniform Edition. (London: Heinemann.)

1930   A FLOOD: Short Story. (New York: The Harbor Press.)

1930   THE PASSING OF THE ESSENES: A Drama in Three Acts. Limited Edition of a further Revision of *The Apostle*. (London: Heinemann.)

1930   APHRODITE IN AULIS: Novel. Limited Edition. (London: Heinemann.)

1931   THE PASSING OF THE ESSENES. Uniform Edition. (London: Heinemann.)

1931   APHRODITE IN AULIS: Revised for the Uniform Edition. (London: Heinemann.)

1932   MUSLIN. Uniform Edition. (London: Heinemann.)

1932   ESTHER WATERS. Uniform Edition. (London: Heinemann.)

1932   THE UNTILLED FIELD. Uniform Edition. (London:
       Heinemann.)

1932   THE LAKE. Uniform Edition. (London: Heinemann.)

1933   PERONNIK THE FOOL. With engravings by Stephen
       Gooden. (London: Harrap & Co.)

1933   A COMMUNICATION TO MY FRIENDS: Autobiography.
       Limited Edition. (London: Nonesuch Press.)

1933   CONFESSIONS OF A YOUNG MAN. Uniform Edition.
       (London: Heinemann.)

1933   " HAIL AND FAREWELL ! ": AVE. Uniform Edition.
       (London: Heinemann.)

1933   " HAIL AND FAREWELL ! ": SALVE. Uniform Edition.
       (London: Heinemann.)

1933   " HAIL AND FAREWELL ! ": VALE. Uniform Edition.
       (London: Heinemann.)

1933   THE PASTORAL LOVES OF DAPHNIS AND CHLOE AND
       PERONNIK THE FOOL. Uniform Edition. (London:
       Heinemann.)

1933   A MUMMER'S WIFE AND A COMMUNICATION TO MY
       FRIENDS. Uniform Edition. (London: Heinemann.)

INDEX

INDEX